In Plain Sight

IN PLAIN SIGHT

*Impunity and Human Rights
in Thailand*

Tyrell Haberkorn

THE UNIVERSITY OF WISCONSIN PRESS

Publication of this book has been possible, in part, through support from the
Center for Southeast Asian Studies at the University of Wisconsin–Madison.

The University of Wisconsin Press
1930 Monroe Street, 3rd Floor
Madison, Wisconsin 53711-2059
uwpress.wisc.edu

Gray's Inn House, 127 Clerkenwell Road
London ECIR 5DB, United Kingdom
eurospanbookstore.com

Printed in the United States of America

This book may be available in a digital edition.

Library of Congress Cataloging-in-Publication Data

Names: Haberkorn, Tyrell, author.
Title: In plain sight : impunity and human rights in Thailand / Tyrell Haberkorn.
Other titles: New perspectives in Southeast Asian studies.
Description: Madison, Wisconsin : The University of Wisconsin Press, [2018] |
Series: New perspectives in Southeast Asian studies | Includes
bibliographical references and index.
Identifiers: LCCN 2017010439 | ISBN 9780299314408 (cloth : alk. paper)
Subjects: LCSH: Human rights—Thailand. | Impunity—Thailand. |
Thailand—Politics and government.
Classification: LCC JC599.T5 H33 2018 | DDC 323/.04409593—
dc23 LC record available at https://lccn.loc.gov/2017010439

ISBN 9780299314446 (pbk. : alk. paper)

For
the unlikely anarchist
and all those who struggle against impunity
in Thailand

Freedom. It isn't once, to walk out
under the Milky Way, feeling the rivers
of light, the fields of dark—
freedom is daily, prose-bound, routine
remembering. Putting together, inch by inch
the starry worlds. From all the lost collections.

—ADRIENNE RICH, "For Memory"

CONTENTS

PREFACE

In a review of Susana Kaiser's *Postmemories of Terror: A New Generation Copes with the Memory of the "Dirty War,"* published in *Aan* (Read) magazine, a Thai progressive literary and cultural quarterly, Pakavadi Veerapaspong wrote, "If it is not too much to ask, perhaps one day there will be a book that a Thai will write on the topic of 'memories after dictatorship,' like the Argentines. Or, perhaps we will have to live our lives in a Thai-style nightmare, and pass the pride in a Thai-style inhumanity that the guardian spirit of the country has given with unending compassion on from generation to generation?"[1] Pakavadi wrote her review shortly after the military crackdown on red shirt protesters by the Abhisit Vejjajiva government in April and May 2010. The violence began with attacks on protesters on the night of 10 April 2010 and concluded with sustained violence on 14–19 May. Ninety-four people were killed during the protests, the majority of whom were civilians, and over two thousand were injured.[2] The crackdown came after the red shirts occupied central Bangkok for a prolonged period calling for elections and greater space for political participation. Abhisit was the fifth prime minister to hold office following the 19 September 2006 coup, which ousted the former elected prime minister Thaksin Shinawatra and his Thai Rak Thai (TRT) party, which was formally dissolved shortly after the coup. The coup put in motion a cycle of color-coded contention between royalist-nationalist yellow shirts who supported the coup and populist-democratic red shirts, some of whom supported Thaksin and some of whom wanted a greater democratic transformation.

Abhisit was appointed prime minister on 17 December 2008 and remained in office until the elections called for by the red shirts were finally held on 3 July 2011. The Pheu Thai party, a reconsolidation of the TRT after its dissolution, won the election, and Yingluck Shinawatra, Thaksin's younger sister, became prime minister. Although the April–May 2010 violence was the impetus for Pakavadi's examination of the questions raised by Susana Kaiser about memory, truth telling, transition, and reconciliation in Argentina, she noted that throughout her life she had witnessed a lack of accountability for state violence against citizens in Thailand. She despaired that a book about "memories after the era of dictatorship" would never be written in Thailand because she had seen dictatorship return multiple times. She urged readers to remember that the way to fight dictatorship is to record the truths about the repression and violence one has experienced or witnessed.[3]

During the first two years of Yingluck's government, the possibility of an era without dictatorship began to seem possible in Thailand. Although lèse majesté prosecutions under Article 112 did not slow down, progressive activists mobilized to launch a campaign to reform the law and court observation of Article 112, and Computer Crimes Act cases became a way to both raise consciousness and display solidarity with those standing trial. There was a series of five independent, semi-independent, and state investigations into the April–May 2010 crackdown, and inquests began in the cases of the civilian deaths. In December 2013 former prime minister Abhisit Vejjajiva and former deputy prime minister Suthep Thaugsuban were charged with premeditated murder for their roles in ordering the April–May 2010 crackdown.

But Yingluck's rule and the broader series of transformations taking place were not welcomed by some elites and their middle-class supporters. Catalyzed by the proposal of an amnesty bill that might have provided Thaksin with a path of return to Thailand after living in exile since the 2006 coup, an extended series of protests by the People's Democratic Reform Committee (PDRC), which included yellow shirts and strident royalist-nationalists, began in November 2013 with the aim of forcing Thailand to the brink of crisis. Yingluck stepped down as prime minister on 8 December 2013, and a new election was scheduled for 2 February 2014. But her critics, who feared that she and the Pheu Thai party would be reelected, were not satisfied. They acted to obstruct the election and continued to create chaos until they succeeded in setting the stage for the twelfth coup since the end of the absolute monarchy. On 20 May 2014 General Prayuth Chan-ocha declared martial law, and on 22 May he and a military junta calling itself the National Council for Peace and Order (NCPO) launched a coup. Claiming to act in the service of ending corruption and returning happiness to the people, the NCPO brought back the repressive measures of arbitrary detention, constriction of freedom of expression and thought, the use of military courts to try civilians for crimes against the crown and state, and other forms of violence that recall the regimes of Field Marshal Sarit Thanarat (1958–63) and Thanin Kraivichien (1976–77), which followed in the immediate wake of the 6 October 1976 massacre and coup.

Today a clear end to dictatorship is not in sight. The possibility of writing the "memories after dictatorship" is foreclosed for the immediate future. This does not mean that the dictators, who return again and again, are the only authors of history. In the introduction to *A People's History of the United States*, Howard Zinn writes, "We must not accept the memory of states as our own. Nations are not communities and never have been. The history of any country, presented as the history of a family, conceals fierce conflicts of interest (sometimes exploding, most often repressed) between conquerors and conquered, masters and slaves, capitalists and workers, dominators and dominated. . . . In such a world of conflict, a world of victims and executioners, it is the job of thinking people, as Albert Camus suggested, not to be on the side of the executioners."[4] In this spirit, the history of impunity I write in this book is one that aims to explicitly challenge the repressive organs of the state and their ongoing evasion of accountability.

∾

I researched and wrote this book over a six-year period beginning in 2011 as I moved among Thailand, Australia, and the United States. It is a great pleasure to thank the many institutions and individuals who made this book possible—and inspired me to remain hopeful even as what I learned about the history of impunity suggested the opposite. Any errors and lacunae that remain are mine alone.

My primary institutional home as I wrote this book was the Department of Political and Social Change in the College of Asia and the Pacific at the Australian National University. The department is a rare community of interdisciplinary scholars committed to both rigorously challenging and steadfastly supporting one another. In particular, I would like to thank

Allison Ley, Daungyewa Utarasint, Ed Aspinall, Greg Fealy, Marcus Mietzner, Nick Cheesman, Prajak Kongkirati, Risa Jopson, Robert Cribb, Rungrawee Chalermsripinyorat, Tony Reid, and Virginia Hooker for their advice and encouragement. I thank Craig Reynolds for his sharp questions, generosity with materials, and shared commitment to writing about and against the violent state.

Archival and field research between 2012 and 2016 was supported by a Discovery Early Career Researcher Award from the Australian Research Council (DE120101838, Impunity and State Violence in Thailand). I developed the structure and drafted the first half of the book during 2014–15 while a fellow at the Radcliffe Institute for Advanced Study at Harvard University, where Judith Vishniac and Sharon Bromberg-Lim facilitated the creation of a warm and critical community of thinkers and scholars. The members of the Human Rights Writing Group, especially my next-door neighbor Sugi Ganeshananthan, offered lively conversation and productive criticism. The Boston dim sum collective—Pitch Pongsawat, Pandit Chanrochanakit, Pinkaew Laungaramsri, and Aranya Siriphon—brought hope and shared analysis to the first months following the 22 May 2014 coup.

The National Research Council of Thailand granted me permission to conduct research and helped me gain access to the National Archives and Ministry of Foreign Affairs Archives. During 2013 and 2014, I was affiliated with the Department of History at Chulalongkorn University. For making this possible, and for their questions, I thank Chalong Soontravanich, Suvimol Rungcharoen, Thanapol Limapichart, Villa Vilaithong, and Wasana Wongsurawat.

Librarians at the Thai National Archives, the Ministry of Foreign Affairs Archives, the Office of the Juridical Council Library, the US Library of Congress, and the Widener Library at Harvard University helped me locate a range of materials, including many I did not imagine existed. Saowapha Virawong at the National Library of Australia tirelessly helped me find rare and out-of-print Thai materials. I thank Andrew Snyder, Charissa Iloure, Jasmine Chia, Preedee Hongsaton and Yupaporn Tarungsri for providing excellent research assistance and sharing their perspectives on, and outrage over, impunity with me.

Parts of this book were presented at Chulalongkorn University, Chiang Mai University, Mahasarakham University, the Sirindthorn Anthropology Center, Candide Books, Kyoto University, the University of Copenhagen,

Lund University, Stockholm University, the University of British Columbia, the University of Wisconsin, Cornell University, Harvard University, Columbia University, the Australian National University, and the annual meetings of the Association for Asian Studies. Audiences in each of these places challenged my interpretations of state violence and pushed me to think in a range of academic and activist frames. In particular, repeated invitations and generous engagement from Karin Zackari at Lund University, Duncan McCargo at Columbia University, Sinsawat Yodbangtoey at the Pridi Banomyong Institute, and Bencharat Sae Chua at Mahidol University gave me an opportunity to sharpen my ideas. Unchalee Maneeroj wrote critiques of two lectures I gave at Chiang Mai University for *Fa Diew Kan* magazine, and reading her analysis in Thai made me think anew and deepen my analysis in English.

An earlier version of the material in chapter 1 was published as a fictional account in Thai as "An Accidental Confession: A History of Arbitrary Detention in Thailand," trans. Warisa Kitthikhunseri, *Aan* 4, no. 2 (2012): 104–13 ["คำสารภาพบังเอิญเกิด: ว่าด้วยประวัติศาสตร์การกักขังโดยมิชอบ," วริศา กิตติคุณเสรี, ผู้แปล, อ่าน 4, no. 2 (2555): 104–13]. An earlier version of the section of chapter 3 on the *thang daeng* killings in Phatthalung was published as "Getting Away with Murder: State Violence and Impunity in Phatthalung," in *State Violence in East Asia*, ed. Sung Chull Kim and Narayan Ganesan (Lexington: University Press of Kentucky, 2014), 185–208. An earlier version of chapter 4 was published in Thai as "A 'Hidden Transcript' within the Amnesty Law: The 6 October 1976 Coup and Massacre," trans. Ponglert Pongwanan, *Aan* (December 2014): 166–83 ["'คำให้การเร้น' ในกฎหมายนิรโทษกรรม: รัฐประหารและสังหารหมู่ 6 ตุลาคม 2519," พงษ์เลิศ พงษ์วนานต์, ผู้แปล, อ่าน (ธันวาคม 2557): 166–83] and in English as "The Hidden Transcript of Amnesty: The 6 October 1976 Massacre and Coup in Thailand," *Critical Asian Studies* 47, no. 1 (March 2015): 44–68. The invitations from Ida Aroonwong to write for *Aan* and both her criticism and her enthusiasm inspired me to think and write in new ways.

I feel very lucky to have again worked with the University of Wisconsin Press as I researched, wrote, and revised this book. Gwen Walker's acute questions pushed me to think and write with greater clarity, and her unflagging support was essential to the manuscript's completion. Sheila McMahon shepherded the book through the editing and publication process, and Janet Opdyke's copyediting improved my prose. Kevin Hewison and an anonymous reader for the press offered productive comparative and theoretical suggestions for revision. Thongchai Winichakul's difficult and generous questions helped me figure out the broader argument about the logic of impunity in Thailand hidden between the lines of the accounts of individual lives. His advice in intellectual work, political struggle, and the points at which they intersect, especially after the 22 May 2014 coup, helped me through many impasses.

Trudi Gershinov of TG Design made the extraordinary cover for this book. The image of the line of prisoners bound to one another is based on a screen-printed cover of the November–December 1979 issue of *Human Rights in Thailand*, the newsletter of the Coordinating Group for Religion in Society. The organization dissolved in the mid-1990s and I was unable to identify the artist who created the original print, and so I gratefully acknowledge her/him here.

Doreen Lee remains my first reader, and I thank her for her lyricism and deep sense of justice. In addition to the readers for the University of Wisconsin Press, the entire manuscript was read by Carolyn Strange, Frank Munger, Hui Yee Tan, Nick Cheesman, and Samson Lim. Their comparative readings pushed me to rethink my assumptions and were very helpful as I revised the manuscript. Carolyn Strange finished her book about state execution and mercy as I was writing this book, and her understanding of both compassion and history pushed me in new directions. I am also grateful to Ana Dragojlovic, Alexandra Dalferro, Ben Tausig, Jennifer Solomon, Mark Selden, Patrick Pierce, Tze Loo, Thak Chaloemtiarana, Tamara Loos, Jim Glassman, and Thitiya Phaobtong for their friendship and advice on writing. My family—my mother, siblings, nieces, and nephews—were patient when I came home only to disappear to write and offered endless encouragement as I struggled to finish the book.

My greatest gratitude is to those in Thailand who told me stories of the state's evasion of accountability, helped me navigate the court system and the prisons, offered suggestions of what to read and learn, answered my endless questions with patience, and shared their hopes for an end to impunity. Although there are some people I cannot name, here I would like to thank Achara Ashayagachat, Angkhana Neelapaijit, Bencharat Sae Chua, Chaithawat Tulathon, Ida Aroonwong, Mutita Chuachang, Nattakant Akarapongphisak, Patporn Phoothong, Pipob Udomittipong, Ponglert Pongwanan, Pronthip Mankong, Pratubjit Neelapaijit, Puangthong Pawakapan, Comrade Saovalux Po-ngam, Sarayut Tangprasert, Thanapol Eawsakul, Yukti Mukdawijitra, and everyone at iLaw, Prachatai, and Thai

Lawyers for Human Rights. In particular, I am grateful to Coeli Barry, Thanet Aphornsuvan, Rassami Paoluengthong, Grant Peck, Chiranuch Premchaiporn, Eef Vermeij, and the unlikely anarchist for their insights about injustice and their generosity in sharing its opposite in the form of bike rides, art, *ba mi*, and *khana*.

This book is dedicated to the unlikely anarchist and all those who struggle against impunity in Thailand, with the hope that one day it will be possible to write the memories and histories *after* dictatorship.

ABBREVIATIONS

ACAA	Anti-Communist Activities Act
AFSC	American Friends Service Committee
AI	Amnesty International
AID	Agency for International Development
BPP	Border Patrol Police
CAT	Convention against Torture and Other Cruel, Inhuman or Degrading Treatment or Punishment
CCA	Computer Crimes Act
CCP	Chinese Communist Party
CCRS	Center for Coordinating Religion in Society
CD	compact disc
CDRM	Council for Democratic Reform under Constitutional Monarchy
CED	International Convention for the Protection of All Persons from Enforced Disappearance
CGRS	Coordinating Group for Religion in Society
CIA	Central Intelligence Agency
CMU	Chiang Mai University
CPT	Communist Party of Thailand
CRES	Center for the Resolution of the Emergency Situation
CSD	Crime Suppression Division
CSOC	Communist Suppression Operations Command
DSI	Department of Special Investigation

FIST	Federation of Independent Students of Thailand
ICC	International Criminal Court
ICCPR	International Covenant on Civil and Political Rights
ICJ	International Commission of Jurists
IESCR	International Covenant on Economic, Social, and Cultural Rights
iLaw	Internet Dialogue on Legal Reform
ISOC	Internal Security Operations Command
JPF	Justice for Peace Foundation
JUSMAG	Joint United States Military Assistance Group
MFA	Ministry of Foreign Affairs
MoE	Ministry of Education
NACC	National Anti-Corruption Commission
NARA	National Administrative Reform Assembly
NARC	National Administrative Reform Council
NCPO	National Council for Peace and Order
NHRC	National Human Rights Commission
NLA	National Legislative Assembly
NSCT	National Student Center of Thailand
OAG	Office of the Attorney General
PAD	People's Alliance for Democracy
PDG	People for Democracy Group
PDRC	People's Democratic Reform Committee
PPP	People's Power Party
PTP	Pheu Thai Party
SPT	Socialist Party of Thailand
TRCT	Truth and Reconciliation Committee of Thailand
TRT	Thai Rak Thai
UCL	Union for Civil Liberty
UDD	United Front for Democracy against Dictatorship
UDHR	Universal Declaration of Human Rights
UF	United Front against Dictatorship
UN	United Nations
UNESCO	United Nations Educational, Scientific and Cultural Organization
USIS	United States Information Service
USOM	United States Operations Mission
VDV	Village Defense Volunteers

NOTE ON LANGUAGE,
TRANSLATION, AND DATES

All translations in this book are mine unless stated otherwise. The Thai words in this book have been transliterated into roman characters with the exception of the bibliography. Both the original Thai and an English translation of the bibliographic information for Thai-language materials are included to aid readers in locating my sources.

For transliterated words, I have followed the guidelines of the Royal Institute outlined in "Principles of Romanization for Thai Script by Transcription Method," with two exceptions. With respect to individual names, if there is already a transliteration familiar through general use, I have used it rather than following the Royal Institute guidelines. I have transliterated "professor" as *ajarn* rather *ajan* due to personal preference.

Finally, in Thailand, dates are calculated in terms of the Buddhist era (BE), which is the common era (CE) plus 543 years. This means, for example, that 1932 CE is 2475 BE and 2016 CE is 2559 BE. Although I use CE dates in the main body of my text, when citing Thai-language sources, I first specify the BE publication date and then include the CE date in brackets immediately following.

IN PLAIN SIGHT

INTRODUCTION

Impunity as State Formation

ON THE FIFTIETH ANNIVERSARY of the Universal Declaration of Human Rights (UDHR), 10 December 1998, the United Nations (UN) issued the "Declaration on Human Rights Defenders" in recognition of the importance of the defense of human rights, the shared responsibility of all humans to defend them, and the need for protection of defenders in light of the significant risks they face. Article 1 stipulates, "Everyone has the right, individually and in association with others, to promote and to strike for the protection and realization of human rights and fulfillment at the national and international levels." The declaration was the product of over fourteen years of work by individual defenders and nongovernmental organizations out of the recognition that those who protect rights often face reprisals in the form of violation of their own rights, particularly in states in which legal and institutional protections are either slim or nonexistent.

The life and struggles of Chiranuch Premchaiporn and the life, struggles, and death of Somchai Neelapaijit offer sharp evidence of the risk of taking up the call to protect human rights in Thailand. On 6 March 2009 Chiranuch Premchaiporn, the executive director and web board moderator for Prachatai, the leading independent online media outlet in Thailand, was arrested and accused of ten counts of violation of the 2007 Computer Crimes Act, with involvement under Article 112, the section of the Criminal Code that criminalizes alleged lèse majesté. Her crime was not removing ten comments with alleged antimonarchy content from the Prachatai web board *quickly enough*. If convicted, she faced a maximum prison sentence

3

of fifty years. She pled innocent. On 30 May 2012 she was found guilty of one of the ten counts and sentenced to a fine and eight months' imprisonment, which was suspended for one year. In the count for which she was found guilty, she allowed a comment deemed to impugn the king to remain online for twenty days before removing it; in the instances in which Chiranuch was judged innocent, she removed the comments within one to eleven days after they were posted. This decision was upheld by both the Appeal and the Supreme Courts in the name of protection of national security and the institution of the monarchy.

On the evening of 12 March 2004 Somchai Neelapaijit, a lawyer and human rights defender, was pulled out of his car by five policemen and then disappeared. One day earlier Somchai had filed a torture complaint on behalf of five young men charged with national security crimes. Angkhana, Somchai's wife, and human rights activists pushed for prosecution in the case of the disappearance, and the five policemen were indicted in 2004. There is no category of disappearance within Thai law, and so the five policemen were instead charged with robbery, assault, and coercion. Although there were witnesses who saw Somchai being pulled from his car, a host of evidentiary and procedural problems and interference meant that only one of the policemen was convicted, on 12 January 2006, for the relatively minor crime of coercion and sentenced to two years in prison. The Appeal and the Supreme Courts overturned this decision and exonerated all the police officers.

The contrast between the outcomes in these two cases is stark and is therefore worth repeating. A journalist, activist, and human rights defender can be found guilty and sentenced to a prison term for allegedly allowing a post containing content critical of the monarchy to remain online for too many days before being erased. The murderers of another human rights defender and lawyer who was pulled from his car in plain sight and disappeared can be exonerated of all crimes, including the theft of his car. The perpetrators can be exonerated even when their actions are witnessed by a number of bystanders.

Impunity, by which I mean the persistent and repeated failure to secure accountability for state violence, has been produced by means of the intimidation of citizens, weak institutional structures, the unwillingness of state officials to find their colleagues responsible, and the unquestionable and shadowy presence of the institution of the monarchy in the polity. The systematic suppression of critical ideas that question the monarchy and other institutions of authority by citizens in Thailand and the prevention of holding state officials accountable for violent actions perpetrated against citizens are twin processes that generate impunity. Unmasking the identities, interests, and networks of those who facilitate this twin set of processes remains impossible in the present moment. This book is a history of this impossibility.

BEYOND REGIME CHANGE

The production and consolidation of impunity cuts across the continual regime changes that have punctuated the many years since the end of the absolute monarchy on 24 June 1932. Between 1932 and 2017, the country experienced twelve successful—meaning that power was seized—coups, seven failed coup attempts, twenty-eight prime ministers, and twenty constitutions.[1] Modern Thai history is frequently periodized by means of these coups and changes in government. During regimes both dictatorial and democratic, the state has consistently used extrajudicial violence, understood here as the use of injurious or fatal violence against citizens, as a form of repression. Dictatorships have ended and there have been gradual returns to elections and more participatory politics, yet there has never been a transition to democracy that has included an accounting of the violence and rights violations perpetrated by the previous regimes. While there have been investigations in several instances, and prosecutions in several individual cases, there has never been a criminal conviction for mass extrajudicial violence, and convictions even in individual cases have rarely withstood appeal. Witnesses recant or disappear, and evidence is lost. Often the law has worked to create, rather than prevent, impunity for extrajudicial violence either by making it difficult to prosecute state officials or by designating categories of citizens who are beyond the protection of the law. Human rights—as a collection of ideals, a set of legal instruments, a platform for diplomacy, and a series of social movements—variously coexist with, fail to apprehend, and challenge impunity in Thailand. Impunity is rarely a secret process but rather one that takes place in plain sight. At every stage—the instance of state violence, the evasion of accountability, and the creation of evidence and the historical record—the public nature of impunity makes it pedagogical for both state perpetrators and citizens.

Acknowledging yet departing from the calendar of frequent regime changes, this book offers a new history of postabsolutist Thailand viewed through the lens of impunity. Beginning with the end of the absolute monarchy on 24 June 1932 and concluding with the immediate aftermath of the 22 May 2014 coup, I provide a chronological account of the production of impunity through the examination of a series of different events and periods of state violence in Thailand. Although I do not treat the years between 1932 and 1944 in detail, I locate 1932 as the beginning due to the promise of progressive social and political transformation represented by the end of the absolute monarchy and the failure of this promise to be fully realized. Three premises and lines of inquiry recur throughout the book.

First and primary, by elaborating on the way changes and continuities in the forms of impunity that protect perpetrators have become institutionalized, I treat impunity as a constituent part of state formation and nation building. Impunity may seem to be contingent each time a set of state perpetrators escapes accountability, but its effects over time are not. Each time a state official is exonerated or simply not prosecuted for arbitrarily detaining, torturing, disappearing, or murdering a citizen, it becomes easier for violence to occur again. Over time, injustice comes to structure relationships between state officials and citizens. To put the argument in other words, rather than the monopoly on legitimate violence being the defining characteristic of the state, as Max Weber and others have argued, the exercise, repetition, and lack of accountability for illegitimate violence is the defining characteristic of the state.[2]

By arguing that state formation is accomplished through the production of impunity, I am proposing a different way of understanding the state, which argues that extrajudicial violence and also those forms of violence that are provided with a gloss of legality through executive orders, court decisions, and other legal instruments but remain illegitimate uses of violence, as well as violations of human rights, are the actions by which the state is formed and secures compliance from its citizens. Unlike some models of the state, including those of the Thai state such as the "bureaucratic polity," "network monarchy," and "deep state," by proposing that impunity is a form of state formation rather than an analysis of key actors or institutions, I am instead shifting attention to how key actors and institutions are formed and, in particular, how they do so by visiting violence on the people.[3] The reason why securing accountability remains difficult, if not impossible, is because perpetrators aim to avoid individual punishment and also because the patterns of abuse and impunity are essential to maintaining the power of the institutions of which they are a part, that is, the police, military, and judiciary. In other words, the illegitimate use of violence and the subsequent securing of impunity for it are not expressions of the power of state institutions or officials but rather the very means through which they secure power. Further, the political and historiographic erasure of previous instances of impunity is a key part of state formation, rather than incidental to it, and the empirical content of this book both illustrates and aims to directly challenge it.

Second, by tracing the twin rise of state engagement in human rights and the institutionalization of human rights violations, the book demystifies human rights principles and institutions and demonstrates how they can be used to cover up, rather than only prevent, repression. Siam was one of the initial forty-eight countries that voted in favor of the UDHR in 1948, and the official position of the state has always been one of support for human rights.[4] But the relationship between the stances on human rights taken internationally, such as in reporting to the UN or offering input on international human rights treaties, and the protection of human rights domestically has never been straightforward or unitary, at least partially due to the fragmented nature of the state. The Ministry of Foreign Affairs (MFA) and the Office of the Council of State, or Krisdika—which is composed of legal scholars and practitioners, serves as a law drafting and legal advisory body to other parts of the state, and has frequently formulated the official state positions regarding human rights—have not always taken the same position as the army or the police. Summary detention and execution during the late 1950s, for example, coexisted with radio programs about the UDHR and sustained and supportive engagement with the drafting of the Convention on the Prevention and Punishment of the Crime of Genocide. The contradiction here, and the ways in which the state did not recognize it as a contradiction, or at least not as an irresolvable one, reveals the constant flux in the meanings of both "human" and "rights." This flux is affected by changing domestic, regional, and international politics and relations.

Third, by detailing the failures to break the links between legal institutions and violence over time, the book identifies the ways in which the legacies of impunity affect individuals, communities, and the nation. By placing the production of impunity side by side with the different challenges to impunity made by victims and survivors of state violence, occasional civil servants, and, particularly beginning in the 1970s, the international and domestic human rights movements, the new history of modern Thailand I construct in this book is not a seamless one of state domination but also records and takes account of the continual and courageous challenges made to it.

I do not, and cannot, provide an exhaustive account of all instances of state violence, the production of impunity, or struggles to discover the truth and forge justice since the end of the absolute monarchy. Much like Michel-Rolph Trouillot's argument that the identification and exposition of the "particular bundle of silences" that constitute historical narratives is a continual process, writing a history of impunity is similarly recursive.[5] Once one instance of violence or the evasion of responsibility for it is identified, related or resonant stories emerge at the temporal and geographic margins. For example, in 2009, as I was conducting research about the exposure and campaign for accountability in the case of the *thang daeng*, or "red drum," killings, in which several thousand villagers accused of being communists were arrested, tortured, and then burned alive in the southern Thai province of Phatthalung in 1972 during the Cold War, I met an elderly woman who told me that similar kinds of killings occurred during that period in her village in Narathiwat, a province farther to the south. The *thang daeng* killings and the burning of the village of Ban Na Sai, which are taken up in chapter 3, were exposed by chance by students who were in the area for election campaigning during the period of open politics between the 14 October 1973 movement for democracy and the 6 October 1976 massacre and coup when villagers raised the issue. There may have been other villages in which similar forms of violence occurred, yet no one came to inquire and the survivors were too afraid to speak out given both the experience of terror and the ongoing militarization during the Cold War. Further, in Thailand, as well as elsewhere, an end to state violence in the near future is implausible. This means that my goal is not to write a definitive history of impunity for state violence in Thailand. Instead, I offer a partial account in recognition of and response to ongoing violence.

EVIDENCE OF VIOLENCE IN THE ABSENCE OF JUSTICE OR TRANSITION

The available evidence of state violence and the production of impunity is rarely as sparse as one might assume. What is available and access to it may depend on the kind of regime, whether there has been a transition or other kinds of justice processes, laws providing access to information, and contingency. A willingness to be surprised, and to look in both unexpected and obvious places, is necessary.

Upon discovering reams of copious documents in the aftermath of violent regimes, both critics and supporters of those regimes may be caught unaware. Why would a regime keep records of the brutal, and often illegal, actions it took? Why would records be kept of those who were arbitrarily detained and tortured? Why would files about those targeted for assassination be archived when even the fact of their assassination was not duly noted? And yet violent regimes frequently keep extensive records about their actions and opponents. Reasons include the need to maintain bureaucratic logic, a desire to provide evidence to justify the barbarous actions taken, and willful denial that these actions were in violation of both the letter of the law and the unwritten principles of humanity. During a time of repression, neither the end of a regime nor the idea that its documents might one day become public is imaginable. An arrogance born of authoritarianism ensures this unimaginability.

At the moment of transition, or sometimes just prior to it, organs of a repressive regime may have the foresight to destroy their records, such as the National Intelligence Service in apartheid South Africa, which disposed of approximately forty-four tons of microfilm and paper records in 1993.[6] Yet not every regime does so in time. For example, over a hundred thousand documents were found in Tuol Sleng, a former school in suburban Phnom Penh that the Khmer Rouge turned into a detention and torture center, when the regime fell in 1979.[7] Or a regime may feel so secure in the defensibility of its actions that it allows access to its internal documents, and this access provides the evidence to cause its undoing, such as in the case of the military dictatorship of Brazil in place from 1965 to 1984. Activists used limited access to records of military court proceedings to compile a catalog of the regime's violence.[8] In yet other cases, a cache of documents found in an unexpected location years after the end of the regime can illuminate the extent of repression and provide evidence for renewed efforts to seek justice, such as in the case of the accidentally discovered archive of the Guatemalan National Police. Among the evidence of routine bureaucracy found in the more than eighty million pages, there were details about persons detained, tortured, and killed during the civil war (1960–96).[9] In each of these cases, the documents released or found at or after the transition provide clear evidence of the violent actions of the regimes. Material contained in state documents may offer crucial information to victims and survivors and serve as evidence in struggles for justice and accountability.

But what, then, of regimes in which no transition has taken place or the transition has been incomplete? What of state archives and the possibilities of their contents speaking to both obscured histories and state involvement in violence? When documents of the state security forces have not been forcibly or contingently declassified, and instead remain under a heavy cloak of secrecy in the name of national security, what can the often scant public archives contain? Instead of potentially legally actionable content or records of those whose lives were devastated by state violence, deliberations about carefully constructed amnesties, queries about the outer limits of what actions can be taken and still be considered lawful, and expansive absences are present. Innuendo and lacunae reign, and the historian must become a detective to decode a hidden transcript of repression. The phrase "hidden transcript" belongs to James C. Scott, and he uses it to identify the evidence of peasant dissidence and rebellion, even when it seems like the power of the landowners is total.[10] The hidden transcripts of impunity can be found in state archival documents, newspapers, memoirs, and other sources in the public record. Here the question becomes how to read the documents and materials that may exist in regimes that have not undergone transitions against the grain in order to identify a different kind of hidden transcript: indications of complicity and participation in violence, anxiety, and the evasion of responsibility itself—a hidden transcript of domination, then, not resistance. The presence of this hidden transcript, and the contempt and denial of the possibility of being impugned that make it detectable, is itself proof of the violence that has been committed. The often public nature of this hidden transcript is further confirmation of both the violence it aims to mask and the contempt and denial of the possibility of being impugned. Rather than accidental, the presence of evidence of impunity in plain sight ensures that its lessons are transmitted to would-be perpetrators, would-be victims, and society at large. Through the repeated transmission of these lessons, they come to be seen as normal.

This book is grounded in twenty-six months of archival research, court observation, and interviews carried out over eight years in Thailand, including an extended eleven-month period (May 2013 to April 2014). Prior to beginning research, I assumed that as part of the production of impunity there would be no public record of state involvement in violence. My assumption was incorrect. While there is no cache of stockpiled military or police documents such as the one found in Guatemala, at least not one that has been discovered, in the chapters that follow I assemble the available evidence of violence into a history of impunity in postabsolutist Thailand primarily through documentary sources already in the public record: archival documents, parliamentary records, newspaper accounts, legal documents, funeral volumes, memoirs by civil servants, newsletters and other documents of human rights groups, and other accounts.[11] Rather than merely noting this as a matter of context, I examine the forms and availability of documentation as part of the way impunity is secured and maintained by the state. Informed by Robin Wagner-Pacifici, who notes in her work on George W. Bush regime security documents that analysis of "state self-articulation and self-documentation must pose the question of how these documents carry forward these burdens," the chapters that follow are both documentary and methodological.[12] I assemble, trace, and analyze instances of violence largely absent from the scholarly record about Thailand and in so doing develop a methodology for writing histories of impunity that extends beyond Thailand.

But the book and my interest in impunity began outside the archives. Since 2006 I have spent many days sitting in courtrooms observing freedom of expression, disappearance, extrajudicial killing, and torture cases with human rights colleagues. The premise behind court observation is that it is a way to show solidarity with survivors and victims of state violence and also to be a visible reminder to judges that they are being watched. In extrajudicial violence and torture cases involving police, for example, I saw large numbers of police, some in uniform, fill the courtrooms in support of their accused colleagues. I saw them cheer and congratulate one another when their colleagues were exonerated, while survivors of violence, or their families in the cases of the dead, were within arm's reach. I saw men on trial for what they wrote or said walk into a courtroom shackled as a matter of regulation, unable to return the *wai* with which their supporters greeted them because if they did so they would drop the string attached to their shackles that kept them from tripping.[13] I saw people judged guilty and sentenced to lengthy prison terms for daring to express their ideas about the institution of the monarchy and then return to the courtroom to be judged once again on appeal. A profound disjuncture emerged and forms the backdrop to this research. Certain people can be killed with impunity, and certain others cannot be impugned.

By utilizing a framework that bridges scholarship with a human rights consciousness, I take Alfred W. McCoy's idea that "history itself, the recording of a troubled past, can serve as an antidote to the oblivion that is the prime requisite of impunity" as a methodological imperative to redress ongoing impunity for state violence in the Thai present.[14] What makes writing a history of impunity different from writing a history of state violence, and lends an added urgency to the question of sources, is the concern with redress of violence made explicit by a focus on impunity. The call to accountability for state violence that redressing impunity necessitates is inherently a demand for access to the facts and knowledge of the violence. This is reflected in the principles developed to combat impunity by the United Nations Commission on Human Rights, which comprise the right to know, the right to justice, the right to reparations, and the guarantee of nonrecurrence.[15] The right to the truth means that knowledge about violence that has taken place and the conditions and logics that made it possible must be made available to victims, survivors, their families, and the societies in which it took place. Support of the right to know can include the establishment of truth commissions, the opening of archives, and the preservation of documents. The right to justice means that there must be "prompt, thorough, independent and impartial investigations" to prosecute and punish perpetrators.[16] Although the guarantee of the right to justice is the responsibility of states, victims, survivors, and their families should also have the right to initiate cases against perpetrators. The right to reparations and the guarantee of nonrecurrence mean that the state must provide reparations to victims and victims must be able to pursue redress from perpetrators. The guarantee of nonrecurrence is meant to ensure that rights violations do not occur again. This can be secured through support of the right to know and the right to justice, as well as a combination of institutional reform and the creation of respect for the rule of law and human rights.

While they were developed for human rights practitioners, the principles also highlight what is at stake in investigating and writing a history of impunity.[17] Much like Karl Marx's eleventh thesis on Feuerbach—"The philosophers have only interpreted the world, in various ways; the point is to change it"—the principles are a reminder that the writing of histories of impunity, which could be considered a contribution to the right to know, does not exist outside the injustice or ongoing violence that necessitate it.[18]

THAILAND'S EXEMPLARY INJUSTICE CASCADE

Drawing on a database of 109 transitions to democracy in 86 countries between 1970 and 2011, Kathryn Sikkink argues that there has been a "justice cascade," by which she means that a combination of international, foreign, and domestic prosecutions of perpetrators of human rights violations "comprise an interrelated, dramatic new trend in world politics towards holding individual state officials, including heads of state, criminally accountable for human rights violations."[19] The justice cascade is not accidental but is a result of the human rights movement and the concerted and courageous actions of activists in pushing for accountability for state violence. Sikkink is careful to stipulate that the emergence of the justice cascade does not mean that all state officials who perpetrate rights violations have been successfully prosecuted and punished but rather that the idea that they should be held to account has become a norm. There are three constituent parts to what she calls the "justice norm." First, rights violations, including arbitrary detention, extrajudicial killing, torture, disappearance, and others discussed in this book, "cannot be legitimate acts of state and thus must be seen as crimes committed by individuals."[20] Second, perpetrators of these acts should be prosecuted. Third, perpetrators also have rights that must be protected, and therefore they must be tried fairly (e.g., a show trial cannot result in justice).[21] While the justice cascade has not taken place evenly throughout the world, Sikkink argues that there is an unfolding of "a decentralized but interactive system of accountability for violations of core political rights with fragmented enforcement, which is primarily undertaken by domestic courts" influenced by transformations in international human rights law.[22]

The idea of the justice cascade is a powerful, and hopeful, one. What I learned as I completed the research for this book is that it has not borne out over the last eighty years in Thailand.[23] Sikkink notes that Asia is the region in which there has been the least diffusion of prosecutions, with only 6 percent of domestic prosecutions and 5 percent of foreign and international prosecutions globally having taken place in Asia between 1979 and 2009.[24] The story of impunity in Thailand that I trace in this book is instead an uneven and episodic *injustice* cascade. Accountability for state violence is the exception, not an emerging norm. Evidence of this compounded injustice can be found at both the level of the state qua state, in the series of coups and subsequent series of amnesties for coups most evident in the level of individual actors, and the difficulty of holding state officials who perpetrate violence against citizens to account. The example with which I began, of the contrasting prosecutions of Chiranuch Premchaiporn and the state officials who disappeared Somchai Neelapaijit, is the norm rather than the exception.

This norm of protection of the monarch and dispossession of the people is the result of the incompletion of the 24 June 1932 transformation from absolute to constitutional monarchy and lingering absolutism and inequality between the rulers and the ruled that are so deep seated as to almost seem intrinsic. Although the transformation wrought by the People's Party was described by one of its progenitors, Pridi Banomyong, as effecting "a change from the system of government in which the king is above the law to the system of government in which the king is under the law," the king remains above the law and the Thai people remain under the king.[25] Immediately after the transformation, Rama VII (King Prajadhipok) and many royalists immediately began to oppose this change using both legal and extralegal means.[26] These included, for example, ensuring that in the first permanent constitution, of 10 December 1932, the phrase *phra maha kasat* (great and sacred king) was used rather than simply "king."[27] Even more significant, while the temporary 27 June 1932 constitution stipulated that sovereignty belonged to the people, the 10 December constitution kept this article but immediately followed it with one noting that this sovereignty would be exercised by the king.[28] This fundamental, and unresolved, contradiction has remained present in subsequent constitutions. Alongside these legal maneuvers, which were carried out by royalists on the constitutional drafting committee, royalists also engaged in political surveillance, constant plotting and attempts to overthrow the civilian government, and planned assassinations of members of the People's Party. Although King Prajadhipok and the royalists were unable to fully reverse the transformation wrought by the People's Party, legal and extralegal opposition to democracy became a continuing aspect of Thai social and political life, felt both in the use of Article 112 to limit criticism of the monarchy and in various waves of vigilantism against those who dare to question the place of the monarchy in political life.

A resonant unresolved contradiction in the relationship between the rulers and the ruled is present in what Thongchai Winichakul identifies as the *nitirat baep thai thai* (Thai-style rule of law), which functions as a persistent obstacle to the consolidation of human rights in Thailand. While what appear to be the universal language, discourse, practices, and institutions of law, human rights, and justice emerged and are used in Thailand, the process by which they did so was a collision of *kan pata prap plae* (translation and modification) that reflected and reinforced long-standing relationships between the rulers (including but not limited to the king) and the ruled marked by profound hierarchy and inequality. He notes, "Even though the law stipulates that individuals are equal, equality remains impossible in actual power and social relations."[29] Rather than the equality inherent in "human rights," the original idea of rights that remains operative in Thailand is that of the *amnat saksit* (sacred power) one possesses naturally on the basis of one's position in society.[30] This understanding takes the concrete form of the unequal possession by or application of this power to people differently located in society. With respect to impunity, this means that those in positions of power across state institutions remain *above* the people and therefore possess the *privilege* of not being held to account for actions taken against those below.[31] What makes both the incomplete transformation from absolute monarchy and the lingering ideas of inequality in Thai-style rule of law particularly dangerous is that the dispossession of the people and their rights takes place in a regime that is ostensibly not an absolutist one and in which human rights are respected.

The norm of dispossession of the people became even more pronounced during the final years of the reign of Rama IX, or Bhumibol Adulyadej, who died at the age of eighty-eight on 13 October 2016 after becoming king on 9 June 1946 following the death of his older brother. There is political will among a significant majority of judges and royalists, both those in elite class positions and not, to prosecute citizens for insulting the monarchy in comments made on web boards, in Facebook posts, in text messages, and in theater plays, but not the will to hold the police or military accountable for murdering citizens. One way to understand this discrepancy is to subscribe to the view held by those who justify the recent harsh sentences meted out in the name of protection of the monarchy. Members of the judiciary and the MFA do not deny that there are restrictions on freedom of expression, but they claim that these measures are both necessary and compatible with the protection of human rights due to the unique importance of the monarchy and the figure of the king within Thailand.[32] Rather than uniqueness, however, this is an expression of the profound inequality that structures the polity. The subtext of the claim to uniqueness is that universal ideas about human rights and freedom of expression do not apply where the monarchy is concerned.

There is nothing new about the argument of the uniqueness of Thailand and, in particular, the uniqueness of the role of the monarchy. In his 1978 essay "Studies of the Thai State: The State of Thai Studies," Benedict Anderson argued that scholars of Thailand *assumed* the uniqueness of the country and forewent a critical stance that would have resulted from engaging in comparison.[33] The result, he argued, has been an uncritical view of the monarchy and the propagation of a series of incorrect ideas about it as having protected the country from colonization and functioning as a modernizing force of stability. In contrast, the Chakri kings, the dynasty that has ruled Thailand from 1782 until the present, collaborated with colonial powers for their own benefit and engaged in a series of colonial projects in the north, northwest, and south that have generated instability.[34] Following the 6 October 1976 massacre and coup, the uncritical stance held by many scholars began to change.[35] In the intervening years, a growing body of critical scholarship has been produced, the majority in Thai rather than English, yet the claim to Thai uniqueness has remained a strong tool of those in power.[36]

It may seem paradoxical that I raise the critique of uniqueness along with making an argument for an *injustice* cascade, rather than the more diffuse and common *justice* cascade, in Thailand. Am I not making an argument for Thailand's uniqueness in another register? No. The history of impunity in Thailand and the concomitant injustice cascade is exemplary rather than unique. The difference is important because it makes possible the comparison Anderson argued was necessary. In his work on lèse majesté, sedition, and dictatorship, David Streckfuss brings a comparative lens to the study of repression in Thailand by drawing on Giorgio Agamben's idea of the state of exception. Agamben's idea of the state of exception was influenced by Carl Schmitt's writings on law and the political during the Third Reich and is "a suspension of the juridical order itself," which then defines who is placed outside the protection of the law.[37] Streckfuss argues that a state of exception has dominated Thai politics since Rama IX ascended to the throne and is marked by three characteristics that stress narrow definitions of the moral and the political. First, there is no space for the people in the practice of politics. Second, the ideology of Thainess, or what it means to be Thai, and its accompanying hierarchies of definition and purity dominate public life. The king and, following the 22 May 2014 coup by the NCPO, the coup leader are at the top of this hierarchy as the only truly moral figures in the country. Third, there is a continual pursuit of impossible purity and the exclusion from the polity of all those who do not fit the definition of what it means to be Thai. In the name of purity, the expulsion of corrupt politicians, the prosecution of dissident citizens, and the protection of those at the top of the hierarchy have become moral acts.[38]

I propose a resonant argument in this book. The production of impunity since the end of the absolute monarchy in 1932 in Thailand has relied on the simultaneous production of certain members of the polity as human and others as not fully human. Who counts as human and who does not, and is therefore placed beyond the pale of the protection of the law, shifts over time and across regimes. While the notion that certain members of the polity are less than human has its roots in absolutism aided by Buddhist cosmology, it has been continually reproduced through state violence, prosecutions of dissidents, and the failure to secure accountability for state violence in the years since the end of absolutism. The Thai government cites the sacredness of the monarchy in order to claim the uniqueness of the relationship between the rulers and the ruled in the country. I instead take the position that the unquestionable presence of the monarchy offers an exemplary, but not unique, instance of inequality between the rulers and ruled. This inequality rests on a disregard for shared humanity and basic dehumanization. The example of Thailand's particular injustice cascade, then, may resonate and illuminate moments, events, and explanations of repression, and the notion of the human required to sustain it, elsewhere.

Toward a New History of Human Rights

Examining the relationships between the rulers and the ruled and state formation in Thailand by tracing state violence, human rights, and impunity changes how we understand Thai history. Simultaneously, the history of human rights as a set of ideas and institutions in Thailand raises comparative questions for international human rights history after the promulgation of the UDHR on 10 December 1948. Scholars and practitioners tend to assume that the adoption of human rights principles by states always leads to improvements in human rights.[39] As I conducted the research for this book, I had to cast this assumption aside. In Thailand, human rights have been actively taken up and manipulated by state officials to legitimize and repeatedly cover up state violence. This manipulation is not accidental or the result of a failure to understand the meaning of human rights but rather the choice by the state to make human rights a site of contention and struggle where the relationship between the rulers and the ruled is formed and reflected. This struggle began in the immediate aftermath of the promulgation of the UDHR.

The thirty articles of the UDHR cover civil and political rights, as well as economic, social, and cultural rights. Taken as a whole, the articles are a succinct description of the specific human rights that must be protected in order to make real the ideal contained in the preamble to the UDHR: "Recognition of the inherent dignity and of the equal and inalienable rights of all members of the human family is the foundation of freedom, justice and peace in the world."[40] Forty-eight of the fifty-six UN member nations that gathered in Paris to vote on the UDHR voted in its support.[41]

But despite the eloquence of the UDHR in the service of the individual human, the declaration and the institutions that sprung up around it left the primacy of the nation in place.[42] During the early years of the international human rights regime, bureaucrats, including those of both the UN and member nations, were the primary figures defining, deploying, and writing about human rights. The *people*, the ostensible humans at the center of human rights, were largely absent. Commenting on the early years following the promulgation of the UDHR, Samuel Moyn argues that "the 1940s were not to be the hour for 'human rights,'" which instead came to prominence in the late 1970s with the development of a global human rights movement.[43]

Moyn's timeline is persuasive and partially resonates with the place of human rights—as an institution, movement, and set of ideals—in Thai history. Thailand (then Siam) was one of the forty-eight nations that voted in support of the UDHR. During the nearly thirty years between 1948 and the 6 October 1976 massacre, different Thai state ministries and departments participated in the nascent international human rights regime, including domestic celebrations of the UDHR's declaration, providing commentary to the relevant drafting committees of UN human rights instruments, and contributing to the annual *UN Human Rights Yearbook*.[44] The term *sitthi manutsayachon* (human rights) was used by prime ministers and military dictators throughout the 1950s and 1960s, as I discuss in chapter 2, but it only rarely entered popular discourse before the emergence of the domestic Thai human rights movement in the late 1970s. Rather than a tool used to challenge dictatorship, the language of human rights was one that dictators could speak fluently without having to alter their repressive actions. Field Marshal Sarit Thanarat could even announce that his autocoup, launched against his own government to consolidate his power, of October 1958 would respect the UDHR with no apparent irony.[45]

The contingent constellation of events, globally and in Thailand, that created the conditions for the emergence of both the global and domestic human rights movements, which I examine in chapter 5, offers a partial explanation of this timeline. But this tells us *why* the 1970s rather than *why not* the 1940s. Moyn suggests that the challenge is to understand the failure of human rights in the 1940s and "to come to grips with why they had no function to play then, compared to the ideological circumstances three decades later."[46] Exploring this question in Thailand during the two decades after the promulgation of the UDHR, two decades in which authoritarianism increased, both provides a specific answer to Moyn's question and transforms it. Rather than *why not* human rights for the people, the question becomes *how* and *why* did a series of authoritarian governments take up the language of human rights and participate in the international human rights regime? Thailand was not the only country with an authoritarian government to do so, but the intersections of authoritarianism and the early decades of the UDHR remain understudied, especially in Asia.[47]

Samuel Moyn argues that the beginning of the international human rights regime was characterized by a failure to take it up widely by citizens opposing repressive states because "human rights were compelled to define the good life and offer a plan for bringing it about precisely when they were ill-equipped by the fact of their suprapolitical birth to do so."[48] They functioned as what he calls a moral utopia that came about precisely because World War II and the Holocaust destroyed all existing possible political utopias. Human rights as a moral utopia, without any political or legal backbone, is what made it possible for Siam, then Thailand, to engage in the early years of the international human rights regime with no seeming contradiction even as the ruling governments grew increasingly authoritarian. The political possibility of a transition to communism, in turn, is what made allowing the people to exercise basic rights, such as freedom of thought and expression, political association, and demonstration, so terrifying to Thai and other military, royal, capital, and other elites.

The emergence of both the Thai and international human rights movements in the 1970s generated a set of tools people could use to defend their rights from the violations wrought by the state. The ongoing work of defending human rights by activists, which functions to both protect individuals and contribute to creating a society in which the promises of the UDHR are made real, provides a powerful counter to the use and abuse of human rights by both dictators and career state officials who violate the rights of the people no matter the regime. The birth of the UDHR and the early international human rights regime may have been suprapolitical, but rights and their violation quickly became political acts implicated in the exercise and accumulation of ruling power. Recognition of the use of human rights by dictators as a political act, rather than merely contradictory, accidental, or farcical, is the beginning of wresting them out of their hands. The reason is that doing so is part of returning human rights—as a language, ideal, and set of tools with which to challenge power—to the hands of the people, where they should have been located from the start.

A Guide to Reading

The goals of this book are at once empirical and methodological. The book provides an analysis of instances unknown, or little known, in the English-language scholarship about Thailand and in many cases the Thai-language scholarship as well. The accounts of extrajudicial violence, repressive use of the law, and the failure to hold state perpetrators to account comprise a new history of Thailand complete with a new chronology, new actors, and new unresolved questions.[49] One way to understand the years since the end of the absolute monarchy in Thailand in 1932 is as a period of sustained contention in which the rulers and the ruled have been locked in a struggle over sovereignty across the country's numerous coups, prime ministers, and constitutions. At key moments since 1932, namely, the 14 October 1973 and May 1992 movements and ousters of dictatorship, the people have wrested sovereignty from the hands of the elites. But just as frequently the elites have taken it back, often using tremendous violence to do so, such as during the 6 October 1976 massacre and the April–May 2010 crackdown on red shirt protesters. Despite the transformation to a constitutional regime, sovereignty—the power to rule, to define politics and determine who can participate in the making of the polity, and to set the limits on what can be expressed—remains with the institution of the monarchy, its self-proclaimed protectors, the judiciary, the military, and others allied with them. This power is guaranteed by the letter of the law, the bars of the prison cell, and the guns of the soldiers. Impunity is the force behind this power.

But this is not a book written only for those interested in Thailand. While the empirical material is specific to Thailand, the way in which this new history is sourced—from material in the public record—and sewn together demonstrates a methodology for uncovering and questioning impunity in plain sight in other contexts as well.

The first chapter forms a pair with this introduction to outline key concerns, questions, and methods for those writing histories of impunity. In this chapter I trace arbitrary detention over time as a way to understand the production of impunity through a specific form of violence and also to illustrate how a lens of impunity renders a new historical calendar. When arbitrary detention, which recurs across time and different types of regimes, is placed at the center of analysis, then the importance of the usual markers of continuity and change, such as prime ministers or coups, is replaced with concern about which citizens are targeted and how much room to maneuver there is for those cast as enemies by the state. Beginning in the late 1930s, legal instruments have been used to place groups of individuals beyond the protection of the law five times. State officials identified these groups as "enemies of the nation" during the late 1930s and World War II, "hooligans" under Field Marshal Sarit Thanarat (1958–63), "dangers to society" following the 6 October 1976 coup, "terrorists" in southern Thailand since January 2004, and a range of unlabeled dissidents following the 22 May 2014 coup. While conditions vary across and within each era, members of these groups variously experienced arbitrary detention, interrogation, reeducation, torture, and other violence at the hands of state actors. What each instance prior to the present also shares is that at the conclusion of the crisis, the measure was repealed, often with grave concern noted about the dangers of such a measure to democracy and the people. When the instrument returned in the next moment of crisis, the structure of the law was remembered and put in place, but the note of concern was not. How does the repetition of arbitrary detention over time contribute to the production of impunity, and how can the efficacy of the challenges to it be assessed given its recurrence?

The six subsequent chapters provide a chronological account of the production of impunity through the examination of a series of different events and periods of state violence in Thailand beginning with the promulgation of the UDHR on 10 December 1948 and continuing up to the 22 May 2014 coup. Chapters 2, 3, and 4 address the period between 1948 and 6 October 1976. For nearly thirty years following the promulgation of the UDHR, the Thai state, like others around the world, was able to keep the definition and use of human rights principles under state control. Chapter 2 examines the coexistence of Thai state participation in the international human rights regime during the late 1940s and 1950s and arbitrary, executive power writ large in the case of the dreaded Matra 17 (Article 17). Article 17 of the 1959 interim constitution promulgated by Field Marshal Sarit Thanarat provided him with "the legal basis . . . to order executions and other activities of the absolutely decisive (*det khat*) variety."[50] Sarit used Article 17 to execute six individuals. I examine Article 17 as a pedagogical measure that taught Thai citizens how little protected they were against the ultimate power of the state. Drawing in each instance on the executive orders and newspaper and other documentary accounts, this chapter also records the specific lives lost, and in this way counteracts the oblivion and silence that state killing is meant to engender. In addition, Sarit spoke in support of human rights yet also viewed the arbitrary detention of "hooligans," examined in chapter 1, as well as Article 17, to be necessary and irrelevant to a discussion of human rights. Rather than dismissing the stance of Sarit and many other leaders who followed him as farce, a cynical ploy to curry favor with other countries, or a lack of understanding of the true meaning of human rights, this chapter takes this as a routine aspect of state forma-tion and examines under what circumstances seeming contradictions—summary execution and human rights—do not register as such.

Drawing on parliamentary debate records, accounts by students and vil-lagers, and civil servants' memoirs, in chapter 3 I reconstruct the Cold War violence of the *thang daeng* (red drum) murders in Phatthalung in 1972 and the burning of the village of Ban Na Sai in 1974. In August 1972 as many as three thousand civilians in Phatthalung, a province in southern Thailand, were arrested on the accusation of being communists, interro-gated and tortured, and then immolated in oil drums. While the presence of a dictatorship in 1972 meant that the event did not become public at the time, it was exposed by villagers and students in February 1975 during the period of more open politics following the events of 14 October 1973. In January 1974 the village of Ban Na Sai in the northeast was burned to the ground by counterinsurgency forces, which claimed that it was a com-munist stronghold. In both cases, in the relatively more open political atmosphere citizens publicly exposed these events and pushed the state to investigate and hold the perpetrators accountable. In both cases, inquiry committees were established by the Ministry of Interior and conducted in-vestigations. To date the perpetrators have not been publicly identified and the reports never became publicly available. What is instead available, in the news clipping section of the National Archives, are close to five hun-dred pages of newspaper articles about the violence experienced by citizens in each instance, the public exposure and demand for investigation of each of these events, and the failure of the reports to be released to the public. In other words, the National Archives holds media documentation of the conscious decision not to secure accountability and instead to produce impunity for state violence. Of particular interest are the contradictory statements uttered by state officials and the victims and their allies, what Leigh Payne calls "unsettling accounts" that create "political competition over how to interpret dramatic political events, how to use them, and what they mean for contemporary political life."[51] While unsettling accounts can foster consensus during democratic regimes, during periods of increased extrajudicial violence the public airing of such debates became an opportunity to demonstrate the sheer vulnerability of those who speak out and signaled the coming return of dictatorship.

In chapter 4, I argue that the two amnesties passed in relation to the 6 October 1976 coup and massacre of students at Thammasat University, which ended the period of open politics begun three years earlier and returned the country to dictatorship, was a turning point for impunity in Thailand, and they serve as a temporal and epistemological one for the book as well. The massacre was carried out by state and parastate actors, and the coup government reported that 3,059 people were arrested, 46 were killed, and more than 180 were injured, although unofficial estimates are much higher. Among the 3,059 people arrested, 18, mostly student activists who survived the violence on the morning of 6 October, were held for nearly two years and tried on a range of trumped-up charges, including being communist activists, committing lèse majesté, and attempting to overthrow the government. The first amnesty law, passed on 24 December 1976, legalized the coup and prevented those who had created the conditions for it and seized power on the evening of 6 October from being held to account. The second amnesty law, passed on 16 September 1978, freed the 18 people still undergoing criminal prosecution and dismissed the charges against them. I unexpectedly found archival documents about the drafting of the first amnesty law and read them together with newspaper and other accounts related to the second to argue that the awareness of state involvement in violence and the conscious decision to foreclose accountability, not only the brutal, public nature of the killing on 6 October, was what signaled a transition to the consolidation of impunity in Thailand and Thai state's engagement in human rights.

Chapters 5, 6, and 7 address the period between 6 October 1976 and the present. After 1976, as torture and extrajudicial violence became normalized, there was an abrupt shift in the stance taken by the state on human rights. In addition, at the moment that the state shifted its forms of engagement

in human rights internationally, the Thai domestic human rights movement emerged, with groups such as the Coordinating Group for Religion
in Society (CGRS) and the Union for Civil Liberty (UCL), both of which
worked closely with Amnesty International (AI) and small solidarity groups
outside the country to document human rights violations in Thailand.
Human rights—as a language, set of principles, and range of tools—no
longer belonged to the state alone. This prompted the emergence of a new
consciousness, and panic, among some Thai state actors and organizations.
While evidence prior to the 1976 massacre and coup supports the idea that
the definitions of "human" and "human rights" in use by the state did not
account for the violations of the rights of certain citizens deemed to be
enemies, the evidence of communication among different ministries about
torture and detention following the massacre and coup indicates that there
was a new awareness inside the state that this was no longer tenable and new
strategies of engagement needed to be found. Chapter 5 begins by linking
the emergence of the Thai domestic human rights movement after 6 October 1976 with global transformations, particularly the US government's turn
toward human rights in its foreign policy. Then I turn to specific instances
of the detention and torture of political dissidents between 1976 and 1979.
In contrast to the detailed documentation compiled by the CGRS and AI,
the MFA claimed that there were no cases of torture in Thailand. Drawing
on state archival documents, primarily a series of exchanges among embassies, the MFA, and the ministries of interior and defense, I analyze the
forms of bureaucratic obfuscation that emerged and how different parts of
the Thai state responded to the demands of human rights activists. Next,
drawing on the materials of the CGRS, I create an alternate accounting of
the rights violations that took place during these years.

Chapter 6 turns to a specific form of violence: enforced disappearance.
While there are at least 179 documented instances of enforced disappearance since 1952, and likely many more hundreds of undocumented cases, no
state official has ever been held to account for his role in a disappearance.
Part of the reason for this is a reflection of the overarching story of this
book and the pervasiveness of impunity in Thailand. This chapter begins
with a partial history of enforced disappearance in Thailand and places it
in relation to other forms of extrajudicial violence both in Thailand and
comparatively beyond Thailand's borders. Then, through a close examination of one case, the disappearance of Somchai Neelapaijit and his family's
struggle for justice, it argues that the very form of the law contributes to

the failure to secure accountability and the consolidation of impunity. When Somchai Neelapaijit disappeared on 12 March 2004, he was working on behalf of five men who had alleged that they were tortured by state security officials while they were in state custody. The day before his disappearance, Somchai had submitted a complaint to the court that detailed the forms of torture experienced by the five men. Despite concerted action by his family and human rights activists, Somchai's body has not been recovered and the perpetrators have not been held to account. Instead, what I term a jurisprudence of impunity has emerged across the court decisions rendered in this case. This chapter traces the intertwined struggles to redress justice in Somchai's case and write disappearance into Thai history.

While the absence of Somchai Neelapaijit's body has contributed to the difficulty of securing justice in his case, even a plethora of physical evidence does not guarantee accountability. During the crackdown on red shirt protesters by Thai state security forces in April and May of 2010, at least ninety-four people were killed and more than two thousand injured. Following investigations by several state and independent agencies, and marking a sharp departure from the past, in December 2013 the former prime minister, Abhisit Vejjajiva, and the former deputy prime minister, Suthep Thaugsuban, were indicted for their roles in orchestrating the crackdown. Yet in late July 2014 the case against them was dismissed with a court decision based on logic that departed significantly from the letter of the law. In contrast to the difficulty of holding perpetrators of the April–May 2010 killings to account, those deemed to speak, write, or otherwise act in a manner than insults the institution of the monarchy have been swiftly punished. Peaceful political expression, offhand comments made inside the home, and bathroom graffiti have all been treated as grave crimes against the crown and state. In many cases, the identification of crimes and the reasoning deployed to justify a ruling of either guilty or innocent also depart significantly from the letter of the law. Chapter 7 takes these departures as neither accidental nor unrelated but rather as foundational and reflective of a logic informing social and political relations in the Thai polity. Drawing on legal documents, writings by political prisoners, and court observation, I compare the legal logics surrounding the proceedings related to the April–May 2010 crackdown and several Article 112 cases. Refracting the question of who continues to be excluded from the protections of human rights, this chapter offers a specific set of answers to the question of who can be killed with impunity and who cannot be impugned and considers what this means about the power of law and who counted as human in late reign Rama IX Thailand.

This book is marked by the return of dictatorship with the 22 May 2014 coup and concludes with a reflection on writing histories of impunity in a time of military rule. The pen of the writer is no match for the guns of soldiers or the keys of the jailers who guard those locked up by the authorities. What the pen, and the writer who holds it, can do so is ensure that their actions are not left unrecorded.

I

The Repetition of
Arbitrary Detention

STATE VIOLENCE, IMPUNITY, AND HUMAN RIGHTS are largely
absent from historical writing about modern Thailand. Scholars who have
taken up the post-1932 period tend to divide their analysis along the temporal lines of coups and regimes.[1] Although instances of mass state violence are
mentioned in these works, especially those centered around the 14 October
1973, 6 October 1976, and May 1992 uprisings and killings, they are addressed as discrete events on the margins rather than central. Smaller-scale
instances of violence and the routine use of law as a form of repression are
absent from these histories. Even the new forms of Thai-language historical writing that emerged after 1973 and 1976, which brought out the experiences and voices of the people rather than those of kings and elites, left
these topics unaddressed.[2] The picture of modern Thai history that emerges
is fundamentally incomplete and elides the way the suffering of the people,
the lack of accountability of state officials, and the people's challenges to
impunity have formed the relationship between the past and the present.

Placing state violence and how impunity for it is secured, rather than
regime change, at the center of the writing of history engenders a new
historical calendar and different understandings of the ways in which social
and political change is both generated and thwarted. In particular, rather
than a trajectory of progress, or even regression, *repetition* emerges as the key
feature of change and continuity over time. By focusing on the repetition
of a form of violence, it becomes possible to see both how accountability is
evaded in a given instance and how this process gathers force.

In this chapter, I take the repetition of arbitrary detention over time as a point of departure and an invitation to think explicitly about how the production of impunity and the construction of history intersect. Although arbitrary detention is a tool of repression frequently used by states against its citizens, there is no clear definition of it in international law.[3] The ICCPR, which links the exercise of basic rights and freedoms to human dignity, prohibits detention as part of Article 9: "No one shall be subjected to arbitrary arrest or detention."[4] The United Nations Working Group on Arbitrary Detention developed the definition of the following three categories of detention deemed arbitrary: (1) when there is no legal basis for the deprivation of liberty, (2) when a person is deprived of liberty guaranteed by either the UDHR or the ICCPR, and (3) when a person has been deprived of his or her liberty without the benefit of a fair trial.[5]

Arbitrary detention in Thailand is explicitly legally codified, and categories of individuals subject to it have been created through executive order, national legislation, and a combination of both. This began with a law and a drafted, but never realized, program of psychological training programs for "enemies of the nation" in 1944 and then returned with arbitrary detention and training of individuals deemed to be "hooligans" under Decrees 21 and 43 of Field Marshal Sarit Thanarat beginning in 1958; the detention and reeducation of individuals deemed to be a "danger to society" under Order 22 of the National Administrative Reform Council (NARC) following 6 October 1976; detention and training of individuals suspected of actual or possible involvement in terrorism under the provisions of martial law and emergency rule in southern Thailand since 2004; and, most recently, the detention and attitude adjustment of dissidents following the 22 May 2014 coup by the National Council for Peace and Order (NCPO) first under martial law and then under Article 44, which replaced martial law in April 2015. Although the targets change, the terms of detention, the absence of either the court or access to legal counsel, and the concomitant attempt to change the thinking of those detained have remained nearly constant across time.

Although held under different legal instruments, the basis for all these detentions was ideological, not legal. The prisoners never appeared in a court or before a judge, let alone underwent a trial before they were detained. They were released from detention after undergoing training, reeducation, or attitude adjustment programs of varying forms and lengths. What these instances also share is that at the conclusion of the crisis, the measure was repealed, often with grave concern noted about the dangers to democracy and the people of such a measure. In the case of Decrees 21 and 43 of Sarit, the repeal was prefigured by a Supreme Court decision ruling on arbitrary detention under the instruments. When the instrument returned with slight modifications during the next moment of crisis, the structure of the law was remembered and put in place, but the note of concern was willfully forgotten or simply not acted on. Although the majority of those detained were not tortured or disappeared, there were cases of both in each period. Knowledge of these cases circulates over time, producing fear and uncertainty at any given moment. While those within the state recall the structure of the law, citizens recall the stories of those who were detained and tortured and those who were taken and never returned home.

While these forms of law create what Giorgio Agamben calls a "state of exception," in which detainees are placed outside the protection and view of the law, the vast majority of those detained are permitted to return to the national community from which they were removed. Rather than being placed in a state of exception, those arbitrarily detained in Thailand are, to use a formulation of Judith Butler's, simultaneously dispossessed and contained. She asks, "What does it mean to be at once contained and dispossessed by the state?"[6] The history of arbitrary detention in Thailand, in which those targeted under the law are denied the protections offered by the polity to its members but then are allowed, even expected, to return to the polity, offers one answer to her question. I identify containment as confinement within boundaries determined by the state.[7] To be dispossessed is to be deprived or denied (of space, thought, or control over one's life) by the state.

Retrospectively, the history of arbitrary detention can seem specific to the political regimes that generated these categories: "danger to the nation," "hooligan," "communist," "danger to society," "terrorist," and "dissident." These categories of individuals targeted for arbitrary detention are not equivalent, and one may be tempted to see a progression—or its opposite—over the sixty years between 1944 and 2014. Rather than collapsing the different forms of detention into one another or trying to rank them in terms of severity, the question instead is to understand how arbitrary detention affects both the lives of those detained and the broader context of daily life in Thailand. In the case of arbitrary detention, impunity is produced *not* through the failure to hold those responsible for it to account but through its failure to even register as a crime.

The choice of arbitrary detention to consider the meaning and effects of the repetition of a form of violence over time is informed by Manfred Nowak, the former UN Special Rapporteur on Torture (2004–10), who highlighted the importance of examining conditions of detention for two primary reasons. The first is that detainees are "one of the last taboos, even in so-called 'open societies.'" The second is that, "as soon as they are behind bars, detainees lose most of their human rights and often are simply forgotten by the outside world. . . . How a society treats its detainees is one of the best indicators for its human rights culture in general."[8] If conditions of detention can tell us about the human rights culture, then tracing detention over time is a way to track the history of this culture and also the tensions among violence, democracy, and security that underline the justifications for the concomitant rights violations and the production of impunity. The dangers posed by the restriction of liberty are forgotten in the service of protecting the nation, and the institutionalized deprivation of liberty becomes regularized as a form of violence and an acceptable strategy of the repressive state. This new history begins in 1944 with an early arbitrary detention law that was never fully realized.

PSYCHOLOGICAL TRAINING SCHOOLS, 1944

Thailand was invaded and occupied by the Japanese Imperial Army on 8 December 1941. The governments of both Field Marshal Phibun Songkhram (16 December 1938–1 August 1944) and Khuang Aphaiwong (1 August 1944–31 August 1945) officially collaborated with the Japanese and the Axis powers in World War II.[9] Martial law was declared on 10 December 1941, and this provided the authorities with extensive powers to ensure order, including seven days of arbitrary detention.[10] After Field Marshal Phibun was replaced with Khuang, the Royal Thai Army found the latitude for suppression under martial law to be lacking.

On 21 January 1945, at the beginning of the last year of the war, the Thai parliament passed the Act for the Internment of Those Who Are a Danger to the Nation during Emergency Times.[11] The law provided for the detention of people deemed to have committed, prepared to commit, or plotted to commit violations of Articles 97 to 115 of the Criminal Code, which delimited offenses against the king and kingdom. If there was any person who violated, or might violate, these measures, then the police commissioner was to arrest them and immediately notify a committee set up under the law. Once this committee of people—rather than a judge or panel of judges in a court—determined that there had been a violation, or might be a violation, of these articles, the person in question could be detained. During this process, fifteen days of initial detention were permitted. Then the committee had to issue an order either stating that the person was a danger to the nation and should be detained further or providing additional time for investigation. The law left the specific places of detention to the discretion of the committee, or the committee aided by the minister of interior, but it was to be a place where he or she would no longer pose a danger to the nation. The length of detention was also left to the committee's discretion. David Streckfuss argues that this law was the beginning of the increased militarization of the judiciary and the idea of "abnormal times," in which martial law was declared and "normal political and legal functions of society were suspended and a temporary, specialized set of laws and procedures took effect to maintain security and peace" until the rulers deemed that such measures were no longer necessary.[12] Although the membership of the first committee was included in the Royal Thai Government Gazette, the law was never put into effect.[13] After the war, the law was formally repealed, on 9 May 1946, as part of the repeal of seven laws enacted to address the emergency times of the war.[14]

Even though the law did not go into effect, the ideas within it, and in particular those that animated its drafting, provide a starting point from which to both date and understand the relationship between the rulers and the ruled and the role of arbitrary detention in forging this relationship within the postabsolutist Thai polity. A series of letters, committee meeting minutes, and a position paper on psychological training schools is present in the collection of the files of the Office of the Juridical Council, or Krisdika, at the National Archives in Bangkok.[15]

The position paper was titled "Regarding Psychological Training Schools," although the small black print of the title was overshadowed by the large, red "Secret" label stamped across the top. The paper was dated 28 October 1944, and the author was only identified by the name Adul. No department or title was specified, although the stance taken means that he can be assumed to have been in the army. Adul complained that martial law did not provide the government with sufficient powers to definitively maintain public order. Yet under the broad authority granted by the act, the commander in chief of the army had established psychological training schools in which the police could detain persons they had arrested or investigated so as "to produce order and [provide] psychological training in

order to make [them] into good people [*khon dee*], for a specific or unspecified period, but no longer than wartime."[16] He explained that there
was interest in some quarters in closing the psychological training schools
because "psychological training was something that should not be carried
out and was in excess of the power granted under martial law."[17] Adul
made a particular plea for psychological training, and arbitrary detention,
on the basis of the nature of political crime. He explained, "Political crimes
or crimes about politics often have wily, tricky tactics different from those
of nonpolitical crimes. The confusing and complicated series of steps is
very different, and it is difficult to present evidence to the court to punish
[political crime] like ordinary crime."[18] Adul provided the example of someone who communicated with enemies outside the country. He claimed that,
although there might not be enough evidence to prosecute such a person
under the Criminal Code, such communication must be prevented.[19] He
acknowledged that opposition to psychological training existed but suggested that this could be resolved by changing the name of the schools. He
wrote, "If calling it a psychological training school is felt to be inappropriate vis-à-vis nice feelings, the name can be changed. There is one important point: people who act or possess behavior that is in opposition to the
peace, order, and safety of the country should be interned, not detained,
for the period of time needed to resolve the situation."[20] Adul, as well as
some at the Krisdika, noted the difference between *kak tua* (internment)
and *kak khang* (detention). Although their view seemed to be that internment was less harsh than detention, at least partially because it was tied to
the period of war, those subject to it experienced the same arbitrary loss of
liberty whether it was called detention or internment.

On 30 October 1944 the army directorate sent an urgent and secret
letter to the prime minister saying that the former commander in chief had
issued an order under martial law to allow the police to arrest and send
people for psychological training to become "good people," and a new law
should be royally decreed to formalize and extend this practice.[21] The term
"good people" is a vague code word meant to identify everything that one's
opponents or critics are not. The prime minister's office opposed the royal
decree of such a measure and wrote to the Krisdika on 15 December 1944
to request that they examine and draft a law for passage by the parliament
instead. It explained that the army had complained that under martial law
it only(!) had the authority to search, draft, ban, seize, occupy, destroy a
dwelling, or force a person to leave an area but not the power to compel a

person who is a danger to public order to undergo psychological training.[22] The prime minister's office was not completely opposed to psychological training, but it wanted to establish it with consensus from the parliament rather than through a unilateral royal decree.

When members of the law drafting committee met at the Krisdika on 18 December 1944, they did not discuss the idea of psychological training schools as out of hand, although the law that was passed with their advice did not contain the phrase. Instead, their discussion turned on the justness of preventive detention, political crime, and the meaning of fascism. The jurists did not have a strong stance vis-à-vis fascism but rather treated it as part of the contemporary and global context in which they operated.

The meeting began with a discussion of the meaning of the phrase *phai thang kanmuang* (political danger), to whose perpetrators or potential perpetrators the psychological training would apply. Prince Wan Waithayakon, a committee member, noted that the clearest case was the theft and sale of secret government documents to foreigners. Pichan Bulyong (René Guyon), the Belgian adviser to the committee, argued that there were two kinds of threats: external and internal.[23] He raised the question of what psychological training might involve and offered the interpretation that it should be "more [like] cultural training. It is not about politics. It should be noted in the law that it is cultural."[24] Prince Wan disagreed and maintained that the measure had been useful during the prior government as a form of punishment and had nothing to do with culture.[25] He further noted, speaking very frankly, that if there was enough evidence to prosecute a person, prosecution should be used. But if there was not enough evidence to punish a person, then internment should be used.[26]

Prince Wan's candidness did not sit well with everyone present. Wisut Krairuk, another committee member, said, interspersing Thai and English, "It is an *Idea* of *Fascism*. The court should examine this issue because people are more afraid of this psychological training than being placed in the square [of a prison cell]."[27] Pichan raised the specter of fascism through comparative law and noted that there was a provision in the Italian penal code to detain people suspected of being social dangers.[28] Perhaps discomfited by the debate, Prince Wan jumped in to say that this was only a preventive measure to be used during wartime.[29] Wisut pushed him further and argued that, given that the courts were used in Italy, why could they not be used in Thailand? Was the prince concerned with *khwam yutthitham* (justice) or publicity? Prince Wan replied that he was unconcerned about justice but worried that if the courts were involved, the examination of evidence and subsequent discussions would be public.[30] He further explained that this was why he used the phrase "internment camp," declaring, "The wrongdoing is not a crime, and internment is not a criminal punishment."[31] Perhaps unintentionally, in his support for it Prince Wan provided a clear definition of arbitrary detention.

Pichan then said, "As I have listened, I do not think this internment is about psychological training schools or *mental training schools* at all. But I understand it to be a *concentration camp idea*, because a *concentration camp* is about holding those who present as dangers to the nation in custody."[32] Pichan's neutral use of "concentration camp" suggests that knowledge of the genocide taking place in concentration camps in Europe had not reached Thailand by the end of 1944. Wisut's criticism did not prevent the law from being sent back to the prime minister's office and then passed by the parliament. The war ended before the law went into effect, and thus before people were arbitrarily held under it in psychological training schools, concentration camps, the simple four walls of a cell, and before a beautiful name had been designed to obfuscate it. Even though it was never implemented, the ideas behind the law survived in subsequent arbitrary detention laws and orders. The ideas that justice can be dismissed in the service of expedience and detention can be given a melodious name to allay the fears of the people. They rest on a misunderstanding that it is the distasteful name of detention or the place of detention, and not the possible violence that one might experience there, that animates fear.

Discipline within the Family, 1958

Field Marshal Sarit Thanarat came to power on 16 September 1957 after launching a coup against Field Marshal Phibun Songkhram's second government (8 April 1948–16 September 1957). He launched an autocoup, a coup against himself, on 20 October 1958 in order to further concentrate power in his hands, after which he abrogated the 1952 Constitution and declared martial law. Until February 1959, Sarit ruled exclusively through executive orders, at which point a temporary constitutional charter was put in place, which remained in use until 20 June 1968. Thak Chaloemtiarana argues that Sarit "believed that modernization and progress must start as a correct state of mind, much as a father might view the upbringing of his children (then 'development') as necessarily starting with proper moral education."[33] Sarit practiced a form of justice he described as *det khat* (decisive), perhaps most embodied in Article 17, taken up in chapter 2, an executive order authorizing him to take any action he believed necessary for the nation and under which six persons were summarily executed during his regime.

A few weeks after his autocoup and declaration of martial law, on 2 November 1958, Field Marshal Sarit issued Decree 21, which defined the category *anthaphan* (hooligan) and provided for detention for those deemed guilty of it. Hooligans were defined as individuals who, either through their own actions or by supporting the actions of others, "bully, persecute, coerce, or harass and disturb the people."[34] Hooligans' actions created fear and were cast as posing significant dangers to the contentment of citizens. Many were engaged in illegal professions; gambling dealers were cited as an example of hooligans who posed an economic danger to the nation. Hooligans needed to be dealt with "for the happiness of the people and the progress of the homeland."[35] Those suspected of being hooligans could be apprehended and detained for investigation; during the first thirty days of detention, the arresting official did not have to bring the case before a court. However, after thirty days, if the arresting official wanted to extend the period of detention, the case had to be sent to court and a detention order issued following the standard procedures of criminal law.[36]

In January 1959 Sarit issued Decree 43, which further specified the implementation of Decree 21. In this decree, the role of the court vanished. Instead, in a decentralizing move that reappeared in Order 22 of the NARC, Decree 43 delegated a vast amount of power concerning the detention and release of suspected hooligans to the director of police in Bangkok and to provincial governors in all areas outside Bangkok. During the first thirty-day period of investigation, "If those individuals continue to exhibit the habits and behavior of a hooligan, then [the provincial governors and director of police] have the power to order those individuals to go to an occupational training center."[37] Every three months each case was to undergo review and a decision made as to whether it was appropriate to release or further detain each hooligan. No time limit was placed on the length of detention. Citing one of Sarit's funeral books, Thak offers a yearly breakdown of the arrests and detentions between 1958 and 1963. In total, 7,539 people were arrested under Decree 21. Of that number, 2,743 were detained for thirty days only, while 4,738 were sent to a detention center for further training.[38]

According to Thak, many of the more than seven thousand persons who were detained under Decrees 21 and 43, "puzzled over their arrests."[39] In concert with other measures, the intention of arbitrarily detaining hooligans was "to intimidate young people into adopting a more 'traditional' proper social life."[40] When the suspected hooligans were released, Sarit told them that "he did not hate them but had to act for the good of the 'family.'"[41] In this sense, Sarit, correctional officers, and the Thai state writ large took over the training and instruction of individuals cast as "children" in social and political life. While not cast out of the nation, hooligans were not conceived to be full citizens. Instead, they were children who might become acceptable members of the polity following "vocational and moral training," the precise content of which was left officially undefined.[42] Yet most notable here is Thak's comment that many of those detained did not know the reason for their arrest. Further, without checks in the form of the courts (or any authority beyond the director of police or a given provincial governor) on how the detentions were carried out, how can it be confirmed that those detained had truly exhibited this behavior? Those who arrested and detained suspected hooligans could not be certain, and it is impossible for those tracing this history to be certain either. What is at issue with arbitrary detention is not only the presence or lack of physical mistreatment. Even if the actions taken while an individual was detained could be seen as benign, the structure permitting them was not benign. The uncertainty acted as a form of dispossession by removing those accused of being hooligans from the people of the nation while also ensuring that members of the people could come under suspicion of being hooligans at any time.

An Escape and a Nullification, 1960 and 1975

Those suspected of being hooligans were not guaranteed protection under the criminal code yet could find themselves subject to it. Decree 43 specified that criminal law covering escape applied to them; if they tried to leave the training center without permission, it was considered a criminal offense.[43] Paradoxically, this meant that the only way suspected hooligans could come before a judge was to attempt escape.[44] Mr. Yiem Phunman found himself in exactly this situation.

On 3 August 1960 Mr. Yiem Phunman escaped from detention in Surin province, where he had been held in a vocational training center for hooligans in the compound of the Surin provincial police station. His detention had been ordered eight months earlier, by provincial order 582/2502, issued on 24 November 1959. He was arrested three days after his escape, on 6 August 1960, and punished for fleeing under Article 190 of the Criminal Code. Mr. Yiem confessed to the allegations made against him.

Yet, despite his confession, the Criminal Court found him innocent. Contrary to the provisions of Decrees 21 and 43, which specify that the detention order must be renewed every three months, there were no further provincial orders regarding Mr. Yiem after the initial one declaring him a hooligan in need of reform. Therefore, he had fled from detention that was itself illegal and so was not guilty of violating the law. The prosecutor appealed, citing the broad powers of detention granted to officials under Decrees 21 and 43. The Appeal Court ruled in favor of Mr. Yiem again, citing the illegal, arbitrary nature of his initial detention. The prosecutor then appealed to the Supreme Court, which ruled that, given that there was no additional order of renewal after the initial provincial order, the detention of Mr. Yiem was illegal. The Supreme Court further affirmed that Decrees 21 and 43 did not provide for unlimited detention but for detention for vocational training of a specific category of person.[45]

Assessing the broader effect of the Supreme Court decision is difficult. The decision may not have affected anyone other than Mr. Yiem, his family, and his community. The Supreme Court decision named as excessive and limited the absolute power of the executive. Yet the decrees were not repealed for another fifteen years. Much like the majority of the members of the law-drafting committee at the Krisdika, who did not oppose arbitrary detention as long as it was not *too* arbitrary, the Supreme Court judges further codified the practice of arbitrary detention of "hooligans" but otherwise left it untouched.

On 9 December 1963 the dictatorship of Field Marshal Sarit Thanarat was replaced with a dictatorship led by Field Marshal Thanom Kittikhachorn. Thanom and the other members of his ruling junta, Narong Kittikhachorn and Praphat Jarusathien, ruled for almost ten years before they were forced out of power following the 14 October 1973 movement for democracy. After the changes wrought by the ouster of the dictators, arbitrary detention, particularly that established by executive decree, no longer had a place in Thai political life.

On 12 February 1975 the government of Sanya Thammasak nullified Decrees 21 and 43 with the passage of the Occupational Training Law of 1975. While the law retained some aspects of Sarit's decrees, there were critical differences. Appended to the law was a note, which explained that

Sarit's decrees had been nullified because they were "inappropriate and not in line with a democratic regime."[46]

One of the significant changes between Sarit's decrees and the 1975 act was how those subject to detention and training were described in the text of the instruments. Rather than creating a category such as "hooligan," this law instead labeled those affected by it as "individuals who ought to undergo occupational training."[47] Six categories of actions that indicated the need for training were specified.[48] In contrast to the earlier Decrees 21 and 43, and Order 22, which followed in the next year, if an individual was suspected of committing these actions, a warrant had to be issued for his or her arrest, detention, and investigation. If after seven days of detention additional time was needed for investigation, the court had to be addressed again. Following investigation, the decision to send an individual for occupational training had to be made by a court. The length of detention was capped at two years. This law is striking in its reinstatement of the court's power to monitor detention and set limits on its length.[49]

This act and the note appended to it indicate that those individuals drafting and passing laws were aware that arbitrary detention was dangerous to something called *democracy*. Although precisely what constitutes *democracy* is a matter of some debate, here it was clear that it does not include the incarceration of individuals without the presence of evidence verified in front of a court. I do not want to uncritically celebrate courts and the officials who work in them as the penultimate guarantors of justice and fairness; at times they may be and at others they may stand in its way. What is certain, however, is that when a case is brought to court, it becomes a public event. As such, what takes place and what decisions are made become public knowledge. They can then be made the subject of scrutiny and debate.

Endangering Society, 1976

The absence of arbitrary detention from the polity was short-lived. In the days immediately following the 6 October 1976 massacre and coup, the NARC, the ruling junta, issued a series of executive orders circumscribing many aspects of Thai social and political life. Political parties were disbanded (Order 6), newspapers censored (Order 10), and radio and television censored and encouraged to broadcast programming in support of the nation, religion, and king (Order 17).[50] Following these orders, on 13 October 1976, Order 22, the legal instrument authorizing the detention of individuals deemed a *phai to sangkhom* (danger to society), was issued.

Order 22 began with the following explanation of its raison d'être:

> As it is apparent that there are kinds of individuals whose actions are a danger to society, individuals whose behavior disturbs the peace and well-being of the people, or whose actions are a threat, or cause economic or security losses for the nation, it is appropriate to proceed by bringing the individuals with these aforementioned behaviors to resume being good citizens for the peace and well-being of the people and the progress of the homeland.[51]

Through arbitrary detention and reeducation, the wayward dissidents were promised *return*. Reeducation included acceptance of "democracy with the king as head of state" as the only legitimate form of government.[52] In the preamble cited above, there is an allusion to the creation of an undivided nation. The first step in creating this undivided, progress- and happiness-filled nation was to identify individuals within it who were a (potential) *danger* to it. Then, once these "dangers to society" had been reformed and returned as good citizens, happiness and progress would ensue. While the violence leading up to and on 6 October 1976 was justified as having been directed against alien non-Thais, Order 22 instead created a category of people neither inside nor outside the nation.[53] Those deemed a danger to society were problematic elements existing within Thai society itself who could return, if they cooperated.

Expanding on the categories named in the Occupational Training Law of 1975, Order 22 identified nine categories of individuals who were a danger to society.[54] In early 1977 the Ministry of Interior published and distributed a manual to help bureaucrats cope with the complexities of dealing with those deemed a danger to society. The manual separated the nine categories of dangerous citizens into two broad categories: individuals who disturbed the order, peace, and well-being of the nation; and politically dangerous individuals (including those who agitated to create negative impacts in society and those who intended to create regime change).[55]

Like Decrees 21 and 43 under Sarit, the administration of the order was placed in the hands of the Ministry of Interior and decentralized. Roles for the Bangkok Metropolitan Police, the Department of Corrections, and provincial governors were created within the text of the order. In addition, human rights and candid reports suggest that the army and the Internal Security Operations Command (ISOC), the interagency army-police-civilian counterinsurgency coordinating body, were also involved in detentions under Order 22. Once an individual was identified as a potential danger to society—by the police, ISOC, army, or civilian informer—Order 22 allowed detention for up to thirty days while an investigation into the suspected individual's activities was ongoing. After the initial thirty days, if the individual continued to exhibit actions or behaviors that were deemed a danger to society, he or she could continue to be held. The Ministry of Interior was charged with the establishment of review committees. These committees were to decide every sixty days if each individual should be detained further or released. No limit was specified regarding the total length of detention.[56] In other words, indefinite detention was possible. At no point was a court or any authority other than the director of police or provincial governor required to authorize the detention of an individual. Those deemed a danger to society did not have the right to a lawyer or outside review of their cases.

It remains difficult to create anything more than a very partial picture of what arbitrary detention under Order 22 was like. The most basic records of the order are fraught with numerical and categorical discrepancies. The total number of individuals detained under it remains unknown. Given that detainees were held by a wide range of security agencies in Bangkok and across the country, this may not be surprising. The reported number of those detained varied widely and changed during and after the period Order 22 was in force. According to a report by the Department of Corrections, 2,188 people had been detained as of December 1976.[57] As of March 1977 the CGRS, the Thailand-based human rights group established in the aftermath of the coup, reported that 8,000 people had been arrested since October 1976 and perhaps 2,000 remained in detention.[58] By June 1977 the CGRS estimated that 1,105 people remained in detention, with 20 percent of that number being political detainees.[59] A late 1977 newspaper account cited a source within the ISOC claiming that arrest lists included over 60,000 names.[60] In a US Library of Congress country study of Thailand published nearly ten years after the nullification of Order 22, John B. Haseman reported that 12,000 people had been detained during the three-year period in which the order was in force.[61] The lack of a consistent record indicating how many individuals in total were detained under Order 22 may be both an outcome of the decentralization of its administration and one of the intentions behind that decentralization.

Even in the case of the detainees under the direct supervision of the Department of Corrections, there were notable discrepancies in state record keeping. In its 1976 annual report, the Department of Corrections noted that on 13 October 1976 it had changed the category *anthaphan* (hooligan) to *phu fuk obrom* (misconduct).[62] It further noted that 2,188 people had been arrested under Order 22.[63] These detentions were duly reflected in the charts and diagrams showing the proportion of each kind of prisoner represented in the total national prison population. But after the 1976 report, the category "misconduct" disappeared without a trace.[64] Not only did the category disappear, but the diagrams showing the proportion of each kind of prisoner disappeared as well. Since arrests continued until the order was nullified in 1979, this absence is jarring. Given its initial willingness to report on the detentions, what caused the Department of Corrections to cease including the existence of the detainees in its annual report? Even before one questions the various abuses of detainees that may have taken place under Order 22, an official accounting of the precise number of detainees remains impossible.

In an attempt to allay the fears generated by Order 22, shortly after it was issued the NARC's public relations division "emphasized that students, laborers, and those people who had become exploited or become unintentionally involved in communist-inspired activities were regarded as innocent persons who would be forgiven."[65] In a special report issued over a year after the order was promulgated, the reeducation centers were noted as being "for those who didn't realize the wrongness of what they had done in the past."[66] The European Co-ordinating Committee for Solidarity with the Thai People argued that the form of Order 22 "permits every possible abuse, and legitimates every arbitrary act of the military, the police, and the para-military groups . . . [and] gives local officials the power to detain 'suspects' for at least 30 days without informing the legal authorities and without advancing the slightest proof of guilt."[67] Although Samak Sundaravej, minister of interior, claimed that there would not be torture or beating of detainees, there were no concrete checks in place to ensure that this did not occur.[68] Although some people reported that their experiences in arbitrary detention were characterized by fear, intimidation, and humiliation rather than physical mistreatment, there is evidence that torture and disappearance did occur.[69] The process by which those deemed a political "danger to society" in Chiang Mai province were arrested, detained, and released provides one possible elaboration of the European Co-ordinating Committee's warning. The very public nature of this process in Chiang Mai functioned to offer a modicum of protection from torture or disappearance to those arrested, yet it simultaneously extended and expanded the order's repressive and arbitrary nature.

The Karunyathep (Angel of Compassion) Center was established within the walls of the old city in Chiang Mai near Suan Buak Hat in 1968 by the Communist Suppression Operations Command (CSOC).[70] When the CSOC became the ISOC after 14 October 1973, the latter continued to administrate the Karunyathep Center.[71] After the 6 October 1976 coup, the center was pressed into service under Order 22 as a detention center for forty-one *political* "dangers to society" in Chiang Mai.[72] In contrast to reports from other centers, persons detained at the Karunyathep Center did not report experiences of violence or torture. They reported being given three meals a day, going on sightseeing trips to important national and religious sites in the city, and playing Ping-Pong and badminton. Yet they were locked in every night, subjected to interrogation, and never given the reason for their detention.

Thai Niu, the largest Thai-language daily newspaper in Chiang Mai, printed the text of Order 22 two days after it was issued by the NARC.[73] The language used to describe those deemed a danger to society was unambiguous. In addition to "danger to society," the order used the phrases "the evil of society" and "that which is blemished, impure, tainted" to refer to those arrested.[74] On 17 October 1976 a front-page article reported that police officers and army soldiers had captured the first wave of "dangers to society."[75] Concurrent with the arrests, there were publicized searches of campuses, bookstores, and private houses for subversive literature and other materials.[76] On 16 October more than one hundred members of the police participated in a search in which 7,878 books were seized from Chiang Mai University (CMU) dormitories.[77] Fearing seizure and the criminality it would imply, the owners of two big boxes containing 257 books discarded them near Wat Rampoeng, a temple near CMU.[78] Individuals were urged to call the police and request a search (of their own or others' houses) if they thought something might be awry because "documents and printed materials are a great, serious danger to the security of the country."[79]

For individuals who did not discard, bury, burn, or otherwise dispose of their leftist or progressive books, possession became a strong liability. For example, a senior teacher from Sanpatong district was arrested because he was allegedly interested in communist ideas and "had helped students who went to organize the masses in various villages in Sanpatong many times."[80] When officials searched his house, they did not find weapons, but they did find twenty-six books allegedly about communism and destroying the absolute monarchy, including a transcript of a speech given by Pridi Banomyong, a member of the People's Party who had called for the transformation from an absolute to a constitutional monarchy in 1932. Similarly, when a rural development researcher in Samoeng district who had graduated from CMU was arrested, the police searched his house and found seventy allegedly communist books, five music-for-life (folk music about peoples' experiences popular after 14 October 1973) tapes, and a map of Samoeng.[81] The newspaper report of his arrest did not explain why each item indicated the need for detention. His possession of a map of Samoeng district hardly seems subversive, or surprising, given that he worked as a rural development researcher in that district.

Ajarn L., a secondary school teacher, was arrested in late October 1976 during the initial sweep. The people who arrested him were not wearing uniforms and used their own vehicles rather than official state vehicles. They did not tell him where they were taking him. They simply knocked on the door and told him to gather clothes and toiletries and come with them. He explained to me that he did not know where he was being taken—whether he was going to be killed and thrown in the river or otherwise detained. He told a neighbor to write down the license plate numbers. If there was no news about or from him in the next day, the friend was to give people the numbers.

When he arrived at the Karunyathep Center, he felt relieved. He was photographed by a newspaper. At this point, he felt very safe because he knew that the information about him was out in the open and had been made public. He noted that the newspaper misspelled his family name and printed the misinformation that his house had been searched. His house was not searched before he was detained.

Including the senior teacher from Sanpatong, the development researcher from Samoeng, and Ajarn L., the detainees deemed dangers to society were kept behind the walls of the Karunyathep Center in small, wooden houses on stilts. Each house held six to eight people, and the detainees were kept in gender-segregated groups. As a part of their classes on good citizenship, state officials and other visitors came to the center. On 27 November 1976 the supreme patriarch, or head Buddhist monk, visited the center. He told the detainees, "Consider that this follows from the laws of karma. Those who commit evil deeds inevitably receive their fate."[82] His speech was published as an excerpt in *Thai Niu*, and there was no indication as to whether he made this observation in direct reference to the situation of the detainees at the Karunyathep Center. His comments may have been part of a general lecture about Buddhist teachings, but he may also have been blaming the detainees for their own detention. If so, the supreme patriarch left little room for a critique of the state's immoderate actions and practice of arbitrary detention.

Five individuals were released in mid-November. The remaining thirty-six political dangers to society were released with great fanfare on 14 December 1976.[83] Chalor Thammasiri, the governor of Chiang Mai province, organized a party and ceremony, releasing the detainees back into the society they had endangered a few months earlier. A photograph of the party, complete with a banner in the background reading "Ceremony to end re-education and release, Karunyathep Center, Civilian, Military, and Police Intelligence Center, Region 5," appeared on the front page of the *Thai Niu* newspaper.[84]

After presenting the detainees with certificates of completion, Chalor gave a speech. Adding a counterinsurgency edge to pop Buddhism, he said:

> The advice I want to give to those released can be summarized like this. Each of us is born with different opinions. It is the freedom of each person to have different opinions. Some people might be persuaded by others to believe in what they believe, and sometimes consequently they are induced to go down the wrong path. Therefore, in our hearts, we must force our consciousness to not become an instrument of other people.[85]

Thus the released detainees were described as people who had been deceived and were urged to make sure that they did not become tools of anyone else's thinking again. Perhaps a strong and repeated emphasis was placed on the detainees as people who were tricked because acknowledging that they might have *chosen* to read Mao or Lenin, to work with the Socialist Party or farmers' and workers' groups, or to join a discussion group about injustice in society was threatening to the Thai state.

After the party, each person was given a small amount of money to use to return home. All released detainees were compelled to report to the center every month.[86] In addition, former detainees with whom I spoke noted that all the released people deemed dangers to society were followed and observed both overtly and secretly by intelligence officials from the center over the next few years.

Physical mistreatment is not the only dangerous practice in the hands of the state. The identification of a kind of thinking as criminally danger- ous is concerning because it reflects a deep fear of explicitly dissenting perspectives, or in fact *any* perspective other than the state's. The people detained and reeducated as part of the Karunyathep project were deemed to have been either deluded or tricked into the wrong kind of thinking. The idea that one could possess criminally dangerous thinking not out of any action of one's own but only through misunderstanding or trickery reflects the state's contempt for citizens and their critical consciousness. The presentation of certificates of completion—a ritual practice referenc- ing graduation—served as a material reminder of this contempt.

What is striking about the extensive newspaper coverage of Order 22 in Chiang Mai is that it made arbitrary detention a public act that took place in plain sight of all in society. This offered those arrested, like Ajarn L., a sense of safety. Once his case was in the public eye, he felt safer because he felt as though he would not simply disappear from sight. Yet this pub- licness also operated as part of the repressive work of Order 22. The *Thai Niu* photographers could not be waiting at the Karunyathep Center for Ajarn L. unless they were called beforehand. The graduation party at the center could not be covered unless this was prearranged by *Thai Niu* and the appropriate officials either within the provincial administration or the ISOC. Is it possible that this publicness was intended to reach those who could be called the indirect, unnamed subjects of Order 22? Readers of *Thai Niu* in Chiang Mai learned about the state's arbitrary arrests, deten- tion, and shaming of their neighbors and colleagues every evening with the arrival of the newspaper. Thus the very publicness that reassured Ajarn L. of his safety may have reminded readers of their own lack of safety.

NULLIFICATION, 1979

Order 22 was nullified on 7 August 1979 under the government of Prime Minister Kriangsak Chomanan. The nullification freed all the people still under detention. If anyone was still to be investigated, a warrant of deten- tion from the court had to be procured within two days. A note appended to the nullification law recalled the nullification of Decrees 21 and 43 four years earlier. Commenting that the order had given state officials the power to investigate, detain, and train people in detention centers, the law noted that detainees had been deprived of their freedom and the ability to practice their professions and take care of their families. Identifying the arbitrary nature of the order, the law noted that some detainees might not have done anything wrong but were detained out of spite by police or government officials. The appended note then explained that this order had given police and government officials too much power. Using the language of Order 22 itself, the note explained that this, in fact, posed a very great danger to society and to a democratic government.[87] Like the earlier nullification of Decrees 21 and 43, the 1979 law ending the use of Order 22 judged it to be out of sync with democracy. Under Order 22, those deemed a danger to society had to be temporarily removed from society in order to protect it. The nullification order seemed to share a similar sense of the temporary: arbitrary detention, while not appropriate during a democracy, was appropriate at other times. But are the effects of using the law to remove certain individuals from its protection only temporary? The repetition of arbitrary detention across time suggests that they are not.

Displacement inside the Nation, 2007

The three southern border provinces—Yala, Pattani, and Narathiwat—were placed under martial law in January 2004 and under emergency decree in July 2005.[88] The reason given by the central Thai state for the abrogation of rights under these two measures has been the need to stem a rising Islamic insurgency. In contrast to the other seventy-four provinces in Thailand, the majority of residents of which are Buddhist, the majority of residents in the three southernmost provinces are Muslim. More than ten years after the declaration of martial law and despite several attempted reconciliation processes, an end to the conflict remains elusive.[89] Simultaneously, the forms of violence used by different state actors against citizens have developed, morphed, and multiplied in official, as well as hidden and unofficial, forms, with documented cases of torture and disappearance.

In addition to the seven days of detention permitted under martial law, the emergency decree adds another thirty days before charges need to be brought against a given individual. During the first thirty-seven days, detainees are often held in temporary sites of detention and cannot see family members or other visitors, which means that the risk of torture is greatest during this period. Detainees do not have access to lawyers during the initial thirty-seven-day period of detention.[90] In addition to the official pretrial detention permitted under martial law and emergency rule, state officials took significant latitude in excess of the law in 2007, resonant with the psychological training schools operated by the army prior to 1944.

In 2007 authors of an internal ISOC document raised the concern that Thailand was acquiring an international reputation for mistreating, repressing, and terrorizing Muslim people in the south.[91] This was not a desirable image, so a new strategy had to be developed. Ideally, the authors noted, a strategy would be developed that would be amenable to observers outside Thailand but would also eliminate the problems in the three southernmost border provinces by removing the culprits fomenting unrest from the area. An idea was proposed that "training" programs would produce peaceful, state-abiding Thai citizens. Incorrect thinking would be corrected, pride in being citizens under a system of democracy with the king as head of state would be fostered, and a group of people who could serve as "good examples" for others would be created.

Resonant again with World War II–era arbitrary detention and Prince Wan's idea of who should be prosecuted in court and who should instead be subject to detention, the ISOC was more concerned with efficacy than justice. A three-point typology recurs across documents outlining problems and possible strategies for resolving unrest.

- Group 1 was composed of individuals who break serious laws and for whom there is clear evidence of wrongdoing. These are individuals who should be prosecuted using the justice system to the fullest extent, with a transparent and just prosecution.
- Group 2 was composed of individuals who are involved in wrongdoing but for whom there is not enough evidence to bring a case. If a case is brought, these people will go free. This will be bad for the justice system and have serious psychological warfare consequences as well.
- Group 3 was composed of individuals who *kratham pid lek lek noy noy* (commit a little bit of wrongdoing) and could go either way—to support the state or the militants.

Members of groups 2 and 3 were those who were seen as appropriate to target and invite or arrest for "training" *outside* the three southernmost border provinces.[92] *Physical removal* of individuals was articulated as central to the strategy. Cases in which there was strong evidence against the accused should go through the justice system—transparently and justly. Those cases without clear evidence could not and so must be resolved outside the system. In other words, those who were placed in the grayest legal area were those who might or might not have done something wrong. One was *almost* safer, at least from unclear, arbitrary arrest, if there was clear evidence that could be marshaled against one; resonant with the experience of Mr. Yiem Phunman, detained as a "hooligan," nearly fifty years earlier, once one is deemed to have clearly violated the law, then one enters the judicial process and appears before a judge. They were *almost* safer because individuals in the first category still faced thirty-seven days of administrative detention before evidence had to be presented showing that they should remain under arrest.[93]

A young man named M. was seen as a member of group 3.[94] The provisions of martial law and emergency rule allow for searches of houses of suspected militants to be carried out by army or police forces at any time. Security forces knocked on M.'s door one morning at 3:30 a.m. in late June 2007 and left a few hours later, declaring that he was innocent and free of connections to terrorism. But the next day he was asked to come to the local police station to sign a new statement. Over the next month, he was shuttled between army bases and temporary detention centers. He was never informed of the reason for his detention—although one army officer told him that he was "50% innocent." In late July 2007, still without having been apprised of the reason for his detention, M. was given two choices. If he wanted to go home one day, he could attend a four-month "occupational training" course, for which he would receive 12,000 baht, or approximately 350 US dollars, upon completion, as well as assurance that he was completely innocent. His slate would be wiped clean. *Or* if he did not want occupational training, the police could bring official charges against him and he would spend at least two years in jail without bail before his case even made it to the first court hearing. M. chose the first option along with close to four hundred other detainees who traveled outside the southern provinces under emergency rule to begin "training" programs in Chumpon, Ranong, and Surat Thani provinces.

The daily schedule for these detainees included time for eating, prayers, and sports. Seminars on Thainess, the correct way to read the Koran, and great religions of the world were part of each week, as well as optional courses in job-training skills.[95] The decision to move the detainees out of the three southernmost provinces for the occupational training course caused tremendous hardship for their families. Yet the location of the camps also provided the basis for a challenge within the Thai judicial system. Once the detainees were moved out of the area under emergency rule, the official provisions permitting administrative detention up to thirty-seven days no longer applied.[96] Families of detainees along with human rights advocates, including the Thailand-based Working Group on Justice for Peace and the Hong Kong–based Asian Human Rights Commission, brought parallel suits challenging the legality of "occupational training" in the provincial courts of Chumpon, Ranong, and Surat Thani. On 30 October 2007 all three courts ruled that "the army's actions in sending residents to the camps may not have been unlawful, but the men taking part in the job-training schemes could return home if they wished."[97] When he was arrested, M. was told that he was 50 percent innocent. One might say that the court decision was 50 percent just.

Even after the court decision, however, M. and the others could not return home. Citing an army order containing a list of 399 prohibited individuals dated 22 July 2007, one month after the sweep leading to the arrests began, Lieutenant-General Viroj Buacharoon, then the Fourth Army Region commander, declared that those on the list could not return to Pattani, Yala, Narathiwat, or Songkhla provinces for six months. The names of all those who participated in the occupational training program were on the list.[98] Following queries from human rights advocates and the families of the detainees, on 17 November 2007, Lieutenant-General Viroj nullified his order and allowed M. and the others to return home.

M. was meant to return to his community after occupational training ended and the expiration of the six-month ban on returning to the three southern border provinces was lifted. Instead of being placed *outside* the Thai nation, M. was instead displaced and dispossessed within it. More significant, the detention of M. and the others is simultaneously containment as Thai citizens who can do good for the nation and dispossession as Thai citizens who might not do good for the nation. Rather than the docile, state-loving citizens ISOC hoped to produce, this program produced fear and insecurity on the part of citizens. M. and those around him learned that it is possible to be arrested, threatened with long-term detention and criminal charges, and forced to undergo "training," even if the police search your house and admit that nothing incriminating was found.

COUP ERA CRIMINALIZATION OF DISSIDENT THINKING, 2014

Martial law was extended to the entire country on 20 May 2014, and two days later, on 22 May, General Prayuth Chan-ocha led a coup by the NCPO. Using the provision of martial law that permits seven days of detention, during the first days following the coup the NCPO carried out a series of mass summons and arrests. This included raids and arrests of people at home, notification through university deans for some faculty and students, and, during the first months following the coup, public summons through orders broadcast on television and the radio. The public summons were announced sporadically throughout each day. One did not know if, or when, one's name might be read out on television, heralded by interruption of the usual broadcast day and the appearance of a junta spokesperson on the screen.

The junta consistently refused to release its own numbers detailing how many people had been summoned, detained, and released or the location of places of detention. According to the Internet Dialogue on Legal Reform (iLaw), a Thai nongovernmental organization that works to improve citizen access to law, during the first two years of rule by the NCPO at least 992 persons were summoned to report to the junta or visited at home by military officers and at least 527 were arrested.[99] Concomitant with the arbitrary detention of dissidents, there has been a broader suppression of freedom of thought, including ongoing intimidation of academics and students who dare to question the junta.[100]

The length of detention of persons summoned varied widely, from those who were questioned and then released on the same day to detention for the full seven days possible under martial law and detention in excess of the legally permissible seven days. Treatment also varied, and it has included verbal intimidation, threats of murder, and torture. On their release, detainees were compelled to sign a statement corroborating that one was not tortured or coerced while in detention and agreeing to refrain from all political activities or travel outside the country without the junta's permission. If one did not comply, one was subject to rearrest and processing in a military court.[101]

Not everyone who was summoned chose to report to the junta. The potential penalty for not reporting was being subject to military court proceedings and up to two years in prison and/or a forty-thousand-baht fine. In several cases, individuals who waited several weeks before reporting, such as labor activist Jittra Kotchadet and law professor Worachet Pakeerut, were then charged in the military court system.[102] Others, including scholars, students, activists, and former political prisoners, refused to report at all. In particular, former political prisoners feared for their safety and even their lives if they reported to the military, and some chose the path of flight and exile. Thantawut Taweewarodomkul, a former political prisoner convicted of violation of both Article 112 and the Computer Crimes Act, who was released after three years behind bars following a royal pardon in July 2013, explained why he opted for exile rather than reporting to the junta.

> The first reason is that I could not accept the seizure of power by the junta, the NCPO. I cannot accept any seizure of power without the necessary agreement from the people. . . . This is the primary reason why I did not report myself to the NCPO. . . . Another reason is that I could perhaps no longer trust the Thai judicial process. After I had once withstood and struggled to call for justice in a lèse majesté case in which I was sentenced to 13 years with no release on bail [for appeal], I could no longer trust the process. I fought and called for the right to bail and asked for fairness of different kinds. But I never received any compassion. What was once faith [in the system] became resentment. . . . But that . . . was in the civilian court. This would be even more [unfair] because it was military court, which is much more absolute. If they pressed charges, if they framed me in any way, I might not have any right to counter it. . . . If you were me, and a crowd of prisoners had stomped on you with their feet with the connivance of the wardens simply because you opened your mouth to excuse yourself, you would well understand my feelings. I was slapped and kicked simply for opening my mouth.[103]

Thantawut's concerns grew out of his prior experience of imprisonment in the Bangkok Remand Prison.

While the majority of those arrested after the coup were released without being criminally charged, the continued force of first martial law and then Article 44, after 1 April 2015, as well as the restrictive political atmosphere meant that they could be rearrested at any time. Thanapol Eawsakul, a writer, human rights defender, and the editor of the journal *Fa Diew Kan* and the press of the same name, was arrested on 23 May 2014 during a peaceful protest against the coup. He was summoned formally on 24 May 2014 and detained for a total of seven days for *prap thasanakati* (attitude adjustment), the phrase preferred by the NCPO, in contrast to the "psychological training," "occupational training," and "reeducation" of earlier eras. He was rearrested on 5 July 2014, because his Facebook posts after his first release made the junta uneasy, and released after five days of detention.

In an account he wrote following his release after his first period of detention, Thanapol offered insight into the junta's decision to detain its opponents.

> What we have to realize is that what has taken place before us is without any basis in law or reason. General Paiboon Kumchaya [deputy commander in chief of the army], who spoke at the end and interviewed us individually on the day of release, said that, "the thing that we did was against the law, but it was at the right time." The process of going to report oneself is a political method. This is a request for cooperation. If one provides it, then one can return [home]. But if one does not cooperate with the soldiers, they say that they will use "harsh medicine" to take care of things.[104]

General Paiboon's comment reflects the logic behind the coup and a self-aware military. The law may be inflexible, but the coup-era polity is flexible enough to allow for transgression of the letter of the law when the rulers deem it necessary. Within this illogic, the arbitrary detention of writers, scholars, human rights defenders, and other citizens does not register as detrimental to society, as the nullifications of Decrees 21 and 43 and Order 22 specified. Instead, arbitrary detention and attitude adjustment are two more strategies of politics to which the possibility of the unknown violence of "harsh medicine" helps to ensure compliance.

History toward an End to Arbitrary Detention

During periods of crisis since World War II, arbitrary detention has been used to identify categories of undesirable citizens, remove them from society, threaten and attempt to indoctrinate them, and then allow them to return to their lives and communities. This practice, and its recurrence, rests on a simultaneous contempt for and fear of the people, contempt because the state authorities choose to deny the people a modicum of justice by bringing them before a court prior to detention, and fear because this denial is based on a self-aware recognition by the authorities that their suspicions might not hold up in a court of law.

Arbitrary detention continues unabated with impunity in Thailand because the criticisms made in nullification laws and the occasional Supreme Court decision against it do not stick and are erased in the next era when the very instrument criticized a few years earlier is dusted off and revised to suit the current crisis. The frequently public nature of arbitrary arrests and detention means that the targets of arbitrary detention extend beyond the individuals who experience it directly to the broader society. The arrests of those deemed to be hooligans and dangers to society were reported in the newspapers, and the authorities often called the newspapers themselves. Arbitrary arrests in communities in southern Thailand were frequently carried out publicly. The first wave of summons to detention following the 22 May 2014 coup were broadcast on television and radio. Even those who do not experience arrest and detention themselves witness that of their neighbors, colleagues, and strangers. Not only are many of those who are arrested uncertain about the reason(s) for their arrest, but many of those who are not arrested fear arrest later or wonder why they were spared. This uncertainty, combined with the possibility of being tortured or disappeared, is behind the fear generated by arbitrary detention.

The lessons of the history of state violence and impunity are different for various members of the polity. Writing about the use of torture by US state security forces, Alfred W. McCoy points to the different ways in which repetition exists for perpetrators and activists. Citing the outrage of human rights activists when reports of US torture in Iraq and Afghanistan surfaced, McCoy notes that torture by US forces is nothing new, having been carried out, exposed, and then forgotten six times in forty years.[105] The Central Intelligence Agency (CIA) remembered, but human rights activists did not share "the bureaucratic influence and deep institutional memory of the U.S. intelligence community."[106] The ad hoc nature of human rights actions and exposures around each instance of the use of torture necessarily only examined the given instance with which they were confronted without tracing continuities or addressing the roots of the problem. Forgetting and the elision of patterns of violence become key parts of the production of impunity.[107] What would interrupt the recurrence of the violence, whether torture in the case of the United States or arbitrary detention in Thailand, would be holding perpetrators to account, but this is elusive in both countries, despite the differences between them. In the absence of accountability, McCoy argues that "historical memory, though heavily contested, remains the most salient antidote."[108]

Even without finding precise evidence that, for example, the NARC after 6 October 1976 examined Field Marshal Sarit's Decrees 21 and 43 before drafting and promulgating Order 22, the repetition of arbitrary detention indicates that there is a strong institutional memory within the state of its use as a strategy of repression and control. Countering this memory of the state with a critical history of arbitrary detention is a strategy of dissent that can be used until there is an end to arbitrary detention. One history of arbitrary detention is that written in and by the laws that facilitate it. But perpetrators of violence and the policy architects who make it legally possible are not the only ones who can remember. By tracking the repetition of arbitrary detention over time, a new understanding of the relationship between the past and present emerges. Progress and movement toward democratization are not inevitable, but challenges to injustice continue even under repressive conditions. The challenges to arbitrary detention in the forms of unexpectedly just court decisions, documentation by human rights activists, and the daring of victims and survivors to fight state repression continue, alongside the repetition of arbitrary detention and other forms of state violence. Remembering these challenges, and the courage that underlies them, is a necessary tool in the struggle to end both state violence and impunity.

2

The Birth of Human Rights and the Rise of Authoritarianism

THE NAME OF FIELD MARSHAL SARIT THANARAT, whom Thak Chaloemtiarana called a "paternal despot," is often spoken of in Thailand with reference both to his *det khat* (decisive) approach to rule and to the fear generated by the swift justice, or injustice, he meted out as part of it.[1] During the six years in which Sarit held power (16 September 1957 to 8 December 1963) at the helm of what King Bhumibol characterized as a "good dictatorship," he created a long list of victims of repression.[2] In addition to the so-called hooligans detained under Orders 21 and 43, discussed in chapter 1, hundreds of communists, socialists, and other dissidents were imprisoned for long periods of time under Sarit, some under the Anti-Communist Activities Act (ACAA) and some by executive decree. In the most significant instrument of his regime, and his most enduring legacy, Sarit took the tyrannical exercise of power in arbitrary detention and expanded it writ large. This instrument was Article 17, which was included in the brief 1959 interim constitution promulgated after his autocoup on 20 October 1958. This constitution remained in force until 1968. Article 17 provided Sarit with "the legal basis . . . to order executions and other activities of the *det khat* (absolutely decisive) variety."[3] The text of the article was explicitly vague about when this could be done: "Whenever the Prime Minister deems it appropriate for the purpose of repressing or suppressing actions, whether of internal or external origin, which jeopardize the national security or the Throne or subvert or threaten law and order, the Prime Minister, by resolution of the Council of Ministers, is empowered to issue orders to take steps accordingly. Such orders or steps shall be considered legal."[4] The measure provided Sarit with the authority to take any action he deemed necessary without pause or review. The only requirement was that he inform parliament of the action taken. Article 17 is an example of the tidy legislation of impunity, complete with the exercise of summary, and arbitrary power. Sarit used the measure to summarily execute six people, in addition to five more who were executed following orders he issued as the head of the ruling junta prior to the existence of the interim constitution.[5] Significance accrues to Article 17 from the loss of these lives and is then magnified by the extended legacy of the measure in the form of use under the subsequent regime of Thanom Kittikhachorn, Narong Kittikhachorn, and Praphat Jarusathien and its recurrence under later dictatorships, including that of the NCPO following the 22 May 2014 coup.

What makes Sarit's authoritarianism pertinent to understanding the history of impunity is the fact that he did not disavow human rights. On the contrary, he viewed his *det khat* authoritarianism as compatible with human rights and framed his autocoup as inaugurating a regime that would respect the UDHR.[6] Human Rights Day celebrations and reporting for the *UN Human Rights Yearbook* continued as usual while he was in power. An indication of tension is present in the absence of any mention of Article 17 in the final reports sent by the MFA to the UN and in the available drafts produced by the Krisdika for the MFA.[7] Why was Article 17 absent? Perhaps it was because the measure and its provision for summary execution were in conflict with Articles 10 and 11 of the UDHR, which provide for a fair and public hearing before an impartial tribunal and stipulate that a person accused of a crime is innocent until proven guilty.[8] Another possibility is that Sarit and the bureaucrats writing the reports did not view Article 17 as pertinent to human rights. Although it is not mentioned in the reports, there was also no attempt to hide it. The exercise of Article 17 was public, with each execution announced through either an order or a statement from the Office of the Prime Minister and circulated further in newspaper and radio reports.

In different ways, Sarit affirmed his support of the UDHR for both the domestic audience of Thai citizens and the international bureaucrats of the UN. Why did he bother? It is tempting to dismiss Sarit's actions as farce, a cynical ploy to curry favor, or the missteps of a person who did not understand the meaning of the UDHR. There may be truth in these three explanations. But the more compelling question to ask is under what circumstances does this seeming contradiction—summary execution legalized by executive order and support of human rights—not register as such?

This chapter takes this question and the contradiction at its core as empirical and methodological points of departure. I begin by retelling the history of the years leading up to the exercise of Article 17 by placing Sarit's rise to power and early Thai state engagements with the international human rights regime side by side. During the first ten years after the promulgation of the UDHR, the meaning of human rights presented by the MFA and other Thai state agencies was in flux and shifted back and forth between more and less progressive interpretations. This flux ended when Sarit came to power. His speeches and actions defined human rights anew and in opposition to the UDHR, even as he claimed he would uphold it. This is reflected most clearly in the five orders and statements he issued under Article 17 to inform parliament of the executions of six people. Each of these documents is a record of the logic developed to justify the execution of a person deemed guilty only by Sarit and therefore also a record of the production of impunity. By reading the orders and statements against Sarit's comments on human rights, it is clear that they are also an attempt to justify his departures from the UDHR. This, too, is part of the early history of Thai state engagements with the international human rights regime.[9] Attending closely to how Article 17 was institutionalized may provide clues to the ease of its recurrence under later regimes. In turn understanding how the histories of authoritarianism and human rights intersected from the beginning, rather than assuming that they would be naturally opposed, may provide clues as to what would be needed to tear them apart.

Human Rights as Politics Narrowed

On 20 June 1933, General Phraya Phahon, one of the military members of the People's Party, led a coup against the civilian government of Phraya Manopakorn Nititada. Less than a year after the transformation from absolute to constitutional monarchy, the rule of the country was in the hands of the military. For the next ten years, this remained the case, first under the leadership of Phraya Phahon and then under Field Marshal Plaek Phibunsongkhram. A brief interval of rule by a series of civilian prime ministers began on 1 August 1944 and swiftly ended on 8 November 1947 when a group of officers calling themselves simply the *khana thahan* (military group) launched another coup.[10] They cited corruption, inefficiency, and widespread crime as the reasons why a coup was necessary.[11] Lieutenant-General Phin Chunhavan, Colonel Phao Sriyanond, Colonel Sarit Thanarat, and Colonel Kat Katsongkhram were involved in the initial putsch, with Field Marshal Phibun Songkhram in the background as a symbolic figure.[12] Foreshadowing Sarit's later significance, Thak Chaloemtiarana argues that his support of the coup was crucial to its success as he commanded the First Regiment in Bangkok. This was the largest group of soldiers that participated in the coup and therefore, with Sarit's support, "the coup plot had the firepower it needed."[13]

The coup returned the military to its pre-1944 place of political prominence. The ten years that preceded Sarit's first coup were filled with instability resulting from struggles for power between Phao and Sarit and from Phibun's attempts to regain his prior role in the polity.[14] For six months after the coup, Khuang Aphaiwong served as prime minister, but he was forced to resign by the junta and Phibun again stepped into the role on 8 April 1948. Until another coup was launched on 29 November 1951 by the same *khana thahan* in order to consolidate its power in the aftermath of two attempted coups and two attempted rebellions, parliament continued to exist and there was an "uneasy accommodation" between the junta and some vestiges of parliamentary democracy.[15] After the 1951 coup, which criminalized political parties and brought back the 1932 constitution and a parliament that was half-appointed and half-elected, the regime no longer *had* to accommodate democracy. But by 1955 Phibun had relaxed restrictions on press freedom and permitted public criticism of government and speeches on democracy on Sanam Luang, a large grass field bordered on one side by the Grand Palace and on another by Thammasat University, used variously for royal cremations, protests, and other activities.[16] According to Thak, however, these were not the actions of a democrat but rather an attempt to curb the power of Sarit and Phao, his chief opponents and competitors for power.[17]

Phao and Sarit both accumulated wealth through "the wholesale plunder of the state's coffers," but they used different means to amass political power.[18] The US government, particularly the CIA and the military, provided material, tactical, and other support to both the Thai police and the army beginning in 1950.[19] After the 1947 coup, Phao was appointed deputy director of police, and after the 1951 coup he rose to the rank of general and became the director general of police. He and his cronies, known as the

"Knights of the Diamond Ring," or, in Thai, simply *asawin Phao* (Phao's knights), enforced their own summary justice long before it was legalized by Article 17. This included the torture and murder or disappearance of Phao's political and personal enemies, including Tieng Sirikan, a progressive politician from the northeast, and Porn Malitong, a politician who had mocked Phao. Both men were strangled, and then Tieng's body was burned and Porn's thrown into the Chao Phraya River. These and several other cases were exposed after Sarit's coup and Phao's simultaneous exit from power and exile, but writing in 1977, Thak noted that no extensive accounting of the violence of Phao and his *aswin* had been made.[20] This remains the case up to the present. Revealing the paradox of impunity in which state violence is known but cannot be addressed, Thak commented, "While the violent tactics of the police were well known and talked about, those actions were condemned only at the gossip level. Official investigation was impossible, for the crimes were committed by the police themselves."[21] The semipublic nature of this knowledge about state violence and its perpetrators is what makes impunity pedagogical. The lack of investigation and unresolved nature of most incidences teaches perpetrators that they can use violence without being held to account and teaches citizens that they are vulnerable to this violence.

In contrast to Phao's use of terror, Sarit consolidated his power through a swift rise up the ranks of the army. He went from the rank of colonel during the 1947 coup to that of field marshal by 1955. He became commander in chief of the army on 24 June 1954.[22] As part of a reorganization of the army, with US support and financing, Sarit systematically installed his supporters in key positions.[23]

The competition for power among Phibun, Phao, and Sarit led to social and political conditions that Craig Reynolds characterizes as "semi-free, semi-unfree."[24] Both tremendous repression, as the lives of the people became expendable to Phao in his quest for power, and unexpected opportunities to criticize the leaders and imagine a different society coexisted. Although large numbers of communist, socialist, and other dissidents were arrested as part of a US-supported anticommunist counterinsurgency, their imprisonment did not stop the publication and spread of dissenting ideas.[25] Jit Phumisak first published *The Real Face of Thai Feudalism Today*, his thoroughgoing Marxist critique of feudalism in labor and social relations during the postabsolutist period, in 1957.[26] Kulap Saipradit, imprisoned from November 1952 to February 1957 as a participant in the peace movement, also wrote and published actively during this period. This included an internationalist socialist novel written while in Australia, *Until We Meet Again* (*Chon Kwa Rao Cha Pop Kan Ik*), which was first published in 1950; and the two volumes of his novel *Looking Ahead* (*Lae Pai Khang Na*), a fictional critique of the failure to make the promises of the 1932 transformation real, the second volume of which he completed in prison.[27] Alongside the proliferation of leftist literature that challenged the Thai and international orders of the day, there was a range of socialist and communist alliances, and the Communist Party of Thailand (CPT) held its second party congress in 1952.[28]

This is the context in which Thailand voted in favor of the UDHR and different state ministries and figures, primarily the MFA, Ministry of Education (MoE), Krisdika, and various prime ministers' offices, celebrated human rights and participated in the early activities of the international human rights regime. Although it seems logical from the vantage point of the present that the tenets of the UDHR could have been used to oppose Phao's violence and the imprisonment of Kulap Saipradit and others, human rights remained firmly in the hands of the state. Across annual events celebrating the 10 December anniversary of the UDHR, a faint transformation in the subject of human rights can be detected. As concerns about the spread of communism grew, what began as tension between the protection of individual rights and the protection of the nation narrowed and the individual became less central. The differences across and within early Thai state engagements with human rights reflect both the "semi-free, semi-unfree" nature of the period and the usual heterogeneity always present within any state.

The tenth of December is both Constitution Day and Human Rights Day in Thailand. The first Thai Human Rights Day celebration took place in 1951 on the third anniversary of the UDHR at the urging of the UN Information Center in Jakarta. The center asked that ten thousand copies of the UDHR be disseminated in Thailand. Henri Fast, the center director, said that the General Assembly had no funds available for this and the MFA or another Thai state agency would have to provide financial support. Fast maintained that the printing did not need to be fancy and could be done "on ordinary newsprint paper or any other cheap paper. It could have altogether eight pages, each three by six inches and no special cover. So you can see that this is not very elaborate."[29] He concluded his letter by reminding the MFA that UN member nations were obligated to observe

Human Rights Day and providing copies of the UDHR would benefit both the UN and the Thai people. The MFA then duly conveyed this request to the Office of the Prime Minister. The minister of foreign affairs, Naivorakarn Bancha, cited the UN statute describing the responsibility to observe the day and also emphasized that spreading information about the UDHR would "be of benefit to our Thai citizens, too."[30] He closed his letter by noting that the MFA was not in possession of funds with which to do this, and he asked the prime minister to arrange for funding from the Ministry of Finance. In early November the Cabinet met, agreed to print the UDHR leaflets, and assigned the task to the Constitution Day Celebration Committee.[31]

The ten thousand leaflets were prepared and distributed prior to 10 December, with five thousand distributed to schools by the MoE, three hundred sent to the MFA, one hundred sent to the Office of the Prime Minister, and the remainder sent to the United Nations Educational, Scientific and Cultural Organization (UNESCO).[32] The archival file provides little information on the reception of the copies of the UDHR, but there are many questions one could pose about this first distribution of it. For example, what were the grade levels of the students who received the five thousand copies distributed by the MoE? Did teachers lead discussions on the meaning of the UDHR? Did students talk among themselves about human rights or go home and talk to their parents about them? Did teachers and students save their copies of the UDHR or were they cast aside or the paper used for other purposes?

A letter from Phra Dulyaphak Suwaman, the permanent secretary of the Ministry of Justice, hints at the UDHR's reception within the judiciary at the time of this first celebration. He noted that the Ministry of Justice decided that it was not responsible for disseminating the UDHR broadly in society but would support it by "distributing it to government offices" and the Bar Association, which might consider disseminating it to its members through the "distribution [of copies], lectures, or adding it to the Bar Association's legal training curriculum."[33] The archival file does not tell us whether the permanent secretary did what he said he would or how the Bar Association reacted, but his letter can be understood as an early assertion that human rights, especially as defined in the UDHR, were viewed as relevant to the judicial process.

In 1954 the observance of Human Rights Day was institutionalized. The UN flag was flown along with the Thai flag at government offices across the country. The MoE published and disseminated copies of the UDHR to secondary schools, vocational schools, and schools for the handicapped throughout the country, and teachers were instructed to inform students about the importance of the day. The MFA organized the reading of the text on national radio. In addition, Prime Minister Phibun gave a brief speech on the UDHR, which was also broadcast on the radio. Phibun used the opportunity to juxtapose the fight against communism and the protection of human rights. He began by noting that it was essential to fight communism because Thailand was a *seri prachathipatai* (liberal democracy) regime. He then explained that opposing communism was necessary "because the communist ideology wants to destroy the liberal democratic regime, the nation, religion, king, culture, and our Thai traditions and cultures. The methods of the communists are numerous and diverse, including propaganda, infiltration, and provocation [intended] to destroy unity between people in the nation. . . . Therefore, it is our shared duty to oppose it. The government is confident that it will be able to surmount these obstacles through the unification of our lives and hearts into one nation."[34] He ended by shifting to discuss rights and said that the UDHR embodies "the principle to protect and promote the right of all the masses of the world to be secure, for the progress of society, [and for] a good standard of living accompanied by great liberty and freedom."[35] Phibun left the link between respect for human rights and the struggle against communism implicit. Liberal democracy did not extend to tolerance of the choice to believe in socialism or communism.

The next year, on 10 December 1955, information about the UDHR was spread through a fifteen-minute conversation on national radio. From 7:30 to 7:45 a.m., two civil servants from the MFA, Thalungchai Chatprasert and Thongtum Kaimolsuk, discussed "The Development of the Universal Declaration of Human Rights."[36] The conversation began with a brief exchange about the origins of the declaration and an assertion that the universality of the rights meant that they applied to all people equally regardless of their ethnicity, sex, language, or religion. As the MFA also broadcast a reading of the UDHR on the radio, the pair put details of the thirty articles aside and instead talked about the origins and functions of the UDHR and where human rights fit into the country's life and politics. Thongtum explained that news about the UN tended to be about politics, but the organization worked in many other important areas. Thalungchai then jumped in and described human rights as being part of this nonpolitical and yet significant work, stating, "The matter of human rights is carried out quietly, gradually. There is no thrilling or sudden news like [one sees with] political issues. But they are of great importance and benefit to ordinary people."[37] The conversation then turned to the UDHR as the beginning of a longer process of protecting rights that would necessitate changing laws. Thongtum explained that the weight of the UDHR was elsewhere: "I understand the aforementioned declaration to be an announcement of ideals. It is not legally binding. But I think this declaration is absolutely psychologically influential."[38] Thalungchai then noted that this influence could be seen in laws, conventions, and constitutions.[39] Given the importance of the UDHR, Thongtum was very proud that Thailand had a role in its dissemination. Thalungchai said that it was the government's role to ensure that "the people are fully aware of their rights."[40] He then went on to link rights to responsibility, saying, "I want to clarify as well that when we have rights, we must also have duties. They go together as a pair. To put it concisely, we have to use our rights in a sincere manner that respects the rights of the country and holds the collective good as important."[41] His comments assume that such duties belong to individuals, not the state. What about situations in which the laws are in conflict with the UDHR or are otherwise unjust? Does the admonition to follow them still apply? Who determines the common good? As Thalungchai commented, perhaps human rights in 1955 were not as exciting as independence, elections, or other tumults in politics, but these questions, their answers, and *whose* answer was accorded authority are all unmistakably political.

SARIT AND HUMAN RIGHTS

Unlike Phibun, Sarit was uninterested in liberal democracy or even maintaining the appearance of it. He had come of age politically during a period in which "force became the political common currency in an unprecedented way," and he adopted the strategy as his own.[42] Once Sarit took power, the limited freedom of expression and political participation allowed by Phibun vanished. Instead Sarit, who cast himself as the father of the country, mediated political participation by traveling to "visit his 'children' around the country, listen to their concerns, and suitably interpret their demands."[43] Sarit brought a new, far less sanguine approach to human rights to the prime minister's office as well. In Revolutionary Announcement No. 4, issued on the day of his autocoup, he addressed the UDHR and dismissed it. The announcement noted that the revolution "will respect and protect human rights according to the Universal Declaration on Human Rights made by the assembly of the United Nations. [The revolution] will not do anything out of step or to violate the Declaration, other than if there are situations in which it is truly necessary to do so in order to ensure the safety of the nation."[44] Rather than redefining human rights to mean something other than the tenets contained in the thirty articles of the UDHR or valorizing the collective over the individual, Sarit created an immediate and clear exception.

References to human rights and the UDHR in Sarit's Human Rights Day speeches reflect a hardening of this position. On 10 December 1960 he used most of his speech to defend the lack of a permanent constitution and reassure the people that the unelected legislature always had them in mind.[45] Sarit arrived at the subject of human rights only in his final paragraph. He emphasized the importance of the collective and stated that the rights of any given individual were no more important than the human rights of all in society. He then explained that during the past year he had encountered people who cited human rights as a justification for terrorism, which he could not abide. Heartfelt, he noted,

> During the past year, I have met with some problems on the matter of human rights. They are not official [problems] but are matters of individuals who have disturbed the tranquility of the people and destroyed national security. They have tried to cite human rights to support terror. I cannot accept this. I will struggle against these actions until I have used up all of the fight I have in me. I will support human rights—but in a way that is good and right. I will support human rights in a way that allows humans to be together in peace and happiness. And I will absolutely not allow anyone to claim human rights for creating terror among the people or to damage the nation.[46]

Sarit did not specify the context of his comments or disclose *who* or *what actions* of terrorism were behind his statements. He repeated this sentiment two years later, during his final combined Constitution/Human Rights Day speech on 10 December 1962, declaring, "I will not allow anyone to cite the Universal Declaration of Human Rights as a tool to destroy the unity and security of the homeland."[47]

The clearest, and most dangerous, demonstration of Sarit's understanding and position on human rights, however, was his promulgation and use of Article 17. Extrajudicial violence and law overlap directly in Article 17. To be clear, what makes this measure a form of extrajudicial violence is that those executed under it were denied any form of review or appeal of their alleged crimes. The measure made it possible for *any* action deemed necessary by the prime minister to become legal upon being carried out. By providing a layer of legality to what would otherwise be considered violent crimes carried out by the executive, Article 17 supplied a veneer of the rule of law and a guarantee of impunity.[48] Although this can only remain at the level of conjecture because Article 17 and human rights are never discussed in relation to one another in the official record, given the primacy of references to terror in the explanations of the use of the measure and the sheer abrogation of the UDHR that it represents, Sarit's comments about exceptions to it likely referred to Article 17.

Sarit used executive orders to execute five people for alleged arson after his autocoup on 20 October 1958 and before the promulgation of the interim constitution on 28 January 1959.[49] Then, between 26 June 1959 and 24 April 1962, he executed six more for alleged rebellion, communist activities, and heroin production under Article 17. Although Sarit used the measure as a legal basis for his extrajudicial actions, he also expressed his personal commitment to them. In early November 1958 he said, "Whatever is right or wrong, I alone will take responsibility for carrying out policies that I deem most correct and which will lead to the happiness of the people."[50] After the first execution, which was of a shop owner who had paid someone to burn his shop down in order to obtain the insurance money, Sarit claimed that he had had no other alternative. He further explained, "Whether it is just or not, I do not fear. I only hold on to the thought that with every breath I take I think only of the happiness of all Thais. This is my greatest wish, which has led me to make this drastic decision. I will assume sole responsibility if there is any."[51] What makes these statements worthy of consideration is that, given the terms of Article 17, Sarit did not have to claim personal responsibility. One interpretation, offered by Thak Chaloemtiarana, is that Article 17 was not only the hallmark of dictatorship but was also "the modern legal basis for a *phokhun* style of leadership, which was key to Sarit's concept of political administration. Sarit as the head of the Revolutionary Council was the head of the national family and had to be able to enforce his will."[52] But rather than a benevolent *phokhun* leader who looked after his children, as the title of Thak's book reflects, Sarit was a despotic father, a despot who clothed repression in familial language. What kind of father kills his children? Sarit's assertion of personal responsibility—and his pointed discard of the meaning of justice—may have been paternal actions, but they also revealed the limits of the legalization of extrajudicial violence.

What gave Article 17 a veneer of law is that each execution was accompanied by an order signed by Sarit or a statement issued by the prime minister's office. These are documents that mark the executions and also provide a logic for the necessity of each one. Sarit often placed himself personally in the investigation and explained the dangers posed to the nation if the person was not eliminated. These orders and declarations were necessary to legalize the execution, but they also reflected the very spare nature of this legality. The paper on which they were printed was the only difference between the executions under Article 17 and the extrajudicial killings carried out by Phao and his knights to deal with his opponents. If the UDHR can be read as the articulation of an ideal of what results when human rights are protected, the series of orders and statements about the use of Article 17 function as the obverse. These orders and statements represent an anti-ideal of the violation of human rights.

This anti-ideal was created through an emphasis on three principles that run counter to the protection of human rights. The first is the dehumanization of the alleged perpetrators. The second is the valorization of the monarchy over the lives of the people through repeated reference to the threat to the crown posed by the actions of the alleged perpetrators. The third is the execution of the alleged perpetrators, even though their crimes remained only alleged as they were killed following swift and shoddy investigations. Thak argues that Sarit consolidated his power by controlling the people and elevating the monarchy.[53] The Article 17 executions are both an example of the simultaneity of these two strategies and an illustration of the human cost of the accumulation of this power.

EXECUTING ARTICLE 17

At 5:30 p.m. on 26 June 1959, Sila Wongsin was shot by a firing squad of six and became the first person to be officially executed under Article 17.[54] The announcement of the execution, signed by Sarit himself, began with a description of Sila's grave crimes. Sila was a northeasterner who cast himself as a god and a king, and this enabled him to recruit people "to create terror and proceed against the law of the land, which is subversion of the security of the kingdom and the crown."[55] In particular, the announcement claimed that Sila led a group of people who attacked and killed five civil servants in Nakhon Ratchasima on 29 May 1959. Sarit did not explain precisely how the attack on the five civil servants would affect the monarchy, but the mention of it augmented the importance of the monarchy and highlighted the danger posed by Sila's actions. Sarit himself traveled to Nakhon Ratchasima and listened to the police question Sila. After hearing the interrogation, Sarit concluded that Sila was dangerous and must be executed.

Less than a month after the alleged attack, Sarit asked the director of police to arrange Sila's execution. After noting the time of execution in the declaration, Sarit offered his condolences for the loss of the lives of the civil servants. He said, "As the loss of the lives of government officials is greatly saddening for the people and the government, I want to take this opportunity to express my profound sorrow to the families of those who lost their lives. The government will provide you with good support from now on."[56] Neither condolences nor support were offered to Sila Wongsin's family. Sarit's generosity as a father was limited to the good children of the nation.

The announcement concluded with a foreboding warning and a promise that this would likely not be the last execution. Sarit stated, "As the head of the government, I would like to firmly make it generally known that the government will use every avenue to secure the kingdom and the crown. The government will decisively and immediately suppress all actions that constitute subversion or agitation or threaten the peaceful order, whether they take place inside or outside the kingdom."[57] The centrality of the crown and the preservation of order in the kingdom alongside the complete absence of the people is how this declaration contributes to the creation of an anti-ideal in opposition to the UDHR.

Less than a month later, on 6 July 1959, Sarit issued the next order under Article 17. This time, Supachai Srisati, the first of four alleged communists to be executed, was the victim. The order in this case had the least detail of all five documents issued in relation to Article 17. The police arrested him on 30 June 1959 after attempting to do so for a long time. Even though only seven days passed between the arrest and the execution, which was arranged by the Ministry of Interior and carried out in secret at Bang Khwang Prison, the investigation was completed by high-ranking police in a *robkhop lae thiengtham* (circumspect and impartial) manner.[58] Sarit himself joined the investigation and interrogation. The conclusion was that Supachai was a representative of unspecified foreign communists in Thailand and served in their politburo. He performed important, also unspecified, duties and possessed instruments to aid him in these duties. Although they were not noted in the order, these instruments included printing and mimeograph machines, five guns and bullets, radio and telegraph transmitters, pamphlets, and money from communist countries.[59] Like Sila Wongsin, Supachai was a threat to the nation, the crown, and peaceful order. These actions were evidence of *kan khai chat* (treason), and without his elimination there might be foreign intervention in the country. In this case, the possible threat to sovereignty served as the justification for summary execution and violation of the UDHR.

Two years passed before Sarit ordered another summary execution. Khrong Chandawong and Thongphan Sutthimat were arrested on 6 May 1961 and accused of being communist separatists who planned to use weapons and foreign fighters to separate the northeast from the rest of the country. Khrong was a former teacher and member of parliament from Sakhon Nakhon who had been imprisoned between 1952 and 1957 along with others arrested on charges of rebellion and communism.[60] Their propaganda aimed to turn people against the kingdom by slandering "every Thai government in every era" (*rathaban thai thuk yuk thuk samai*).[61] Khrong himself had insulted the king and queen in order to generate hatred and reduce respect for the crown. Thongphan was Khrong's trusted right-hand man.[62] In addition to their ideological crimes, the pair had engaged in theft in Sakhon Nakhon, Udon Thani, and Nong Khai. Taken together, all these actions constituted a grave threat to national security and the crown, and so Sarit ordered the Department of Police to arrange the execution to ensure their protection. Although the two had been held by the Special Branch police in Bangkok during the investigation, on the morning of 31 May 1961, they were flown back to Sakhon Nakhon and executed by a six-man firing squad using carbine rifles.[63]

Communism played only a minor role in the next summary execution. In contrast to the first three uses of Article 17, in which Sarit issued an order, the final two uses were also accompanied by statements from the office of the prime minister. These statements were longer and more expansive in their development of a logic for the executions than the orders had been. In this case, Liang Ho Sae Lao, an alleged heroin producer, was executed at 5:00 p.m. on 29 August 1961. Although Liang Ho denied that he was guilty, the available evidence left no room for doubt in Sarit's mind. The statement began by establishing the context for the execution by means of an explanation of the *phai antharai to chat* (severe danger to the nation) posed by heroin.[64] Compared to opium, which had recently become difficult to acquire after its sale and consumption were criminalized, heroin was cheaper and more addictive.[65] Heroin damaged one's body, mind, and will to work. The only mention of communism was in the broad context of the dangers of heroin and not tied directly to Liang Ho. According to the office of the prime minister, "The government has reason to believe that the distribution of heroin in Thailand is one part of the communists' plan of terror, which is intended to subvert the entire Thai nation."[66] The monarchy was not mentioned, perhaps because Sarit himself was involved in the heroin trade.[67]

The statement noted that prior to the arrest of Liang Ho, the government had carried out educational campaigns about the dangers of heroin and warned that producers caught would be punished with the greatest severity. The office of the prime minister characterized producers as "depraved people who secretly produce heroin for distribution with an aim only for wealth without thinking about the negative effects on humankind."[68] This is the only Article 17 document that mentioned humans other than civil servants or the king and queen. Due to the dangers posed by heroin, there was swift movement after Liang Ho was arrested on 16 August 1961. His actions, it was claimed, were planned, coordinated, and "monstrous to the people and the nation."[69]

The office of the prime minister then noted his Chinese ethnicity, claiming, "This behavior indicates clearly that he is an individual who has harmed the nation and Thai people. He has dwelled here for twenty years, and this is a grave betrayal. He should not be allowed to live on Thai land any longer."[70] Liang Ho's threat to the nation and necessary expulsion were ethnicized. This is the only Article 17 document in which ethnicity is mentioned, and other crimes did not merit denial of a place within the country. Since he was the only heroin producer executed by the Sarit regime, it is impossible to know if Sarit also would have said that ethnically Thai heroin producers were not actually Thai and also did not deserve to live in Thailand any longer. The link among ethnicity, danger to the nation, and expulsion foreshadows the accusation that the dissident students at Thammasat University in October 1976 were not Thai and therefore should be killed.

Summary justice meted out under Sarit had a pedagogical element automatically built into it that was enhanced through the circulation of news reports about the executions.[71] But in the statement about the execution of Liang Ho Sae Lao, these pedagogical aims were put into words. The execution was being carried out "so that it will be clear to all the people that the government counts the production and sale of heroin to be a grave crime that is a subversion of the security of the kingdom. It is a [form of] destruction of the health and sanitation and potential of the people in the nation. Therefore, it is of direct harm to the nation. No one should emulate him."[72] Less than two weeks passed between the arrest of Liang Ho and his execution, which was arranged by the Ministry of Interior and took place at Bang Khwang Prison.[73] The audience for the summary executions under Article 17, and the swift manner in which they were carried out, was people of all ethnicities living in Thailand. Sarit aimed to create order by frightening ordinary people into complying with the law.

As the Cold War continued, the dangers of communism grew ever graver in Sarit's eyes. Sarit's final use of Article 17 was the execution of Ruam Wongphan on 24 April 1962 for alleged *kan kabot thorayot to prathet chat* (traitorous rebellion against the nation).[74] The length of time between arrest and execution was longest in this instance. Ruam Wongphan and thirty-eight others were arrested and accused of communist activities and rebellion on 23 February and 1 March 1962. Sarit's government chose to highlight this case and produced the lengthiest Article 17 document in relation to it because it determined that this was "a case that is greatly important because the accused intended to subvert the security of the kingdom and the crown and overthrow the rule by democracy with the king as head of state in order to transform it into a communist regime. This is a severe danger to the utmost independence and sovereignty of the nation."[75] The severity of the danger to the nation posed by Ruam also prompted the authorities to carry out a detailed investigation. The description that follows indicates that this may not have been the case with respect to this investigation and prompts the question of *detailed* in comparison to what. Given that summary execution and a life were involved, what other kind of investigation would be carried out? And what about crimes against ordinary citizens? What was the nature of the investigation in these sorts of cases?

The statement then describes Ruam and his activities. A brief and partial history of the CPT, or the counterinsurgent state's version of the history of the CPT, is woven between the lines of the development of a logic that made his execution necessary. In 1949 Ruam became a member of the party and left Thailand to receive communist training abroad. In 1952 he returned to Thailand for a brief period and then left again. In 1956 he returned to Thailand permanently. Ruam was from Suphanburi, and he and seven others comprised the provincial committee of the CPT. They had successfully built cells in the subdistricts of districts in the province.[76] The authorities had to stop Ruam or his success might have spread across the country. Sarit alleged that Ruam's prominence within the party is what made him a comparative threat, as "he is an important, high-ranking person of the Communist Party of Thailand. He is a person who is a graver danger than many others who have committed this crime."[77] He and his colleagues set up a *khana kammakan patipat ngan chao na* (farmers' work committee) led by the CPT to spread communist ideology and agitate and provoke farmers in rural areas to become enemies of the state. The statement then argued that their attempts to organize in the capital failed because city dwellers did not believe their propaganda. Reflecting a long history of looking down on rural people by the central state and other elites, the office of the prime minister explained, "Taking this to the farmer brothers and sisters is easier and more convenient because the communists can make contact with and cajole them into believing more easily" than they can people in the city."[78]

The office of the prime minister then turned to the evidence gathered through the investigation. All thirty-eight arrested people other than Ruam spoke in a single voice: "All of the accused confessed and maintained that Mr. Ruam Wongphan was the ringleader who induced them to become communists."[79] He shared illegal books and newspapers with them as part of their indoctrination. The uniformity of this statement raises a question. Did all thirty-eight really accuse Ruam? Or were differences in their accounts papered over to strengthen the statement about his execution? And if they all did make the same statement, were they tortured or otherwise coerced by their interrogators?

According to the statement, all thirty-eight said that during the indoctrination sessions Ruam had slandered the government and unspecified important people so that they would be indoctrinated to detest the government and those important people. In addition, a majority of the thirty-eight said they were told that if they became party members the party would forgive their debts and give them land, tractors, money, and high positions in the future. Then the statement addresses *phi nong chao thai* (Thai brothers and sisters) directly and declares that they would see that the lies of Ruam were no different from the lies told to people in other communist countries. The statement then used the term *rao* (we), which had not been used in any of the prior Article 17 orders or statements. In a direct appeal to the people, it reads, "At this time, we know well the situation of the citizens who have swallowed this [ideology] and that they suffer, being forced to do hard labor as no more than slave laborers."[80] The majority of the thirty-eight said that after they had applied for membership in the party, they received none of the assistance promised by Ruam. After their arrest, they came to recognize the lies of the communists.

For these reasons, the prime minister decided to take decisive action. The documents seized during the arrest would be displayed on Sanam Luang as each one was evidence of the severe crimes Ruam had committed against the government, legislature, religion, and king, who was "ultimately loved and respected by the Thai masses."[81] This is the sharpest expression of royalist nationalism to emerge in the orders and statements related to executions authorized by Article 17. The statement went further, noting that Ruam did not deserve *khwam metta* (compassion) because his crime was of the highest nature. This was not a political crime "because it is subversion of the security of the kingdom and the crown, a grave threat to the tranquility of the nation . . . [and] a traitorous rebellion against the nation."[82] Perhaps. I would argue instead that the denial of the political nature of the crime by the office of the prime minister must be read as acknowledgment of its political nature. Regardless, the power to decide what was a political crime and what was subversion worthy of execution must be acknowledged as power that can only be held by a dictator who has attained office by illegitimate means. Ruam Wongphan was executed by firing squad on 24 April 1962 at Bang Khwang Prison.[83]

By the end of Sarit's regime, it was apparent that human rights and authoritarianism could not coexist without one or the other sustaining fractures. The fractures are evident in the orders and statements he released to justify the logic for the summary execution of six people under Article 17. Each document developed an argument for why the individual in question must be executed and, in turn, how he was less than human and too dangerous to remain alive. The utopian ideal of human rights protection contained in the UDHR had to be countered with an anti-ideal of the urgency of the preservation of the crown and the nation. The orders and statements went beyond the utility of fulfilling the requirement for the prime minister to report each use of Article 17 to create a logic for the valorization of the monarchy and the nation over the lives of the citizens.

THE LEGACIES OF ARTICLE 17

Sarit Thanarat died at age fifty-five on 8 December 1963. Yet the spirit of Article 17 survives until the present. Like the repetition of arbitrary detention across regimes, the use of executive orders by dictators contributes to the production of impunity through both the individual acts of extrajudicial violence authorized and made nominally legal and the normalization of this process over time. During the fifty-five years between Sarit's first use of Article 17 and the 22 May 2014 coup by the NCPO, five similar measures have been included in constitutions promulgated by military regimes. The repetition is marked by two primary changes: the expansion of the range of the measure and, beginning in the late 1970s, the emergence of the human rights movement and explicit challenges to the exercise of summary executive power.

On 9 December 1963, one day after Sarit's death, Field Marshal Thanom Kittikhachorn became prime minister. The 1959 interim constitution remained in force until the 1968 constitution was promulgated on 20 June. From the time he entered power until the 1968 constitution was promulgated, Thanom used Article 17 to execute eleven people, imprison thirty-four people, and seize Sarit's assets.[84] In response to the investigation and seizure of Sarit's assets, his widow, Thanphuying Vichitra Thanarat, sued the government and pushed the Constitutional Court to evaluate the legality of Article 17.[85] The Constitutional Court ruled the measure valid and legislation was promulgated that asserted that the government could not be prosecuted for actions undertaken in the name of Article 17.[86] The Constitutional Court ruling and the passage of an extra law to bolster the use of Article 17 signaled the willingness of a greater range of state institutions outside the dictatorial executive to legalize and normalize the exercise of absolute power.

The 1968 constitution did not have a measure comparable to Article 17. But on 19 November 1971 Thanom launched an autocoup to consolidate his power and abrogated the constitution. Thailand remained without a constitution for over a year, until 15 December 1972, when the 1972 constitution, which contained an expanded Article 17, was promulgated.[87] During the interim period, Thanom issued executive orders to execute thirty-seven people and imprison sixty more.[88] Then Thanom used the new Article 17 to execute two people, imprison eighteen, and detain nineteen. Thirteen of the nineteen detained under Article 17 were the student and citizen activists who had called for a new, democratic constitution in early October 1973 and launched the movement that resulted in the ouster of Thanom and the installation of a civilian government. The outcome of the arrests—which prompted protests large enough to cause the dictator and two of his colleagues, Narong Kittikhachorn and Praphat Jarusathien, to flee the country and the immediate transition to a (more) democratic government—can be read as indicative of the displeasure with dictatorship felt by many Thais and as an indictment of Article 17 itself.

With the ouster of Thanom and his colleagues and the beginning of a more democratic period, one might imagine that Article 17 would have been repealed immediately. However, a new constitution was not promulgated until 7 October 1974. Until then the 1972 interim constitution remained in force. Beginning in late October 1973, at the behest of popular calls, the measure was used to investigate and seize the assets of Thanom, Narong, and Praphat, at least partially with the idea of using the funds to repair the damage done by state forces when they repressed activists during the protests surrounding 14 October 1973.[89]

A return to arbitrary executive power went along with the return to dictatorship following the massacre and coup of 6 October 1976. A string of subsequent constitutions contained measures with different numbers but content identical to that of Article 17 in the 1972 constitution: Article 21 of the 1976 constitution, Article 27 of the 1977 constitution, and Article 200 of the December 1978 constitution.[90] Under Article 21, 28 people were sentenced to prison terms and 10 were sentenced to death for alleged crimes, including rape, murder, forgery, drug trafficking, and weapons sales. Under Article 27, 134 people were sentenced to prison terms and 7 were sentenced to death. Under Article 200, 179 people were sentenced to prison terms and 25 were sentenced to death. In June 1981 human rights activists noted that, although it remained in force, Article 200 was no longer being used; yet all 179 people summarily sentenced to prison terms remained incarcerated.[91] The activists' descriptions of how they came to be behind bars resonate with the accounts of those executed under Article 17 during Sarit's regime: "None of them had any opportunity to go to court. Almost all of them were accused as guilty by the police. Many of them said that they were innocent and were threatened to accept such false accusations by the police after they had been arrested."[92]

The difference was that in that moment a coalition of relatives of the prisoners, activists in the nascent Thai human rights movement, and their international allies organized to demand the prisoners' release. In late 1981 Marut Bunnag, the minister of justice, chaired a committee convened to review the cases of the 179 people still imprisoned, who were known as the "Forgotten 200." The committee recommended that they be pardoned as a group as this would be swifter than either the passage of an amnesty law or review of individual cases by the courts.[93] As part of the royal pardon granted on the occasion of the Rattanakosin Bicentennial, 120 people were pardoned on 26 April 1982.[94] The fifty-nine not pardoned were those who had been accused of drug trafficking or threatening national security, offenses excluded from the pardon, and the government maintained that their arbitrarily determined sentences remained valid.[95]

Nearly ten years passed before the measure recurred in yet another new charter. The 1991 charter promulgated on 1 March 1991 following General Suchinda Krapayoon's 23 February 1991 coup against the civilian government of Prime Minister Chatichai Choonhavan contained an article, numbered 27, that was identical to the earlier Articles 17, 21, 27, and 200. But the interim charter was revoked nine months later when the 1991 constitution was promulgated on 9 December.

Twenty-three years passed before military dictatorship and a similar measure returned to Thai politics. Following the 22 May 2014 coup by the NCPO, Article 44 of the 2014 interim constitution brought executive authority back. This time the categories for which orders could be used extended to all instances in which "the Head of the National Council for Peace and Order is of the opinion that it is necessary for the benefit of reform in any field and to strengthen public unity and harmony, or for the prevention, disruption or suppression of any act which undermines public peace and order or national security, the monarchy, national economics or administration of state affairs, whether that act emerges inside or outside the kingdom."[96] On being announced, orders or actions become immediately legal and constitutional. During the first two years of rule by the NCPO, General Prayuth Chan-ocha issued seventy-one orders under Article 44.[97] Unlike earlier uses of executive orders, these orders have not authorized the summary execution or imprisonment of individuals. Instead, Article 44 has been used to authorize broad, summary policy interventions by the junta. This includes, for example, the use of Article 44 to replace aspects of martial law after it was revoked on 1 April 2015, particularly the provision allowing arbitrary detention for up to seven days without charge and in undisclosed places of detention.[98] Other orders issued have authorized the extension of police investigation and arrest powers to military officers, the transfer and appointment of civil servants, actions to address lottery ticket sales, the seizure of land from villagers, and many other actions that can be taken without prior judicial review or public discussion.[99] Like Sarit sixty years earlier, Prayuth denies that his regime violates human rights and maintains that his actions are necessary to reform the country and return happiness to the people.

But the institutionalization of the violation of human rights cannot lead to happiness or justice. Instead, through the repetition of orders such as those issued under Articles 17, 21, 27, 44, and 200, extrajudicial violence has been legalized and state officials placed beyond the reach of account-ability. The frequent, extravagant exercise of power, Kasian Tejapira argues, poisons and wounds Thai society. The form of injury is the spread of extra-judicial violence by state officials, and the symptom of the severe injury is the inability of society to stem this expansion.[100] The dispossession of the people's right to intervene in injustice, too, is an effect of the exercise of executive power and the blurring of the line between law and extrajudi-cial violence.

3

The Burning of
People and Villages

What is the law there for? If you only have to be suspected of being a terrorist or a Communist, and [the state] can shoot you and leave you for dead or burn down your village or do whatever they wish, it would be better to just get rid of the courts and judicial system.

—Villager from Ban Na Sai, quoted in Chaiwat
Suriwichai, *What Took Place in Ban Na Sai*

[We have] laws [stipulating] that people who act wrongly are judged via a judicial process. But when the administrative class makes themselves those who decide [on matters of justice], the lives of the people have no meaning.

—SUTHAM SAENGPRATHUM, *Sieng Puangchon*,
15 February 2518 [1975]

DURING THE FIFTEEN YEARS during which it was in force (1959–74), Article 17 provided the prime minister with absolute power to issue executive orders to take whatever actions—including the six executions that took place during the regime of Field Marshal Sarit Thanarat—he deemed necessary to address what he judged to be grave dangers to the nation. Four of the six persons executed—Supachai Srisati, Khrong Chandawong, Thongphan Sutthimat, and Ruam Wongphan—were accused of being communists. During this same period, as well as extending before and after it, an extensive body of law provided a broad range of state officials with the power to restrict and violate the rights of citizens in the service of confronting the creeping threat of communism. From the moment of the transformation from absolute to constitutional monarchy on 24 June 1932, elites feared a further transformation into a socialist or communist society.[1]

77

Beginning in 1933, nineteen different legal measures, including acts, junta announcements, junta orders, and announcements by the Ministry of Interior, came into force as part of the suppression of communism.[2] A range of actions critiquing the status quo, communist or not, came to be cast as such during this period and became the object of such suppression.

The fear of communism by monarchical, military, and capitalist elites, as well as the concomitant state repression to stem it, reached its height in the 1960s and 1970s and was particularly intense by 1975 with the transitions to socialist governments in Vietnam, Cambodia, and Laos. This was also the period in which the CPT was at its height before its dissolution in the 1980s. The legal foundation for counterinsurgency was laid much earlier and the promulgation of draconian anticommunist measures reached its zenith during the regime of Field Marshal Thanom Kittikhachorn (1963–73). The first in a repressive trilogy was the Anti-Communist Activities Act (ACAA) of 1969, passed on 12 February of that year.[3] The ACAA of 1969 built on the ACAA of 1952, which had defined an initial meaning of "communist activities" and provided for basic sanctions of individuals who participated in them, to set out requirements for designating a place a "communist-infiltrated area" and then provided the military, police, and civilian officials engaged in counterinsurgency efforts with a great deal of authority to restrict the rights of individuals in those areas.[4] This included forbidding people to enter the area, preventing people from leaving their homes, and requiring individuals to report to the authorities at set intervals. The ACAA of 1969 also allowed for those accused of violating it to be detained for up to 480 days before being formally charged. This is 396 days longer than the maximum 84 days of precharge detention permitted under the Criminal Procedure Code. David Streckfuss argues that the combination of the strictures of the law and Cold War anticommunism created "the basis for the complete militarization of Thai society."[5]

In 1971 Field Marshal Praphat Jarusathien, one of the other members of the dictatorial triumvirate, claimed that within six months all traces of communists and communism would be eradicated from Thailand.[6] Within a year, on 16 February 1972, the second key repressive measure of this trilogy, Revolutionary Announcement No. 78, was passed.[7] Under this announcement, autopsies did not have to be conducted on individuals suspected of violating the ACAA who died while in state custody if doing so would be an obstacle in suppressing communism or dangerous to the officials engaged in that suppression. The third measure issued during Thanom's regime was Revolutionary Announcement No. 199, which came into force on 11 August 1972.[8] This announcement made it possible for those suspected of violating the ACAA to be detained for the entirety of an investigation or "as is deemed necessary for the security of the country and the peace and order of the people. As a result, legally stipulated procedures and length of the detention of suspects does not need to be adhered to."[9] In other words, those accused of being communists could be detained indefinitely.

Taken together, Jaran Kosanan notes, these two announcements created a legal way for state officials to arbitrarily detain and execute any citizen.[10] All that was necessary was that the citizen or citizens in question be suspected of being communists. While Article 17 limited this authority to the prime minister and ensured that records of all executive excesses were kept, as an order had to be issued each time the measure was used, the series of anticommunist measures gave unbridled authority to a wide range of officials and removed the possibility of keeping records by creating exceptions in terms of places of detention and autopsies of deaths in custody. The names of Supachai Srisati, Khrong Chandawong, Thongphan Sutthimat, and Ruam Wongphan were recorded and are known because they were executed under Article 17, but the names of thousands of others are not known. What Thai citizens learned during the Cold War was that the boundary between an ordinary villager and a communist was nonexistent at worst and extremely flexible at best in the eyes of the state. What Thai citizens learned is that when they suffered as a result of the state collapsing the boundary between the two, they had no recourse to law. These lessons were acute in Phatthalung and Ban Na Sai, two areas designated as "communist infiltrated" in the south and northeast, respectively.

In August 1972 citizens were arrested, or simply taken, in large sweeps across districts throughout Phatthalung province and brought to detention camps for interrogation. They were accused of engaging in communist activities or providing tacit support for them. While some detainees were released after being interrogated, others were tortured and killed. At night, after being beaten until unconscious or with irons around their necks, citizens were placed in empty two-hundred-liter oil drums at the edge of the detention camps, doused with oil, and burned alive. While the bodies were burning, truck engines were revved to partially mask the screams. The engines only partially masked the evidence of what was occurring because those detainees who survived recalled both the screams and the sound of the engines. Villagers and students estimated that several thousand people in Phatthalung, perhaps as many as three thousand, were killed as alleged communists in this manner. These killings are known as the *thang daeng* (red drum) killings due to the method of murder employed by the state.

At 6:00 a.m. on the morning of 24 January 1974, gunshots were heard by the residents of Ban Na Sai, a village in Nong Khai province. A few minutes later, state security officials, including Border Patrol Police (BPP) officers, counterinsurgency officials, and members of the Village Defense Volunteers (VDV) came to their doors and told them to leave their homes immediately and assemble in the village temple.[11] A few moments later, the villagers watched their houses and rice barns burn to the ground while they were prevented from leaving the temple by the state officials who surrounded them. In total, 106 homes were destroyed and many villagers lost their year's rice supply, which had been harvested only a month earlier, and cash and other valuables that they had not had time to retrieve. Three people, a family composed of a mother, a father, and a small child, did not leave their house and were killed.[12] Whether they were shot or burned alive is not known.

When thinking about the burning of Ban Na Sai and the *thang daeng* killings, whether the CPT was active in Nong Khai and Phatthalung is not at issue. Both provinces had areas that were strongholds of the CPT. Instead, what is of concern is understanding how violence emerged in response to both an actual insurgency and the fear of a possible insurgency. What is of concern is that people were killed as communists when they were not and understanding how it was possible to blur the line between communists and ordinary villagers. Also of concern is how it became state policy, official or unofficial, to arbitrarily select people to be brutally killed.

These two events became front-page news in Thailand during the three-year period between the ouster of the dictatorial triumvirate of Thanom Kittikhachorn, Narong Kittikhachorn, and Praphat Jarusathien during the events of the 14 October 1973 movement and the return to dictatorship with the 6 October 1976 massacre and coup. This period is well known as one in which student, farmer, worker, artist, and other progressive movements emerged and flourished after long years of dictatorship. The same political opening that created the conditions for these movements also created the conditions for calls for accountability for violence and other illegal actions perpetrated by state officials. The burning of Ban Na Sai and the *thang daeng* killings in Phatthalung were exposed and became public knowledge almost by accident when student activists visited these areas to propagate democracy in February 1974 and February 1975, respectively.[13] While the open murder of citizens was possible under a dictatorship, within the context of open politics, survivors and student activists demanded that the state officially investigate the killings, and the state was forced to respond.

In both cases, the sequence of events following the initial exposure and the ultimate response by the state began when student activists learned of the violence and shared it with fellow activists and the press in Bangkok. Survivors of and witnesses to the violence spoke out in situ and traveled to Bangkok to speak in public and to meet with state officials to demand accountability. Various state officials, including members of the security forces, bureaucrats, and politicians, offered a range of counteraccounts. In response, the Ministry of Interior established a committee in each instance and tasked it with carrying out an investigation to determine the truth among the varied and often contradictory accounts. Despite promises to release committee reports to the public and take legal action against state officials who had broken the law, the reports were not released, nor was any legal action taken against the perpetrators. In 2017 the reports were still unavailable to the public.

The exposure and series of actions and inaction that followed the two events demonstrated both the excesses possible under dictatorship and what lingered of them even after the removal of the dictators. While the exposure by students and villagers was marked, and made possible, by the events of 14 October 1973, the failed investigations and lack of accountability for the perpetrators foreshadowed the return to dictatorship, which came a year and a half later in the form of the 6 October 1976 massacre and coup. The state refutations of accountability for the burning of Ban Na Sai and the *thang daeng* killings heralded the production of impunity that contributed to making it possible for unarmed students to be accused of being alien communists and killed in broad daylight on 6 October 1976. In considering the failed investigations into the burning of Ban Na Sai and the *thang daeng* killings, and the 6 October 1976 massacre, it is not surprising that the ACAA and related laws remained in force until several decades later.

In *Unsettling Accounts: Neither Truth nor Reconciliation in Confessions of State Violence*, Leigh Payne examines state confessions in four nations—Chile, South Africa, Brazil, and Argentina—that were undergoing both democratization and a range of judicial processes focused on past violence. Payne argues that "confessions do not settle accounts with the past; rather, they unsettle them."[14] Public discussion and accounts of what happened do not create a single truth about the past but instead facilitate what she calls "contentious coexistence." This mode of being and relating socially and politically in the aftermath of violence "rejects infeasible official and healing truth in favor of multiple and contending truths that reflect different political viewpoints in society" and "is stimulated by dramatic stories, actors, or images that provoke widespread participation, contestation over prevailing political viewpoints, and competition over ideas. Contentious coexistence, in other words, is democracy in action."[15] Payne's analysis is provocative and hopeful, suggesting that it is precisely at the moment that past state violence becomes public, even when denied by the perpetrators, that it becomes challengeable by citizens. It is this sense of possibility that makes contentious coexistence a part of democratization. But what happens when exposure of past violence and confessions of state involvement occur not in a period of democratization but while a nation is precariously perched between democracy and dictatorship and hurtling toward the latter? Is it possible that at this point, exposure, discussion, and ultimately a lack of accountability contribute to the production of increased impunity, manifested in the failure to stop the violent actions of state officials and hold them accountable, including the failure to revoke the laws that stand in the way of accountability?

This question is the point of departure for the remainder of this chapter. More than forty years after both incidents occurred, what is known about the killings in Phatthalung and the burning of Ban Na Sai remains plagued with inconsistencies, lacunae, and a persistent lack of resolution. The series of events that led to the burning of Ban Na Sai and the reason it was burned remain unknown, with the state claiming that it was the work of CPT members and students and survivors claiming that it was the work of state officials. The duration of the *thang daeng* killings is unknown, although survivor and family accounts cite 7 August 1972 as the beginning of the arrests. Estimates of the number of people who disappeared and were murdered vary widely; some state officials estimate that there were approximately eighty deaths, while student activists claim that there were as many as three thousand. Most troubling, the precise nature of state involvement in both incidents—including units, motivation, actions, and record keeping—remains obscure.

In Vince Boudreau's terms, the burning of Ban Na Sai, the *thang daeng* killings, and the subsequent failure to secure accountability were both instrumental and exemplary.[16] The public production of impunity both served to silence the immediate dissent and provided a pedagogical reminder to dissident (and nondissident) citizens of the lack of paths of redress and justice open to them. My contention in the cases of the burning of Ban Na Sai and the *thang daeng* killings is not only that the public exposure of these events, and subsequent failure to hold state officials accountable, led to the further consolidation of impunity but that an end to impunity can, and perhaps must, begin with understanding this process. This means tracing how the violence was exposed, how state officials responded, and how the decision not to take action to hold them responsible emerged publicly and in plain sight. Although state documents about the two events, particularly the final reports commissioned by the Ministry of Interior, or the broader context of counterinsurgency operations do not exist in the National Archives, extensive news reports about the exposure and failure to hold the perpetrators to account were clipped and filed by National Archives staff. Reading these reports, in tandem with survivor and student accounts and the spare recollections made after the fact by state officials, allows questions of how citizens' fear of violence at the hands of state officials is consolidated, how state officials systematically evade responsibility, and ultimately how justice is foreclosed to come to the surface.

The Burning of the Village of Ban Na Sai

On 24 January 1974 the burning of Ban Na Sai, a village in Nong Khai province, which is located across the Mekhong River from Laos, was reported in the newspapers without much fanfare. After a battle between Thai state forces and "communist terrorists," the communists burned the village and fled. The BPP asserted that, despite the proximity of the village to Laos, this was an *thammada* (ordinary) battle.[17] But when activists from the Prachachon Phua Prachathipatai (People for Democracy Group, or PDG), a group of current and former student activists led by Thirayuth Boonmee and Chaiwat Suriwichai, visited the area to propagate democracy in early February 1974, people told them that this was not true. State officials, not members of the CPT, had burned the village.[18] The end of dictatorship meant that it was newly possible to call for government accountability, and the PDG decided to carry out an investigation into the burning of the village of Ban Na Sai.

Over the next three months, divergent accounts of the event circulated in public. Villagers dared to speak about their experience of violence at the hands of state officials even as they were publicly condemned as communists. A range of state officials offered muddled and often shifting accounts of what had taken place. Three primary investigations with three different conclusions emerged. The PDG concluded that state security forces had burned the village. The provincial government did not come to a conclusion about who burned the village but provided compensation to the villagers. The national government offered a partial conclusion that the village had caught fire during fighting between the CPT and state forces, but it never released its findings to the public. A columnist for the *Daily Niu* opined, "The venting of the villagers and the report of the state are as different as the sky is from the ground."[19] A *Thai Rat* editorialist commented that the accounts were as different as black and white and that if state officials were found to have broken the law they must be prosecuted because their actions caused decent officials to *rap khwam suam sia* (be dishonored) during a time in which counterinsurgency was essential to the preservation of the nation.[20] The stance of the *Thai Rat* editorialist—that the primary problem created by the burning of Ban Na Sai was the dishonoring of officials rather than the violence visited upon citizens—was an unspoken undercurrent in the two government investigations. During the Ban Na Sai controversy in the early months of 1974, the possibility of accountability for state violence against citizens created by the 14 October 1973 movement flashed up and then slipped away. The impossibility of accountability came to rest on the truth of the villagers' accounts and the attendant implications in excess of any potential impact on counterinsurgency. As activists demanded accountability, state officials aimed to both evade potential prosecution and ensure that they, not the villagers, would remain the arbiters of truth.

On 8 February 1974 several members of the PDG traveled to Ban Na Sai by oxcart. Chaiwat said that when they arrived, "Everyone felt dispirited and full of great sorrow when we saw the state of the village. More than one hundred small, little houses had been burned down."[21] The shock of what they witnessed convinced the PDG that they had to expose the burning of the village to the public, and three days later, they returned with a camera and tape recorder to make a record of what had taken place.[22]

As the PDG began to share their findings with the press, public interest in the burning of Ban Na Sai began to grow. On 15 February Thirayuth took four villagers to meet the prime minister: Lom Kanchanasan, the village headman; and three male villagers, Ang Yodsaeng, Sanga Sombatdee and Sakorn Chantawee. They met with the prime minister for close to two hours. Ang Yodsaeng, a military veteran of World War II, asked the soldier who knocked on his door on the morning that the village was burned down if he had time to collect his citizen ID and veteran cards before going to the temple. The soldier's reply was to ask him if his veteran card could shield him from bullets. After listening to the villagers, Sanya said that he was gravely concerned and would ensure that a prompt investigation was carried out. He sympathized with the villagers and pulled out 500 baht (at that time, approximately 20 U.S. dollars) from his wallet and handed it to Lom, who kept 200 baht and gave the others each 100 baht. Lom commented on the morals and compassion of the prime minister, and said that his eyes filled with tears at his remarks. He planned to save the money as a keepsake of the prime minister's sincerity. Speaking after the meeting, Sanya warned that the event was complicated and careful work was needed to ensure that the truth—a truth based on the facts of what happened— came out.[23] A little over two months later, Sanya deemed the truth to be too dangerous.

For the PDG and allied activists, the truth was not something that needed to be investigated but was rather the uncomplicated result of listening to the villagers. They organized a large mass protest on Sanam Luang on 20 February 1974 that was attended by ten thousand people. The event began with a pledge by all present to only speak the truth. They intended to discern what had taken place in Ban Na Sai and not to attack the state.[24] The PDG, along with the National Student Center of Thailand (NSCT) and the Federation of Independent Students of Thailand (FIST), issued a joint statement. They began by asserting that they believed the villagers' account of what had taken place. In contrast, they condemned the actions of some state officials as "brazen lying to the people."[25] They called on the government to provide compensation, clarify the facts, punish those responsible using the judicial system, and in the long term, "acknowledge the truth that the Communist suppression policy is without effect and must be improved."[26]

The PDG's call for the truth was met with a sharp and polarized response. The PDG was alternately accused of being leftist instigators, traitors, Vietnamese, and a tool of the CPT. The Nong Khai governor accused them of organizing public events in the province without asking for permission and claimed that they had slandered civil servants as *thorrarat* (tyrants).[27] The villagers who spoke out about what they had witnessed, especially the four who came to Bangkok, were accused of being both communists and supported by elected politicians, and so therefore untrustworthy.[28] Within this context, on 22 February Sanya announced that the national government would carry out an investigation. A day later, the PDG announced that they would cease their organizing and wait for the release of the national government's report.[29]

The PDG kept their promise and waited until 11 March, after the national government declined to release their results to the public, to disseminate their results. The PDG then made their announcement that 106 houses in Ban Na Sai had been burned down and three people had been killed by state authorities. The PDG's assessment was that the evidence in support of this was incontrovertible.[30] Along with their conclusions, the PDG's report also included interviews and testimonies from various figures in Ban Na Sai, including Lom Kanchanasan. His account suggested that he and the other villagers were uneasily caught between the CPT and the Thai state, a common inconvenient truth during the Cold War.

Lom was born in Ubon Ratchathani province and moved to Ban Na Sai in 1969. The village had a constant presence of VDVs beginning in 1966; while the majority were well behaved, some took advantage of the villagers and demanded free food and alcohol. Similarly, CPT cadres sometimes came to the village and asked for rice. The villagers handed over the rice because they were afraid of what would happen if they refused.

At 10:00 p.m. on 16 January, CPT forces came into the village, killed one VDV, and fled. At 2:00 p.m. on 17 January, thirty armed CPT fighters came into the village, looked around, and then left. When they returned the next day, state forces were waiting for them and so they fled into the neighboring mountains. The state forces followed them and fighting ensued. One state official was killed and two were injured.[31] On 19 and 20 January, the village was peaceful. Then, at 1:00 a.m. on 21 January, villagers carried a small baby buffalo that had died to an area behind one of the village rice mills to be cut up. The VDVs patrolling shot at them and so the villagers fled.

At dawn on 24 January, the majority of the villagers were awake and beginning their morning chores. They heard heavy gunfire and ran back into their homes. A loud voice ordered all the villagers out of their homes. The voice warned that anyone who did not do so would be killed. A group of over one hundred VDVs, BPP, and army soldiers rounded the villagers up and led them to the temple. Then the villagers watched their houses burn down. As the village burned and the fire grew hot, the villagers were sent to a swamp at the edge of the village. Five women and fifteen men, including Lom, were selected out of the group and searched for weapons.

They were then taken to the village school to be interrogated. At this point, Lom thought that he was going to be killed, but he and thirteen others were released. The remaining six were taken to the district police station but later released. During the period in which he participated in the exposure of the burning of Ban Na Sai, Lom was accused of being a member of the CPT and received a series of death threats. He was told he should eat his favorite foods, because he would soon be eating a bullet.[32]

In his conclusion to the PDG report, Chaiwat Suriwichai remained unequivocal in his assertion that the village was burned down by state officials and framed his support for the villagers' articulation of the truth by explaining the state's inaction as based in tyranny that lingered from prior to 14 October 1973.[33] He called on readers to be impartial and to "use discretion to make a decision and search for the truth about this event. You will have to attempt to open your hearts, remove your prejudice and old beliefs in order to have equality, liberty, and solidarity . . . without forgetting that this equality, liberty, and solidarity must be for every Thai person equally, not only for one group of people, not only for students and people in Bangkok."[34] The provincial and national investigations ensured that acknowledgment of the truth, let alone equality, liberty, and solidarity, remained an unrealized hope for the people of Ban Na Sai.

The first to contradict the PDG account was Khamphon Klinsukhon, the governor of Nong Khai province. After speaking with villagers who maintained that their homes had been destroyed by state officials, he said that none of the villagers had told the truth.[35] He then offered a timeline of events beginning on 16 January that differed from that offered by Lom Kanchanasan. Khamphon said that on 16 January communist fighters came into the village and burned a VDV uniform, killed one VDV, and injured two others. Then, at 4:00 p.m. on 17 January, a special police force came to clear the area of communists. One policeman was shot dead and four were injured. On 21 January communists burned a bridge close to the village that had been built by state officials. On 24 January state security forces engaged in fighting with communists who had taken over the village. Khamphon insisted that the village then had to be *kwad lang* (purged) since the communists were in control.[36] He did not describe the details of this purge but asserted that communists had set off a bomb in order to burn down the village with the complicity of the villagers in order to embarrass the government.

The governor's accusation rings hollow because it is difficult to imagine how or why the villagers would have been willing to sacrifice their homes and possessions, including in many cases their rice for the next year, in the service of *embarrassing* the government. Perhaps the governor deployed a misplaced logic of counterinsurgent psychological warfare and claimed that the people themselves sacrificed what the government was willing to destroy for them. The governor's accusation of the villagers' alleged complicity also seems untrue given that no villagers were prosecuted in connection with the burning of the village. Under the ACAA, providing support to the CPT, even a handful of uncooked rice to a hungry cadre, was sufficient grounds for arrest and prosecution. The governor's subsequent actions suggest that he understood the falseness of his words because he distributed rice, food, and blankets to the villagers in mid-February.[37]

The governor also appointed an investigatory committee in mid-February, albeit one composed entirely of state officials.[38] The report was one hundred pages in length and was presented in both Nong Khai and at the Ministry of Interior on 8 March. It recommended that the villagers be provided with social services but was inconclusive on the question of who burned Ban Na Sai. Nineteen civilians were interviewed, including a final interview with Phisamai Na Nakorn, a member of the right-wing Village Scouts.[39] Phisamai was well acquainted with all the VDVs, BPP officers, and other state security officials in the area and claimed that "nearly all were good people." She saw people clad in green setting fires but did not know if they wore the uniforms of one of the branches of the Thai state security forces or that of the CPT.[40] Her uncertainty was enough to exonerate the state officials, but many former residents of Ban Na Sai, including Lom Kanchanasan and Ang Yodsaeng, no longer felt safe living in the area and moved away.

The national report was even more inconclusive than the provincial report because it was never finalized and therefore not released to the public, even in summary form. Similar to the provincial report, the lack of a public conclusion was itself an assessment of who burned the village of Ban Na Sai. Had the CPT burned the village, with or without the villagers' complicity, this could have been made public without hesitation. As Jaran Kosanan astutely notes, despite the other changes wrought by the events of 14 October 1973, neither the illegality of communism nor the legality of extensive violence in the service of repressing communism changed.[41] Shortly after the PDG broke the news of the burning of the village to the public, General Kris Sivara, the commander in chief of the army, said, "If it is proven that it is the actions of the officials that persecuted the people, then it must be held to be a very grave issue and there must be punishment. At the same time, if it comes out that the burning of the village was done by the officials in order to suppress the Communists, then this is not at all a grave issue."[42] General Kris's comments suggested that burning villages was business as usual for the army. General Saiyud Kerdphol, the director of the CSOC, the primary military-police-civilian counterinsurgency agency, noted that the burning of the village would have a significant impact on communist suppression, but that could be fixed. If the officials were behind the burning of the village, they must have had a good reason to do so. He did not think they would act in a *sia sathi* (lunatic) fashion.[43] General Saiyud claimed that the path forward included legal and other remedies. Whoever had committed wrongdoing would be dealt with under the relevant laws. In addition, *silatham lae kanmuang* (moral and political) means would be used to create understanding so that the people would not choose to align themselves with the communists.[44] The national investigation that ended without a conclusion was perhaps meant to do so.

A week after Prime Minister Sanya Thammasak met with the four villagers from Ban Na Sai, he established a national investigative committee to report to the cabinet. Chaired by Winyu Angkanarak, the deputy permanent secretary of the Ministry of Interior, the other members of the committee were the secretary-general of the Department of Local Administration, which oversees provincial governments; General Saiyud of the CSOC; and the national police commissioner. The national committee declared its neutrality, but, like the provincial committee, it was composed solely of state officials. If any state officials were found to have broken the law, they were to be prosecuted. The committee visited Ban Na Sai from 24 February to 1 March and reported that it had carried out a full survey of the village.[45] During the week that they spent in the village, Winyu and his fellow investigators divided the village into fifteen squares and inspected them on foot, taking many photographs and asking villagers what they had seen. Winyu claimed that he was followed by a Vietnamese spy but persisted in his work. They spoke with thirty villagers and nine state officials. Winyu noted, "There were villagers who spoke the truth and those who did not. The words of many villagers were in conflict."[46] Winyu did not assess the truthfulness of the state officials.

Within a week of returning to Bangkok, the committee submitted a sixty-page report to the cabinet, with a lengthy appendix composed of drawings, photographs, and documents. Winyu said that he was satisfied with the report.[47] A cabinet meeting was held on 19 March, and the decision was made not to release the full report to the public but to release a partial version and then carry out a further investigation.[48] The report stated that the fire had been caused by an exchange of gunfire between state security officials and communist fighters who had entered the village on 23 January, one night before the village was burned. Sanya said that the precise details of how this occurred could not be released to the public at that time and instead called on the committee to do further research before its release at an unspecified time in the future. The only other piece of the report released to the public declared that the state should provide financial assistance and other social services to the displaced villagers.

Winyu awaited further instructions.[49] On 2 April he was sent to carry out further investigations without any time limit placed on him. At this time, the national government maintained that whoever had committed the crimes would be prosecuted under the law. The minister of interior said that the majority of the remaining work had to do with the issue of *kho thet ching* (facts).[50] Initially, he said, the reason why the identities of those behind the burning of the village could not be revealed was because the committee had to remain neutral.[51] By 13 May the official reason for the nonrelease was "because at this time there are issues of livelihood of the people which must be urgently addressed."[52] Perhaps the unofficial reason was that only certain kinds of truth were compatible with neutrality. In May, Winyu told reporters he would do whatever the prime minister asked him to do, but he would not speak about Ban Na Sai in public anymore.[53]

Neither Winyu nor Sanya spoke in public about Ban Na Sai again, and it became one in a lengthening list of unresolved state crimes in the years leading up to the 6 October 1976 massacre. If there was firm evidence that the CPT had burned the village, this would have been readily revealed to the public. But if the truth was that the state security forces had burned the village, as the inconclusive provincial and national government reports suggest, then this could not be confirmed to the public.

The exposure of the burning of the village of Ban Na Sai existed uneasily in a period of open politics sandwiched between two periods of dictatorship during the Cold War. While this may have been business as usual for counterinsurgency forces, as the comments of General Kris and General Saiyud suggest, state officials could no longer treat it as such, or at least not in public. But the political transformation from dictatorship remained incomplete and the truth spoken by the villagers did not register as impartial enough to be acknowledged. The version of events narrated by state officials was cast as the only true and impartial one.[54] What made this dangerous was that the facts of the burning of the village and the impossibility of holding the perpetrators accountable created what could be called a threatened existence for the people, rather than Payne's contentious coexistence. The people, like the truth of the violence visited upon them by the state, were out in the open. Less than a year after the exposure of the burning of Ban Na Sai quieted down without resolution, another cycle of the exposure of state violence, calls for accountability, a series of investigations, and an ultimate failure to secure accountability was centered on an earlier, and even more brutal, instance of state violence in Phatthalung province in southern Thailand.

THE BURNING OF PEOPLE IN PHATTHALUNG

Yongyut Dusithamo, a teacher and VDV from Khaochaison district in Phatthalung province, undertook a particularly proactive response to Field Marshal Praphat's 1971 statement that all traces of communists and communism would be swiftly removed from Thailand.[55] Teacher Yongyut recruited a group of young men and instructed them to create the appearance of having fought with communists. Thirteen young men were given five guns and twenty bullets per night. After 9:00 p.m. every evening, they shot the guns into the air and ran through the rice fields, trampling the stalks and destroying the rice. Teacher Yongyut also provided a chicken for them to kill to create blood-laced evidence of their encounter with the communists. This nightly killing of a chicken was necessary since the communists were not real. With the chicken blood as evidence of their presence, the young men could report that the communists always fled. After using their allotted bullets, the young men ran to tell the nearest village headman in a given area that they had fought the communists but they had escaped.[56]

Teacher Yongyut and fellow VDVs who used similar strategies produced the impression that there was both a formidable communist presence in Phatthalung and justification for increased financial support for their activities. Through their nightly fights with a chicken, his volunteers produced an image of communists so fierce that they always escaped, unstoppable even when wounded. If this many communists allegedly existed and needed to be eliminated but did not really exist, then who would be killed in their place?

One answer is in the way the *thang daeng* killings unfolded. While a range of experiences are described in the various *thang daeng* accounts, common to all is a high degree of arbitrariness. Villagers were asked to tell state officials which of their neighbors and colleagues were communists. In some cases, this was an informal process and in others villagers were actually placed on the payroll of the CSOC as spies. One could end up on the communist blacklist due to a dispute over an unrelated issue with a neighbor, and so the blacklist became a means of eliminating one's enemies.[57] The stories of two other teachers in Phatthalung—Teacher Lim and Teacher Ploy—illustrate the grave implications of the arbitrary blacklists.

On 7 August 1972 Lim Phaosen was taken from his home and never returned. Teacher Lim left his house in the morning to observe a school in another district as part of his work as the acting head teacher in his village. While he was out, an army soldier came looking for him. His mother-in-law, Kloy Ketsang, said he was not home and told the soldier to come back later. The soldier searched and found Teacher Lim in the other district and forced him to come with him. He took Teacher Lim home and asked him to change his clothes, as he was wearing a sarong, and then took him to a nearby army camp to meet his superiors. Chaweewan, Teacher Lim's eight-year-old daughter, was home from school while this series of events was occurring and pleaded with the soldier not to take her father away. Chaweewan and her grandmother cried and begged the soldier to let them come to the camp too, but he refused. When Khruawan, Teacher Lim's wife, arrived home in the evening, she became concerned. Teacher Lim suffered from a chronic illness and had not taken his medication with him. But the soldier had not told Kloy or Chaweewan where he was taking Teacher Lim.

Chom Kaewpong, another man from Teacher Lim's village, was also taken on 7 August 1972, but he was released a few days later. Chom told Khruawan that he had seen Teacher Lim at the camp where he was held. She quickly prepared a supply of medicine for Teacher Lim and rushed to the stated camp. When she arrived at the army camp where Chom had been held and released, the soldiers told her that they had not arrested Teacher Lim and he was not there. Khruawan then went from camp to camp in Phatthalung but did not find Teacher Lim or anyone who had information about him. She went to neighboring Songkhla and Pattani provinces but was still unable to find her husband. Finally, she learned from a survivor of Thachiet camp, in Mod subdistrict, that he had been burned in a *thang daeng*. The same person told her that the reason why Teacher Lim had been killed was that he had opposed the corrupt dealings of a locally influential person who wanted a contract to build a new school. Teacher Lim had worked as a civil servant for over ten years, but Khruawan was unable to obtain his death benefit or even his last month's salary. The reason: there was no body and no death certificate.[58]

In contrast, Ploy Prap-in, age thirty-nine, was a teacher who narrowly escaped the *thang daeng*. On 10 August 1972 he was taken and stuffed with others from his village into a General Motors truck and transported to Thachiet camp. In language reminiscent of the earlier and later periods of arbitrary detention discussed in chapter 1, Teacher Ploy was told that he was not being *chap* (arrested) but was *choen* (invited) to the camp. Once one is arrested, there are certain procedures and record-keeping mechanisms that must be followed under Thai criminal procedure law. "Invitation" is a slippery linguistic trick of obfuscation. If Teacher Ploy was "invited," it was an invitation without the possibility of refusal.

On his arrival at Thachiet, the officials there accused Teacher Ploy of working with his colleague, Teacher Lim, to foment unrest. They were allegedly planning to make photocopies of tracts supplied by the Peoples' Liberation Army of Phatthalung to distribute in the market. Then they were going to burn government buildings, including a health center, and kill army soldiers and VDVs. At the close of this interrogation, Teacher Ploy was told that if he did not confess to these crimes, he would be killed in a *thang daeng*. A soldier took Teacher Ploy to a large tent at the edge of the camp. He saw blood staining the ground near the tent. When he entered the tent, he saw more than sixty villagers, many of them with obvious marks of torture on their bodies. His fellow villagers told him that if one was called for interrogation at night, then one was going to be killed. The villagers told Teacher Ploy that even though the soldiers guarding the tent told those who left at night that they were being released, this was not true. Instead, people were forced to sign a statement confirming that they had been released, and then they were killed. Every night those inside the tent saw the fires as the oil and bodies in the *thang daeng* burned.

On his fifth night in the tent, Teacher Ploy was taken to be interrogated. He was forced to sign a paper stating that he had been released. Then a high-ranking officer came into the room and said that he was innocent and would be taken back to the tent. Teacher Ploy was held for seven more days. During those days, he underwent *kan fuek obrom* (training) in the camp. He was very surprised to later find himself the subject of documents distributed by trainers of the CSOC. Apparently, he and Teacher Lim had turned themselves in to the CSOC and confessed to planning to distribute communist documents and destroy government property. He had neither turned himself in nor confessed. After his release, Teacher Ploy remained afraid but felt lucky to be alive and returned to work.[59]

Actually being a communist was not a requirement for being taken by the authorities given the wide parameters for detention provided by the ACAA, and reports indicate that the first to be arrested were those who knew about the corrupt, abusive actions of state officials, such as Teacher Lim. Within this context, personal connections could lead to either one's death or one's survival, as in the respective cases of Teacher Lim and Teacher Ploy. Aside from the use of blacklists, there were mass arrests in many villages. A large number of people would be arrested in a sweep, and then those deemed innocent would be released after interrogation.[60] Those who witnessed such operations reported that a large number of security officials—fifty to sixty in the middle of the night or one hundred during the day—would surround the house of an alleged communist.[61]

On their arrival at the camp, detainees were accused, like Teacher Ploy, of plotting and/or committing crimes against the Thai state. In the days that followed their initial detentions, many detainees were interrogated multiple times and frequently tortured. Villagers who were taken and those close to people who were taken reported that forms of torture used during interrogation included electric shock, withholding food, and being beaten and kicked in the chest and head until one passed out.[62] Throughout the period of detention, physical torture was accompanied by the fear of what might happen when the security forces ceased their interrogation. Would one be released, like Chom Kaewpong and Teacher Ploy? Or would one be killed in a *thang daeng*, like Teacher Lim?

When the *thang daeng* killings were perpetrated in late 1972, the dictatorial and severely anticommunist regime of Field Marshal Thanom Kittikhachorn, Field Marshal Praphat Jarusathien, and Colonel Narong Kittikhachorn ensured that there would be no public outcry or opposition. Nor did the villagers immediately begin to speak out about their experiences following the 14 October 1973 movement and transition to more open politics. Instead, like the burning of Ban Na Sai, the *thang daeng* killings came to light unexpectedly during democracy propaganda and consciousness-raising by students in early 1975.

The first national election was set for 26 January 1975. In the weeks and months preceding the election, many student activists traveled throughout the country spreading information on democracy and teaching people how to participate in politics. While doing this work in southern Thailand, Phinij Jarusombat, a fourth-year law student at Ramkhamhaeng University and the head of the political wing of the National Student Center of Thailand (NSCT), heard stories about the *thang daeng* killings from villagers he met. After hearing about sweeping arrests, detention, torture, and killings in the *thang daeng*, Phinij wanted to launch an investigation to obtain a fuller picture of what happened in Phatthalung province in 1972. When he returned to Bangkok, he brought the issue to the attention of his colleagues in the NSCT.[63]

Similar to the investigation carried out by the PDG of the burning of Ban Na Sai, the NSCT and the United Front against Dictatorship (here, UF), a progressive network of students and nonstudents, formed a committee in early February 1975 to study and then disseminate information about *thang daeng* to the public. Their logic was that this was likely not an isolated case and the Thai people needed to know what had happened during the previous dictatorship.[64] In the month that followed, the NSCT and UF brought villagers from Phatthalung to Bangkok and then sent a delegation of students, doctors, and journalists to Phatthalung. The villagers were brought to Bangkok to provide an opportunity for survivors of *thang daeng* to share their experiences with the people and media directly. Then they were to meet with the newly elected government of Prime Minister Seni Pramoj to decide how to provide justice to the survivors and the families of those who were killed or disappeared. Finally, while the villagers were in Bangkok, the NSCT and UF wanted them to meet with General Kris Sivara, the commander in chief of the army, to figure out how to ensure their safety, as they remained afraid of state security forces.[65] In the meantime, the delegation from Bangkok would use its time in Phatthalung to compile as much specific information about the *thang daeng* case as possible in order to present it to the government.

The NSCT planned an event on Sanam Luang as the centerpiece of its exposure of the *thang daeng* killings. In preparation for the event, Phinij Jarusombat and a group of villagers, including Samart Rakradej, a village headman who helped the NSCT organize the collection of evidence and the names of people killed in *thang daeng*, met with the prime minister and other state officials to inform them of their plans.[66] Together with the Socialist Party of Thailand (SPT), the NSCT called for the dissolution of the Internal Security Operations Command (ISOC), which the CSOC had been renamed after 14 October 1973.[67] The SPT viewed the ISOC as "creating great suffering for the people and the most vile criminal."[68]

Even before the event on Sanam Luang, villagers in Phatthalung who intended to speak out became the targets of criticism and threats. On 9 February a group of NSCT activists went to Phatthalung because the villagers who were planning to come to Bangkok had been threatened by four *khon luek lap* (unknown figures) who followed them and warned them "not to bring the issue to the public in Bangkok."[69] On 10 February there were reports of a *thalaengkan muet* (murky declaration) to the effect that the conduct of the students was "a violation of the law and a dishonoring of Thai people" that would create chaos.[70] The language about dishonor is resonant with that used in the case of the burning of Ban Na Sai. Yet what law was being violated by the exposure of state violence and *who* stood to be dishonored by its exposure? Honor is something that must be earned; it does not follow automatically because one wears the green uniform of the state security forces. While it is tempting to dismiss this statement solely as a feeble attempt to discredit those involved, taking it seriously reveals the existence of multiple layers of impunity. The *law* that was being violated was not one contained within the Criminal or Civil Code but rather the unchecked, unquestioned power of the state permitted between the lines of the ACAA and related measures. By bringing to light what happened during the *thang daeng* killings, students made this latent law visible. If anyone was being dishonored, it was the citizens.

Despite these threats, the NSCT, UF, and SPT continued with the plan for the event on Sanam Luang. On 14 February at 4:00 p.m., there was a "Hyde Park"–style public hearing under the banner "Report of Killing the People by Throwing Them into Red Barrels and Burning Them," which was attended by more than twenty thousand people.[71] Approximately thirty villagers from Phatthalung traveled with Samart Rakradej to Bangkok to attend the event, and nineteen spoke about their own and their families' experiences of *thang daeng*.[72] One said that villagers had called on officials in Phatthalung, but no action had been taken. This had "caused many people to feel afraid up to today."[73] Although participating in the event on Sanam Luang was frightening, by joining with others, this villager suggested that participation was also transformative.

On Sanam Luang, students and villagers made two demands: dissolve the ISOC and compensate those whose family members were killed. The

ISOC was identified as the common thread in the various accounts of terror in Phatthalung. While most of those who came to Sanam Luang supported the exposure of the *thang daeng* killings, a few members of Krathing Daeng, one of the right-wing parastate groups active in Thailand between 1973 and 1976, also attended the event.[74]

A day later the two demands had become six.

1. Protect the people of Phatthalung who had brought the issue into the open, including both those who had spoken out about the issue and those who had called for the government to accept responsibility
2. Compensate people who were tortured by state officials or whose relatives were killed
3. Remove soldiers and VDVs from the area
4. Punish officials who had exceeded the law
5. Dissolve the ISOC
6. Repeal the ACAA.[75]

The new set of demands went beyond identifying the ISOC as the perpetrator of the killings and asking for compensation to addressing the broader contexts of fear and the dangers of counterinsurgency. The demands that accompanied the exposure of the *thang daeng* killings were stronger than those associated with the burning of Ban Na Sai. Rather than simply evaluating the effectiveness of counterinsurgency, the students and villagers called for the ISOC, the primary counterinsurgency agency, to be eliminated. With the extended set of demands, the issue of holding the many different actors involved accountable also came to the fore. On 15 February the Phatthalung villagers met with Minister of Interior Atthasit Sitthisunthorn at his home in Bangkok. When presented with the demands, he said that it was "the first time he had received an official complaint about the case" and "although no official protest had been lodged it is the duty of the provincial authorities to take the 'serious matter' up as soon as possible."[76] Since almost three years had passed since the killings took place, Atthasit believed that a period of study and research was needed before a response to the six demands could be made.[77] By the end of the month, Atthasit had ordered the Ministry of Interior to compile an official report on *thang daeng*, but his response to the demands led to the proliferation of other responses and rumors. One of these rumors cited an unnamed source within the army who said that an internal report commissioned by General Kris claimed that "government troops were 'used' by village headmen to kill 16 personal enemies in a rival group" who were engaged in a rivalry over "mining and sexual relations issues." Ten people were allegedly arrested in that sweep but later released.[78] While it is impossible to determine whether this particular account is true, many within the state itself confirmed that the arrests were arbitrary and based on personal conflicts in a given village or district. As students, doctors, and journalists prepared to travel to Phatthalung, rumors proliferated and tensions in Bangkok and the south increased.

While a range of state officials reacted negatively to the events exposing the *thang daeng* killings in both Bangkok and Phatthalung, the lengths to which they went to prevent the exposure in Phatthalung were dramatic. Abdulmanee Abdullah, a villager from Phatthalung who worked with the CSOC prior to *thang daeng* but later resigned and joined in the efforts to expose the killings, commented that those who dared speak about the events lived in an *anachak haeng khwamklua* (kingdom of fear).[79] Abdulmanee and others who joined in the exposure were threatened and followed by assassins.[80] Members of the security forces who participated in the *thang daeng* killings clearly did not expect their actions to become the object of public scrutiny, and they stood to suffer if they did. If the reaction to the exposure and those who spoke out can be read as diagnostic of the dangers of speaking out, the risks increased as the exposure moved from Bangkok back to Phatthalung itself. In other words, it may have been more dangerous to break one's silence locally, where the killings occurred, than in the national center of Bangkok. The increasingly violent reaction to the exposure of the *thang daeng* killings was both caused by and indicative of the disappearing space for dissent in Thailand in mid-1975.

These risks did not stop people from speaking out, however, and shortly after the NSCT began its exposure, a group of Phatthalung villagers told *Daily Time* newspaper of their willingness to be witnesses if the state decided to investigate. They shared their addresses and names with the newspaper, which published them. Somnuksang, a lawyer, told *Daily Time* about his brother, Chamsangkaew, who had been accused of supporting the CPT in 1972.[81] He was interrogated and harangued by the village headman in front of his fellow villagers while Chamrat Mahapol, the provincial head of the CSOC, watched from the sidelines. One month later, CSOC officials came for Chamsangkaew, but he had fled to Bangkok. Banjong Khaekpheng, a teacher, was taken and investigated by the CSOC for allegedly fomenting bad feelings against officials among villagers and being a communist at the time of *thang daeng*. Like Teacher Ploy, he was recognized by one of the CSOC officials and released from the tent before he was killed in a *thang daeng*. Kawisak Oonruang, a lawyer, heard a loud noise outside his door while he was sleeping. He thought the noise was a villager with a problem. When he opened the door, he was surprised to see a mix of sixty CSOC officials and VDVs. When Kawisak started to close the door, one of the CSOC officials accused him of trying to flee as a dirty communist. Kawisak was not taken to an army camp but was interrogated in a field belonging to the local headman. Many people he had helped, or sat and chatted with while drinking, were there as VDVs, and one of them told the CSOC to release him. When these three came forward with their stories in February 1975, all were ready to be witnesses.[82]

Immediately after the event on Sanam Luang, the NSCT and UF formed a committee to organize their trip to Phatthalung to interview people like Kawisak, Banjong, and Somnuksang. They met with General Kris about their planned trip and to ask for cooperation from the army and the ISOC, as one of the other rumors that circulated in mid-February was that soldiers were going to shoot at the students if they went south. General Kris assured the NSCT committee members that they would be safe in Phatthalung.[83] Set for 17–22 February, journalists from *Athipat, Prachathipatai, Prachachat, Daily Time, Thai Rat, Bangkok Post*, and an international news wire service also planned to make the trip.[84] Sixty students, including representatives from Chulalongkorn, Thammasat, Mahidol, and Ramkhamhaeng universities, were going to split into six groups to visit different parts of the province. Two members of each group were to be medical students from Mahidol University, who would provide services for villagers without access to public health centers.[85] The primary purposes of the trip were to support villagers who were speaking out, to gather evidence and the names of people who were killed or disappeared during the *thang daeng* killings, and to build networks that would continue working for justice on the issue.[86] In a broader sense, the NSCT planned to use the trip as an opportunity to learn about additional problems faced by villagers in Phatthalung and southern Thailand.[87] The breadth of those involved in the exposure of the *thang daeng* killings was wider than those involved in the case of Ban Na Sai, and the reaction was more extensive as well.

From the first moment of their arrival in Phatthalung, members of the delegation met with resistance from local officials.[88] Asa Monkholsiri, a district officer, was one of the loudest voices interfering with the NSCT delegation. Soon Khamnurak, who had three nephews who died in *thang daeng*, said that Asa Monkholsiri called a district meeting on 20 February and told everyone present not to believe the newspapers. Instead, they should only believe village headmen and other state officials. According to Soon, Asa "said that the students were going to incite us to go to the jungle. They did not come to spread democracy. If we didn't believe him, we would suffer more."[89] Another report alleged that Asa gave villagers food, clothing, and other items and told them to keep quiet about *thang daeng*.[90] Asa told *Prachathipatai* newspaper that he did not tell people not to talk to the students. During his time as district officer, he said, only two young children had come to see him about relatives who allegedly disappeared during the *thang daeng* killings. At the same time, however, he said that the news about *thang daeng* was a strategy of the CPT to convince people to go to the jungle.[91]

When the students arrived in Ban Phut subdistrict, Asa turned his warnings into action. He used a megaphone to attack them verbally, and his verbal intimidation was matched by the presence of fifty armed soldiers. Asa and the soldiers finally left, and then the students organized a debate and discussion. Many villagers spoke, and the conclusion was that at least two hundred people were killed in Ban Phut. Saphak Panui, who had worked as a patroller for the army in 1972, said that typically seven or eight people were killed each evening. He said that the soldiers drank while they killed people and the bodies burned.[92]

Asa Mongkholsiri was not the only person against the NSCT investigation. A deputy district officer, Surinthorn, told villagers that the students came to agitate and instructed them not to talk to students. In particular, he claimed that if they talked to students, "it will cause [our] homeland to become chaotic and return to dictatorship again."[93] Posters were also put up urging the students to leave and go back to studying and reading books.[94] When students went to one village in Khaochaison district, they saw a poster that read, "Dear children, commit yourselves to studying. Don't create divisions. Now they live together peacefully already."[95] In another part of Phatthalung, students faced accusations that they had come to burn down the market and incite the people to riot.[96] The truth becomes dangerous when it is visible in plain sight.

Given the intimidation and harassment they faced, Phinij Jarusombat estimated that the NSCT delegation covered only one-tenth of the affected communities. Despite these difficulties, they collected the names of 809 people who were killed or disappeared during the *thang daeng* killings.[97] Perhaps unintentionally, the efforts of Asa Mongkholsiri and others to silence villagers and intimidate the NSCT delegation signaled the need for exposure. These efforts can be seen as a form of denial of wrongdoing in which "perpetrators acknowledge the stories of victims and survivors and challenge the regime's justifications."[98] Similar to the burning of Ban Na Sai, after which the state provided social services but refused to reveal the full results of the investigation, if the stories of *thang daeng* did not matter, why would Asa dispense free items in an attempt to silence them? Why would soldiers be willing to spend the day watching as Asa shouted at the students? Why would posters be put up in communities telling students to go back to reading books, rather than seeking knowledge of recent events? And what forms of violence and intimidation did not make it into the newspaper and other reports about the exposure?

What was at stake, it seems, was not only the issue of the facts of the *thang daeng* killings but the capacity of the security forces to control life in Phatthalung in a broader sense. The importance of maintaining this control was particularly clear in the way state officials who were invested in keeping the killings hidden reacted to state officials who joined the exposure efforts. For example, Chamlong Porndetch, who was appointed governor of Phatthalung province in early 1975, came into constant conflict with the provincial head of ISOC, as well as district-level officials in Phatthalung. As soon as news of the NSCT and UF's exposure of the *thang daeng* killings broke in early February 1975, Chamlong expressed a wish to learn more about the events, which had occurred before he became governor. On his arrival in Phatthalung, he was made very aware that the people were afraid.[99] Chamlong told Phinij Jarusombat and the NSCT, "I have heard news about this kind of assassination of the people. But I don't have witnesses or evidence because the people are terrified. They are afraid to talk openly with civil servants about it."[100] While Chamlong supported exposure and risked his position, and even his safety, to push for further investigation, his colleagues fought, both openly and secretly, to put a halt to the exposure and his involvement in it. In mid-1975, after facing death threats and constant harassment, Chamlong asked the Ministry of Interior to transfer him to another province. In a different political moment, perhaps when Thailand was not hurtling toward a return to dictatorship, Chamlong Porndetch and his allies might have been able to force the emergence of accountability within the Ministry of Interior or the state security apparatus that it attempted to monitor. Yet in mid-1975 his position within the bureaucracy was not even secure enough to keep him safe from threats. If dissenting state officials can be threatened or forced to resign or flee for their lives, then what might happen to ordinary citizens?

Far from uniform, from the very beginning of the exposure of the *thang daeng* killings, citizens and state officials offered a range of often contradictory statements, what Payne calls "unsettling accounts," which she says create "political competition over how to interpret dramatic political events, how to use them, and what they mean for contemporary political life."[101] In a time of democracy, competition over the interpretation of a violent past might "not end by killing off democracy or saving it. Instead, it puts into practice the art of competition over ideas and the possibility of building consensus around democratic values."[102] But even more so than during the exposure of the burning of Ban Na Sai in early 1974, extrajudicial violence was on the rise in Thailand in mid-1975, and the public airing of the debate became an opportunity to demonstrate the sheer vulnerability of those who speak out.[103]

When he met with villagers who came to Bangkok in mid-February 1975, Minister of Interior Atthasit said that a committee would be formed to investigate the allegations and if state officials had acted improperly they would be held accountable.[104] The Ministry of Interior could call any former or current employees to Bangkok for questioning, but it had to ask the Ministry of Defense for permission to investigate members of the army.[105] Viang Sakornsin, inspector general for the southern area, was appointed to head a two-person committee to investigate the killings.[106] Viang and the second committee member, Montri Trangan, were given seven days to carry out their investigation.[107] Unlike the inconclusive reports of the provincial and national governments about the burning of Ban Na Sai, the summary of the investigation released to the press in late March 1975 stated that, although innocent citizens had been killed in *thang daeng*, it was a much smaller number than that offered by students and villagers. Rather than thousands, seventy to eighty people had been killed. The report concluded that no punishment of state officials was warranted because it would cause them to feel discouraged in their important work of fighting insurgency.[108] The ISOC could not be dissolved because it was needed to continue the fight. Shortly after the summary of the report was released, the

NSCT criticized the hidden nature of it and the apparent protection of wrongdoing by state officials.[109]

The assertion that state officials should not be punished for murdering citizens because it might cause them to feel discouraged recalls another contradictory acknowledgment of violence and refusal of accountability by a state actor. Police Major Anan Senakhan, a maverick and often inconsistent figure vis-à-vis progressive politics in the mid-1970s, publicly acknowledged in early February 1975 that the *thang daeng* killings had occurred. In 1972 he was responsible for collecting and distributing the police news from the southern region, and so he was aware of the sweeping arrests and killings. Anan disputed the number of people who were killed, arguing that it was not three thousand but approximately three hundred. He personally knew of only two people who had been killed. Yet, despite this knowledge, Anan urged people not to think of soldiers as monsters lacking humanity. Instead, they were "people who love the homeland too, [and so] we should have sympathy for them too."[110] The difficulty with this sentiment is that if perpetrators are not held responsible they are the *only* ones who receive compassion.

Without accountability for perpetrators, compassion for survivors of torture and those who died in the *thang daeng* killings lacks meaning. Shortly before the release of the summary of the Ministry of Interior report, a new government headed by Kukrit Pramoj, Seni's brother, came to power. As 1975 wore on, overt intimidation and violence against progressive activists increased, and while the NSCT inquired as to how the Kukrit government was going to address the *thang daeng* killings, it was unable to force Kukrit to take action.

What occurred during the exposure of the *thang daeng* killings, the calls for state accountability, and ultimately the foreclosure of the possibility of accountability was a process resonant of and complementary to what occurred in the case of the burning of Ban Na Sai. As the period of open politics began to come to a close, state officials could openly acknowledge their crimes in a way that was not possible in the immediate aftermath of the 14 October 1973 movement and the end of dictatorship. Through the wide exposure of the *thang daeng* killings, citizens across Thailand learned the precise extent of what could be done to them by security forces if they became real or perceived enemies of the state. They also learned that even if there was a broad public exposure, including a large demonstration in the center of Bangkok and high-profile meetings among survivors, activists, the commander in chief of the army, and the prime minister, it was possible that no one would be held accountable for the violence. They learned that a committee appointed by the state could acknowledge that there was wrongdoing by security forces and then decide not to punish them. The truth exposed during the public debates and conversations about the *thang daeng* killings was that the lives of the people were dispensable.

TRUTH DEFERRED

What is most troubling about the burning of Ban Na Sai and the *thang daeng* killings is not that they occurred and were never brought to light but rather that they were exposed, the state investigated its own wrongdoing and strongly suggested or outright confirmed that state officials had murdered villagers and destroyed their homes, and in the end it chose to do nothing. During the event on Sanam Luang, Sutham Saengprathum, a student leader, explained, as quoted in one of the epigraphs to this chapter, "[We have] laws [stipulating] that people who act wrongly are judged via a judicial process. But when the administrative class makes themselves those who decide [on matters of justice], the lives of the people have no meaning."[111] Sutham's idea of the law left no space for the unchecked power of the state. The people's lives were being stripped of meaning because they could not be protected by the law. In another sense, when members of the administrative class acknowledge that they have committed crimes but then allow these crimes to go unpunished, the lives of the people who suffered and died become *filled* with meaning. Their lives, and deaths, become a permanent reminder of the ability of the state to kill its citizens with impunity. They become a reminder of how state officials can get away with wanton destruction and murder. And when state officials cannot bear the public airing of this impunity, and so silence the truth, the lives of the people are further endangered.

As the Cold War came to an end in Thailand and globally, this was reflected in transformations in law and policy. In April 1980 communism was partially decriminalized with the issuance of Order 66/2523 by the government of General Prem Tinsulanond, which provided amnesty for citizens who had joined the CPT provided that they were willing to turn themselves in to the authorities and therefore acknowledge their wrongdoing.[112] The ACAA was finally nullified in 2000, though with no apologies.[113] There has been no attempt to prosecute state officials for the crimes they committed during the Cold War. Further, memoirs written by state officials involved in the burning of Ban Na Sai and the *thang daeng* killings published after the Cold War ended underline what was, and remains, at stake in ensuring the security of both the state's version of the truth and its concomitant impunity.

In 2001, twenty-six years after the burning of Ban Na Sai, Winyu Ang-khanarak, the former permanent secretary of the Ministry of Interior, who later went on to serve as the director-general of the Department of Local Administration, published a memoir of his years as permanent secretary, *Heart of the Permanent Secretary*.[114] The chapter "The Incident of the Ban Na Sai Fire" recounts his role in the investigation. He begins by noting that although he uses real names elsewhere in the book, in this chapter he does not do so.[115] Yet he does not adhere to this completely, and the combination of the details he reveals and the names he cites offers a much different, and sharper, picture of both the burning of Ban Na Sai and its exposure than did his comments to the press at the time of the investigation. Ban Na Sai, he writes, is 140 kilometers east of Nong Khai city. There were 137 families in the village, which had a total population of 1,537.[116] Winyu then provides a version of events leading up to the burning of Ban Na Sai that clarifies what the provincial governor may have meant by "purge" and indicates that the responsibility for the destruction of the village lies squarely with state officials.

In mid-January 1974 there were several skirmishes between state officials and CPT forces. On 22 January CPT forces blocked a main road into the village. On 23 January a plan was made to send state officials to the village. On 24 January two hundred officials went to take back Ban Na Sai.[117] The results of this operation are not detailed by Winyu, and instead his time-line jumps forward to the exposure and investigation. When Winyu and his committee carried out their survey of the village, they found that 102 houses had been burned along with 82 rice barns, 3 rice mills, and 2 monk's cells.[118] They collected 239 pages of documents and 140 photographs.[119] The committee recommended that the state officials involved should be prosecuted under the Criminal Code. Winyu presented the results to the cabinet, which then questioned him and other members of the committee for one and a half hours. At the end of the meeting, General Kris Sivara, the commander in chief of the army, who was sitting next to Prime Minister Sanya, said to him in a loud voice, "*Chao*" (done), a word used by gamblers to indicate the end of a round or game.[120] General Kris's precise meaning was made clear by what happened next and the way Winyu describes it in his memoir. He quotes a *Thai Rat* article that noted, "Khun Winyu was very anxious because even though they had summarized the results of the investigation for the Cabinet, the Cabinet would not agree to release [the results] to the public. This caused him torment. Wherever he went, people surrounded him."[121] Although Winyu did not state explicitly who burned Ban Na Sai, his recollection of the one word General Kris uttered speaks volumes. It was as if the game was up and the sore loser overturned the card table. The Thai army is nearly always a sore loser.

In the case of *thang daeng*, the indicative recollections appear in the memoir of Pallop Pinmanee, a soldier who, nearly forty years after the incident, became a general and the deputy commander of the ISOC. Almost as an aside in a book about his role in the Krue Se mosque massacre in 2004, General Pallop revealed his role in the *thang daeng* killings.[122] Rather than the clarity provided by Winyu's account of the burning of Ban Na Sai, General Pallop's account instead provides another layer of obfuscation to what is known about the burning of people in Phatthalung.

During the time of *thang daeng*, General Pallop served as the chief of operations for a unit in the midsouth, including Phatthalung. During a patrol in Ban Phut in Kong Ra subdistrict, his unit was ambushed and three were killed and more than ten injured. At this point in Pallop's story, recall that Ban Phut was the same village where I noted that student activists and villagers in 1975 collected the names of over two hundred villagers who had been killed. General San Chitrapatima, the commander of the Civilian-Police-Military Task Force, was angered and demanded that the culprit behind the ambush be identified. Normally Pallop (who was not yet a general) would not have been involved in interrogation, but General San cited his experience in Laos and placed him in charge of finding the culprit.[123]

Pallop and his troops surrounded Ban Phut, identified and arrested twenty-seven suspicious people, and detained them in the village temple. But then things got out of hand. Pallop writes, "There was one teenager, about nineteen or twenty years old. While I was questioning him, he was trying to provoke me. I did not say anything. . . . I poked with one foot, not quite a kick."[124] Then an intelligence officer for the CSOC, who had been one year ahead of Pallop at the military academy, told him to leave and said he would finish the interrogation. Pallop got up because, as he said, "When an older brother wants to do the interrogation, he does the interrogation."[125]

He walked no more than twenty steps before hearing a "plock" sound. The young man had a seizure, fell to the ground, and was dead. All that General Pallop's senior had done was kick the young man under his chin. When Pallop returned, he was shocked and trembling because he had never seen combat. Pallop himself was surprised, and recalled that he said, "Damn. . . . What are we going to do?"[126]

Then Pallop turned and saw a red oil drum. His time in Vietnam flashed before him. Faced with a lack of latrines, the soldiers had cut oil drums in half, put diesel fuel in them, and used them as toilets. When the oil drum was full of their waste, they burned it. He ordered his soldiers to empty the drum, which was filled with sand. They then burned the body of the dead young man and threw the remains into the river. The problem, Pallop wrote, was that the truth that they burned one person had morphed into the fiction of burning many people.[127]

The remaining twenty-six people he detained in Ban Phut witnessed the entire series of events because it was carried out within the temple compound. He released ten of them and sent sixteen on to the police. They were later released as well. Pallop concludes his account by casting his behavior as having been in the service of the truth: "Therefore, I maintain that I burned one person, because this story is mine. I did not burn hundreds, thousands, as is bandied about. I do not want the truth in this story to be twisted. The nature of noble soldiers such as myself, who have become experts in battle, is that we are courageous enough to accept what we do. I do not want this to be turned into a crime. I want the next generation to know the truth because I was there and performed my duties during the incident."[128]

General Pallop, who reduces the number killed from even the seventy to eighty in the entire province counted by the Ministry of Interior, let alone the over two hundred in Ban Phut counted by the students, to one, seems to want to reduce the significance of the event by reducing the number of lives lost. A number of questions remain between the lines of his story, even if we consider his account to be true. The first of these questions centers on the meaning of his acceptance of responsibility. By insisting that only one person was killed, rather than attempting to shift the blame by arguing that other units in the midsouth had carried out the *thang daeng* killings, is it possible that General Pallop was the actual figure behind them? If so, his ability to make this claim in print, over forty years after the killings and in the context of a book in which he refutes the accusations against him with regard to a more recent instance of state violence, suggests the lasting strength of impunity in Thailand.[129] The second question, what might be cast as a question about humanity and the Thai army, is one that can be posed but not answered. Although under Revolutionary Announcement No. 78, bodies of communist suspects who died in state custody did not have to be autopsied if doing so would be dangerous to the authorities or an obstacle to counterinsurgency, what danger did this young man pose? In General Pallop's detailed account of his ingenuity and how the body of the young, insolent man came to be burned, he may have revealed more than he planned. His unit burned and disposed of the body of the young man in the same fashion that it burned its own urine and feces. Did doing so, rather than returning the young man's body to his family to be properly mourned, make the Thai nation safer from the alleged dangers of communism?

In the cases of the burning of people in *thang daeng* in Phatthalung and the burning of the village of Ban Na Sai, the investigations failed to secure accountability not because the committees could not determine the truth but because the state could not bear the burden of the truth. Although there were different versions of these events circulating, the fragile democracy at the time meant that rather than Payne's "contentious coexistence," the exposures and debates around both incidents heralded the impending return to dictatorship. By going out of their way to advocate in public for their versions of what happened, which are often at profound odds with the accounts of victims and survivors, state officials may both reveal themselves as perpetrators of crimes and expose a flaw in the logic of impunity. The very confidence that facilitates the exercise of state violence is often left behind as evidence at the time or resurfaces in later recollections. This is evident in General Pallop's account of *thang daeng* years later and evident in the ways in which state officials crafted a way to avoid accountability for the 6 October 1976 massacre. The realization and tracing of how accountability is elided are inseparable from the truth of state violence that such cover-ups aimed to erase.

4

The Hidden Transcript
of Amnesty

AMONG THE TWELVE SUCCESSFUL COUPS, the one that occurred on 6 October 1976 is exemplary due to the public and extreme nature of both the brutality of the accompanying violence and the measures through which impunity for it was secured. The coup came less than three years after the movement for democracy, on 14 October 1973, ousted the three dictators—Thanom Kittikhachorn, Narong Kittikhachorn, and Praphat Jarusathien—whose power had been consolidated in the seventh coup of 17 November 1971. The period between 14 October 1973 and 6 October 1976 witnessed unprecedented political participation by previously marginalized groups, including workers and farmers, and also the creation of a space in which to ask previously unbroachable questions. This was the context in which students and citizens were able to expose the burning of Ban Na Sai in 1974 and the *thang daeng* killings in Phatthalung in 1975. But the changes taking place in Thai society, which pointed to a reconfiguration of both social relations and material interests, were not welcomed by all. The difficulty of turning the exposure of these two events into accountability, and in particular the virulent indifference of the state reaction to the calls for justice for the *thang daeng* killings, signaled the growing backlash to a more progressive society in which formerly marginal groups were participating in politics. Capitalists, landlords, royalists, conservatives, and other elites viewed their actions as dangerous and in need of repression. What began as fear turned into violent panic. Beginning in 1975, intimidation, harassment, attacks, and targeted assassinations of progressive and leftist activists grew in frequency.[1]

When Thanom Kittikhachorn returned to the country on 19 September 1976 to be ordained as a monk, leftist and progressive students were suspicious of his claim that the reason for his return was religious in nature. In response, student activists began protesting his return as a warning sign of a potential return to dictatorship. Two labor activists were hanged in Nakhon Pathom province on 25 September 1976 while posting flyers as part of these protests. The students suspected that the activists were hanged by the police.[2] Four to five thousand students massed inside the gates of Thammasat University to continue their protest, and on 4 October they performed a skit that included a reenactment of the hanging as a critique of police violence.[3]

Emboldened by Cold War fears heightened by the transitions to communism in Vietnam, Laos, and Cambodia in 1975, the right wing, both inside and outside the state, first criticized the students and then openly called for them to be repressed. On 5 October, *Dao Siam*, a right-wing Thai-language newspaper, reported that the skit about the murdered labor activists was actually a mock hanging of an effigy of the crown prince and that the student activists wanted to destroy the monarchy.[4] Right-wing forces circulated copies of a photograph and the newspaper article about the alleged mock hanging of the crown prince.[5] Dissident students were accused of being Vietnamese, Chinese, and/or communists, all three being code names for persons whose activities were treacherously un-Thai. On 5 and 6 October these accusations were taken one step further when the armed forces radio called for mobilization against the students massed inside the walls of Thammasat University.

This call for mobilization turned into violence shortly after 2:00 a.m. on the morning of 6 October. The unarmed students and activists were beaten, hanged, and killed by an angry mob of state and parastate forces. That evening, the National Administrative Reform Council (NARC), a military junta led by Admiral Sangad Chaloryu, announced that it had successfully launched a coup and ousted the elected prime minister, Seni Pramoj. The NARC reported that 46 people had been killed, 180 injured, and 3,059 arrested at Thammasat University, although the unofficial estimates were higher.[6] Those arrested were the survivors of the massacre; no arrests were made for the assaults and murders of the students and other activists massed inside the university. More than forty years later, the perpetrators of the violence still enjoy complete impunity; there has never been a public state investigation of the violence, let alone anyone held to account for it.[7] This impunity is both cause and effect of what Thongchai Winichakul argues is the silence, ambivalence, and ambiguity surrounding the event for both those who survived it and Thai society as a whole.[8]

There is nothing unusual about the fact that state officials and their civilian co-conspirators got away with murder on 6 October 1976. Even if only the three years between 14 October 1973 and 6 October 1976 are examined, let alone the periods before or since, impunity was the established norm for state violence, as chapter 3 makes clear. What makes impunity for the 6 October 1976 massacre remarkable is that a legal trail was documented and accessible. Unlike the archival lacunae in the cases of the burning of Ban Na Sai and the *thang daeng* killings in Phatthalung, the production of impunity in the 6 October 1976 massacre was documented, archived, and left in plain sight.

In the two years following 6 October 1976, two different amnesty acts centered on that day were promulgated. The first, the Amnesty for Those Who Seized the Administrative Power of the Country on 6 October 1976 Act, was promulgated by the National Administrative Reform Assembly (NARA) on 24 December 1976.[9] The second, the Amnesty for Those Who Committed Wrongdoing in the Demonstrations at Thammasat University between 4 and 6 October 1976, was passed by the National Legislative Assembly (NLA) on 15 September 1978.[10] Neither law mentioned the massacre or the deaths of the students or even admitted that violence had taken place at Thammasat University. On the surface, the first amnesty seems to have been an ordinary amnesty for participants in the coup fomented by the NARC. The second appears to have been an amnesty to end the legal proceedings against the Bangkok Eighteen, the eighteen students and activists who survived the massacre but were being prosecuted for grave crimes, including revolt, lèse majesté, and communist activities committed during the protests.[11] Yet both amnesties went beyond their stated goals to cover the massacre itself.[12]

There are no direct references to the massacre or the specific acts of violence that took place at Thammasat University, but examination of state documents related to the drafting and passage of the first amnesty, combined with a close reading of the much sparer record connected to the second one, suggests that they were paramount in the minds of those behind the two laws. Here absence reflects a sharp presence. Through the careful use of language, the first amnesty prevented murderers and coup makers from being held to account. By granting forgiveness for crimes not committed, the second amnesty blamed the victims and survivors of the violence. Common to both amnesties was the assertion that their passage was good for the well-being of the country and the Thai people. The combination of the two amnesty laws first created and then consolidated impunity for the coup and the massacre that preceded it.

Writing less than a year after the massacre and coup, Benedict Anderson criticized observers who cited the frequency of coups in Thailand and viewed this one as typical. Instead, the 6 October 1976 coup marked a historical turning point because it "was not a sudden intra-elite coup de main, but rather was the culmination of a two-year-long right-wing campaign of public intimidation, assault and assassination best symbolized by the orchestrated mob violence of October 6 itself."[13] Not only was the violence public, but through the drafting, debate, and passage of the two amnesty laws, the evasion of responsibility for it became public as well. While the two amnesties constitute an exceptional instance of the elaborate, public, legal production of impunity, they also reflect one aspect of the general form of the relationship between the rulers and the ruled in Thailand. State perpetrators are routinely not held to account for violence committed against citizens, and at best the injustice experienced by citizens is not made worse when they dare to call for justice.[14]

The archives of the state, at least those open to the public, rarely offer up a source in which violent actors state both their actions and their desire to obscure those actions in order to retain power and avoid responsibility. In Thailand, available state and other documentary sources must be read against the grain, which means with attention to absences, gaps, discordant statements, and unexpected revelations. The two amnesties for 6 October 1976 that I examine in this chapter are the clearest example of what I call, borrowing and adapting a term from James C. Scott, a hidden transcript of repression. In "The Prose of Counter-Insurgency," where Ranajit Guha outlines a strategy of reading colonial documents against the grain in India, he does so in order to discern dissident peasant voices and locate the evidence of dissidence and rebellion.[15] This is what Scott calls the hidden transcript present even in what seem to be accounts of the total domination of marginalized subjects.[16] Impunity instead demands a reading of state documents against the grain in order to identify a different kind of hidden transcript: indications of complicity and participation in violence, anxiety, and the evasion of responsibility by the state itself. Scott's hidden transcript highlights the presence of resistance to oppression, which is sometimes actively hidden as part of the practice of domination and sometimes obscured in plain sight due to the failure of observers to apprehend its presence. When I began the research for this book, I expected to meet with the former. Instead, I have often found the evidence of violence and the failure to secure accountability in publicly available documents.

The evidence available about the political and legal processes leading to the promulgation of the two 6 October 1976 amnesty laws is uneven and ambiguous. The first amnesty was debated and revised by the lawdrafting committee at the Office of the Juridical Council, or the Krisdika. In 2007 the Krisdika files from its inception to 1979 were transferred to the National Archives in Bangkok. Since then, the forty-three-page file on the first amnesty law, which includes the initial and revised drafts of the law, as well as the minutes of meetings about the revisions, can be read by anyone with access to the archives.[17] In addition, the minutes of the debate in the NARA are available in their entirety. In contrast, although the second amnesty law falls within the temporal limits of the Krisdika documents sent to the National Archives, there is no corresponding file for it, indicating that either the Krisdika was not consulted, it was consulted but the minutes were not recorded, or it was consulted, minutes were taken, and they were removed from the files sent to the National Archives. Additionally, while the law was debated in the NLA, the deliberations were secret, so there is no official record available. Instead, the story of the debate and passage of the law must be culled from newspaper records. While the record of the debate in the NLA was made secret, individual members were not bound by a gag order. What the partial, fragmented, uneven nature of the evidence means is that, as in John Roosa's analysis of the September 30th Movement in Indonesia, certainty is neither possible nor the goal.[18] What is possible instead is to cast doubt on what is currently known and to elucidate what is not known about the 6 October 1976 massacre and coup and the methods by which those responsible have not been held to account.

The contradictory position of the available information about the two amnesty laws—for example, the public accessibility of the Krisdika file about the first amnesty affirms the right to know and yet the ambiguity of the information contained within it cannot aid in concretely moving toward either the right to justice or the right to reparation—makes it a rich point of departure for considering a series of political, legal, and analytical questions about accountability, evidence, amnesty, and the persistent challenges of securing justice after state violence. In particular, first, what are the legal mechanics through which violent actors escape accountability? Second, what are the legal and political functions of amnesty when no crime has been committed? Third, and finally, might accountability for past violence still be possible, and if so, under what conditions?

THE FIRST AMNESTY

On the morning of 23 November 1976 seven of Thailand's brightest legal minds, including one external guest from the Krom Phrathammanun (Department of the Judge Advocate General) in the Ministry of Defense, gathered for an urgent meeting of the law-drafting committee at the Krisdika.[19] For two hours, the seven men at the Krisdika meeting vigorously discussed the 6 October 1976 coup, the differences between an amnesty and a pardon, and the various needs an amnesty should meet.

The 6 October 1976 coup was the eighth coup since the end of the absolute monarchy in 1932. Every previous coup had been followed by either an article in the relevant postcoup constitution or a stand-alone amnesty law formally legalizing the illegal actions of the coup makers.[20] In this case, the final article of the 1976 constitution, promulgated on 22 October 1976, addressed the coup. Article 29 stipulated, "All the actions, announcements, or orders of the head of the National Administrative Reform Council that were carried out, announced, or ordered before the date that this Constitution came into force, all that was related to the administrative reform of the country, irrespective of their manner or form and irrespective of their legislative, administrative, or judicial force, including the actions of those in compliance with the announcements or orders, shall be considered lawful." Given this seemingly comprehensive measure, why was a separate law necessary? It was necessary because, while the coup itself was not remarkable and a few words could have been changed in an earlier law and pressed into service to protect those behind it, the massacre that took place several hours before the coup was unprecedented. The proximity of the two events raised particular legal and political problems, and, as became clear during the deliberations on the first amnesty bill, the law needed to account for this proximity while also concealing its significance.

When the members of the law-drafting committee met to discuss the amnesty for the coup, they did so in a building that was approximately a five-minute walk from the location of the massacre. The Krisdika complex consists of a series of buildings between the Chao Phraya River and Phra

Athit Road, which meets the back gates of Thammasat University next to the faculties of economics and political science. The violence against the students on the morning of 6 October 1976 was incited by language and ideology that cast them as neither Thai nor human. In the rhetoric of the rightists, eliminating them was necessary to preserve the nation, religion, and monarchy. But inside the meeting room at the Krisdika, a far less glib story unfolded. For the majority of those involved in drafting the new constitution, the presence of the final article legitimizing the coup was sufficient. But for a vocal minority there was a strong concern that Article 29 was insufficiently comprehensive.

In response to a request from the prime minister's office, the secretary of the law-drafting committee sent out an urgent call for a meeting on 22 November 1976. The prime minister's office had drafted a law in response to concerns about the constitutional provision and wanted feedback on it. The committee met the next day (23 November) and sent a revised draft back to the prime minister's office the following day.[21] The text of the revised draft was the one that became law a month later, on 24 December 1976, when the Amnesty for Those Who Seized the Administrative Power of the Country on 6 October 1976 was promulgated.

The amnesty law was short, composed of only four articles. The crucial one was Article 3. The draft version read:

> All the actions, announcements, or orders of the head of the NARC, or the actions, announcements, or orders of the NARC that were carried out, announced, or ordered before the day this law goes into force, including related to the administrative form of the nation by the aforementioned individuals, irrespective of their manner or form and irrespective of their legislative, administrative, or judicial force, these actions, announcements, and orders, including the actions of those following the announcements or orders, irrespective of whether they were carried out by someone in the position of a principal figure, a supporter, a person acting for another, or a person who was used, are actions, announcements, and orders that are lawful. No individual can be prosecuted for them.[22]

The revised, final version read:

> The entirety of actions taken due to the seizure of the administrative power of the country on 6 October 1976 and the actions of individuals connected

with those aforementioned actions were undertaken with the intention of fostering the security of the kingdom, the crown, and public peace. The entirety of the actions of the NARC or the head of the NARC or those who were appointed by the NARC or the head of the NARC, or those who were ordered by someone appointed by the NARC or the head of the NARC that were carried out for the reasons noted above, including punishment and the bureaucratic administration of the country, all of the aforementioned actions, irrespective of their legislative, administrative, or judicial validity, irrespective of whether they were carried out by someone in the position of a principal figure, a supporter, a person acting for another, or a person who was used, and irrespective of whether or not they were carried out on the aforementioned day or before or after that day, if the actions were unlawful, the person is absolved from wrongdoing and all responsibility.[23]

The changes in the new draft are subtle but significant. The most visible among them is in the final sentence. Both versions stipulated that the actions covered by the amnesty would be considered lawful, but the initial draft then mandated that no one could be prosecuted for any actions covered by the amnesty. The final draft went further and absolved everyone involved in actions covered by the amnesty from any wrongdoing and all responsibility. There were five coup amnesty laws promulgated prior to this one, and each included provisions to make the actions covered by it lawful. In the most recent amnesty law prior to this one, which was for the 1971 coup that Thanom Kittikhachorn launched against himself in order to consolidate his power, this was expanded to include absolution from wrongdoing and all responsibility.[24] Prosecution was not mentioned in any of the earlier laws, which suggests that explicit concern over it may have arisen with this coup and the events surrounding it, including the massacre.

In the letter introducing the revisions, the Krisdika noted that it had changed the draft in order to "make the individuals who seized the administrative power of the country on 6 October 1976 entirely absolved of wrongdoing and responsibility instead of a measure prohibiting prosecution as in the original draft. This is in order to bring it in line with the principles of amnesty so that it will be legislation that expunges the illegal actions that individuals committed on, before, or after 6 October 1976, in order to achieve the result that they never committed any wrongdoing, not only that they cannot be prosecuted [for it] in court."[25] In other words, the Krisdika wanted a law that would not only mechanically prevent prosecution but would also, at least legally and perhaps politically and historically, justify the coup and the events surrounding it.

The discussion of accountability at the Krisdika emerged along three broad questions on which many amnesties, not only this one, tend to turn: (1) who was covered, (2) what period of time was covered, and (3) what legal changes were engendered by it?

Who was covered? This was a primary concern raised by Serm Winichai-kul, the chair of the committee, at the beginning of the meeting. He noted that with regard to Article 29 of the constitution, "They are probably afraid that the provision in the constitution is not clear enough or broad enough to protect them."[26] Who *they* or *them* included was not made clear, although who was not to be included was very clear. Sompop Notrakit, a committee member and secretary-general of the Krisdika, acknowledged that there were two groups involved on 6 October: "The incident on that day involved two groups: 1. the group of students that also demonstrated in order to reform [change] the government; 2. the National Administrative Reform Council."[27] But by casting the students as engaged in an attempt to change the government, they were presented as persons in need of pun-ishment, not persons who deserved redress for the violence they experi-enced at the hands of state and parastate actors and their fellow citizens. Major General Sawat Oorungroj, the representative from the Ministry of Defense, was very clear in his request to the Krisdika. After the revised draft was read aloud, he commented, "The revised draft is very good. Our objec-tive is that we want a law promulgated that will protect individuals from [the rank of] private on up."[28] The chairman concurred, noting, "This draft is universal. It shields everyone."[29] When another person present (name un-specified in the minutes) raised the concern that perhaps it was too broad, the representative from the Ministry of Defense reiterated his concern that privates who were following orders needed to be covered as well. No fur-ther changes were made.

There is no direct mention of the need to protect any state official who carried out or was otherwise involved in the beating, rape, lynching, and murder of students on that day. But the combination of the mention of the students involved in the incident and the need to protect soldiers from the rank of private on up suggests that this was a concern. While the secretary-general may have wanted to ensure that the students then behind bars would not be amnestied, the more immediate issue that remained unspoken was the legal and moral consequences of the dead students. Similarly, although it is not elaborated, the urgency of writing the amnesty in such a way that *privates* were covered suggests that this amnesty was not only meant for those who took over the government. Why would privates need to be protected in the case of a coup, one at least tacitly supported by the king, no less? They needed to be protected because the amnesty was intended to protect the perpetrators of both what it seemed to be on the surface—the seizure of administrative power on the evening of 6 October 1976—and the violence at Thammasat University that preceded it that morning. It is a consequence of the amnesty and the concomitant foreclosure of any investigation, let alone prosecution or remedy for the victims and survivors, that the precise roles of privates, as well as higher-ranking soldiers and police, the BPP, the Village Scouts, other state and parastate actors, and ordinary citizens are unknown.

What period of time was covered? A further indication of the expanded intention of the law is suggested by the discussion about what period of time was covered by the amnesty. Early in the meeting, the secretary commented that the draft did "not include 'preparation' that was carried out before power was seized."[30] He noted that in the amnesty for the coup carried out by the Thanom Kittikhachorn government against itself in 1971, the amnesty mentioned the actions before and after the seizure of power.[31] The secretary-general later noted, "Time is at first an issue of 'before the reform' and after is 'after the reform.' Before the reform there was no official name, so then use 'individuals.' After the reform, it was then called the 'National Administrative Reform Council.'"[32] He again raised the issue of preparation, commenting, "The provision in the constitution does not include 'preparation.' When this part is left out, it is not total. Before 6:00 p.m. on 6 October 1976, it was not yet called the 'National Administrative Reform Council.' The constitution therefore does not shield the preparation to reform the nation's administration."[33] But then the secretary-general suggested even broader phrasing: "Let me propose it to be '. . . that was carried out due to the seizure of power . . .' which is broader and includes 'preparation' also."[34]

On the one hand, there was nothing unusual about a discussion of ensuring that preparation for the coup was covered. A coup does not arise out of thin air. Alliances must be forged and plans made. What makes it notable here is that, in combination with the concern that privates be covered and the comment that the incident at hand involved both the students and the NARC, preparation could include the dispersal of protests at Thammasat

University before 6:00 p.m., when the NARC was established. The massacre on the morning of 6 October is not mentioned in the text of the law, but it does not have to be. The temporality of the law and its breadth mean that the events that morning were covered by it.

What were the legal changes engendered by the amnesty? In a comparative analysis of amnesties globally, Francesca Lessa and Leigh Payne defined amnesties as "legal measures adopted by states that have the effect of prospectively barring criminal prosecution against certain individuals accused of committing human rights violations."[35] While this is what Article 29 of the constitution accomplished, the men in the meeting room at the Krisdika wanted to go further. At the beginning of the meeting, the chairman summarized the initial draft and commented, "Right. The principle of amnesty is that wrongdoing has occurred, but it has been exculpated. It does not legalize those actions. The draft as written is that the things that were done were 'right,' but the people who did them still engaged in 'wrongdoing.' They have not been absolved yet."[36] In doing so, they drew on the well-established role of amnesty laws in Thailand to perform what David Streckfuss argues is a process of ritual purification. He explains that the repeated passage of amnesty laws is a process that gathers salience and legitimacy within a Thai Theravada Buddhist framework and entails the resetting of the political order through sacrifice, violence, and the production of virtue. Streckfuss describes how coups and amnesty laws function politically, and his use of the past tense in his general description also suggests how they serve as the writing of a particular form of history: "The political order was reset. A new order was established by men of virtue (with guns). Their virtue allowed them to seize power not for themselves, but for the whole social and political order. However, they had to ritually purge themselves of the necessary violence by declaring an amnesty."[37] While this process acquires a particular meaning within a Theravada Buddhist context that prizes a continual process of purification and the cultivation of virtue, the result is also an explicitly secular one: avoidance of criminal prosecution. The string of amnesty laws and the foreclosure of even the possibility of prosecution for criminal acts therefore serve as incentives for would-be coup makers.[38]

An exchange between the chairman and the secretary-general clarified the difference between the measure in the interim constitution and amnesty as they intended to use it.

CHAIR: We wrote to make the law correspond to the constitution that pre-
scribes "these are lawful actions . . ." but does not prescribe that those who
carried out these actions are "right [lawful]." We will therefore issue a law
that will purge wrongdoing and acquit in line with the principle of
amnesty. This principle is that there was wrongdoing, but acquittal is
granted.

SECRETARY-GENERAL: The constitution only says that the actions were "lawful," but an amnesty will acquit and absolve the people. They will be completely innocent, the result being that they committed no wrongdoing."[39]

Quietly, the chairman and the secretary-general confirmed that wrongdoing had been committed on 6 October. The context of the wrongdoing
was not specified, but were they writing an amnesty to apply to the coup
only, their careful attention to detail would not have been necessary. The
goal seems to have been to go beyond preventing prosecution and to
inscribe, at least legally, the actions and actors on 6 October as correct and
completely free of wrongdoing.

Yet it is what may seem like a marginal comment about amnesty during
the meeting that is most thought provoking and unsettling. The preamble
to the final version of the law reads, "Whereas the National Administrative
Reform Council seized the administrative power of the nation and dissolved the constitution on 6 October 1976, it did so with the purpose of
resolving a situation that was a danger to the nation, the institution of the
monarchy, and the people and to establish a form of administration that
was appropriate to the country's situation, the economic foundation, and
the sentiments of the people in order to create well-being for the Thai
people and progress for the nation."[40] While the institution of the monarchy is only one of the three key institutions mentioned, throughout the
discussion of the two amnesties, the valorization of and emphasis on the
protection of the monarchy were key. The protection of the monarchy was
the stated reason for the massacre, and citing it was part of the way the
amnesty was justified.

The question of the collective was raised, almost parenthetically, during
the meeting during which the draft law was revised. The secretary-general
noted, "This amnesty must only protect issues of the collective. This is in
particular issues that are about the collective seizure of power. It cannot
shield the carrying out of actions that were done for personal reasons,
actions done out of rage, killing people for personal reasons on the day

of the seizure of power, etc."[41] The secretary-general's comments here are strange. First, which collective did he mean? The amnesty and the very actions that necessitated it reflect the narrowness of any possible conception of the Thai people. Second, *personal* acts of hatred-fueled killing would not be covered by the amnesty. Through the lens of the Krisdika, perhaps the *political* acts of rage that characterized the massacre could be interpreted as violence in the service of the collective. What they failed to recognize, and what is apparent even to those who have only seen photographs of the massacre, is that all the killings were also personal.

Were this a leisurely, academic discussion about the legal principle of amnesty—such internal discussions on various topics were and are frequently held at the Krisdika—then perhaps the secretary's comments would be inconsequential. But this was anything but a theoretical discussion. It was an urgent, two-hour meeting called to discuss a draft amnesty law that had to be revised and returned to the cabinet within a day. A month later the revised draft became law. Despite the stated intention of the secretary, all the actions of 6 October 1976, even those that were personal, hateful, and detrimental to the common good, were included within the amnesty law. The minutes provide sufficient evidence to suggest, if not confirm, that this was the actual intention of the law.

Five days after the Krisdika sent the revised draft law back to the cabinet, Lieutenant-General Sawai Duangmanee submitted it to the NARA, an assembly of 340 members appointed after the coup. Lieutenant-General Sawai was a former prosecutor in the Bangkok Military Court and former head of the Department of the Judge Advocate General in the Ministry of Defense. Rather than clarifying the purpose or precise parameters of the amnesty law, the expedited debate of it in the NARA on 17 December 1976 only deepened its ambiguity.[42] Those present voiced no opposition to the bill, only a range of different reasons to support it. Unlike the discussion at the Krisdika, neither the students nor Thammasat University were mentioned by name. This acute absence and the broader ambiguity of the amnesty's objects was further underscored by the individual nature of the appeals made by the members who spoke in favor of its passage.

Lieutenant-General Sawai began by arguing that Article 29 of the constitution left many loopholes, and therefore "it is appropriate for the assembly to provide protection for those who acted in the interests of the nation and the Thai people."[43] Then he identified those who might be affected by the loopholes, describing their situation as follows: "The head of the Reform

Council did not invite them. The Reform Council did not invite them to help. They saw their friends go, and so they went."[44] His choice of words is significant: "*their friends*"? They, whoever they were, state officials or civilians, saw their friends go *where*? To Thammasat University to repress the students there? To Government House to seize power? To Thammasat and then Government House? Then Lieutenant General Sawai offered concrete categories of actors who might not be covered by the law. He mentioned the drivers who brought their bosses to the Reform Council. Although they would not be seen as guilty following basic logic, they were guilty in terms of the law "because it [driving] was support that made the seizure of power succeed."[45] This was one of the least ambiguous moments in the debate. The persons he was concerned about could be placed in time and space: drivers of the generals who comprised the NARC. When he continued, however, the ambiguity returned. He pleaded, "In addition, I ask you to please examine the Reform Council, the vendors who sold things, sold food, the clerks, the radio, television, and telegram people. The water, electricity, the various tents who all went to support."[46] These people were not protected by the constitution, yet "they went out of duty. They went to help out of goodwill for the Reform Council."[47]

Although there was no precedent for it in Thailand, it is possible to understand the legal reasoning by which the drivers of members of a junta who launched a coup might be prosecuted for their role in it, and therefore one could conclude that Lieutenant-General Sawai was discussing amnesty for the precise actions of the coup. But this does not hold with his next set of categories, particularly food vendors. Under what legal conditions could a food vendor be prosecuted for his or her role in a coup? Did he mean, for example, that if Admiral Sangad Chaloryu, the head of the NARC, ate chicken rice on the morning of the coup, the vendor who made and sold it to him could be found guilty of supporting the seizure of power by sustaining Admiral Sangad? Or was Lieutenant-General Sawai referring to those who sold the goods and snacks that sustained the rightist mobs outside Thammasat?

Next Lieutenant-General Sawai turned to his own role and possible culpability. He narrated his involvement: "I myself received an invitation to offer my legal opinion. I went to assist for many days. But [according to] the invitation I received, I was not invited by the head of the National Administrative Reform Council and I was not invited by the National Administrative Reform Council or someone appointed by the National Administrative

Reform Council. I am not sure if I would be exculpated or not. I am not 100 percent sure about myself. That all those who went to explain different laws, many laws that we examined together in meetings, for example, the communist law, the gun law. We gave assistance about many laws. There were representatives from many different departments and ministries. There were police, administrators, officials from the Krisdika. There were officials from many ministries, fifty or sixty at one meeting. Do you think that these people were ordered by the head of the NARC or the NARC?"[48] Since they were not, they would not be protected by the constitution. Lieutenant-General Sawai noted that planning had gone on for many months and then asked, "Why are we not going to protect them when they gave assistance in an undertaking that was in the interest of the country?"[49]

I have quoted at length from Lieutenant-General Sawai's comments here because the content of his rhetorical plea for support for the amnesty raises questions about precisely what he wanted the amnesty to cover and also the nature of the massacre and coup. Although he referenced many months of planning, he did not say when or where the meeting (or meetings) was held or who invited him. Even if the amnesty was only meant to cover the coup and my attempt to discern a further meaning is folly, his comments suggest that the coup was not only a military affair but a broad undertaking involving a range of jurists and other civil servants. If his comment about the meeting with fifty or sixty participants was about the coup, then it suggests that the NARC's seizure of power was not the result of an intra-army contest but a carefully planned, broad-based toppling of the elected government of Prime Minister Seni Pramoj from the inside out. However, his mention of "communist law" and "gun law" suggests that this meeting was not about the coup but instead was about what kinds of repressive measures, for example, would be legal and possible under the ACAA and what kinds of exemptions of investigation it might make possible.[50] The ambiguity of Lieutenant-General Sawai's comments means that both assessments can only be speculative.

Lieutenant-General Sawai concluded his introduction of the law by appealing to the assembly's compassion and asking it to pass the amnesty so that "we might consider it as a new year gift for all of them"[51] so that the *phu mi kiat* (honorable people) and their families would not face suffering and hardship in the future. What a gift! Was Sawai joking or did he always exaggerate when he addressed the assembly? A blanket protection from prosecution for crimes for which one might face the death penalty is a gift of a far different order than a fruit basket for the new year. Combined with Sawai's reference to preventing families, including his, from suffering, this statement reflects an inability to think of those killed at Thammasat or the Bangkok Eighteen as human. Like the clear centrality of the monarchy throughout the drafting and passage of the two amnesties, the idea of humanity operative in Thailand was already narrow, and the amnesties, as well as the actions that made them possible, further cemented this. The suffering of those killed, injured, or imprisoned after the massacre, and that of their families, did not register in this discussion. The floor was then opened for debate.

No opposition to the draft bill was voiced. A statement from one of the few female representatives stands out for both her admission of involvement and her simultaneous ambiguity about the nature of that involvement. Mrs. Chongkol Srikanchana began by noting that the possibility of the death penalty disturbed her. She explained, "The incident took place on 6 October, but I have wondered for around two months if someone was going to provide an amnesty for those who participated in the work of that time. I am an ordinary citizen-housewife that went to join and dance wildly with them. The reason is not so important, that was trespassing to make the Government House [the government of Prime Minister Seni Pramoj] fall. Something like that."[52] In her comments during the debate at the NARA, Mrs. Chongkol does not explain what she means by "*ten yeng yeng*" (dance wildly), but in an interview she gave fifteen years later, her account of that day indicates that she and other self-identified housewives were demanding to meet with the prime minister to call for his resignation, and when he did not respond to their demands they went to storm Government House.[53] On arrival they discovered that a coup had already taken place.[54] She explained, "When I learned about the laws, many of my friends expressed concern."[55] Like Lieutenant-General Sawai's perplexing reference to food vendors, the combination of Mrs. Chongkol's admission of excess in "dancing wildly," her agitation over the possible death penalty, and her friends' concern suggests that she might not have been referring to the seizure of power by the NARC on the evening of 6 October but perhaps meant the violence that preceded it. Under what conditions could someone who cheered on a military junta as it fomented a coup face the death penalty? She concluded by beseeching the NARA to pass the amnesty bill: "Therefore, I beg you, honorable representatives and respected chair, the reason for the proposal of this draft amnesty law, I ask you to offer your fullest support, but just now I see that of all of you no one opposes it because you likely see the need to give [amnesty to] the people and everyone that joined in those actions out of loyalty to the monarchy and the nation."[56] To Mrs. Chongkol, a claim of loyalty was sufficient for exoneration of grave crimes, including her own.

The first reading of the law passed with a vote of 302 persons in favor and no votes against. During the second reading, the only discussion was about the possible removal of the words *"nuang nai"* (due to) from Article 3.[57] Lieutenant-General Sawai argued that it would be better to keep them in so that the broadest possible protection would be offered. By a vote of 281 to 3, the words stayed.[58] The final, third reading of the draft was brief. The first amnesty passed with no votes against it.[59]

THE SECOND AMNESTY

While Lieutenant-General Sawai was occupied with ensuring that the first amnesty was passed so that he, and many unnamed and unidentified others, would not face prosecution for unspecified crimes, the Bangkok Eighteen were already living behind bars. Under orders issued by the NARC shortly after it took power, they were to be tried in a military court, rather than a criminal court, which made them ineligible for bail. They waited eleven months before the formal proceedings against them began in the Bangkok Military Court on 5 September 1977. Each was charged with a different combination of crimes, including communist activities, violating national security, insulting the heir apparent, assembling to use force and weapons to create chaos, trespassing, resisting officials who were doing their duty, and possessing unlicensed and illegal weapons, bullets, and bomb-making materials. The possible sentences each person faced if convicted varied, but for some they included life in prison or the death penalty. But the prosecution only had the chance to call eleven of its eighty-three witnesses to the stand before the case was halted due to the passage of the second amnesty bill, the Amnesty for Those Who Committed Wrongdoing in the Demonstrations at Thammasat University between 4 and 6 October 1976. On 16 September 1978 the case against the Bangkok Eighteen ended and they were released.

Significant political changes inside and beyond Thailand occurred in the twenty-one months separating the two amnesty laws. Right-wing jurist Thanin Kraivichien, who had been appointed prime minister by the NARC, was ousted in a military coup on 20 October 1977 led by General Kriangsak Chomanan. In comparison to Thanin, who envisioned a twelve-year return to democracy, General Kriangsak began to relax the strictures the

NARC and then Thanin had put in place.[60] Both nationally and internationally, the human rights movement began to exert wider influence and specific pressure on Thailand.[61] Even the US government, one of Thailand's most important allies in its counterinsurgency efforts over the previous twenty years, began to pay attention to human rights. Excessive repression in the name of counterinsurgency, at least publicly, began to be untenable.

General Kriangsak personally pushed through the second amnesty, calling it a "surprise" (using the English-language word) for the young people he considered to be his *luk lan* (children, grandchildren). But was the amnesty actually, or primarily, for the Bangkok Eight? In an April 2013 interview, Vasant Panich, one of their lawyers, recalled the case and suggested otherwise, saying, "This case did not end with the charges being dismissed. Once testimony began, the 6 October amnesty law was passed, and it ended everything. They claimed to forgive the students, but in actuality they forgave themselves because a lot of students were killed. Everything ended due to the amnesty."[62] When the case was dismissed, the prosecution had presented only 10 percent of its evidence; the rest of the prosecution's evidence and all of the defense's evidence remained unheard. Writing about the proceedings, Thanapol Eawsakul and Chaithawat Tulathon argue that very quickly after the questioning began, the plaintiffs became the defendants. During cross-examination, the lawyers for the defense not only questioned the allegations made against the Bangkok Eighteen but began to illustrate the violent actions committed by state and parastate forces on 6 October. They noted, "Each meeting of the trial of the 6 October case, rather than being an examination to prove the guilt of the students and citizens, instead became an exposure of the violence of the side that wanted to construct a dictatorship out of the events of 6 October."[63] Had the defense witnesses, including the Bangkok Eighteen themselves, given testimony, the prosecution, as well as the repressive parts of the state behind it, might have had a great deal to fear. The actual events of the morning of 6 October—and perhaps what came before and was planned to come after—would have been revealed. The first amnesty—and the broad protections that were so carefully crafted into it—may have become untenable if evidence about the perpetrators and the planning for the massacre had been revealed. It was better to foreclose this possibility.

The nature of the evidence available about the drafting and passage of the second amnesty makes it difficult to ascertain whether it was the compassionate gesture of Kriangsak, the auto-amnesty (amnesty promulgated by the perpetrators for the perpetrators) described by Vasant, or a combination of the two. Unlike the first amnesty, there is no file in the Krisdika records concerning the second amnesty.[64] The draft bill was debated and passed by the NLA, whose 360 members had been appointed by the National Policy Council with the king's approval after General Kriangsak entered office.[65] Yet, unlike the records of the debate in the NARA for the first amnesty, the record of this debate was not made public.[66] However, the arc of the second amnesty bill, including the excitement preceding it, Kriangsak's role, and even the debate in the NLA, was reported in the newspapers.

General Kriangsak claimed that he had been considering an amnesty from the very first day he entered office.[67] In February 1978 he spoke publicly about an amnesty, noting, "If the court judges and releases the eighteen people, we can hold that each is innocent. But if the court decides to punish the eighteen people, the government will be ready to pass an amnesty that day."[68] Over the next six months, the fate of the Bangkok Eighteen was a matter of public concern. Passage of an amnesty by the NLA was one of the three options that could result in their release; the withdrawal of charges by the prosecutor or the use of Article 27, the measure of the 1977 constitution that gave the prime minister executive power in exceptional cases, were the other two. In September 1978 the head of the Department of the Judge Advocate General, Lieutenant General Saming Tailanka, said that the use of Article 27 would be a subversion of the court's authority.[69] An amnesty was acceptable in his book and he noted that precedent existed in 1957 when all those being held on political charges were amnestied.[70]

After a cabinet meeting on 12 September 1978, General Kriangsak was laughing and in a good mood when he told a reporter from *Matichon* newspaper, "What I am thinking of is justice. On this matter, wait. I will surprise you. For now, not yet."[71] He made the amnesty personal, commenting, "I believe that those in jail are my children, my grandchildren, and also accepting individual responsibility.[72] He also said, "I decided this matter myself. The king was not involved in any way. The king was not involved in this matter at all."[73] Why did General Kriangsak make explicit that the amnesty was his idea? Was it because, as he was accused of doing, he was using this as a strategy to campaign for a possible future run for elected office? Or was it because the monarchy was not in favor of amnesty? Initially, Kriangsak had said that alleged violations of Article 112, the measure in the Criminal Code that stipulates penalties for lèse majesté, would not be covered by any amnesty, but this exemption fell away over time.

Prasit Narongdetch, minister of communications, commented that "this is a sensitive matter. Please don't bring our highly revered institution into it at all. The government should dare to accept responsibility for its actions. However, I ask you to trust that we would never do anything that would irritate the feet of their majesties."[74] The matter of the monarchy remain sensitive when the draft second amnesty entered the NLA two days later.

Like the first amnesty in December 1976, the second amnesty was given an expedited review and all three readings were carried out on 15 December 1978. Usually only 100 or so of the 360 members attended meetings, but approximately 260 were present for this one, which was described as *kheuk khak* (lively).[75] Another newspaper described it as *prachum kan khapkhang pen prawatisat* (a meeting with record attendance).[76] General Kriangsak himself introduced the bill in the first reading.

The second amnesty law begins with a preface explaining that the government had examined the situation carefully: the case had gone on long enough and presumably would continue to do so for some time. The law notes, "If the case proceeded until completion, it would cause the defendants to sacrifice even more of their educational and professional future."[77] It explains that the reason the wrongdoing took place was because the protesters' youth caused them to fail to truly understand the situation. As the government had a desire to build unity within the nation, and it was therefore appropriate to *hai aphai kankratham* (forgive them for their actions). This would create the opportunity for those who had committed wrongdoing, including those who were being prosecuted and those who had fled, to act correctly and in the interest of the nation. While the preamble to the first amnesty law explained that those who had carried out the coup and the actions that preceded it had done so to save the nation and foment progress, this one instead claimed that the students had acted out of ignorance and were being given a chance to participate in progress. To be clear, this was the very "progress" put in motion by the coup and the massacre that preceded it.

In terms of the key questions of who was covered, what time period was covered, and what legal changes were engendered by the amnesty, Article 3 was again the most important measure: "All actions by whomever, which took place or were related to the demonstrations inside Thammasat University between 4 and 6 October, whether they were committed inside or outside the university, and whether the actions were taken by a principal figure, a supporter, a person acting for another, or a person who was used.

If the actions were unlawful, the person is absolved from wrongdoing and all responsibility."[78] In the initial draft, the location was specified as at the university "*reu sathanthi eun dai*" (or in other locations), but in the final version it was changed to "*reu nok mahawithayalai*" (or outside the university).[79] In other words, anything and everything that took place during those three days at the university or elsewhere was covered. The amnesty came with a caveat, however. Article 5 mandated, "The amnesty following this law does not provide the right for those amnestied to complain or demand any rights or benefits."[80] To be clear, then, this meant that the students who were pardoned could not claim compensation for wrongful arrest, but perhaps it also meant that they could not then accuse state officials of committing violent crimes at Thammasat University.[81] Article 5 complemented the preface, which began by describing the students' youth and lack of understanding. Together these functioned as a denial of their agency that legally, politically, and epistemologically consolidated the power of those behind the massacre, coup, and amnesties.

The first reading of the second amnesty passed by a vote of 208 to 1. The slight change to the wording noted above was made in the second reading, and it, too, passed with only a single vote against. In the third reading, the second amnesty became law with a vote of 180 to 1.[82] The sole opposition vote was from Mr. Sa-nga Wongbangchuad. Sa-nga opposed the amnesty bill for a variety of reasons, including concern about the alleged acts of lèse majesté committed by the students and a belief that there were more pressing matters, such as economic difficulties, to attend to before passing the amnesty.[83] He commented, "Allowing the eighteen people to come out is not the right way to help the country. This is a matter related to the institution of the monarchy. If we hold to the principle of compassion, ten thousand other people in prison all ought to be amnestied and released."[84] General Kriangsak's response to this criticism was that the social and political costs of not passing the amnesty were too high. Once the amnesty had been passed, he would turn his attention to economic problems.[85]

Although Sa-nga was the only member who voiced opposition, the number of those who voted indicates that a large number chose to express their opposition by not voting. One of these members was Khunying Wimon Chiamcharoen, an outspoken rightist and prolific writer also known by her pen name, Tomayanti. She raised her hand and said that she felt slighted by the second amnesty because she had consistently made sacrifices to protect the three institutions of the nation, religion, and king. On 6 October

one hundred thousand citizens turned out to oppose the students, and therefore she believed that the case against the students should be completed in
court. She walked out and did not participate in the voting.[86] There was
also a curious silence from an important category of members: retired and
active military personnel, who accounted for 200 out of the 360 seats.[87]

When the bill passed, there was applause in the assembly. As he got into
his car after the vote, General Kriangsak said, "Today I am very relieved
and most content."[88] He flew to see the king at 8:00 p.m. on 15 September
at the palace in Narathiwat.[89] There was no mention in the newspaper of
the opinion of the king or queen. Like his colleague the minister of communications, Kriangsak discouraged discussion of the involvement of the
monarchy, noting, "Don't mention it at all. Don't involve him. Let it be a
government matter."[90] But the monarchy's assent can be assumed. General
Kriangsak flew to Narathiwat because the amnesty bill, like all other Thai
laws, needed the signature of the king to go into force.

The next day the bill became law and the Bangkok Eighteen were released.
Only three days later, the MFA reported that the image of the country
abroad had improved.[91] Not even a week later, the US government issued
a statement describing the amnesty as an important step toward reconciliation.[92] Domestically, General Kriangsak faced some criticism and was
accused of being a communist by rightist groups.[93] This criticism did not
have concrete effect on his term as prime minister, however. He remained
in office until he retired and handed over power to General Prem Tinsulanond in March 1980. Both amnesties remain in force to this day.

TOWARD UNDOING IMPUNITY

In an editorial published one day before the second amnesty was debated
and passed by the NLA, General Kriangsak's notion of the amnesty as a
surprise was sharply critiqued. The author commented, "The people of the
world were already astonished that many different institutions and sides
aroused the most brutal slaughter of students and citizens in [Thai] history.
The arrest and prosecution of the survivors multiplied this surprise twofold.
If the Kriangsak government is going to blot out this shock or expiate the
sins of the perpetrators of 6 October, this is supposed to please, rather than
surprise, everyone, as he said."[94] The fifth article of the second amnesty,
which prohibited the released students from filing charges against those who
imprisoned them or attacked or killed their fellow citizens on the morning of 6 October, reflected what can accurately be called the status quo of

impunity for state violence. The legal prohibition against calling for justice was reinforced by the experience of the Bangkok Eighteen. Their experience was witnessed by the entire nation: the massacre, the prosecutions, and the amnesties were public events. What citizens learned is that a group of people can be engaged in a legal protest against encroaching dictatorship when an angry, fear-driven mob of state and parastate actors can carry out a massacre against them. Then, the surviving victims of this massacre can be detained for nearly a year, charged with grave crimes, and then be tried in a military court. Next, when it becomes domestically and internationally untenable to continue prosecuting the survivors for crimes that they did not commit and the real perpetrators begin to feel uneasy about their status, they can be released. But this release is conditional. The amnesty implied that the survivors were guilty and in need of forgiveness, and their release depended on their acceptance of the status quo of impunity for state violence.

The "hidden transcripts" of the two amnesties for the 6 October 1976 massacre and coup reveal the careful, calculated legal moves taken to protect those who were behind it. Despite the rhetoric in the streets and on the radio about the need to protect the nation, the coup and the massacre that preceded it unsettled some inside the state–perhaps because they were aware of the extralegal status of the massacre, perhaps because they worried about their own culpability and perhaps because they were aware that the violations in need of amnesty were not only those of the criminal code but of the more basic code of being human. The Krisdika file and NARA debate record about the first amnesty and the newspaper reportage about the second amnesty do not offer judicially viable evidence of the evasion of state responsibility for violence. Instead, they offer enough details and ideas to provide an account of how impunity for the massacre was produced through the passage of two amnesty laws that did not mention it.[95] What I have done in this chapter is reconstruct the legal maneuvers by which the perpetrators of the massacre and coup forgave themselves, blamed the survivors, and, in so doing, evaded accountability. In my account, I have been purposefully circumspect. Given the partial nature of the information available, certain conclusions can only be gestured toward and a series of questions remain.

What John Roosa notes in *Pretext to Mass Murder* is that rather than confidently identifying the figure(s) definitively behind the September 30th Movement, he aims to "bring us a bit further through the labyrinth, mark some dead ends, and point to the most promising paths for further research."[96] In the case of the 6 October 1976 massacre and coup, there is much that is not known as long as the impunity holds. But there are three questions that the available evidence about the two amnesties suggests, and that are significant in this particular instance as well as in a broader frame of understanding the role of impunity in state formation. First, what kinds of internal state discussions took place following the massacre? Did officials inside the Krisdika, Department of the Judge Advocate General, and other departments and ministries discuss the violence at Thammasat University? Second, when and how was the link among the violence at Thammasat, the coup, and the possibility of an amnesty law made? What kinds of collusion among different agencies, institutions, and individuals occurred? What kinds of background legal reasoning took place prior to the coup, such as the meeting mentioned by General Sawai when he spoke in support of the first amnesty in the NARA? Third, were there any critics of the massacre inside the state? Were any of the legal experts at the Krisdika uncomfortable with their roles as the protectors of murderers?

Given how much remains unknown about the planning and involvement of different actors and agencies in the 6 October 1976 massacre, it may seem premature to raise the possibility of undoing impunity, which means securing accountability. Yet, as the principles to combat impunity suggest, securing knowledge and securing accountability about past violence are necessarily linked. Without facts and clear evidence about violence, impunity cannot be challenged. Similarly, impunity provides protection against questions being asked and sufficient information found about state violence. To date, neither the first nor the second amnesty has faced legal challenge. The seven men who met at the Krisdika in November 1975 had remarkable foresight. Nearly two decades before the emergence of the "justice cascade"—the name given by Kathryn Sikkink to a rapidly expanding call for individual criminal responsibility for grave human rights violations—they acted to foreclose any possibility of accountability.[97] But who is to say that this will last forever? As events in the Southern Cone and Central American over the last decade have illustrated, amnesties, even those put into place by murderous military juntas, do not necessarily last forever.[98]

5

Accounting for Human Rights at the End of the Cold War

THE 6 OCTOBER 1976 MASSACRE AND COUP are often described as an ending: the violent break during which the nearly three years of open politics that began with the students' and people's movement of 14 October 1973 abruptly came to a close. But 6 October 1976 also marked the beginning of a period of human rights violations in which the brutality of the massacre was extended through the arbitrary detention, torture, disappearance, and extrajudicial killing of those who were labeled one of the nine types of "dangers to society" under NARC Order 22, were accused of being communists under NARC Order 22, or simply ran afoul of local state officials.[1] During the first four years after the massacre, under the regimes of Thanin Kraivichien and General Kriangsak Chomanan, political dissidents were targeted in particular, and then the tactics used against them melted back into the toolbox of routine suppression of citizens during the eight years of rule by General Prem Tinsulanond.[2]

Citizens experienced arbitrary detention, torture, disappearance, and extrajudicial killing, along with summary execution, prior to 1976. But various Thai state agencies did not comprehend the arbitrary detention or summary execution of certain citizens deemed to be enemies as rights violations. As part of the Thai government's vigorous participation in early UN human rights reporting and other activities between 1946 and 1976, the Krisdika and the MFA prepared annual reports on the state of human rights for the UN. Although the reports covered many years of dictatorship in the 1950s and 1960s, and therefore periods in which arbitrary detention and summary execution were official government policy, there was no mention of these actions in the final reports and no reference to the need to conceal them in the drafts of the reports present in the Krisdika files in the National Archives. Torture, extrajudicial killing, and disappearance were not mentioned at all, although there are known, and likely many more unknown, cases.[3]

From the vantage point of the present, this lacuna appears to be a glaring contradiction, but it also reflects the early Cold War origins and history of the UN human rights regime and its exclusions. Those who were arbitrarily detained and executed were frequently accused of being communists or otherwise cast as grave dangers to national security. They did not register as part of the *human* in human rights for Thailand and many other states at the time, resonant with the treatment of those defined as terrorists in the early years following the events of 11 September 2001.[4]

But after the 6 October 1976 massacre and coup, the contradiction of the Thai state as a promoter of human rights principles internationally and perpetrator of human rights violations at home could no longer be sustained. There are three primary reasons behind this shift, one specific to Thailand and two others inflected by global transformations. The first reason is that the violence perpetrated by state forces and parastate civilians at Thammasat University on the morning of 6 October 1976 was criminal in nature and the perpetrators were keenly aware of this. The careful drafting and urgent passage of the first amnesty law in December 1976 was catalyzed by this awareness. The second reason was the reduction of the communist threat to Thailand. During the 1960s and much of the 1970s, particularly in the immediate aftermath of the transitions to communism in Cambodia (17 April 1975), Vietnam (30 April 1975), and Laos (2 December 1975), the possibility of a similar transition in Thailand was palpable to military, royal, capital, and other elites.[5] This led to the development of a sophisticated counterinsurgency program and created the social and cultural context for the massacre, coup, and ensuing return to dictatorship. After the massacre, thousands of students and other leftists fled to the jungle to join the Communist Party of Thailand (CPT), some because they agreed with the party's Maoist-Leninist approach to social change and others to avoid arrest or assassination in the cities. But the normalization of relations between the Thai and Chinese governments in the late 1970s and an amnesty for those who had joined the CPT in 1980 led to the fragmentation and slow dissolution of the party. The specter of communism began to lift. The third reason was the unexpected salience of the international and domestic human rights movements. Samuel Moyn has argued that the rise of the human rights movement in the 1970s, rather than the drafting of the Universal Declaration of Human Rights (UDHR) and the beginning of the UN human rights regime in the 1940s, is the key to comprehending the salience of human rights up to the present.[6] Human rights "served as a moral utopia when political utopias died," including those of socialism, communism, and unfettered counterinsurgency.[7]

The utopic human rights movement that emerged then was not the static tool of statecraft centered in New York and Geneva that the Thai government had taken up with enthusiasm from the very beginning as one of the original forty-six states to sign the UDHR but instead a set of tools that directly challenged the state in the service of the protection of those who lived inside its borders. The human rights at the center of the new movements were heterogeneous and at once comprised a set of ideas about how individuals were to be treated, a collection of internationalist citizen activists who viewed the urgency of protecting others as one without national borders, and a range of perspectives on the state's role in protection at home and abroad. Moyn further argues that the emergence of this newly defined notion of human rights centered around a constellation of events in 1977.[8] Although Thailand has not figured in the analyses by Moyn and other historians writing about human rights, this calendar holds for the human rights movement in Thailand, as well as the advocacy in Washington, London, and around the world about human rights in Thailand. A series of contingent events coalesced to at once launch the Thai human rights movement and prompt a quiet transformation inside the Thai state, or at least in the ministries whose work became a target of human rights critics. The first Thai human rights documentation group, the Coordinating Group for Religion in Society (CGRS), was founded in 1976 but began work in earnest in 1977. Donald Fraser, the US congressman from Minnesota who chaired the House Subcommittee on International Organizations, presided over hearings on human rights in Thailand in June 1977. After winning the Nobel Peace Prize in 1977, Amnesty International (AI) drew on information provided by the CGRS to launch its first Thai campaign in 1978. During this campaign, members of AI sent letters to Thai embassies in their own countries and to the MFA expressing concern that political prisoners were being held without bail, tortured, and subjected to lengthy trial processes. In contrast to the silence that prevailed during the Fraser hearings, in which the Thanin government declined to nominate a civilian representative to speak on its behalf, the MFA felt compelled to respond to the AI letters. But it did so with uniform denials. No one was being tortured or deprived of due process in Thailand. In contrast, the CGRS compiled a meticulous and detailed series of hundreds of accounts of torture and other rights violations that were taking place, including descriptions of the very same individuals noted in the MFA letters.

Moyn foregrounds the contingent rise of human rights in the 1970s as one that "came out of a combination of separate histories that interacted in an unforeseeable explosion," and Stefan-Ludwig Hoffman calls for "a genealogy of human rights that narrates their history not teleologically as the rise and rise of moral sensibilities, but rather as the unpredictable results of political contestations."[9] Tracing the different accounts of detention and torture in the US House hearings, the MFAs files, and the CGRS newsletters, I offer a partial history of the unforeseeable and unpredictable rise of the human rights movement in and about Thailand. By placing the profound discrepancies between the different accounts at the center, this is also a history of the production of impunity in two distinct yet related ways. First, examining the new consciousness about human rights that became operative within the MFA and the new forms of bureaucratic obfuscation that emerged reveals how responding to complaints of human rights violations became part of the process of evading accountability and producing impunity. Second, the gaps between the accounts illustrate how impunity for state violence limits who has the power to name the truth about state violence or whose accounts of what happened are accorded authority and whose are dismissed.

Reflecting on these discrepant accounts makes it possible to understand how the process of creating an accounting of human rights violations is shot through with questions of evidence and politics—such as what information to include, what details to elide, who to consult, and how much to risk—questions that are no less urgent for scholars than they are for state officials or human rights activists.

THE UNITED STATES AND HUMAN RIGHTS IN THAILAND

The history of US involvement in the human rights movement in Thailand begins with military and security intervention, or what might instead be characterized as involvement in creating the need for a human rights movement. Beginning in early 1950, through the vague moniker the Sea Supply Company, the American CIA began to provide weapons and training to

General Phao Sriyanond, director-general of the police.[10] Resources flowed to support the existing branches of the police, including the Santiban (Special Branch), as well as to establish the elite paramilitary Border Patrol Police (BPP), characterized by its close connection to both the CIA and the Thai royal family.[11] In October 1950 the two governments signed the Mutual Defense Assistance Agreement and established the Joint United States Military Assistance Group (JUSMAG) in Bangkok to coordinate military cooperation.[12]

Throughout the 1950s and 1960s, the US state security and military forces provided extensive financial, tactical, and technical support to their Thai counterparts. As the United States waged war in Vietnam, Thailand became the base for its counterinsurgency activities in the region, and a large number of Thais fought with the US military.[13] At its height, there were seven US airbases in Thailand.[14] Their joint efforts aimed at curtailing communism inside Thailand were equally vigorous. In 1965 General Praphat Jarusathien, one of the three ruling dictators, set up the Communist Suppression Operations Command (CSOC) as a military-police-civilian counterinsurgency coordinating agency with the support of US ambassador Graham Martin and the CIA.[15] The CSOC, renamed the Internal Security Operations Command (ISOC) after 14 October 1973, carried out military and ideological attacks against the CPT, socialists, leftists, and others who were cast as dissidents.[16] During the three years of open politics between 1973 and 1976, and particularly by 1975 when transitions to communism in neighboring countries raised the fear of regime change in Thailand, both the Thai state security forces and the CIA supported right-wing parastate vigilante groups. These included the Village Scouts, Krathing Daeng (Red Guars), and Nawaphon.[17]

In May 1975 Prime Minister Kukrit asked the United States to withdraw its military forces. The US military, which had 27,000 troops in Thailand at that time, withdrew all but 250 by 20 July 1976.[18] Although the United States had no direct hand in the 6 October 1976 massacre at Thammasat University and the subsequent coup, the relationship between the two countries and their myriad military and security forces remains an essential factor in understanding the two events and the years of human rights violations that followed. This is not because the individuals who beat and killed the students were CIA agents but because of what were, as E. Thadeus Flood argues, "the cumulative effects of almost a quarter century of careful cultivation by the U.S. of an essentially fascist-minded, repressive, reactionary, privileged military elite, faced with a majority of farmers and laborers who have been stripped of the dignity of political, social, or economic recognition."[19] The challenge is to track the intertwining of US and Thai counterinsurgency ideologies rather than trying to identify instances of violence in which the perpetrators carried US passports. When the ideology, if not the relationship, unraveled, both its forms and their implications came into sharp relief.

Although much US intervention in Thailand during the years between 1950 and 1976 was carried out in secret and without the knowledge of the US Congress, this changed after the 6 October 1976 massacre and the global turn toward human rights. In the United States, although President Jimmy Carter's statement during his inaugural speech on 20 January 1977 ("Our commitment to human rights must be absolute, our laws fair, our national beauty preserved; the powerful must not persecute the weak, and human dignity must be enhanced") is often cited as the moment when US foreign policy shifted toward human rights, the hearings held by Representative Donald Fraser, a Democrat from Minnesota, were less visible but more important.[20] Between 1973 and 1978, as chairman of the Subcommittee on International Organizations of the House Committee on International Relations, Fraser presided over 150 hearings on human rights and heard the testimony of more than five hundred witnesses, including many who had suffered at the hands of regimes closely allied with the United States.[21] The hearings were foundational for Carter's human rights policy, and the information they brought to light forced changes within the State Department.[22] For Fraser, advocating for human rights was a corrective after the US war in Vietnam, and in his hearings he emphasized addressing human rights abuses perpetrated by regimes allied with the United States rather than those by communist countries.[23]

Writing about the Argentine human rights movement, Lynsay Skiba noted the profound irony that this produced. Lucio Garzón Maneda, an Argentine lawyer and human rights activist who testified before Fraser's subcommittee, along with his colleague Gustavo Roca, in September 1976, viewed the hearings "as the first international defeat of the military junta." He reflected thirty years later that they "never imagined that they would confront the junta from the capital of its most powerful supporter."[24] Like Lucio Garzón Maneda, Puey Ungpakorn, who was rector of Thammasat University at the time of the 6 October 1976 massacre and fled abroad the evening of the coup after being briefly detained, confronted the Thai regime through his testimony before Fraser's subcommittee.[25] Puey spoke truth to power in his testimony before Fraser's subcommittee, and its importance is evidenced in its reverberations among his supporters and detractors alike.

The hearings were held in a second-floor room in the Rayburn House Office Building on two consecutive Thursdays: 23 and 30 June 1977. When the hearings began at 10:30 a.m. on 23 June, Donald Fraser explained that the human rights situation in Thailand was of concern because it signaled a step backward for the country. The long-standing relationship between the two countries underlined this concern, and one of the purposes of the hearings was "to explore whether U.S. policy and assistance programs contributed to the demise of democracy in Thailand."[26] For slightly over five hours across the two days, this question, as well as the precise details of the 6 October 1976 massacre and subsequent political detentions and other rights violations, was addressed by five speakers.[27] In addition to their verbal testimony, all but one of the speakers submitted prepared written statements. The speakers and their disagreements reflected the range of perspectives on human rights violations in Thailand, from criticism to complicity and the indolent pace of change within the US State Department.

On 23 June, David Morrell and Stewart Meacham gave testimony. Morrell, then a lecturer in politics at Princeton University, had spent more than five years in Thailand, and his comments were largely based on a paper he coauthored with three other scholars submitted beforehand to the subcommittee.[28] In his brief verbal testimony, he highlighted the scale of violence during the massacre and the complicity of the monarchy, noting that this coup was different from the others because "this time the royal family, fearful for the future of the country in the wake of Communist victories in Indochina, lent its unmistakeable support to the forces of the right."[29] Morrell advised the Congress to support decentralization, political participation by all, and freedom of expression. He concluded by warning that continued US military support for the repressive regime would be like "spraying gasoline over smoldering embers" and would strengthen the CPT.[30]

The next person to give testimony, Stewart Meacham, was the former director of Quaker International Seminars and former national secretary for peace education for the American Friends Service Committee (AFSC). The AFSC was very active in the movement opposing the US war in Vietnam and then became a constant voice for human rights beginning in the late 1970s. In his written testimony, Meacham foregrounded Thailand as a test case for Carter's stated commitment to human rights. He wrote, "If

this policy can be applied to our relations with Thailand it can be con-
vincingly pursued elsewhere. . . . Our government cannot press the Soviet
Union on human rights, or other socialist countries for that matter, unless
we are willing to press our friends."[31] Meacham then framed his verbal testimony within the language and framework of human rights and the UDHR.
He argued that Articles 3 (right to life, liberty, and security of person), 5
(freedom from torture and cruel, inhuman or degrading treatment or punishment), 9 (freedom from arbitrary arrest, detention, or exile), 10 (fair and
public hearing by an independent and impartial tribunal), 19 (freedom of
opinion and expression), 20 (freedom of peaceful assembly and association),
21 (right to participate in politics and public life), and 23 (rights to work, to
equal pay, and to form unions) had all been violated during the massacre
and following the coup. The UDHR is not legally binding, but Meacham's
invocation is an early example of its use to shame the regime and place the
rights violations it committed in a universally known framework.

After the 6 October 1976 massacre, the violation of human rights became
"an undergirding dimension of power in Thailand."[32] Meacham took on
the US Department of State directly by criticizing the prepared statement
submitted by Robert Oakley, deputy assistant secretary in the Bureau of
East Asian and Pacific Affairs, who gave verbal testimony a week later. In his
written statement, Oakley alleged that those tried in Thai courts had the
same rights as those tried in US courts.[33] In contrast, Meacham asked, with
respect to those undergoing political trials in his written statement, "Are
they being tried? Will they be tried? What are they charged with? Have
they the right to defense counsel? Will the trials be in open court? . . .
[These questions] are of great concern to Thailand, but not many Thais are
in a position to ask them."[34] In his verbal testimony, Meacham highlighted
the difficulty of obtaining information about people who were detained
and commented of Oakley's submission that it was "an extremely strange
statement to be made about the Thai situation where people are being held
on very vaguely stated charges, under situations where their opportunities
for trial are equally vague and uncertain, and where people can be held for
time periods which can be extended and extended again."[35] The difference
between the perspectives of Meacham and Oakley was not one of degree
but of the very nature of the political and legal order in place.

Meacham took a harder line on US responsibility in his concluding
suggestions than Morrell had done and called for an investigation into
how a range of US government organizations, including the United States

Operations Mission (USOM), the Agency for International Development (AID), the United States Information Service (USIS), JUSMAG, and the CIA, operated in Thailand and what kind of relationship they had with the US military and the Department of State. Invoking the emerging internationalist citizen created during the early years of the human rights movement, Meacham called for US citizens to ask "where we are as a people when these kinds of situations can arise and would go virtually unheeded were it not for the determination of a committee such as is conducting this hearing today."[36] One answer to this question was found in his own actions and those of others who joined the burgeoning human rights movement as workers, volunteers, and writers of petition letters. The individual, humanist sense of responsibility, and the power to effect change that motivated his question, was behind the new movement.

During the discussion at the conclusion of the first day's testimony, Fraser pressed Morrell and Meacham for details on detention and the use of torture in Thailand. Fraser wanted to know the precise number of people who had been arrested and detained on political charges. Meacham and Morrell agreed that accurate information was very difficult to locate, even in Thailand and if one were a Thai state official.[37] Fraser also began a line of questioning about torture that continued into the next week. Meacham explained that evidence existed of what he termed "a kind of, you might say, improved type of tiger cage."[38] Tiger cages were a specialized prison cell used in Con Son Prison in South Vietnam. They were very small and caused constant pain and suffering due to the lack of movement possible for those incarcerated in them.[39] Meacham called for an inquiry into the situation of approximately 140 people being held at the Setsiri Road police headquarters "in tiger cages that are very small, very compact little boxes, that are dark, there is no light that comes into them. People are let out of them only once a month and are otherwise kept in the dark tiger cages."[40] The tiger cages used in Thailand were 1.5 meters long by 1 meter wide and 1 meter high.[41]

When the hearings reconvened a week later, Robert Oakley was the first to give testimony. He repeated the assertion that he had made in his written testimony that the rights of those accused and prosecuted were similar in Thailand and the United States.[42] Oakley then made a series of contradictory statements about human rights, the State Department, and the Thai government. He said that all those currently being held on political charges were being held without due process.[43] Perhaps this was a quiet admission of the presence of political prisoners in the United States, but it was instead likely a careless statement made in direct opposition to his previous comment. Oakley then said that he knew of no cases of torture in Thailand, but it "may have occurred in isolated instances of which the State Department is not aware."[44] This can be read as a quiet confirmation of the use of torture. Oakley further notes that President Carter's views on human rights had been conveyed to the Thai government and "it is our judgment that the Government of Thailand understands these views and that it is, for its own reasons, becoming more concerned about the issue of human rights."[45] Although the reason for Oakley's contradictory comments may have been ordinary incompetence, they can also be read as a visible record of the confusion, and therefore the transformation, going on inside the State Department. The mechanisms and challenges of this transformation were brought out further during Fraser's rigorous questioning of Oakley, following which Fraser concluded, "I appreciate the fact that the Department is, I think, being increasingly sensitive to a broad range of concerns than has been their experience in the past."[46]

Puey Ungpakorn's testimony began with an exchange between him and Fraser about the absence of any representatives of the Thai government in the room. Puey characterized it as "a pity" that no one was present.[47] Fraser explained that, although it would have been inappropriate for there to be a Thai government official present, the subcommittee had informed the Thai embassy of the hearings and invited it to provide names of nongovernment representatives "that they think would help to round out the testimony that we are going to hear."[48] Puey responded, "That is my point exactly. My reason for saying this is that it would be better for you to hear both sides of the story."[49] This detail of the invitation extended and declined was ignored by those who criticized Puey later.

Puey submitted his account of the chronology of the events of 6 October 1976 as one part of his five-part written testimony, but in contrast to the written testimony of Morrell, Meacham, and Oakley, Puey's was not printed in the record of the hearings.[50] In his verbal testimony, Puey detailed the range of human rights violations and restrictions on expression and daily life since the massacre and coup. The lack of publicity and information about political detentions and prosecutions was a result of the care taken by the Thai government to avoid arresting well-known figures in the cities so as "not to antagonize international public opinion."[51] One of the effects of secret arrests was "deceiving foreign observers, especially embassy people, into thinking that there is fair play in dealing with accused and defendants."[52] This confirmed Morrell's and Meacham's testimony about the difficulty of finding information about detentions and directly refuted Oakley's statement, or perhaps provided a context for it.

In his recommendations to the US government, Puey warned that Thailand was on a path to civil war. Referring to the long-standing relationship between the two countries, he underscored the growing importance of human rights for both activists and governments and called on the US government "to use your influence to bring the Thai authorities back to the right path on the human rights issue. The stands that the new U.S. administration and Congress are taking on these issues have heartened us all over the world. . . . The Thai government and military groups are sensitive to American opinion. This is a country where you can save a good number of lives and spare a great deal of suffering. Don't be deceived by the benign appearance of the dictators, [for] they always hide something from you, and the best of your Embassy in Bangkok could easily be deceived."[53] Although Oakley had left the hearing room immediately after giving his own testimony, Puey concluded by responding to Oakley's comments, saying, "I am puzzled whether he really believes everything that the Bangkok government has told him directly via the Embassy or the facts as independently acquired by the U.S. intelligence coincide with the government of Bangkok. I wonder."[54] Although the US military withdrew the bulk of its forces in 1976, the CIA never announced a full or partial withdrawal. Just as its actions prior to the coup remain obscure, those undertaken afterward are as well.

The final witness to give testimony was W. Scott Thompson, a professor in the Fletcher School of Law and Diplomacy at Tufts University. He defended the need for the return of order in Thailand after the lack of it during the three years prior to the coup and given the transitions to communism in neighboring countries.[55] He identified the problem as stemming from the US withdrawal rather than the long years of US presence. More than any other witness, except Stewart Meacham, Thompson used the frame of human rights, but he used it to dismiss rights rather than calling for their protection. Clearly unaware of the longtime Thai government use of and involvement in human rights, he said, "Democracy and human rights may be a long time in coming to Thailand. It is not something to which the Thai people are accustomed, however high are the aspirations for it on the part of the talented Thai intelligentsia."[56] Then, directing a similar sentiment to Fraser, he concluded his testimony by asking, "So if we are truly concerned about human rights, ought we not hear more about truly totalitarian states and less about the domestic affairs of a friendly country like Thailand, for whose development we bear so much responsibility?"[57] What makes these statements similar is Thompson's failure to understand that human rights were coming to be seen as basic and universal rather than a luxury for elites or those he perceived to be living under the most repressive regimes. Amid what he experienced as the disorder of the 1973 to 1976 period, he missed the broad demands for democracy and justice made by students, workers, farmers, and others. His final question contained its own answer: it was precisely because the US government bore so much responsibility for the state of affairs in Thailand that it warranted concern.

During the subsequent question and answer period, Fraser again turned to the issue of torture and asked Puey if he had confirmed evidence of it. Puey provided extensive details about the kinds of torture used, including the burning of people with cigarettes and forcing people into cloth sacks and beating them until they confessed. He further noted that there were many survivors willing to testify as long as their names were not used.[58] The gravity of the situation and Puey's own position within it were made clear when he spoke of always carrying a suitcase with him in the months prior to the massacre and coup and leaving Bangkok under the threat of being lynched by right-wing parastate forces.[59] Fraser asked for clarification, and Puey confirmed that he was being targeted by right-wing parastate forces. Thompson did not comment on Puey's description of what might have happened if he had not left the country, perhaps because he was beginning to realize that what had taken place in "friendly" Thailand was not so different from the situation in the "truly totalitarian states" he had in mind.

Although a representative of the Thai government was not present at the hearings, a response from inside the military was swift. A week after the conclusion of the hearings, General Kriangsak Chomanan, the deputy supreme commander of the armed forces who launched the coup against the Thanin government a few months later, gave a speech titled "Human Rights in Thailand" to a group of foreign journalists, diplomats, and businesspeople at the Foreign Correspondents' Club in Bangkok.[60] Kriangsak began by dismissing the newfound interest of the United States in human rights, noting, "There is great excitement among the democracies over human rights. I don't understand why. In Thailand, we were excited about them a long time ago. We have struggled for human rights and will continue to do so to maintain them."[61] Kriangsak then offered his definition of basic rights, which included freedom from hunger; access to shelter, clothing, medical treatment; the ability to travel freely; the ability to obtain an education; and the protection of physical bodies, families, and property. Subversion, communism, the influx of Indochinese refugees, and the drug trade were obstacles to Thailand's achievement of these rights for all. Kriangsak made no mention of torture or detention, not even to justify them in relation to the suppression of subversion or communism. Nor did he mention Puey Ungpakorn or Donald Fraser or note that hearings on Thailand had been held in the US House of Representatives. But he closed his speech with a sharp punch line that indicated his interest in the hearings and their content: "Mr. Robert Oakley, Deputy Assistant Secretary of State for East Asian and Pacific Affairs, has spoken fairly and positively on the subject of human rights in Thailand."[62] Rather than dismissing human rights, by giving this speech so soon after the hearings, Kriangsak underlined their importance. His reference to Thailand's long-standing engagement with human rights and his quick response can be read as a realization that the definition of human rights was no longer only the province of the state but was a new area of contestation between states and between a state and its people.

Six months later, former prime minister Kukrit Pramoj made a direct attack on Puey, the US government, and the hearings.[63] His muddled and mean-spirited analysis appeared in his weekly column in *Sayam Rat*, a newspaper he owned.[64] Using the language of rights, Kukrit wrote that Puey "had a complete right as a Thai person" to say what he said in the US House of Representatives and that other Thais have a "complete right" to agree or disagree with him.[65] He then wrote, "As Dr. Puey is a Thai. Dr. Puey perhaps must love his country like other Thais and perhaps has the loyalty to the nation, religion, and king like other Thais as well."[66] Kukrit's use of the conditional *khong* (perhaps) here is equivalent to suggesting that Puey did not love his country and was disloyal to its three pillar institutions. Given that the accusations of being un-Thai and disloyal were used to motivate violence on 6 October 1976, the meaning of the allegations in Kukrit's words is unmistakable. He then claimed that Puey's testimony was the result of bias and claimed that others, if they had experienced what he experienced, would also have been biased. He himself, he said, would have been tens or hundreds of times more biased had it been him.[67] In other words, Puey was not angry enough. This is how Kukrit dismissed Puey's testimony without addressing its content.

Then Kukrit turned to the United States, Puey's partner in crime. Puey could not have gone to give testimony on his own and therefore must have done so at the invitation of the US Congress. In Kukrit's view, Puey's presence was unnecessary, as the US ambassador to Thailand could have provided whatever information was needed. This indicates the preexisting cozy relationship between Thai elites and US diplomats, which was one of the very reasons for the hearings. Kukrit continued, commenting, "Or if it was the view that they really had to listen to the facts from the mouth of a Thai person, there is an abundance of other Thais."[68] Kukrit was apparently unaware that the Thai embassy in Washington had declined to nominate a representative to come and offer a *Thai* perspective different from Puey's. In his view, to learn the truth about a matter, an impartial person must be asked. He seemed unable to acknowledge that it was precisely Puey's experience of violence that equipped him to speak the truth about the massacre and subsequent regime. Kukrit concluded by questioning whether the behavior of the United States was that of a friend.

Those in the burgeoning human rights movement in Thailand had a much different view of the hearings and Puey's testimony. Phaisan Wongrawisit, later ordained as Phra Phaisan Visalo, who at that time was working for the CGRS, traveled to Mexico for a conference shortly after the hearings and stopped in the United States to see human rights friends, including Stewart Meacham. Years later, Phra Phaisan reflected on the way Puey's example and clarity of truth inspired his own actions.[69] He wrote that Meacham told him, "The U.S. congresspeople seemed very satisfied with Ajarn Puey's testimony and [were] impressed with him as a person as well. We heard this and were happy because the views of these congresspeople may cause the Thai government to improve the human rights situation somewhat."[70] Given the rights violations that the CGRS continued to document in 1977 and subsequent years, it is impossible to address the effects of the hearings with any precision. But I am confident in making the assessment that given the unease that the hearings caused for Kriangsak and Kukrit, who were not ordinary citizens but a general and future coup maker and a former prime minister with a royal title, rights violations would likely have been even worse had the hearings not taken place.

HUMAN RIGHTS IN THE MFA ARCHIVES

Every Thai government ministry is advised to send all documents twenty-five years and older to the National Archives. There are exceptions to this advisory. Any material that relates to the institution of the monarchy or national security can be retained by the original ministry for seventy-five years or in perpetuity if deemed necessary.[71] In addition, some ministries simply choose not to send their documents, and the archives lacks the authority to compel them to do otherwise. Even with these caveats, as I have noted throughout this book, there are documents available that provide partial information sufficient to piece together accounts of state involvement in violence and the erasure of responsibility for it. This is particularly the case with respect to records about human rights. Rather than dismissing or attempting to obscure information about human rights, different ministries and agencies within the Thai state have often been interested in highlighting their actions in support of them and in so doing setting their definition.

The MFA is one of the government ministries that chooses to archive the vast majority of its own materials rather than sending them to the National Archives. When I was reading the Krisdika files about human rights in the National Archives, I saw references to MFA documents but could not locate them in the partial files present. A colleague alerted me to the MFA Archive, a semipublic archive to which access is granted on a case-by-case basis. In particular, I was interested in reading the MFA side of correspondence with the Krisdika related to the submissions to the *UN Human Rights Report* and materials about an August 1977 human rights monitoring visit by Ramsey Clark, a maverick former head of the US Department of Justice, and Wen-hsien Huang of AI, for which the Krisdika had provided the MFA with translations of various laws.[72] In mid-2013 I requested permission to use the MFA Archive and explained in my application that I was interested in international law and international organizations. To use the phrase "human rights" seemed like it might result in my application being deemed too controversial and therefore likely to be delayed or turned down, so I opted for less precise language. It took twelve months for my application to be processed, by which point I had given up hope of being granted permission.

But in July 2014, two months after the 22 May 2014 coup, I spent two weeks in the MFA Archive. Users of the archive are not permitted to search the computer database but must wait for the archivists to select materials for them. On the morning I arrived, I was led to a table in the middle of a room of catalogers and two boxes filled with files on tax treaties and maritime organizations were placed in front of me. After waiting so long to be granted permission to use the archive, I was both dismayed and uncertain about what to do next. After two days of reading about tax treaties and the laws of the sea, I asked the head archivist if I might look at documents about human rights and international organizations. I left the archive with the expectation that the next day I would come back to an empty table.

I returned the next morning to find two thick binders on the table. The first was labeled "Amnesty International and Petition Letters about Various Cases in Thailand, 1978–1979," and the second "Amnesty International Calls for the Thai Government to Release Political Prisoners in Thailand (Ordinary Cases Aside from the 6 October 1976 Case and the Case of the Members of the Coordinating Group for Religion in Society), 1978–1979."[73] The two binders were filled with correspondence and other files related to AI's first campaign in Thailand, which was an appeal for the release of political prisoners launched in April 1978. It identified four categories of political prisoners in Thailand: (1) those arrested prior to 6 October 1976 and accused of violating the ACAA; (2) the Bangkok Eighteen, the eighteen students and activists who watched their friends being murdered by state officials and parastate forces on 6 October 1976, were then charged with a range of grave crimes, and spent nearly two years in prison undergoing processing in the military court before being released following the second amnesty passed in September 1978 for the 6 October 1976 massacre and coup; (3) those accused of being a "danger to society" under NARC Order 22 following the 6 October 1976 coup; and (4) those arrested after 6 October and accused of violating the ACAA.[74] Across these four categories, AI was concerned that political prisoners were being held without bail, tortured, and subjected to lengthy and delayed trial processes. Members of AI and other human rights and student organizations sent letters to Thai embassies in their own countries and to the MFA reiterating these concerns and requesting updates on specific cases. These letters set off a flurry of correspondence within and beyond the MFA.

Neither photocopying nor the taking of photographs was permitted, and so I spent the next week and a half reading the contents of the two binders. They contained eighty-eight letters from individual AI members inquiring about specific political prisoners. A total of twenty-eight political prisoners were mentioned in the letters.

1. Bunchob Chuay-punth
2. Vanta Rungfa
3. Kao Sae Heng
4. Noonong Kanjanapukdt
5. Jeng Sae Tan
6. Somboon Banlusilpa
7. Vichai Banlusilpa
8. Somjit Mothasin
9. Chuay Jool-pukdt
10. Navin Aphanram
11. Chao Chainarong
12. Montri Unrat
13. Thongchan Srinual
14. Sao Saokaew
15. Boonrueng Sri-udom
16. Suphap Pasa-ong
17. Udom Pakakrong
18. Suthep Chotampai
19. Viruthana Te-rin
20. Srisamarn Suebboonwong
21. Daeng Srisuk
22. Prasit Phitsuwong
23. Sanga Naem-suksai
24. Somphong Sanleum
25. Somnuk Beuw-kaew
26. Promma Nanock
27. Phisit Phathanaseri
28. Surin Suanpan

The binders contained the original letters and their envelopes. Some of the handwritten letters were on thin airmail paper or aerogrammes while others were on whimsical stationary or lined notebook paper. The letters were personal and often eloquent and were addressed to either the minister of foreign affairs or the Thai embassy in the author's country.

Katherine Pettus, a member of AI in Honolulu, inquired about the case of Navin Aphanram, a worker-activist arrested in Om Noi along with eight others on 30 March 1976 and charged with a range of alleged crimes, including communist activities. On 5 May 1979 Pettus wrote a letter to the Minister of Foreign Affairs. "Life is a short blessing at best," she wrote, "even when you get to live it in freedom, [and] if you must suffer jail and torture, it is a terrible misery. Freedom is the most precious thing in life[;] you are a freeman, you know what I mean, and I appeal as one human being to another, for the life and freedom of Navin Aphanram."[75] Katherine Pettus and other writers wrote in the tenor of AI activists at the time: at once respectful of the leaders to whom they appealed and also steadfast in their belief in human rights and the urgency of their universality.[76]

The letters and their authors were viewed with derision by some within the bureaucracy, and a letter from the Thai embassy in the Hague back to the MFA offered the opinion, "Some of the accusations against the Thai government seem to lack an understanding of the law. They view only one side of human rights to an extreme."[77] A side comment in a letter sent from the MFA to the Ministry of Defense in July 1978 indicates why it chose to engage the international human rights movement rather than throwing the letters away, which would have been another option: "Let us offer the observation that the reports of organizations about human rights in Thailand are based partially on facts [already] provided by the Thai government. But this is insufficient for the organization, which then looks for additional information from other sources, in particular from different newspaper accounts. These accounts may be incorrect. Therefore, providing correct and sufficient information to the organizations will be of benefit to Thailand."[78]

My assessment is that the information collected in the two binders is *not* correct. However, disputing the truth claims made in the materials in the MFA Archive is the beginning, not the end, of analysis. The more compelling questions, as Katherine Verdery asks vis-à-vis the file that the Romanian secret police kept on her, concern "the effects of the existence of these files and the manner in which they are made, circulate, and act."[79] What does the way in which the MFA went about collecting the information to respond to the letters from AI members indicate about the production of knowledge about state violence inside the bureaucracy? Who was involved in the creation and circulation of this knowledge? In other words, this is to examine, in Ann Laura Stoler's terms, "archives-as-process" rather than "archives-as-things," in which archives are taken up "as condensed sites of epistemological and political anxiety rather than as skewed and biased sources."[80] Here, rather than anxiety, the files indicate a growing realization within the MFA that the meaning of human rights was changing and neither they nor other state officials were its sole arbiters any longer, even within Thailand. Within this context, they chose to respond to letters they viewed as baseless with the repeated production of *correct* knowledge.

Copies of any letters sent back to the writers by the MFA were not included in the binders, but what can be read is the correspondence among the MFA, the Ministry of Interior (about cases being tried within the civilian court system), and the Ministry of Defense (about cases being tried within the military court system). In each case, the MFA asked if the political prisoner in question had been tortured and if there had been any undue delays in the judicial process. The Ministry of Interior and Ministry of Defense consistently dismissed allegations of torture as unfounded and assured the MFA that the judicial process was proceeding according to the law. For example, in a July 1978 response to queries about the case of the Bangkok Eighteen, as well as cases involving nineteen other people, the Ministry of Interior wrote, "All the involved officials have proceeded correctly according to the judicial process. There was no abuse of any kind in the interrogation or in order [to attempt] to make the defendants confess."[81] This was the identical response to every query archived in the binders. None of the letters sent back by the Ministry of Interior or the Ministry of Defense in response to the MFA queries confirmed the allegations of torture. It is impossible to discern whether the authors were engaged in the defense of the system common to bureaucracies or in an intentional cover-up of torture and denial of due process. Rather than intention, however, I am compelled to analyze the picture of the recent past that emerges from the files. According to the materials in the binders, there were no cases of torture in Thailand in 1978 or 1979.

Perhaps there is another set of binders in which the ministries of interior and defense provided the MFA with details of the torture state officials carried out. But I suspect not. The MFA could have discarded the letters or written responses denying that any human rights violations were taking place without consulting the ministries. But in taking the queries from AI members seriously enough to inquire about the status of political prisoners, it created a record of itself as a ministry concerned about human rights and willing to engage with the quickly expanding international human rights movement. In participating in creating this record, through the series of letters denying all allegations of torture, the ministries of interior and defense also demonstrated an awareness that even in intrastate communications certain actions could not be acknowledged. As was discussed in chapter 4, only two years earlier, during the drafting and passage of the first amnesty law for the 6 October 1976 massacre, there was nearly open acknowledgment of participation in mass murder during the debate on the draft in the NLA, which was open to the press and the minutes of which were published and remain accessible without any special permission needed in the Parliamentary Library. Like Kriangsak's speech on human rights after the Fraser hearings, the uniformity in the correspondence in the MFA Archive reflects the emergence of human rights as a domain of struggle between people and states rather than one in which states offer the only version of the truth.

The MFA's willingness to engage individual letter-writing activists was short-lived, and frustration with AI soon emerged. In early February 1979 the Ministry of Interior told the MFA that there was no reason to respond to the letters: "The petition letters and requests for information about the progress of cases are therefore simply letters from people who claim that they are individual members of Amnesty International. These are letters in the style of a personal inquiry, not letters from Amnesty International. Therefore, the Thai government does not have to respond to these letters. If the Thai government responds to one letter, then perhaps letters from other members will have to be addressed, and it will be without end."[82] How can governance occur if officials spend all their time responding to queries about violations of human rights that take place as part of this governance? This question belies the point that the series of events and correspondence that went into responding to the queries was itself part of governing the Thai polity. In late February 1979 the protocol for responding to letters changed. Rather than responding to individual letters, the MFA would respond to the main AI office in London, and then AI was to inform its members of the response.[83] This protocol remains in use up to the present day.[84]

I asked the archivist at the MFA Archive if there were any similar binders, and her response was no. Given that one of the binders was labeled as covering cases of political prisoners *except* for the 6 October case, which was that of the Bangkok Eighteen, and the case of the CGRS workers, in which three human rights activists were arrested and accused of being communists, at a minimum, materials dealing with these two cases are likely to exist.[85] This correspondence, and the archiving and preservation of it, is an example of Nicholas Dirks's description of an archive as "the state's instantiation of the state's interest in history."[86] What the binders tell us is that the MFA wanted to create a record of twenty-eight political prisoners who were *not* being tortured. But, perhaps unexpectedly, the very presence of the names of twenty-eight political prisoners in the MFA files is an opening with which to tell a different story. The state may be interested in history, but its control is rarely, if ever, total.

TOWARD AN ALTERNATIVE ACCOUNTING OF HUMAN RIGHTS VIOLATIONS

How, and using what evidence, can the elisions in the MFA files be redressed? If one is concerned that the twenty-eight political prisoners whose names are present *were* tortured, what does one do? A history that counters the one in the MFA Archive must respond to its absences in both content and form. "Content" here refers to the provision of evidence that refutes the uniform denials of the existence of torture, and "form" refers to the writing of a history of the struggle to support survivors of state violence and redress impunity. I examine the establishment and work of the CGRS, the Thai human rights organization whose documentation of human rights abuses was essential to both the Fraser hearings and the AI campaign, to offer a partial counterhistory and in so doing to think through a methodology for assembling one.[87]

The CGRS carried out the most extensive documentation of human rights violations in Thailand between 1976 and the mid-1990s. It was first formed as the Center for Coordinating Religion in Society (CCRS) during a meeting of approximately thirty Buddhist and Christian clergy and laypeople on 17 March 1976 in advance of a protest to push the US military out of the country. Prior to the 6 October 1976 coup, it issued declarations against violence, worked to thwart the impending coup, and organized internal events to exchange ideas about religion and working for society and to learn about the different Buddhist, Catholic, and Protestant groups to which its members belonged. After 6 October 1976, its mission shifted, and it decided "to assist with moral support, a necessity, and to follow the news of how many died and if people were tortured. At that time, there were a lot of terrible rumors circulating widely about the condition of those who were being detained, especially the student leaders, until it was impossible to separate what was true from what was false."[88] They also changed their name from Coordinating *Center* to Coordinating *Group* due to the virulent animosity against the National Student *Center* of Thailand after the coup.

The CGRS made its public debut when its members went en masse to visit detainees in prisons during the New Year's holiday in 1977. On 16 April 1977 the organization was formally voted into existence by twenty-three founding members, "all of whom are committed to struggling for human and social justice through non-violent means."[89] In his testimony before Donald Fraser's subcommittee, Stewart Meacham described the CGRS in terms resonant with Moyn's characterization of human rights as utopian. He argued that after 6 October 1976, citizens who were active in progressive movements and then repressed took four different, distinct paths. They chose to be silent, to go into exile, to join the CPT, or to join the CGRS. He described the latter organization as "operating quietly but openly. . . . They want to maintain communication; they want to do it openly. They want, in the name of humanity and nonviolent approaches and nonpolitical approaches, to make contact with those who are the victims of the repression, are being held in prison or are being suppressed in a variety of ways."[90] To act in the name of humanity after the brutality of the massacre was courageous as well as utopian. From the beginning, the work of the CGRS was focused on collecting, storing, and filing information about where and under what conditions prisoners were being held, the crimes with which they had been charged, and their family situations. During the first few months after the massacre, CGRS began publishing the *Human Rights in Thailand Report* with lists of those arrested, testimonies and letters from political prisoners, updates on trials, and details of other human rights violations. The reports, initially published monthly, were often in excess of one hundred pages of small, English-language print. The audience for their documentation was primarily outside the country, both because circulating the information in Thai in Thailand would have caught the attention and aroused the ire of the state authorities and because they were part of the internationalist wave of the human rights movement during this period.[91] The CGRS sent the information about the violations it had documented to AI, and its reports were often reprinted in the newsletters of a range of solidarity groups set up by Thais in exile, including the Thai Information Center in Sweden, the Union of Democratic Thais in the United States, the Sixth October Front for Democracy in Australia, and others groups in Japan, France, Germany, and the United Kingdom. Inside the country, CGRS representatives visited prisoners and their families and provided material assistance when possible. When letters to prisoners from AI members began to arrive in late 1977, the CGRS made sure that they were delivered.[92] In addition to its human rights documentation and activism, the CGRS also aimed to "develop a strategy so that the various religions can work together for justice, peace and human development."[93] As the organization grew, it was funded by AI, as well as a range of Christian organizations, including Bread for the World (Germany), the World Council of Churches (Switzerland), and the Quakers and Mennonites (United States).[94] By late 1979 the CGRS was aiding in the formation of other human rights groups and aiming "to play a catalytic and coordination function," in the broader human rights movement.[95] Once the regime of General Kriangsak ended and General Prem came to power in 1980, it shifted to publishing its newsletter quarterly, as there were improvements in the human rights situation.[96] In 1980 and 1981 the CGRS joined international solidarity movements calling for justice in relation to the Gwangju massacre in South Korea and in support of the Solidarity movement in Poland.[97]

After the crisis passed, most of the exile and solidarity groups dissolved in the 1980s during the Prem government, except for the CGRS, which kept going until the mid-1990s. Its records were not collected or preserved, and a complete set of its reports does not exist in any one location. More than ten years ago, I began collecting the CGRS reports, as well as publications of the exile groups. I did not locate any of the materials in public repositories in Thailand but rather found them in the Kroch Library at Cornell University, the Widener Library at Harvard University, the Library of Congress, the National Library of Australia, and colleagues' personal collections.[98] The publications contain a much different picture of human rights than that offered by the MFA. They comprise what Doreen Lee, reflecting on student activist materials and their ephemeral nature at the end and in the aftermath of the Suharto regime in Indonesia, calls a "shadow archive," a collection "assembled as a politically motivated project to disrupt, rather than complete, the narrative of state archives."[99]

As I read the reports, I was overwhelmed by the quantity and detail of cases of human rights violations. As a counter to the sanitized, uniform denials of mistreatment contained in the MFA files, I decided to use the shadow archive I had assembled to first literally count the number of each kind of case documented as a way to respond to the zero cases of torture

acknowledged in the MFA files and, second, to create an alternative account
of the experiences of detention of the political prisoners named in the
MFA files.

Working with three research assistants, I counted and cataloged across
the twelve years for which I had materials, 1976–88, which corresponded
to the long period of dictatorship that began with the massacre and coup.[100]
We went through every issue of the CGRS and exile newsletters and counted
the instances of state violence. The method was time consuming but very
simple. We used the categories of the CGRS itself: arbitrary detention,
torture, extrajudicial killing, and disappearance. For each case, we noted
the name, date of incident, location, kind(s) of violence, and any other key
details. Then we pulled out the aggregate numbers by years and kind(s)
of violence (see table 1). The numbers refer to incidents, not individuals—
as some individuals experienced detention, torture, and then either disappearance or extrajudicial killing.[101]

These numbers are likely low as access to information by the CGRS and
others was highly uneven and many victims and survivors may have been
afraid to talk to human rights workers. In the case of detention, the CGRS
itself estimated that there was a total of 8,000 cases in 1976 and 1977 alone,
and other sources offer estimates ranging from 2,100 to more than 60,000.[102]

Table 1. State violence and solidarity in Thailand, 1977–1988

Year	Detention	Disappearance	Torture	Extrajudicial killing
1977	750	38	23	44
1978	269	8	35	57
1979	71	2	2	36
1980	14	0	1	16
1981	11	1	4	45
1982	59	9	3	41
1983	42	0	0	1
1984	86	0	35	36
1985	38	0	7	33
1986	38	0	11	11
1987	30	0	12	13
1988	28	0	15	12
Total	1,436	58	148	345

SOURCE: CGRS, *Human Rights in Thailand Report*, various issues, December 1976–December 1988.

The number of detentions listed, 1,436, reflects only the cases in which the CGRS reported details about a specific individual. During the Thanin and Kriangsak regimes, those targeted were those accused of or labeled as being communists or otherwise having committed political crimes. State perpetrators were primarily military or counterinsurgency officials. By the end of the Kriangsak regime, there was a sharp drop in detentions, but the numbers of other violations remained relatively constant through to the end of the Prem regime. The perpetrators narrowed to primarily police. This reflects what is now known to be the routine use of extrajudicial violence by police in their daily work. The police continue to torture, disappear, and extrajudicially kill civilians today, but the CGRS was the first organization to compile systematic documentation of it.

Why count, especially if the numbers are so low in relation to the likely actual numbers? One reason is that it is a way to refute the zero proffered in the history contained in the MFA Archive. But the point, thinking again of Katherine Verdery, is not only to use this information to say that the state's record is wrong but also to disclose what these numbers tell us. They do not tell us the total number of people detained, tortured, disappeared, or extrajudicially killed. But they do tell us that CGRS staff and volunteers collected information about 1,436 people who were arbitrarily detained, and in many cases they visited them in prison and brought them food or books or visited their homes and brought news of them to their parents or children or vice versa. These numbers, then, reflect the human concern and solidarity felt across prison bars, which was in direct contrast to locking people up and torturing them. The numbers of those disappeared and extrajudicially killed indicate the daring that people still possessed despite repression, the daring to contact human rights workers after a person was extrajudicially killed or disappeared in their communities even though speaking out might mean that one risked becoming the next person on the list.

After compiling the aggregate numbers, I began to look through the CGRS reports for the twenty-eight political prisoners mentioned in the letters from AI activists that the MFA denied were being tortured or subjected to a lack of due process. All except one are mentioned in the shadow archive.

Vanta Rungfa, Navin Aphanram, Suphap Pasa-ong, Promma Nanock, and Phisit Phathanaseri were part of a group of five workers and four students, all labor activists, who had been arrested and accused of communist activities on 30 March 1976 in Om Noi, a district thick with factories on

the edge of Bangkok. They were also accused of firearm possession and
threatening state security. After more than three years of detention, all nine
were acquitted on 15 August 1979 on the basis of insufficient evidence.[103]

Bunchob Chuay-punth, Noonong Kanjanapukdt, Jeng Sae Tan, Chuay
Jool-pukdt, Chao Chainarong, and Udom Pakakrong were part of a group
of eleven teachers and farmers who were arrested in Nakhon Sri Thammarat province in southern Thailand on 23 May 1976 and accused of communist activities. They were also accused of killing twelve soldiers and
burning down a military camp. They were all acquitted on 20 November
1979. Rather than communism, what the eleven shared was having aroused
the ire of the authorities by complaining about local corruption.[104]

Somboon and Vichai Banlusilpa were brothers arrested under Order 22
as being a "danger to society" in October 1976, released in February 1977,
and immediately rearrested for communist activities.[105]

Thongchan Srinual, Sao Saokaew, and Boonrueng Sri-udom comprised
the Surin Three. On 23 June 1976 their house in Surin province was raided
by a group of thirty policemen who claimed that communists had stored
weapons there. During the raid, one policeman was killed and three were
injured. The Surin Three were charged with illegal weapons possession, killing a government official, and communist activities. They were sentenced
to death on 15 June 1977, although this sentence was later commuted.[106]

Viruthana Te-rin was arrested on 6 October 1976 and accused of communist activities.[107]

Surin Suanpan was a former member of the Socialist Party who was
arrested under Order 22 as being a danger to society in July 1977, released
on 7 January 1978, and immediately rearrested for committing sedition.[108]
His allegedly seditious crime had been distributing leaflets criticizing the
Thanin government.[109]

Srisamarn Suebboonwong, Montri Unrat and Suthep Chotampai were
arrested on 22 March 1978 and accused of communist activities after authorities found incriminating books and other papers in their house.[110]

Kao Sae Heng, Somnuk Beuw-kaew, Daeng Srisuk, Prasit Phitsuwong,
Somphong Sanleum, and Sanga Naem-suksai were stevedores in Chonburi
who were arrested on 27 May 1978 for disturbing the peace and public
order while leading a strike by hundreds of stevedores the previous day.
They blocked the harbor and called for increased pay and job security.[111]

The only person listed in the MFA files whose name I could not find in
the CGRS newsletters was Somjit Mothasin.

In some cases, the CGRS compiled a detailed account of the torture experienced, in other cases it reprinted letters written during or after imprisonment, and in still other cases it compiled a life story or only noted an arrest. Three examples—those of Jeng Sae Tan and Bunchob Chuay-punth, arrested in the communist activities case in Nakhon Sri Thammarat, and Navin Aphanram, arrested in Om Noi—illustrate this range and are the evidence of a history of and for human rights.

In a report about the communist activities case in Nakhon Sri Thammarat, the CGRS noted that torture was used extensively and "was aimed at destroying the prisoners' will so that those who could not stand the torment would admit the fake-story made up by the police and military torturists as their confession" and to attempt to make them accuse one another.[112] All three detainees were kept in solitary confinement on a temporary military base, which had been created on the grounds of Wat Tonhong, a Buddhist temple.[113] They were subjected to a range of forms of torture, including "tying the victims' hands behind their back to cause paralysis of the arms, putting them into sacks and giving them series of severe strokes, threatening to drown them into the sea from a helicopter, tying big chains around their necks and pulling hard, and also threatening to shoot through their heads."[114]

At the time of his arrest, Jeng Sae Tan was forty, married without children, and a teacher. The MFA amassed evidence showing that he was not being tortured, but he wrote a series of letters to the CGRS, which it translated and circulated in its newsletter, that offered a different picture. Jeng wrote the letters after he was transferred out of military detention and into the Nakhon Sri Thammarat provincial prison. He described his interrogation and said that he was asked about an attack on the local military base carried out by communists, but he knew nothing about it and so was sent back to his cell. He was taken to be interrogated again later on the evening of the same day. He wrote, "The room was dark. I was to sit in a big chair with my arms locked behind my back. They asked me questions for which I did not know the answers. Suddenly many soldiers surrounded me. They tied an iron chain around my neck and pulled at both ends, asking if I had joined the attack. I said I knew nothing. They kicked me, slapped me, and kicked at my stomach till I fainted. When I became conscious I was in an open building in the temple." The next evening, he was interrogated again, writing, "I was brought to that dark room again. And they treated me with the same method, telling me to confess. But I did not. So they put me in a sack and kicked and hit me. I still did not say what they wanted." Jeng wrote of the final day, "I was brought for investigation again. They threatened me, saying that if I did not confess tonight I would die. I was very afraid and yielded. They taught me what I should say, especially that I should say that I saw Mr. Udom in green clothes, that he and I joined the communist guerrillas attacking the military camp. The investigator wrote down my confession for me. I only had to sign it thereafter, without seeing what they wrote." During the trial, Jeng retracted his confession and said that he had been tortured and coerced into confessing. One of the other witnesses for the defense was a monk. While Jeng, Udom, and the others were being held, the monks had been forbidden to walk on the grassy temple land close to the camp. But one monk heard voices crying out in pain and asking for blankets. He went to the camp with blankets and refused to leave until he was granted permission to enter. He was allowed in and testified in court that he saw Jeng, Udom, and another detainee lying in pain on the ground with obvious injuries from having been tortured.[115] Although the judges did not cite the torture in their decision, they threw the case out due to insufficient evidence that the accused had committed the alleged crimes.[116]

What can be made of the discrepancy between Jeng's account and the assertion of the MFA that he, and others, was not tortured or forced to confess? I am confident in making the claim that Jeng's account is the correct one. But again, this is the beginning, not the end, of analysis. The methods of torture that Jeng cites recur across other accounts, along with mock executions, electrocution, exposure to extreme heat, and regular beating. Torture did not begin in Thailand during the late Cold War—by that time, state officials were well practiced. But this was the first time that details of what took place circulated in public. They circulated in the English-language newsletters of the CGRS, AI, and other groups, and then by 1979 and 1980 in the Thai-language press as well. These accounts moved AI activists to write petition letters out of an internationalist spirit of solidarity. Jan Eckel is critical of the use of detailed testimonies of violence by AI and argues,

> Empathy was key to the Western human rights movement and even at times spurred government action. . . . Very often it was the sheer fact of people being physically maltreated that propelled human rights activists to intervene—at least as much, it seems, as abstract notions of political injustice and

oppression. . . . Skillfully evoked in these accounts and often turning into a forceful impulse to help, empathy was part of a politics of the self. It deeply involved individual activists, both morally and emotionally, and made their feelings the driving force for political action. Paradoxically, aiding those in need provided activists with an opportunity to engage in self-realization through altruistic behavior.[117]

The question of how and why the testimonial form became so powerful during this period is an important one, but Eckel privileges both the West and AI. His criticism contains both the assumption that human rights activism was centered in London and the assumption that victims of state violence and activists opposed to it were necessarily different people. For the activists in Thailand who compiled and translated these accounts, this work was the first step in building a movement that continues today. For Jeng, the writing and circulation of his account of his torture meant that the MFA did not have the only, or last, word on whether he was tortured.

One of the other activities of the CGRS was to take letters written by prisoners out of the prisons by informal means and distribute them to the public. Censorship by prison officials meant that "most of the letters that disclose the real situation in the prison or the real feelings of the prisoners are stopped by the authorities (with the prisoners writing such letters being given severe punishment)."[118] The transmission of these letters was one way that "a prisoner can make his problems reach the ears of people in the outside world."[119] Bunchob Chuay-punth, one of those arrested in Nakhon Sri Thammarat along with Jeng Sae Tan, wrote a series of letters to the CGRS that were translated and published in its newsletter. Writing from the Bangkok Remand Prison on 18 January 1978, he thanked the CGRS volunteers for visiting him, saying:

I feel as if I were among my own closest relatives. Although I wanted so much to talk to you, when I saw you I could not find the words. I was afraid that my words would be wrong. It is the typical feelings of a country man whose life is used up in the rice fields, who struggles throughout his life only for survival, and who never gets assistance from anybody. And now in a far off place I suddenly find mercy from some justice loving people, and I cannot find any suitable words or thanks. The peasant just blinks his eyes like men without consciousness.[120]

Bunchob was aware of both social divisions and the realities of class. But in his next paragraph, he shifted from victim of human rights abuses and villager afraid to speak to asking the CGRS for advice about disseminating his own writing. He had written two stories, one that "tells the life of a young country girl who lost her parents in a big storm. . . . She and her sister had to struggle in the selfish society. It relates the real lives of the country people."[121] The second story was autobiographical and "tells about my own reality, including the injustices I have faced from the local authorities, and the inhuman torture I received from the soldiers."[122] Bunchob ended his letter by asking the CGRS if publication of the two stories could adversely affect his case. The CGRS added a further note calling for translators to convert the stories into English. After his release, Bunchob wrote to the CGRS about his bittersweet return home. As he watched the rice fields pass by as he rode the train from Bangkok to Nakhon Sri Thammarat, he sighed as he thought about how his family had lost its land during his three years of incarceration. But he concluded on a hopeful note: "However, I am glad that I am still alive, and still have a chance to continue to work for peace and freedom. The freedom I gained after the release is not a perfect freedom. I want a real freedom which everybody in this society could share."[123] People whose lives were changed and who came to consciousness during the early years of the human rights movement included those imagined to be its objects rather than its subjects. Bunchob came to consciousness because of his own suffering and the process of putting that experience into writing, not because of the suffering of others.

The CGRS did not publish information about the conditions of detention in the case of Navin Aphanram, one of the worker-activists arrested in Om Noi, whose freedom Katherine Pettus called for in her letter to the MFA. Instead, it wrote and circulated an account of his life. He was born on 10 October 1955 in Buriram province to peasant parents. After finishing grade 4, he was ordained as a novice for three years and studied dhamma until he was sixteen. He went back to school briefly before returning home to work in the fields. Before his eighteenth birthday, in mid-1973, he went to work in a sock factory in a nearby province so that his younger sister could continue her education. After the changes wrought on 14 October 1973, he joined a strike asking for an increase in wages. The management retaliated by accusing him and others of stealing materials from the factory. They were arrested, beaten, and forced to confess. After twenty-nine days, they were released without having been charged. Fired from his job,

Navin went home and again worked in the fields. One evening, old friends from the factory who had also been fired visited him, and then they went together to demand portions of their salaries that had been withheld. First they went to the factory, but when they tried to enter, they were beaten by guards and police. Next they went to the local police station to file a complaint, but instead a trespassing complaint was filed against them by the factory. They were released and in December 1973 went to Bangkok to the Labor Department and the Special Section of Provincial Police. Within a month, the company agreed to pay compensation. Navin stayed in Bangkok and worked with the Labor Coordinating Center, a new workers' rights umbrella organization. He was very active as an organizer and worked in several different factories before taking a job in Om Noi at the Siam Stainless Steel Company, where he worked until his arrest in March 1976. In the account compiled by the CGRS, Navin is depicted as a person with a history of struggling for justice. In a different situation, he might have been the author of an AI letter rather than a prisoner of conscience highlighted in one.

Toward a New History of Human Rights

Samuel Moyn is ambivalent about whether the transformation and increased global currency of human rights in the 1970s "made a practical difference."[124] In the case of Thailand, the work of the CGRS, the concrete improvements in the lives of political prisoners and their families, and the organization's constant challenges to injustice leave no room for ambivalence. But its work also makes possible another, more subtle transformation in the register and writing of history. Writing about challenges to military dictatorships in Latin America in the 1970s and 1980s, Lawrence Weschler connected torture and the writing of history: "History, in this conception, is a battle over who gets to say 'I' (or at the state level, who gets to say 'we'— 'we, the regime . . .' or 'we, the people'), and that, after all, is what torture is all about as well. If, as Elaine Scarry has demonstrated in her book *The Body in Pain*, torture is in its essence a discourse, a teaching, what is being taught is the futility of acting like a subject, of aspiring to anything beyond abject objecthood."[125] These lessons were not lost on either the Thai state security forces or the MFA. But their success was not total. In contrast to the state's attempts to turn political prisoners and others they deemed dangerous into objects, the activism and documentation of the CGRS challenged this at its core. Jeng Sae Tan's account of torture, Bunchob Chuay-punth's letters from prison, and Navin Aphanram's biographical narrative only account for three of the twenty-eight political prisoners who the MFA denied were being tortured or deprived of due process. The specificity of their lives and voices counter the uniformity of the lack of information in the MFA Archive. They are not objects that can be erased but subjects of both their own lives and Thai history. The CGRS documented over a thousand additional instances of human rights violations during the waning years of the Cold War, including many accounts of extrajudicial killing and disappearances. The partial counterhistory of human rights violations and the human rights movement that I have assembled in this chapter is the faint beginning of a much longer account that demands to be written.

6

Disappearance and the Jurisprudence of Impunity

The arrest, detention, abduction or any other form of deprivation of
liberty by agents of the State or by persons or groups of persons acting with
the authorization, support or acquiescence of the State, followed by a
refusal to acknowledge the deprivation of liberty or by concealment of the
fate or whereabouts of the disappeared person, which place such a person
outside the protection of the law.

—Article 2, International Convention for the Protection
of All Persons from Enforced Disappearance

My father had a great deal of trust in justice (it seems difficult to explain
why he had this degree of confidence and trust in the judicial process).
He always said that the court decided whether one was right or wrong.
My father did not unceasingly think that his clients were innocent. If they
committed a crime, then they had to be punished. But the punishment
had to be one that fit the crime, not one that exceeded the crime.
Everything is a struggle in the judicial process, from the Court of First
Instance to the Appeal Court and then the Supreme Court.

—SUDPRATHANA NEELAPAIJIT, "When [My]
Father . . . Was Disappeared"

IN CHAPTER 1, I wrote about the experience of Ajarn L., who was arrested
in late October 1976 and detained as a "danger to society" at the Karunyathep Center in Chiang Mai. The people who arrested him were in plainclothes and arrived in a private rather than an official vehicle. As Ajarn L.
gathered clothes and toiletries, he called out to his neighbors to write down
the license plate numbers of the car. If they did not hear any news of him,
they should raise the alarm that he had been disappeared and search for

him. He was blindfolded before he got into the car, and the fear that he would be killed and his body discarded mounted once he could no longer keep track of the car's route. But when the car stopped and he stepped outside, the blindfold was removed and he was immediately photographed by the local newspaper. His fear of being disappeared dissolved and was later replaced with annoyance that the newspaper had misspelled his family name in the article printed about his arrest.

Ajarn L.'s fear reflected the reality of disappearances during the Cold War in Thailand. The *thang daeng* killings examined in chapter 3 are cases of arbitrary detention and torture but also disappearance, because the identities and fates of those who were burned in the *thang daeng* remain unknown. Progressive activists were disappeared during the years prior to the 6 October 1976 massacre, including those who lived and worked close to Ajarn L.'s home in northern Thailand. Three members of the progressive Farmers' Federation of Thailand were disappeared in Chiang Mai province in August 1975, and two more were disappeared in Lampang province in April 1976.[1] Disappearance remained a common form of violence used by the state during the long years of dictatorship after the massacre and therefore one that the CGRS documented. It documented fifty-eight disappearances between 1976 and 1982 alongside the cases of detention and torture discussed in detail in chapter 5. In some of these cases, such as the disappearance of Jean Sangsakul, a reporter in Nakhon Sri Thammarat province, a person was first arrested and detained for several days by counterinsurgency authorities as a "danger to society." Then, after a certain amount of time, he or she would disappear from custody. When families queried the authorities about the whereabouts of their loved ones, as Jean's wife did, the authorities claimed that they had been released.[2] Many others were arrested by the police and never returned home, such as Pitak Paramal. He was an activist who played a key role in a large protest against the murder of five villagers in Pattani province in southern Thailand in 1975.[3] On 30 October 1977 he was arrested by the police with no charge specified while he was watching a soccer game. Two days later, his brother went to the local police station to look for him. Pitak was not there, and the authorities denied any knowledge of his arrest or fate.[4] In addition to the refusal of the authorities to provide information about those who had disappeared, which amounted to a denial of the disappearance, some also threatened relatives who came to inquire after their loved ones. A young man disappeared after meeting with a district officer in Sakhon Nakhon on 19 May 1981. His older sister, Nupun Mingmitrwan, was threatened with death when she called for an investigation into his disappearance.[5]

But the disappearance of both dissident political figures and ordinary citizens was not only a Cold War phenomenon. The practice began long before the heated years of the late 1970s and did not cease with the slow, rocky transition to a more democratic form of rule after General Prem Tinsulanond left office in 1988. The very nature of the crime of disappearance— that its victims never resurface—makes tracing its history more complicated than other forms of violence I have examined in this book. When the Justice for Peace Foundation (JPF) published a report on fifty-nine disappearances it had documented between 2002 and 2012, it framed its research by noting that the lack of documentation of human rights violations in Thailand was an obstacle to its work and that in its view the cases it had documented were only a fraction of the existing cases.[6] With this caveat in mind, I share the JPF's brief sketch of the history of disappearance to illustrate how much remains unknown.[7]

During the first years of the Cold War, Tieng Sirikhan, a member of parliament from Sakhon Nakhon aligned with Pridi Banomyong, was disappeared by the police on 12 December 1952. Porn Malitong, a politician who opposed General Phao Sriyanond, the police chief (1951–57) and aspiring dictator who ruled with an iron first, was disappeared on 24 March 1954.[8] Haji Sulong, a dissident religious and cultural leader in southern Thailand, has not been seen since he met with the Songkhla chief of police on 13 August 1954 and is presumed to have been disappeared.[9]

After the long years of military dictatorship during the late Cold War ended, disappearance remained a constant feature of the landscape of state violence, including as part of large-scale events such as the military crackdown on democracy protesters in May 1992, the "War on Drugs" in 2002, and counterterrorism operations in southern Thailand since 2004.[10] Individual activists who challenged state power during this period were also disappeared, including Thanong Pho-an in 1991, Somchai Neelapaijit in 2004, and Porlachee "Billy" Rakchongcharoen in 2014.[11] In all these cases, impunity for disappearance has also remained constant. Like other forms of state violence discussed in this book, a combination of threats to relatives of victims who dare to call for justice, such as Nupun Mingmitrwan, collusion among state officials, and a lack of adequate judicial mechanisms and political will has ensured that no state official has been held to account for his actions. Article 2 of the International Convention for the Protection of All Persons from Enforced Disappearance (CED), quoted in the epigraph and which Thailand ratified in March 2017, defines a disappeared person as one who is placed beyond the protection of the law. The history of disappearance in Thailand, then, is also one in which the perpetrators are placed outside the accountability that the law might demand. The knowledge of this dual process is the reason why Ajarn L. was afraid when plainclothes officials showed up at his house in October 1976.[12]

The case of the disappearance of Somchai Neelapaijit, a lawyer and human rights defender, stands out as a partial exception in the history of impunity in Thailand. On the evening of 12 March 2004, five men pushed Somchai into their car near a busy intersection on Ramkhamhaeng Road in Bangkok. The day before his disappearance, Somchai had submitted a petition for justice on behalf of five young men he was representing. The five men, who were arrested shortly after martial law was declared in southern Thailand in January 2004, alleged that they had been tortured while in police custody. Like other victims of disappearance in Thailand, neither Somchai nor his remains have surfaced since the night he was disappeared. What makes this case different from others is that following concerted action by Somchai's family and human rights activists, five policemen were arrested in April 2004 in connection with his disappearance. There is no category of disappearance within Thai criminal law, and in the absence of Somchai's body, the men could not be charged with murder. Instead, they were charged with robbery and coercion with the use of violence. They were prosecuted in a case that went through all three courts and concluded in December 2015 with the Supreme Court exoneration of all five police officers and the denial of the right of members of the Neelapaijit family to be coplaintiffs in the case.

This outcome is why the exceptional nature of this case constitutes a partial gain. To put it in other terms, on the one hand, Somchai's case stands out as a victory in the struggle against impunity because it is the first time that police officers were tried in connection with a disappearance in Thailand. But on the other hand, the police officers were not held to account by means of the judicial process that brought them to trial. Instead, across the three court decisions, a *jurisprudence of impunity* emerges. This is a jurisprudence that both forecloses justice in the specific case of Somchai Neelapaijit and simultaneously makes it more difficult for other victims of disappearance to access justice. What should have been part of the process of securing accountability instead resulted in the dispossession of the right to justice of Somchai's widow and children and the consolidation of impunity.

Tracing the origin of the word "disappeared" in its original Spanish form, *desaparecido*, Marguerite Feitlowitz writes, "It was coined by the Argentine military as a way of denying the kidnap, torture, and murder of thousands of citizens. Then-commander of the army Roberto Viola put it this way: A *desaparecido* was someone who was 'absent forever,' whose 'destiny' it was to 'vanish.' Officially, a *desaparecido* was neither living nor dead, neither here nor there. The explanation was at once totally vague and resoundingly final."[13] The combination of the vague and final nature of the violence is what makes disappearance devastating to those who are left behind. The families of those who are disappeared rarely know the details of the last moments of their loved ones' lives and can never bury them. The lack of information compounds the violence of the disappearance itself. Writing in the context of disappearance in Thailand, Pratubjit Neelapaijit and Anuk Pitukthanin make a resonant argument that the crime of disappearance is one that generates *khwam klum khrua* (ambiguity), which at once distinguishes it from other forms of state violence and makes it difficult to resolve.[14] The ambiguity is a result of the inability to determine with any clarity whether the person who has disappeared remains alive, if the person who has disappeared was murdered or intended to flee, and the identity or identities of the perpetrators.[15] The humanity of the disappeared person is made ambiguous, the roles of the perpetrators are ambiguous, and the relatives of the disappeared persons face ambiguity in resolving the crime as well as their futures. This ambiguity is reflected in the history of disappearance in Thailand, which is marked by an even greater degree of partiality and uncertainty than are the histories of other forms of state violence.

Rather than challenging the vague, ambiguous, and unresolved nature of the disappearance of Somchai Neelapaijit, the jurisprudence of impunity instead replicates it by refusing to identify his disappearance as a crime or even hold the perpetrators to account for a lesser crime. To frame one of the central questions of this book in relation to this specific case, of what use might the pen of the historian be in the face of such jurisprudence? How might scholarship challenge the ambiguity left uncontested and the impunity produced by judges in the series of three decisions in the case of the disappearance of Somchai Neelapaijit?

There is a significant tradition of scholarship that crosses law and history, with Carlo Ginzburg identifying the shared project of judges and historians "to demonstrate, according to specific rules, that x did y, where x can designate the main actor, albeit unnamed, of a historical event or of a legal act, and y designates any sort of action."[16] In one stream of scholarship, scholars read a case file and then offer a different interpretation of the series of events or a different conclusion than the one reached by the judges.[17] A postjudgment alternative vision of justice can emerge in this kind of work—as the rereading generates an imagined holding of perpetrators to account or exoneration of an unjustly convicted person. In another stream, which takes up instances of violence that do not make it to the courts, scholars reconstruct the series of violent events using newspaper and other kinds of reportage.[18] This kind of work results in a sharp outline of the reasons *why* the case has not, or cannot, make it to the courts; these reasons often include evidence of collusion among state officials and intimidation of victims and witnesses.

Both of these approaches can entail reading or rereading evidence against the grain in the service of justice and therefore lend themselves to being used by historians and other thinkers concerned with impunity.[19] Rather than either of these approaches, in the remainder of this chapter I read across and within the three court decisions in the case of the disappearance of Somchai Neelapaijit in order to understand the constituent pieces of the jurisprudence of impunity. The three court decisions are significant legally and politically because this was the first disappearance case to be adjudicated across all three courts, and the Supreme Court decision, in particular, sets the definitive interpretation of the law. But the three decisions can also be read as a form of history authored by the judges. In an essay inspired by Hayden White, "The Plot of Thai History: Theory and Practice," Craig J. Reynolds argues against the dominance of academic historians in the domain of analysis of the past. He calls for recognition that novelists, playwrights, and mapmakers in Siam and Thailand are also engaged in creating meaning about continuity and change between the present and the past.[20] All these figures, knowingly and unknowingly, emplot history and may emphasize continuity even as "events seem to repudiate the past, to challenge held assumptions and to declare the onset of a new epoch."[21] Guided by this methodology, Reynolds writes, "The need for the nation's story to be continuous is the overriding factor that determines what is put in and what is left out of the plot."[22] To Reynolds's list of historians, I would add judges.

The history written by the judges in court decisions is not a transparent retelling of what happened but is instead a record of the struggles that

Sudprathana Neelapaijit, quoted in the epigraph, said her father taught her were present at every stage of the judicial process. During case proceedings in the Court of First Instance, a verbatim transcript of what is said in the court is not produced. Instead, the judges summarize what each witness says, and that is what is recorded. Prior to the conclusion of hearings for each day, what has been recorded is read aloud in the court so any corrections and amendments can be made. Judges are historians in another sense. When they write decisions that are an account of both a given crime of state violence and the attempts to solve it or the failure to do so, their judgments also reflect what is possible at a given moment vis-à-vis accountability in the nation's history. The struggles—between the prosecution and defense or accountability and impunity—can be grasped by examining the presence or absence of ambiguity in the decisions. The precise crime, the identities of the perpetrators, and the status of Somchai's life are made ambiguous in the court decisions, but the court is unambiguous about the facts of his assault and abduction and the lack of rights of victims. In this instance, to put it in Ginzburg's terms, the judges were not attempting to demonstrate that x did y, in which x refers to the defendants and y refers to the action of disappearing Somchai Neelapaijit, but rather that x did z, or partially committed the crimes of theft and coercive assault as accused. In so doing, they pushed the possibility of demonstrating that x did y even farther out of reach.

But just as Reynolds argues that the attempt to "suppress or paper over the painful episodes" in the service of imposing continuity on historical writing never fully succeeds, impunity itself is rarely total.[23] Instead, a combination of what is not ambiguous across the court decisions and the work of human rights activists to create Thai law on disappearance points to the possibility of justice, or a *jurisprudence against impunity* and in the service of accountability. In the remainder of this chapter, I take the three decisions as a form of historical writing and then write against the conclusion of impunity that they imply. This is a history that refuses ambiguity at every possible turn.

THE DISAPPEARANCE OF SOMCHAI NEELAPAIJIT

At the time of his disappearance, Somchai had been a lawyer for twenty-seven years. Throughout his career, he frequently accepted pro bono cases and those that directly challenged abuses of power by the police and army, even though this placed him at great personal risk. In the beginning of the twenty-first century, as tension in the southernmost provinces began to increase, he frequently advocated for poor and marginalized Muslims living in the south.[24] The conflict between the Malay Muslim southerners and the central Thai state, which has waxed and waned since 1902 when Siam annexed the Patani sultanate, intensified again on 4 January 2004 when insurgents carried out attacks on eighteen government targets. In response, the government of Prime Minister Thaksin Shinawatra declared martial law in the three southernmost provinces of Yala, Pattani, and Narathiwat.[25] Somchai was one of the leaders of a group that collected fifty thousand names for a petition to revoke martial law, which contains many measures that restrict rights and facilitate their violation.[26] During the month before his disappearance, Somchai also took on the case of five men— Makata Harong, Sukree Maming, Abdullah Abukaree, Mana-sae Mah-ma, and Suderueman Maleh—who were arrested on 21 February 2004 and accused of being involved in the theft of more than three hundred guns and the burning of schools in Narathiwat province as part of the 4 January surge of attacks. The five men confessed to the accusations made by the police, but they alleged that they had been forced to do so after being tortured. They reported being suspended from the ceiling with ropes, having urine put into their mouths, being electrically shocked, and being kicked and beaten. After their initial arrest, they were transferred to Bangkok, and their families contacted the Muslim Lawyers' Club, which Somchai chaired, for assistance. On 11 March 2004, the day before his disappearance, Somchai submitted a petition for justice from the five men that detailed the forms of torture they experienced to the minister of interior, the police director-general, the attorney general, the chair of the National Human Rights Commission, the Senate Committee on Human Rights and Justice, and the Parliamentary Special Study Committee on the Problem of Bombing.[27] The five retracted their confessions and called on the authorities to investigate the police involved in their arrests. In a letter that accompanied the petition, Somchai wrote, "As a result of the act of torture, the five alleged offenders were forced to confess as demanded by the police officers. Their confession and cooperation in the reenactment of the crime was made possible by their being subjected to physical assault, being threatened, and being denied visits by relatives and lawyers while the interrogation was taking place," and argued that this was both a violation of their rights and in direct contravention of the Thai Criminal Code.[28]

The next day, Somchai met a client in the morning and went to court in the early afternoon. He then met a trainee lawyer who worked in his office and they went to pray and then eat dinner near Ramkhamhaeng University. After dinner, Somchai was waiting for a colleague in the lobby of the Chaleena Hotel, and around 8:00 p.m., when his friend was delayed, he realized that he was tired and decided to go to the home of another friend to spend the night. But he never arrived. Two days later, his wife, Angkhana Neelapaijit, filed a missing persons complaint with the police. Two days after that, on 16 March 2004, his empty car was found abandoned in the parking lot of the Mor Chit 2 bus station. Prime Minister Thaksin Shinawatra's initial sexist, dismissive response to Somchai's disappearance was to claim that he had not been disappeared but had simply run away after an argument with his wife.[29] But then, under pressure from national and international human rights activists, Thaksin launched an initial investigation by the Department of Special Investigation (DSI), and the police and Senate launched investigations as well.[30] In April 2004 five police officers were arrested, two of whom were recorded as having been involved in the investigation and interrogation of Somchai's five clients who alleged that they were tortured and three more who were professionally connected to those two. Police Major Ngern Thongsuk, Police Major Sinchai Nimbunkampong, Police Sergeant Major Chaiweng Paduang, Police Sergeant Rundorn Sithiket, and Police Lieutenant-Colonel Chadchai Liamsanguan were charged with robbery and coercion with the use of violence.[31] The jurisprudence of impunity began to be written at the very first hearing when the police officers entered their unanimous plea of not guilty. The very structure of the law, and in particular the lack of disappearance as a category within Thai criminal law, forms the core of this jurisprudence.

The trial commenced on 12 July 2005 in the Criminal Court in Bangkok. During the first day's proceedings, Angkhana Neelapaijit submitted a motion to serve as a coplaintiff along with the public prosecutor. Article 5 (2) of the Criminal Procedure Code stipulates, "The ancestor or descendant, the husband or wife, in respect only of criminal offenses in which the injured person is so injured that he dies or is unable to act by himself," may join the public prosecutor as a coplaintiff. Although the public prosecutor opposed the motion, the judges granted it because they agreed that the circumstances of the case indicated that Somchai could not act on his own behalf.[32] When the witnesses began to testify on 9 August, Angkhana's and

Somchai's four daughters (Sudprathana, Pratubjit, Kobkuson, and Krong-tham) also joined the case as coplaintiffs. Witnesses gave testimony for the prosecution and defense until 10 December 2005. During the investigation, the court hearings, and their aftermath, witnesses, particularly Angkhana Neelapaijit, faced continual threats and intimidation.[33] The hearings were observed by numerous Thai and international human rights organizations, diplomats, and journalists.[34] Although the assessment of the International Commission of Jurists (ICJ) was that the five defendants had received a fair and public trial that mostly conformed to international standards, it also found "serious irregularities in the overall criminal investigation, in contravention of international standards which has denied the victim's family an effective remedy in international law."[35]

On 12 January 2006 the Court of First Instance returned the verdict that a group of men had pushed Somchai Neelaphaijit into a car and he had not been seen since but that a lack of evidence made all other allegations, except coercion on the part of Police Major Ngern, impossible to prove. Ngern was sentenced to three years in prison. The other four defendants were found innocent. Both the defense and the prosecution appealed the verdict. Ngern remained out on bail while he appealed, and the other four officers returned to work. The Appeal Court decision was handed down in July 2010, but due to a series of procedural technicalities, it was not read until 11 March 2011.[36] The Appeal Court upheld the initial dismissal of the charges against four of the five defendants. In addition, the court overturned the conviction of Police Major Ngern on the basis of a reinterpretation of the eyewitness testimony as being too weak to merit a conviction. I was in the courtroom on the day the decision was read and the defendants and their friends cheered as the decision was read, even though Somchai's family sat within an arm's reach of them. The Appeal Court also ruled against the right of the members of the Neelapaijit family to serve as coplaintiffs in the case on the basis that it had not been proved that Somchai Neelapaijit was dead or injured to the degree that he could not act on his own behalf. Over four years passed before the Supreme Court ruling was read on 29 December 2015. The Supreme Court upheld both the exoneration of all five defendants in the case and the denial of the right of the family members to be coplaintiffs. The series of three decisions comprise a jurisprudence of impunity that used the judicial process to redirect the specificities of the violent crime of disappearance—what Feitlowitz describes as

the vague finality surrounding a person who is neither living nor dead—
toward the legalization of injustice.

The decisions reached by the court can be read as a record that reflects
the investigatory irregularities the ICJ argued prevented the Neelapaijit family from obtaining justice. The series of rulings also amount to an attempt
to erase the assault and murder of Somchai Neelapaijit or, to put it another
way, to make it as though the crime of his disappearance did not occur. But
the version of history written by the court is only that: one version. The
decisions can be read against themselves to identify a contradictory admission of the crime of disappearance and a staunch refusal to take action to
redress it. The reasons for the refusal, which may include lacunae in the law,
a lack of political will, or collusion among the police, judiciary, and other
figures, cannot be discerned from the decisions and may never be known.
Instead, examining the decisions for the interplay between what the court
leaves ambiguous and a few sharp moments devoid of ambiguity both illustrate the investigatory irregularities noted by the ICJ and point to the intertwined urgency of working for justice in the case of the disappearance
of Somchai Neelapaijit and writing his disappearance and that of others
into Thai history. The interplay between the ambiguous and the unambiguous comes into view in the description of the crime, the treatment of
eyewitnesses and other evidence, and the matter of the Neelapaijit family
joining the case as coplaintiffs. In the end, the judges concluded that x (the
defendants) did not fully commit z (theft and coercive assault), and the
question of who committed y (disappeared Somchai) was deferred.

The decision by the Court of First Instance, written by Suwit Phromph-
anich and Omrudee Phongsai, begins with a description of the crime and
charges at hand.

> The plaintiff charges that on 12 March 2547 [2004] in the evening, the five
> defendants cooperated to rob Mr. Somchai Neelapaijit, the injured party, by
> taking his vehicle, registration number Pho Ngo 6786 Bangkok Metropolitan
> Area, valued at 600,000 baht; a Rolex wristwatch, valued at 277,560 baht; a
> Montblanc pen, valued at 7,000 baht; and his Motorola mobile telephone,
> valued at 18,900 baht. The total value of the property criminally taken from
> Mr. Somchai Neelapaijit was 903,460 baht. In the robbery, the five defen-
> dants used injurious force to push and drag the body of Mr. Somchai Neela-
> paijit into the vehicle of the five defendants and hold him there. This was

coercive to compel Mr. Somchai Neelapaijit to go with the defendants. By using injurious force, they caused him to fear for danger to his life, body, and liberty, until Mr. Somchai Neelapaijit had to unwillingly get into the car with the five defendants. The aforementioned injurious force was used in order to facilitate the theft and taking of the possessions, in order to take and seize the items, and to hide the crime and allow the defendants to escape from arrest. At this time it is not known whether Mr. Somchai Neelapaijit is still alive.[37]

The detailed nature of this description belies the underlying ambiguity of the crime. As noted earlier, because there is no category of disappearance in Thai law, the defendants could not be charged with disappearance, and because Somchai's body has not been found, they could not be charged with murder. The detail of the stolen objects is contrasted by the lacuna surrounding the question of whether Somchai remains alive. The final sentence suggests the actual crime without naming it by confirming that at the time of the decision, twenty-one months after the night Somchai Neelapaijit disappeared, his fate remained unknown. Given that coercive assault carries a harsher sentence than theft, it seems unlikely that the defendants would have assaulted Somchai and forced him into their vehicle to avoid being arrested for stealing a pen, a watch, a mobile telephone, and a car, especially because the judges concluded that the defendants had not engaged in theft because they abandoned the car rather than exploiting it for their own purposes and the other items were not found in their homes.[38] The items were presumed to still be with Somchai as they were on his person when he disappeared.

The judges' examination of eyewitness evidence leaves no ambiguity about the series of events leading up to the moment when Somchai disappeared but exhibits a significant lack of clarity about the perpetrators involved. The seven eyewitnesses who testified for the prosecution were unambiguous in their descriptions of the assault of Somchai Neelapaijit and his unwillingness to go with his assailants. They all witnessed a scene by the side of the road in which a group of men was clustered around two cars parked one behind the other. The first eyewitness, Sonthaya Chakraphon, was reported by the court as saying, "The witness heard a voice shouting on the left. He turned and saw two cars parked in a row and saw a group of three to five men, aged around thirty to fifty, pulling and dragging [someone or something] in the vicinity of the left-hand passenger door of the rear car."[39] The witness did not stop to look but used his mobile phone to call the police hotline number 191 to make a report. The second eyewitness, Siem Eiamsamang, also witnessed the pulling and dragging of a person and people getting in and out of cars.[40] The third eyewitness, Chaweewan Yutthahan, was walking out of a nearby lane. She saw Somchai resist his attackers. The judges noted that she said, "The witness heard the voice of a man yelling 'Oy, oy' and then turned and looked to see the man who was being pushed and shoved into a car by another person. The man who was pushing him was tall and wore a black jacket, a white t-shirt, and blackish pants. But the person who was being shoved was resisting. He refused to get into the car."[41] The fourth eyewitness, Sunan Khongkhem, was walking out from a nearby lane with the fifth, sixth, and seventh eyewitnesses to buy food. She saw a person being forced into a car by a group of people and then saw one of this group walk to the other car (Somchai's car) and get into it.[42] The fifth eyewitness, Montri Khaokhong, heard a man calling for help and saw him being shoved into the rear car by four or five men.[43] When the sixth eyewitness, Kamolthip Phromwi, walked by the two cars, she

> saw an older man of approximately fifty years, small framed with white hair and wearing glasses, standing alone. There were approximately four to five men standing by the rear vehicle. The man from the front vehicle walked toward the men who were in the rear vehicle as if he knew them. The witness and her friends then walked past. When they had gone approximately thirty meters, the witness heard the voice of a man asking to be let go. He yelled loudly. The witnesses turned to look. They saw a tall man lock [his hands] around the neck of the elderly man and shove the elderly man into the car. The elderly man tried to use his feet to shove [open] the door of the car. But another man closed the door of the car.[44]

The seventh eyewitness, Adirek Yimwadee, heard a man calling out to be freed.[45] With respect to identifying specific perpetrators, three eyewitnesses felt either certain or reasonably confident in identifying Police Major Ngern as having been one of the assailants.[46]

All three courts discounted much of the eyewitness evidence on the basis that the only piece of information that was without doubt was that Police Major Ngern was present when Somchai was pushed into the car, and this relied on identification made during the investigation process, not in court.[47] The identities of the other assailants were unknown. What is not ambiguous is that the seven eyewitnesses painted a picture of a gang of large men assaulting and pushing a smaller man into a car against his will. Although their accounts do not speak to the final fate of Somchai Neelapaijit, they elucidate the moment when the crime began and his resistance. That none of the seven intervened as the assault occurred, and only one immediately called the police hotline, is a sobering reminder that being in public is no protection against becoming a victim of violence. The five men were not reported to have been in police uniforms, but I suspect that if they had been dressed in the brown of the police or the green of the military, eyewitnesses would have been even less likely to intervene.

During the trial proceedings, all five defendants denied that they were present during either the interrogation of the five young men in southern Thailand or when Somchai Neelapaijit was disappeared. The judges cast only a few doubts on the alibis reported by the defendants, even though they could only be confirmed by other policemen or relatives. Police Major Ngern Thongsuk, whose name had been listed in the arrest records of the five young men, claimed that he was not actually present during the arrest and interrogation of the five men.[48] On 12 March 2004 he claimed that he was not even in Bangkok when Somchai was assaulted and pushed into the vehicle near Ramkhamhaeng University. The prior evening, he and his wife had a terrible argument and he left the house before dawn on the twelfth. He stopped at the Crime Suppression Division (CSD) and gave his two mobile telephones to one of his juniors because he did not want to speak with his wife. If his boss called, the junior was supposed to answer the phone. He then drove to Rayong province, south of Bangkok, to visit his brother. He had planned to stay in Rayong for several days, but he missed his small child and returned to Bangkok the same day. He returned to pick up his telephones around 8:00 p.m., close to the time when Somchai disappeared.[49] Although the judges of the Court of First Instance argued that the claim about leaving his phones at the CSD was false, as there were other ways to avoid talking to one's wife, such as turning the phones off or not answering her calls, no deeper challenges to the veracity of his testimony were recorded in the decisions.[50]

Police Major Sinchai Nimbunkampong, also based at the CSD, told a long, complicated story about his role in investigating a vegetable seller-cum-criminal in Pathumthani, a province neighboring Bangkok, and aiding colleagues involved in investigating a drug case. He worked on these cases for four days and finally returned home on 12 March after 10:00 p.m., where he stayed and relaxed for the next two days.[51] Police Sergeant Rundorn Sitthikhet worked in the CSD under the command of Police Major Sinchai. He was also involved in the arrest of the vegetable seller-cum-criminal.[52] At around 7:00 p.m. on 12 March, one of his juniors borrowed his mobile telephone, as he did not have his own.[53] He got his phone back around 10:00 p.m. and then went home.[54] Police Sergeant Major Chaiweng Phaduang, affiliated with the Tourist Police, said that he was involved in investigating a case in Bang Rak with several colleagues until 7:00 p.m. on 12 March. By 8:00 he was home with his wife in their condo.[55] Police Lieutenant Colonel Chadchai Liamsanguan, Police Major Ngern's commander, whose name was also listed in the arrest records of Somchai's five clients arrested in the south, said he was not present during either the arrest or the investigation. On 12 March he worked at the CSD all day. He ate dinner in the food court of the Tesco Lotus store adjacent to the CSD between 8:00 and 9:00 p.m.[56] As policemen, they were all able to refuse being put in a lineup to be identified by eyewitnesses. Other than challenging Police Major Ngern's assertion that he left his mobile phones at the CSD, the judges who wrote the Court of First Instance decision were unconcerned with the unconfirmable nature of the policemen's alibis. They were all taken to be true. The jurisprudence of impunity leans toward assigning truth to the accounts of the perpetrators more often than to those of the victims and does so to a degree that extends beyond protecting their right to a fair trial.

The reason why several of the policemen were at pains to elucidate the whereabouts of their mobile telephones is that the evidence that the prosecution presented indicated that their telephones were in contact with one another throughout the day on which Somchai disappeared and the day on which his car was found. The evidence produced by the prosecution also placed their telephones in the geographic area where Somchai disappeared. But this was the first time that mobile telephone evidence had been used in a criminal trial in Thailand, and the court ultimately did not accept it because the records introduced were photocopies rather than originals. On the issue of the telephone evidence, even if the technical aspects of it had been acceptable, the judges of the Court of First Instance discounted it by stating, "Even if the aforementioned documents were taken into account, the information about the telephone usage that the plaintiff and coplaintiffs have raised are only facts that demonstrate that telephones were used in that area. It still cannot be taken to assert that the five defendants committed the crimes as charged because the aforementioned documents only demonstrate that telephones with the aforementioned numbers were used in an area that recorded information. The information cannot be taken to assert that the defendants committed the crimes because it is well known that mobile telephones can be used by anyone."[57] Since the judges decided not to admit the mobile telephone evidence, they did not have to pose or answer the question that this comment implies. If the five mobile telephones with numbers belonging to the defendants were used in the geographic area where Somchai Neelapaijit was disappeared and yet they were not used by the five defendants, then who was using their phones and why? Only two policemen testified that they had left their phones with other people. The near absurdity of the question reflects the brazenness of the judges' comments. Even the most circumspect of historians would likely not dismiss the evidence as merely proving that telephones were used in that area; they would have to raise the next question that such an assertion implies. The way in which the judges used the evidence was both to demonstrate that x did not commit y and to inscribe z, disappearance, as an unspoken and unsolvable crime. The second use is what makes this an instance of the jurisprudence of impunity rather than only a single unjust decision. Writing shortly after the Court of First Instance decision was announced, Danthong Breen, a former engineering professor and long-time human rights activist in Thailand, offered a different view of the records than the judges. He noted, "The records contain other information which has not yet been revealed. Apart from assuring conviction in a retrial of the five accused defendants, it is most likely that the conspiracy which lies behind the abduction and the involvement of higher authority will be revealed. The game is certainly worth the candle!"[58] The jurisprudence of impunity also benefits the broad range of individuals involved in the perpetration of a rights violation, including the architects and accomplices as well as the direct perpetrators.

The judges wrote a combination of ambiguity and clarity about the crime against Somchai Neelapaijit into the conclusion of the decision much as they began the decision. The court concluded that what was not disputed was as follows: "The facts that stand without any doubt are that on the day, time, and location as charged, Defendant No. 1 and three to five people together took Mr. Somchai Neelapaijit into the vehicle prepared by Defendant No. 1 and the group, with Mr. Somchai averse to going, and drove away from the area. . . . No one knows whether or not at present Mr. Somchai Neelapaijit is still alive."[59] The repetition of the assertion within and across all three decisions that the status of Somchai Neelapaijit's life was unknown operates as the writing of both the ambiguity of disappearance and the violent dispossession of knowledge that accompanies it into history.[60] The Court of First Instance ruled that the defendants were not guilty of theft because Somchai's watch, pen, and mobile telephone were not found in their possession. As regards Somchai Neelapaijit's car, the judges wrote a measure of uncertainty into their analysis, noting, "The aforementioned behavior and the actions of Defendant No. 1 [Police Major Ngern] and the group indicate that Defendant No. 1 and the group did not have the intention to take Mr. Somchai Neelapaijit's possessions, namely, his car, in any way. Defendant No. 1 and the group perhaps only intended to drive Mr. Somchai's car and abandon it in order to conceal the truth and avoid investigation and arrest."[61] The judges left the crime for which the defendants wished to avoid investigation and arrest unspecified.

The judges then wrote an unexpected and clear articulation of the ambiguity of disappearance into their description of the crime. They noted, "But nevertheless, the crime of robbery was combined with the crime of assault, which is also a crime in and of itself. Therefore, the seizing and pushing of Mr. Somchai Neelapaijit into the car was the assault of Mr. Somchai Neelapaijit. But the plaintiff and the five coplaintiffs did not demonstrate how Mr. Somchai Neelapaijit was physically or mentally endangered. *Perhaps all we know is that no one has found Mr. Somchai Neelapaijit since then. And we do not know if Mr. Somchai Neelapaijit remains alive or not.*"[62] The judges concluded that Somchai Neelapaijit was assaulted but also that as he could not be located the injuries and danger he faced could not be ascertained. The judges called pushing Somchai Neelapaijit into a vehicle a crime, but disappearance was left as an unspoken detail that made it impossible to ascertain the extent of the assault.

All parties to the case appealed. The Appeal Court decision, written by Songsilp Thammarat, Pakorn Wongsaroj, and Rangsan Wichitkraisorn, upheld the exoneration of four of the five defendants and also overturned the conviction of Police Major Ngern, even though the Appeal Court judges maintained that the facts presented substantiated that "on the date and time and the place of the incident as charged, Mr. Somchai Neelapaijit was really taken by a group of criminals into a car."[63] But the judges ruled that the evidence linking Police Major Ngern to the crime was very shaky and therefore did not merit a conviction.[64] The question remains: if Somchai Neelapaijit was pushed into a vehicle and his fate remains unknown, who was responsible for this?

The view of the judges of both the Appeal Court and the Supreme Court was that this was not a question that Angkhana Neelapaijit and her children had a right to ask. Both courts ruled against the Court of First Instance's decision to allow them to serve as coplaintiffs. On this matter, this mismatch between the crime as charged (theft and coercive assault) and the actual crime (disappearance) created an opening for the judges of the Appeal and Supreme Courts to both deny the rights of the victims and write the ambiguity of Somchai Neelapaijit's fate into history.

In their appeal, the five defendants argued that the plaintiff and the co-plaintiffs had asserted that the crime was "acting together to use coercive force and seize Mr. Somchai Neelapaijit and put him into the car belonging to the five defendants. This was coercion to make Mr. Somchai assent to go with the five defendants and make him afraid that his body, life, and liberty were in danger. They did this by using injurious force until Mr. Somchai had to act and agree to get into the car and sit with the five defendants. This does not mean in any way that Mr. Somchai was assaulted until he was injured."[65] The Appeal Court judges reaffirmed that there was no confirmation that Somchai Neelapaijit was dead. The judges further noted that "the five petitioners believe that the five defendants assaulted Mr. Somchai until he was dead or injured until he could not act by himself. It has not been confirmed as true for certain that Mr. Somchai was assaulted and injured until he was unable to act for himself or killed."[66] The Appeal Court then noted that even though as family members of the victim, the petitioners fit the category of individuals covered by the law, the situation was not the one described in the law.

The decision by the Supreme Court went even further, and the three judges, Phanuwat Suphaphan, Somyot Khemthong, and Somsak Khunlertkij, wrote, "Even though the aforementioned charge statement demonstrated that the five defendants used force to assault Mr. Somchai, the plaintiff was unable to confirm that Mr. Somchai was dead; the case therefore cannot be held that Mr. Somchai was assaulted until he died following the meaning of the law. In addition, the contention that the five defendants acted together to use coercive force to push and shove Mr. Somchai into the car of the five defendants is contrary to the charge of the plaintiffs that Mr. Somchai was injured until he was unable to act for himself. And even though in 2009 the Southern Bangkok Civil Court issued an order that demonstrated that Mr. Somchai was a missing person held to be dead according to Article 62 of the Civil and Commercial Code, this was legal death. It was not a case of being assaulted and killed according to the facts. . . . The facts do not demonstrate that Mr. Somchai was assaulted and killed or injured until he was unable to act for himself."[67] By refusing to accept Somchai's death as defined by his having been ruled a person presumed to be dead after having been missing for five years, the Supreme Court does not even acknowledge the possibility of the crime of disappearance. The Supreme Court also noted that "the facts do not demonstrate that Somchai was assaulted and murdered or grievously injured and unable to represent himself." The additional content of the two appeals written by Somchai's widow and children was left unexamined by the court. These decisions denied the right of the family to be coplaintiffs and were an explicit attack on the rights of victims of state violence to seek redress.

The day the Supreme Court decision was read, Angkhana Neelapaijit made a public statement: "Today, the Supreme Court has created a new norm in Thai society. This is the confirmation that families of the disappeared do not have rights in the process of demanding justice in the stead of the person who has disappeared, as there is no evidence that the person who has disappeared has been injured or lost his life and is therefore unable to act for himself."[68] The jurisprudence of impunity affects both the family of Somchai Neelapaijit directly and all possible future families of victims of disappearance.

Perhaps as a confirmation of the failure of the judges to do their job, even as the case was being examined in the court, the investigation into the disappearance continued outside it. The DSI officially took over the investigation on 19 July 2005. On 13 January 2006, a day after the Court of First Instance decision was read, Prime Minister Thaksin Shinawatra, whose knowledge of or collusive role in the disappearance remains ambiguous, commented, "I know that Mr. Somchai is dead. There is an evidence trail. But I cannot say anything yet because it is for the DSI to wrap up and proceed [with bringing a case]. Regarding finding confirmation of the death, we must know that he has died if we are to bring a case of murder. The DSI will be able to wrap up the investigation file during the month of February."[69] After eleven years and three months, in October 2016, the DSI announced that it had closed the case without identifying the culprits. The lengthy, inconclusive investigation, despite early admissions from

Prime Minister Thaksin and others that they knew the truth about what happened to Somchai Neelapaijit, is a concise indication of *why* the case cannot be solved.[70] Knowledge of state violence by prime ministers, high-ranking military officers, officials in the Ministry of Interior, and others is not acquired by accident. Like many other instances of state violence examined in this book, the problem is not a lack of facts or analysis of how the facts articulate together as the truth. The problem is a lack of will to act on this knowledge and hold perpetrators accountable for their actions. These actions, and the collusion that places perpetrators beyond the reach of accountability, are part of the way the Thai state forms and reproduces itself.

A JURISPRUDENCE AGAINST IMPUNITY

At every stage of the struggle for justice in the case of the disappearance of Somchai Neelapaijit, the lack of disappearance as a category within Thai criminal law was a significant obstacle. The gravity of the crime could not be adequately described by the prosecutor, and over the course of the three decisions, the truth that Somchai Neelapaijit was disappeared vanished. Dispossession of the Neelapaijit family's right to be coplaintiffs with the prosecution went along with the erasure of the severity of the crime of disappearance and the death of Somchai Neelapaijit that it entailed. Unlike family members whose relatives are victims of murder or grievous assault, families of the disappeared cannot be coplaintiffs in prosecutions of alleged perpetrators. This at once depends on the denial of disappearance as a crime and reinforces it.

Although changing the law would not automatically redress the problems of the lack of political and judicial will to end disappearance, such a change would provide a minimal tool with which to both prosecute perpetrators and further expose the challenges of doing so. In February 2015, building on years of work by Thai human rights activists, the Ministry of Justice's Department of Rights and Liberties Protection released a draft law that defined the crimes of torture and disappearance and stipulated punishments for them.[71] The Act on the Prevention and Suppression of Torture and Enforced Disappearance was drafted to bring Thai law into compliance as a state party to the Convention against Torture and Other Cruel, Inhuman or Degrading Treatment or Punishment (CAT) and with the CED, which Thailand has signed but not yet ratified. The draft act was submitted to the legislative assembly appointed by the NCPO in late 2015.

At that time, I asked human rights colleagues what might happen with the draft act; they reported that it is likely it will not be passed while the NCPO is in power. The junta was unlikely to allow a law to be passed that could result in its own leaders being punished.[72] This assessment was correct: the legislative assembly ceased their examination of the law in March 2017 and the draft act is on permanent hold. But the draft act will be waiting to be examined, or drafted anew, in the future when the dictatorship falls and there is a return to a more democratic regime.

Putting aside the question of whether the draft act will be passed and when, examining its provisions is a utopian act that makes it possible to imagine what a jurisprudence against impunity might look like. In direct contrast to a jurisprudence of impunity that forecloses accountability both in individual cases and in a collective sense, a jurisprudence against impunity would both facilitate access to justice in individual cases and support the broad protection of rights. A jurisprudence against impunity would have resulted in a different judicial process in the case of the disappearance of Somchai Neelapaijit and established a precedent for additional cases of disappearance to be brought to the criminal courts.

The draft act defines "enforced disappearance" as "the arrest, detention, or abduction or any other kind of action that is a deprivation of an individual's physical liberty done by a state official, or by an individual or group of individuals ordered, supported, or with the complicity of state officials; there is a denial of the arrest, detention, or abduction or any other kind of action taken to deprive the physical liberty of the individual, or the concealing of the fate or location of that individual."[73] If a state official, or a person ordered by a state official, perpetrates an enforced disappearance, the punishment is five to fifteen years in prison and a fine of 100,000 to 300,000 baht. If a disappearance results in grievous injury, the penalty increases to ten to twenty years in prison and a fine of 200,000 to 500,000 baht and in cases of death fifteen to thirty years or life in prison and a fine of 300,000 to 1 million baht. In the draft act, any official senior to the perpetrators who was aware of or complicit in a case of disappearance is subject to a punishment of up to half of the punishment stipulated for perpetrators. The draft act also stipulates that the investigation in disappearance cases should continue until the disappeared person or evidence indicating the death of the disappeared person is located. The draft act allows for a range of individuals to bring a case, including victims, prosecutors, administrative or police officials, members of the committee set up under the draft act to support it, and other individuals acting in the interest of victims. To return to Carlo Ginzburg's shorthand equation for the shared project of judges and historians, were the draft act to be passed, it would be possible under Thai law for the judges to examine and prove that x did commit y, that a perpetrator or group of perpetrators carried out an enforced disappearance.

The series of events described by the seven eyewitnesses in the case of Somchai Neelapaijit falls within the definition of enforced disappearance set by the law. In addition to discarding Somchai's car, which the Court of First Instance judges argued was done in order to conceal a crime, the three court rulings themselves operate to aid in the concealment of Somchai's fate. I am not arguing that there is evidence to prove that the judges colluded with the police and actively worked to hide Somchai's fate, which would make them criminally liable under the draft act. Although this could be the case, my point instead is that a flawed judicial system and set of laws can operate to serve the same effect. If the draft act passed, and the case of the disappearance of Somchai Neelapaijit were to be reopened and prosecuted anew, the facts of his disappearance and fate would be made explicit and devoid of ambiguity.[74] The passage of the draft act would provide a beginning, though not necessarily a just end. To recall Sudprathana Neelapaijit's comment, "Everything is a struggle in the judicial process, from the Court of First Instance to the Appeal Court and the Supreme Court."[75]

Were the passage of the draft act to prompt changes in the way disappearance cases are adjudicated in the future, this would also transform the version of history that judges write in their decisions. Even in the absence of the new law, a resonant and inseparable struggle to write new histories of disappearance that counter the ambiguity surrounding and created by the crime is also necessary. By conservative, partial estimates of the scattered cases of disappearance from 1952 to the present that I mentioned at the beginning of this chapter, there are at least 179 unresolved cases of disappearance, and this number grows to over 5,000 if one adds the suspected deaths that occurred during the *thang daeng* killings in 1972 and the "War on Drugs" in 2002. Drawing on the 59 cases it documented, the JPF identified people close to state officials, including those who worked closely with them in illicit industries, activists and human rights defenders, witnesses, and migrants as those most at risk of disappearance.[76] The JPF also identified three common methods of disappearance across these cases: taking people from the street and pushing them onto a motorbike or car, as in the case of Somchai Neelapaijit; arrest; and inviting people to meet with state officials.[77] A great deal more research remains to be done on the history of disappearance in Thailand, and it will take transformations in law, politics, and accountability to do so.

In his research about disappearance in relation to the mass killings of those suspected or labeled as communists in Indonesia in 1965–66, John Roosa writes about how little is known even sixty years after the killings.[78] The nature of disappearance as a form of violence intended both to eliminate a figure deemed to be an enemy and to sow fear and terror meant that discretion, rather than secrecy, was needed.[79] The primary question that Roosa aimed to answer addressed the ambiguity surrounding the identities of the perpetrators of the disappearances and killings: were they state officials or civilians? Existing scholarship places responsibility with both groups, but Roosa rereads both long-standing and recent scholarship to identify a *lack* of shared responsibility. The identity of the perpetrators is not ambiguous. In the relatively open political atmosphere that has prevailed since the fall of the Suharto regime in 1998, research has revealed that the majority of the perpetrators were engaged in "organizing the civilians, administrating the detention camps, and arranging the trucks to transport the detainees to the execution sites" around the country.[80] This similarity in tactics used throughout the country points to collusion that must have reached up the chain of command to Suharto himself. Roosa calls for scholars to build on new work completed since 1998 to examine how decisions were made within the army. In particular, the necessary questions have become: "When and why did the army high command under Suharto decide upon a policy of mass disappearances? How did they overcome resistance within the army, police, and civilian administration to ensure that the policy was implemented?"[81]

A similar set of questions regarding the military and police is relevant in Thailand. The opening of Thai state security archives may be even farther off than in Indonesia, and the growing authoritarianism of the Thai military regime after the 22 May 2014 coup also marks a difference that affects and constricts the kinds of research and analysis that can be done. But in the absence of declassified official documents—which can obscure or obfuscate in addition to illuminate—one can still engage in analysis and the writing of history against impunity. One place to begin may be compiling a more complete list of the disappeared and those suspected of having been disappeared in order to clarify the contours of what is not known.

Writing the histories of disappearance and other forms of state violence and the ways in which impunity is produced for them is one way to disrupt the version proffered by the state itself. Placing as yet ineligible forms of violence visited upon citizens by state officials at the center of analysis is a way to write a new history and, in Craig Reynolds's words, "to repudiate the past, to challenge held assumptions and to declare the onset of a new epoch" in which the specific lives affected by impunity will not go unnoticed.

7

Who Can Be Killed with Impunity and Who Cannot Be Impugned?

Inequality before the law lies at the root of real history, but official history is written by oblivion, not memory.

—EDUARDO GALEANO, *Upside Down*

FIRST ELECTED ON 9 FEBRUARY 2001, and then in a landslide victory for a second term on 6 February 2005, Thaksin Shinawatra's Thai Rak Thai (TRT) party took a populist approach to governance that differed from those of earlier politicians. The TRT promoted policies, notably universal health coverage and decentralized, autonomous village-level loans and grants, that responded to the peoples' needs and took them seriously as subjects of politics. Thaksin's approach to human rights, however, was no better than those of other politicians. The disappearance of Somchai Neelapaijit was but one of at least eighteen murders of human rights defenders that took place during Thaksin's time as prime minister.[1]

But it was Thaksin's populism, and the figure of the man himself, who was a successful telecommunications entrepreneur before he became a politician, that made many in the corridors of power uncomfortable.[2] Arguing that he was corrupt and aimed to usurp the king, a royalist-nationalist movement began to coalesce to call for his ouster after he was elected for a second term. Operating under the official name People's Alliance for Democracy (PAD), and known colloquially as "yellow shirts" due to the color worn by its members (chosen because it was the color of King Bhumibol), it called for Thaksin's ouster. By mid-2006 this call became one for his removal by any means necessary, including a military coup. On 19 September 2006 the military obliged, and a junta calling itself the Council for

Democratic Reform under Constitutional Monarchy (CDRM) launched a coup while Thaksin was out of the country.[3]

During the years between the 19 September 2006 and the 22 May 2014 coups, the struggle between the rulers and the ruled increasingly took the form of color-coded politics between the royalist-nationalist yellow shirts, who favored rule by a moral few, and the populist-democratic red shirts, including many supporters of Thaksin, who emerged after the 2006 coup and wanted rule by those chosen by the majority. The two sides of yellow and red also map onto the long-standing divides between the relatively prosperous city and center of central and southern Thailand and the relatively tenuous countryside of northern and northeastern Thailand.[4] Coincident with color-coded tension, the specter of royal succession emerged as Bhumibol Adulyadej, the ninth king of the Chakri dynasty and the world's longest-reigning living monarch, aged and began to grow ill.[5]

Over time, the struggle between the yellow and red shirts hardened, and both sides developed strong ideological positions through repeated street protests in and beyond the capital. The protests were both a response to the seeming revolving door of the prime minister's office and one of the factors behind the frequent changes. Between the ouster of Thaksin in September 2006 and July 2011, there were six appointed prime ministers. The seat was occupied for the longest stretch by Abhisit Vejjajiva, leader of the yellow-aligned Democrat Party, who was appointed following a series of judicial machinations in December 2008 and remained in office until August 2011.[6] The appointment of Abhisit as an unelected prime minister only two years after the September 2006 coup accelerated the politicization of the red shirts and what they called the process of *ta sawang* (eyes opening) or an awakening to both the injustice they faced in the present and its long history.

In March 2010 red shirts took to the streets of Bangkok for protests that led to the most deadly incident of mass violence in modern Thai history. Led by the United Front for Democracy against Dictatorship (UDD), the largest red shirt organization, and joined by a diverse range of smaller groups, the protesters planned to stay in the city until a date was set for general elections. Their quarrel was not with Abhisit as an individual but with the method by which he had come to power. The protests initially took place at two primary sites: the area surrounding the Democracy Monument and Phan Fa bridge on Rattanakosin Island, a traditional site of protests, and the glitzy Ratchaprasong shopping area near Siam Square across the city.[7] Organized by province, different areas of the protest sites were populated by tents representing various groups and districts; rice, dried fish, and other provisions were provided by those who stayed home. Middle-class city dwellers complained of the inconvenience and hurled ethnicized epithets at the protesters, referring to them as both buffalos and germs.[8]

While residents and businesspeople treated the red shirts as out of place in the urban space of the city streets, the Abhisit government and its supporters cast them as more squarely out of place in the governing of the polity. The red shirts' call for elections was met by the state with disproportionate violence. Exploiting the suspicion that there was a faction of armed protesters, the so-called men in black, within the majority of unarmed red shirts and the fiction that the protesters aimed to topple the monarchy, the government of Prime Minister Abhisit declared a state of emergency on 7 April 2010 and named Deputy Prime Minister Suthep Thaugsuban director of a coordinating agency, the Center for the Resolution of the Emergency Situation (CRES).[9] Three days later, on 10 April, the CRES presided over the first of a series of military crackdowns that ended with the complete clearing of the city streets of protesters on 19 May. The violence left at least ninety-four people dead, including eighty-eight civilians, and more than two thousand injured.

Eventually the demands of the red shirts were heard, and parliament was dissolved on 10 May 2011 and a general election held on 3 July. Yingluck Shinawatra, Thaksin's younger sister and leader of the Pheu Thai Party (PTP), which, like the PPP (which was dissolved in 2008), was a reconfiguration of the TRT, was elected with the majority of the votes. Following the 2011 election, Abhisit and Suthep remained in government as representatives of the opposition yellow-shirt-aligned Democrat Party.

Within the context of the history of impunity for state violence traced in this book, the crackdown on red shirt protesters in April–May 2010 was business as usual. But what happened next was not. The series of events that followed in the aftermath of the crackdown offered an initial promise of a departure from the history of impunity for state violence. Rather than swift passage of an amnesty law, such as the one that followed the 6 October 1976 massacre, the Abhisit government set up a semi-independent committee to examine the protests and the crackdown, the Truth and Reconciliation Committee of Thailand (TRCT). Members of the government and state security forces, to a greater or lesser degree, cooperated with the TRCT and four other state and independent investigations. Inquest hearings into the deaths began in 2012 in order to determine whether the protesters had been killed by state security forces.

On the basis of the inquests and additional evidence submitted by the DSI, in October 2013 the Office of the Attorney General (OAG) announced that it was pressing charges against Abhisit and Suthep for premeditated murder for giving orders to use lethal force in April–May 2010. This was the first time that individual state officials were indicted for their roles in mass violence perpetrated against the people, and it suggested that perhaps what Kathryn Sikkink calls the "justice cascade" would begin in Thailand.[10] Yet in late August 2014, several months after the 22 May 2014 coup and before the hearings and witness testimony began, the Criminal Court dismissed the case against Abhisit and Suthep. Deploying a logic that departed significantly from the letter of the law, the Criminal Court argued that, as the pair held political office at the time of the alleged crimes, the case could only be examined by the National Anti-Corruption Commission (NACC), the independent agency tasked with examining the malfeasance of officials. If the NACC found the two to have committed an abuse of power, then the case could be examined by the Supreme Court's Criminal Division for Persons Holding Political Positions. While Abhisit and Suthep faced a maximum penalty of death or life imprisonment if convicted of premeditated murder in the Criminal Court, the harshest punishment that this court could mete out would be to bar them from political office. The injustice cascade was resurgent.

In dismissing the charges, the Criminal Court gave a legal and institutional gloss to the already normalized use of violence as a strategy of rule. While those involved in the 6 October 1976 massacre and coup clamored for an amnesty out of an awareness that they could be prosecuted for their actions, the dismissal of the charges by the Criminal Court eliminated the need for an amnesty. There was no need to pass a law retroactively authorizing past illegal actions because the Criminal Court was itself willing to step outside the law. In his weekly column in the *Matichon* newspaper, Nidhi Eoseewong parsed the way this decision defined murder as an act of bad judgment by political officeholders rather than an act for which perpetrators could be found culpable. Nidhi wrote, "If the perpetrator holds political office at the time of the alleged offense, a crime of politics holds a penalty aimed only at restricting his right to be involved in politics. The Criminal Court's view is that the massacre of the people in the center of the city by the people who held political office is merely a crime of politics. And when it becomes a crime of politics, the soldiers who carried out the actions have nothing to do with the crime at all."[11] Rather than a definition of political crime as that which has as its aim the overthrow or change of government, the Criminal Court here defined it as regime-preserving violence underscored by the occupation of the perpetrators.

The dispossession of the people from equal membership in the polity, which is at the heart of preserving a regime, is cast in stark relief when the case against Abhisit and Suthep is placed side by side with another kind of case that occurred during the same period. These are the cases of prosecution for violation of Article 112 of the Criminal Code, the measure that defines and stipulates the punishment for alleged lèse majesté. In contrast to the case against Abhisit and Suthep, violations of Article 112 are not designated as political crimes, and those who are held and prosecuted under the measure are not designated as political prisoners. Similar to the case against Abhisit and Suthep, the Criminal Court departed from written law in this case, which belies the political nature (in the sense of regime preservation meant by the Criminal Court) of both kinds of cases.

Judges drift into discussions of premodern kingdoms in their decisions, give credence to unverified (and unverifiable) loyalty, and castigate defendants as liars in decisions and comments in Article 112 cases. The immediate function of the court's actions in excess of the letter of the law is to create a logic for the harsh punishments meted out to individuals, such as the eighteen-year sentence given to Daranee Charnchoengsilpakul for delivering a fifty-five-minute speech and the fifty-six-year sentence given to Sasiwimol (family name withheld) for seven Facebook posts.[12] Resonant with Nidhi's assessment of the effects of the decision to dismiss the case against Abhisit and Suthep, these repeated decisions institutionalized and normalized repression in the service of preserving the regime.

Similar to the swift prosecution of Chiranuch Premchaiporn and the inability to hold the perpetrators of Somchai Neelapaijit's disappearance to account in court, with which this book began, the departures from the law in these two kinds of cases were neither accidental nor elaborately planned. Instead, they invite a comparison, which I frame as a question: why is it so difficult to prosecute a former prime minister and former deputy prime minister for their roles ordering military operations that led to the deaths of ninety-four people and injuries to more than two thousand and so easy to prosecute ordinary citizens for questioning the monarch? Who can be killed with impunity and who cannot be impugned? The comparison of these two kinds of cases provides a way to glimpse part of the foundational logic informing social and political relations in Thailand during the late reign of Rama IX. The promise of the 1932 transformation to bring everyone within the polity under the same law still has not been kept. Every person who enters a courtroom in Thailand becomes aware of this even before the judges open their mouths to speak: the accused and visitors both sit on wooden benches facing, but lower than, the judges, who sit on plush seats below an ornately framed photograph of the king. By tracing the different positions before the law that Abhisit Vejjajiva and Suthep Thaugsuban and those accused of violating Article 112 hold, an outline of what Eduardo Galeano calls real history, rather than the history of oblivion, which leaves inequality obscured, may become visible.

THE LEGALIZATION OF PREMEDITATED MURDER

Following the April–May 2010 crackdown, there was a series of five investigations into the violence by a range of state, independent, and semistate/semi-independent organizations. Four of these reports were written, released to the public, and debated and criticized during what now stands out as the relatively open atmosphere of June 2010 to late 2013. The law firm of Robert Amsterdam, the legal counsel of former prime minister Thaksin, released a report on the crackdown in the context of the history of state violence in January 2011 under the auspices of an entity called the Thai Accountability Project.[13] The People's Information Center, a civil society coalition of activists, academics, and survivors, carried out an investigation and released its report to the public in August 2012.[14] The TRCT, the semistate/semi-independent body set up by the Abhisit government within the first two months following the crackdown, released its final report to the public in September 2012.[15] The National Human Rights Commission (NHRC), one of the independent organizations set up under the 1997 constitution, carried out an investigation and released its report to the public in August 2013.[16] All four reports agreed on two basic premises: (1) the state used a disproportionate amount of force and (2) there were some protesters who were not unarmed at the red shirt demonstrations.[17] Beyond this basic similarity, significant differences among the reports reflect divergent conceptions of human rights, truth, and justice and therefore multiple ways of identifying and interpreting relevant facts, events, and actors.[18]

The fifth report was compiled during the same period by the DSI but remains classified. The basis of the evidence in the DSI's report differs from that of the four others, as the DSI has the capacity to compel state and citizen witnesses to provide testimony and documents.

Simultaneous with the investigations, a process of postmortem inquests began in 2012. Article 150 of the Criminal Procedure Code stipulates that when state officials have been involved in the deaths of civilians, autopsies and inquest hearings must be carried out. Once the court has ruled on the cause of death in an inquest, the file is forwarded to the OAG for consideration of the next step. The next step is often inaction, even in cases in which state officials have been identified as the perpetrators of murder. This inaction is foreshadowed by the contradictory language often chosen by the courts in cases in which there is incontrovertible evidence that a victim died at the hands of state officials: the court rules that the victim was killed by state officials but notes that this occurred while the officials were carrying out their civil service duties.[19] By December 2016 inquests had been held in thirty of the ninety-four April–May 2010 deaths. Of these thirty deaths, the court ruled in eighteen cases that there was clear evidence that the shots that killed the victim were fired from the military side, but the shooter could not be identified. In the other twelve cases, the direction from which the gunshots came could not be determined.[20]

In a departure from earlier instances of mass state violence, on the basis of the inquest results, as well as sixty-one folders containing 11,242 pages of documentation compiled by the DSI, on 28 October 2013 the OAG announced that it was bringing criminal charges of premeditated murder against Abhisit Vejjajiva and Suthep Thaugsuban for ordering the use of armed force against the red shirt protesters in April–May 2010.[21] Abhisit and Suthep were accused of one count of violation of Articles 288, 84, 83, 80, and 59. Article 288 pertains to murder, and the other articles provide the link between the orders given and the act of murder.[22] Nantasak Poonsuk, spokesperson and director-general of the OAG's special cases division, explained that Suthep had been charged because he gave the order to use armed force during the dispersal of the protesters as the director of the CRES, and Abhisit had been charged because he ordered the use of the emergency decree and appointed Suthep director of the CRES. The view of the OAG was that the emergency decree was not a blank check and the orders to use weapons were in excess of necessity.[23] If convicted of murder, Abhisit and Suthep faced a possible punishment of fifteen to twenty years imprisonment, life imprisonment, or the death penalty under Article 288. Even if they confessed and received the minimum sentence, they would still face a sentence of seven and a half years behind bars.

With the families of the victims of the crackdown as coplaintiffs with the OAG, Abhisit was formally indicted in the Criminal Court in Bangkok on 12 December 2013 and Suthep on 26 May 2014.[24] But on 28 August 2014, less than a year after the OAG filed the charges, the Criminal Court dismissed them. The veracity of the actions in question—that Abhisit announced a state of emergency and appointed Suthep the director of the CRES and Suthep gave the order to state security officials to use weapons against the protesters—was not disputed.[25] Nor was the link between the order to use weapons and the resulting deaths.[26] Instead the charges, their denial by Abhisit and Suthep, the dismissal by the Criminal Court, and an ongoing appeal turn on questions of the interlocking interpretations of legal jurisdiction, duty, and politics.

A combination of problems within existing laws, lack of other needed laws, collusion among state officials, and lack of political will has made it difficult to hold state actors accountable for violence using the criminal justice system.[27] At the time when the OAG filed the charges against Abhisit and Suthep, the NACC was also examining the incident. Like the NHRC, the NACC is an independent organization established by the 1997 constitution. Part of its mandate is to investigate whether high-ranking government officials have committed malfeasance while in office.[28] From the beginning, Attaphon Yaisawang, the attorney general, was explicit about the OAG's authority to examine the case.[29] His position was that this was a case of using or instigating other people to commit or attempt to commit murder, not a case of malfeasance while in office.[30] In other words, Abhisit and Suthep's actions constituted a crime rather than an instance of corruption.

Abhisit and Suthep both disagreed with this assessment and issued statements via the Democrat Party spokesperson shortly after learning of the charges. Decrying the charges as politically motivated, Abhisit said, "I maintain that the fact of what happened in 2010 is that I and Khun Suthep carried out our duties as prime minister and deputy prime minister. We had the duty to maintain public order in the nation. There was a demonstration that the court had ruled illegal and in excess of the limits set by the constitution on demonstration."[31] He was not a murderer but rather a prime minister who had performed his duty of protecting the nation. In contrast, it was the red shirt demonstrators who had violated the law.[32]

Abhisit also maintained that the presence of weapons among the protesters was widely known. Using the familial language often employed by Field Marshal Sarit Thanarat, General Kriangsak Chomanan, and other Thai politicians and military generals to inflect domination with intimacy, he said, "The brothers and sisters, the people, were well aware that the demonstration had become one characterized by armed people hidden among, or moving alongside, the demonstrators."[33] As a result, he and Suthep had acted with "a clear stance that we must lead the country back to normalcy and peace and happiness while avoiding losses."[34] He seemed to have forgotten the loss of the lives of ninety-four people at the heart of the murder charge he faced.[35]

Abhisit's primary focus on the legal reasons why he should not be charged with murder, which he casts as technical and cut-and-dried, reveals a logic of impunity in which any action undertaken in the service of duty cannot be a crime. Contrary to the attorney general's assertion that the emergency decree was not a blank check, Abhisit asserted that he could not be charged in the Criminal Court because he had committed the alleged crime while he was prime minister. He commented that accusing him of murder contained a fundamental contradiction because, "The reports of my wrongdoing and that of Khun Suthep claim that we issued orders while I was in the position of prime minister and Khun Suthep was in the position of the chair or director of the CRES. No matter the instance, these are all orders given as state officials."[36] For Abhisit, the very fact that he was prime minister when he gave the orders means that he could not have committed murder. When people are killed as part of the preservation of order, this does not register as murder. Between the lines of Abhisit's statement, the authority to give orders as prime minister is defined as an authority bereft of accountability.

Suthep was more direct in his refusal of accountability. The attorney general was a member of the committee running the CRES, and either he or a representative was present at every meeting. If Suthep violated the law while he was director of the CRES, he should have been stopped or at least warned at the time. The government had no desire to use armed force against the people, but it was necessary "in order to preserve the peace and order of the country, in order to preserve the law, because there were armed people who entered [the protests] to foment terror."[37] Rather than speaking of his own duty, Suthep instead defended the soldiers and the performance of their duty. The initiation of prosecution had him worried "especially for the soldiers who are the children and grandchildren of the people. There is no one who went out carrying a gun with the intention of slaughtering the people. But it was necessary that they perform their duty and sleep on the streets for many months in order to protect the law and protect the democratic regime. Soldiers lost their lives and were injured and remain disabled. I beseech society, all of the country's brothers and sisters, do not join in the process of Police Lieutenant-Colonel Thaksin [Shinawatra] or Tharit Pengdit [director-general of the DSI] to accuse the troops, the soldiers of the army, who followed my orders—orders given by me as the deputy prime minister that were legal—of being those who committed wrongdoing. It will throw their families into chaos."[38] Given that there was no active plan to try to press charges against individual soldiers at that stage, Suthep's appeal to protect the soldiers and his assertion that they were protecting the law when they, to use his words, slaughtered their fellow citizens, rings hollow. He spoke directly to the soldiers and their families and said that if the attorney general did not heed his call to refrain from prosecuting the soldiers, they were not to worry: "I want to take this opportunity to tell the brother soldiers, do not fret . . . do not fret. I have consulted with thirty or forty lawyers. They are prepared to act as counsel for all the soldiers. To the families of the soldiers, do not be frightened. You did the right thing. Today perhaps you have come under attack. But dhamma must win."[39] He leaves the meaning of "dhamma"—that which is morally correct—unspecified. Perhaps Suthep promised the soldiers his support of their legal defense because if he and Abhisit failed to dissuade the Criminal Court from prosecuting them, they planned to argue that the soldiers, as those who pulled the triggers, should be prosecuted rather than those who ordered that they do so.

Neither Abhisit nor Suthep disputed the actions for which they were being charged (giving orders to use weapons against red shirt protestors) nor the outcome of the orders (deaths and grievous injuries). Instead they mounted a preemptive defense by identifying in turn as a victim (Abhisit) and the protector of potential victims of future prosecution (Suthep). They did not speak of the citizens who were the actual victims of the crackdown in April and May 2010 except to refer to them as those who illegally protested or fomented terror.

Abhisit and Suthep were soon able to let go of their worries. The indictment and accompanying hope for possible accountability were short-lived. On 28 August 2014, a little over three months after the coup by the National

Council for Peace and Order (NCPO), the Criminal Court ruled that it did not have the jurisdiction to examine the case. The court took the same position as Abhisit and Suthep that the action in question was "the issuance of orders in the position of prime minister, deputy prime minister, and director of the CRES, relying on the authority of the 2005 Emergency Decree. It was not an individual criminal act or beyond their civil service duties."[40] As such, the NACC was the only relevant body that could examine the incident, as it could determine whether the actions constituted malfeasance of duty or an abuse of power. If it determined the actions to be an abuse of power, then it should forward the case to the Supreme Court's Criminal Division for Persons Holding Political Positions. In addition to the comparatively minor penalties these two entities could mete out, the transfer to exclusive examination by the NACC ruled out the ability of the family members of those killed to be coplaintiffs.

Despite the restrictions on protest and expression of dissent put in place by the junta following the coup, there was criticism from many different quarters, including the chief justice of the Criminal Court. Both the attorney general and the families of the victims appealed. The criticism lays bare the logic at work in the nonadjudication of this case and outlines its implications: just as the indictment was a historic moment heralding a possible end to impunity, this decision was similarly historic and can be read as an indication of what the 2014 coup meant for impunity.

The first critic was Thongchai Senamontri, the chief justice of the Criminal Court, who wrote the first dissenting opinion of his career in this case. The decision of the Criminal Court, he wrote, violated the right of the families of the victims to pursue justice and was incorrect legally: "This is an interpretation of the law that is devoid of justice and is contrary to the law. When the two defendants denied any wrongdoing, the case should have proceeded through the judicial process to the end point in order for justice to be served for both sides. [The court should] not have made a legal ruling that curtails the right of the plaintiffs and the victims to bring a case."[41] Thongchai argued that the case was within the jurisdiction of the Criminal Court and that the DSI and OAG had correctly followed the Criminal Procedure Code. In contrast to the assertions by Abhisit, Suthep, and the Criminal Court that the case was not a criminal one because their actions occurred while they were carrying out their duties, Thongchai argued that the explanation of their roles as prime minister and deputy prime minister/director of the CRES was relevant only in terms of explaining how their actions caused others to commit murder, not as definitive of the alleged crime. Their actions could not be dismissed as duty or even malfeasance of duty. He wrote, "The offense of homicide of another person is a serious crime. It is not related to the carrying out of civil service duties."[42] The Criminal Court needed to examine the case to determine whether the two defendants "had intended that weapons of war would be used to kill people. This concerns action that is beyond that of a civil service position. It is instigating or using state officials to commit murder. As for whether or not and how the evidence is admissible is another matter."[43]

The plaintiffs had thirty days within which to appeal. The OAG appealed on 17 September 2014. It reiterated that it had indicted the defendants based on Articles 288, 84, 83, and 80 of the Criminal Code, not Article 157, which covers matters of officials performing their duties.[44] The OAG reiterated that, although it noted that the two defendants committed the crimes while they held political office, it was descriptive rather than definitive of the crime in question. It reiterated that the DSI had the authority to investigate, the attorney general had the authority to indict, and the Criminal Court had the authority to adjudicate the case.[45]

The families of those killed during the April–May 2010 crackdown were similarly angered by the dismissal of the charges. Phayao Akkad, who became a leader among the families after the death of her daughter, Kamolkade Akkad, who was a nurse killed in Wat Pathumwanaram on 19 May, explained that she and others were surprised because the courts, the investigators, and the DSI had all collected information about how the protestors were killed by the actions of state officials.[46] Suriyan Phonsila, whose husband, Chanarong Phonsila, was shot and killed on 15 May 2010, said:

> I did not think that the Criminal Court would transfer the case to the Supreme Court's Criminal Division for Persons Holding Political Positions, given that the death of Mr. Chanarong, my husband, is not a matter of politics but a case of murder. . . . As a person who has sustained losses, I will push on to demand justice for my husband. I do not want to make any criticism during this period because I know that anyone who engages in any movement will be arrested. . . . I believe right now that many of the families of those who were killed are likely shocked at today's ruling by the court. And we do not know what to do. Perhaps we can only sit and pray for justice to come quickly. I believe that whatever one does, retribution will follow.[47]

Like Suthep, Suriyan inserted the language of Buddhist morality into her response to the court with the use of the term *phon kam* (retribution). Her comments also make clear that the karmic retribution she awaits is that dispensed by judges in a courtroom, not that meted out by a higher authority at an unspecified date.

On 29 September 2014 Chokchai Angkaew, the lawyer for the coplaintiffs, submitted an appeal that drew on both Thongchai Senamontri's dissenting comments and the attorney general's appeal. The appeal by the families also focused on the importance of the case being examined by the Criminal Court, not by the NACC or the Supreme Court. The families' appeal made clear the limits of duty and order and noted, "Even though the two defendants committed the acts while they were prime minister and deputy prime minister, these were offenses beyond their office because there is no article of law that gave permission for the two defendants to order the murder of people. The accusation of murder following Article 288 of the Criminal Code is therefore not malfeasance of duty as a civil servant, even though the two defendants committed the acts while they were in the position of prime minister and deputy prime minister."[48] The Appeal Court upheld the initial decision of the Criminal Court in February 2016.

There is no written law that permits the murder of the people by the state authorities, but history offers substantial evidence of the inequality among different members of the polity, which results in the murders of some to fail to register as such. The inequality that renders the lives of some citizens—red shirt protesters—dispensable works to simultaneously create another set of lives, the monarch and those close to him, that are indispensable.

THE CRIMINALIZATION OF QUESTIONING THE INSTITUTION OF THE MONARCHY

Although Article 112 has been part of the Criminal Code since its last major revision in 1957, after the 2006 coup there was a rapid increase in its use that David Streckfuss astutely identified as "epidemic."[49] After the 22 May 2014 coup, the use of the law by the authorities intensified further, with at least 90 new Article 112 cases having been brought in the Criminal and Military Courts between May 2014 and December 2016.[50] Such alleged crimes, including performing plays, writing graffiti in bathrooms, and the Facebook posts mentioned earlier, have been treated as grave crimes against the crown, state, and the slippery space between them.[51] At the same time, a range of new state and parastate entities have emerged to aid in the implementation of the law by monitoring public events and scouring social media for possible violations.[52] Any individual can bring a complaint of alleged violation of Article 112 to the police, who are then obliged to investigate and decide whether to send the case to a prosecutor. The prosecutor then decides whether to send the case to court.

Provisions for significant punishment—three to fifteen years per count of defamation, insult, or threat to the king, queen, heir apparent, or regent, with how a count is to be determined left unspecified—is present within the text of Article 112 itself. One striking feature of court commentaries and decisions since the 2006 coup is that the judges have gone far beyond the justification needed by the law in their decisions. In an example of the production of what Thongchai Winichakul calls hyper-royalism, the judges have developed a jurisprudence that centers the monarch as a timeless figure who cannot be impugned.[53] Belief and loyalty are cast as more important than evidence, and citizens are cast as figures always under suspicion and rarely to be believed. Rather than even the bizarre procedural logic offered by the Criminal Court in its dismissal of the charges against Abhisit and Suthep, the tone of the judges in many Article 112 judgments and comments is more akin to that of the opinions expressed by Mo Noi in the best-selling mass paperback *The Karma of Those Who Topple the Monarchy*, in which the crackdown on the red shirts in April–May 2010 is likened to retribution by the gods for daring to occupy a sacred space of the city and the exile, imprisonment, or physical suffering of anyone who dares to question the monarchy is perceived as the righteous reception of one's just karmic desserts.[54]

What makes these (un)just karmic desserts significant is that in the late reign of Rama IX in Thailand they did not exist in a vacuum but rather as one part of the process of creating the monarch as a figure who cannot be impugned and the people, particularly those who were cast as disloyal to the monarch, as those who can be killed with impunity. At the end of his essay about the Criminal Court's dismissal of the charges against Abhisit and Suthep, Nidhi Eoseewong wrote, "Although I have never studied the law, I have come to understand that interpretation of criminal law must rest on the principal that a given interpretation will have far-reaching social consequences now and in the future. Some guilty people may have impunity owing to inefficiencies in the judicial process. But the principle that an action is wrong because it is harmful to the entire society in the short or long term should not be lost simply because some people can get away with it."[55] His analysis is equally relevant in the case of Article 112 prosecutions. What are the broad effects on society and the polity when loyalty becomes more important than evidence in determining guilt? What happens when over time the space in which citizens have the right to express their ideas or question those in power disappears because these actions pose too much of a challenge to a seamless and unquestioned past centered on the monarchy? Two cases adjudicated between 2010 and the 2014 coup—those of Somyot Prueksakasemsuk and Yutthapoom—offer a series of answers.[56]

Somyot Prueksakasemsuk: There Is a Seamless, Unitary Past

On 24 May 2010, in the aftermath of the April–May 2010 violence in Bangkok, Somyot Prueksakasemsuk was arrested and detained by the CRES.[57] He was released after nineteen days with no explanation. Then, on 30 April 2011, he was arrested again and subsequently charged with violating Article 112 in relation to two articles published in *Voice of Taksin* magazine, a print publication for which he was a key member of the editorial team. The reason why I say he was charged *in relation* to the two articles found to be egregious by the prosecutor is that he was not their author. The articles, published under the pseudonym Jit Phonlachan, were written by Jakrapob Penkair.[58] During the long period of pretrial preparations and the trial, despite numerous requests, Somyot was never granted bail.[59] The Criminal Court decision was originally scheduled to be read on 19 December 2012, but it was delayed due to the reading of a comment by the Constitutional Court.[60]

The comment addressed a petition submitted by Somyot, as well as a petition submitted by Ekachai Hongkangwan, who was prosecuted in a separate case for alleged violations of Article 112.[61] If the Constitutional Court accepts the petition of a person currently being prosecuted, the proceedings of the Criminal Court are placed on hold while the petition is examined. The comment addressed whether Article 112 contravenes three provisions of the constitution that protect the rights and liberties of the people. The Constitutional Court's response was unequivocal: it concluded that Article 112 in no way contravenes the constitution.

While the avenue of petition taken up by Somyot and Ekachai is one meant to offer individual citizens a method through which to protect their rights, in this instance the Constitutional Court acted in an antithetical fashion. There is a fundamental tension contained within the constitution that makes this possible. Section 2 reads, "Thailand adopts a democratic regime of government with the King as Head of State." Then immediately following, Section 3 reads, "The sovereign power belongs to the Thai people. The King as Head of State shall exercise such power through the National Assembly, the Council of Ministers and the Courts in accordance with the provisions of this Constitution. The performance of duties of the National Assembly, the Council of Ministers, the Courts, the Constitutional organizations and State agencies shall be in accordance with the rule of law." According to the constitution, sovereignty, then, belongs to both the people and the king. While there may be a context in which this could function democratically, late-reign Rama IX Thailand was not one.[62] This would have required that it be possible to question the relationship between the monarchy and politics or the involvement of the king in regime change, for example, without risking a prison term.

The Constitutional Court framed its comment by further citing Section 8 of the constitution, which elaborates on Section 2 and states, "The King shall be enthroned in a position of revered worship and shall not be violated. No person shall expose the King to any sort of accusation or action."[63] Next the Constitutional Court placed the present-day king within a long, unbroken lineage dating from the thirteenth-century Sukhothai Kingdom (1238–1438 CE) and cast the transformation from absolute to constitutional monarchy in 1932 as one that altered the kind of regime but not the position of the king as head of state in the polity. The Constitutional Court then commented on what this means, offering the following interpretation:

> This demonstrates the great respect, esteem, and admiration held by the people for the institution of the monarchy. The place of the Thai king as the respected and beloved center of the Thai people has been continuous, as shown in age-old royal traditions and legal conventions. The king has administered with virtue and taken action with the intention of the well-being of the people. In particular, King Bhumibol Adulyadej, the current monarch, greatly contributes to the nation and gives royal grace to the Thai people. He visits the people and bestows royally conceived projects in different areas in order to alleviate the suffering and solve the problems and troubles of the people. He teaches the people to subsist in line with the principles of the sufficiency economy by living in line with the middle way, having enough, and being prepared to face changes that might arise.

Ordinary people are aware of the king's conduct and his generosity. They therefore have deep-seated respect, trust, and loyalty for the king and the institution of the monarchy. The long-standing patronage of the Thai king has caused the Thai people to continually respect, love, and admire the king. This is a unique characteristic of Thailand held by no other country."[64]

For this reason, the Constitutional Court explained that the state provides protection because the king is the head of state and the primary institution of the country. The subtext of the claim to uniqueness is that protections that rest on universal ideals of human rights do not apply. The court then noted that Article 112 is a complementary provision of Section 8 of the constitution.

In addition, the Constitutional Court noted that the purpose of Article 112 is to "control the behavior of individuals in society, protect safety, and safeguard public peace for members of society, including strengthening the security in society."[65] The reason it is appropriate to do so is because speech deemed to insult, defame, or threaten the king, queen, heir apparent or regent "may be action that destroys the spirits of Thai people who have respect, love, and are loyal to the king and the institution of the monarchy, and may cause resentment among the people."[66] There is no space for diversity of thought or critical perspectives on the monarchy within the polity in this formulation. If one does not love the king, it follows, then one is perhaps not Thai.

After this introduction, which foreshadowed the Constitutional Court's dismissal of the two petitions at hand and any future petitions, the court turned to specifically address Article 112 of the Criminal Code in relation to Sections 3 (2), 29, and 45 (1, 2) of the constitution. Section 3 (2) of the constitution aims to establish the rule of law as a basis for state administration and states, "The National Assembly, the Council of Ministers, the Courts, other Constitutional organizations and State agencies shall perform duties of office by the rule of law." The petition submitted by Somyot and Ekachai noted that the classification of Article 112 of the Criminal Code as a crime of national security, and the corresponding harsh punishment, was not in line with the rule of law. In response, the Constitutional Court noted that Thailand is a democratic regime with the king as head of state. The court further argued that the monarchy is in a special position, and therefore a special law is just because the monarchy is a primary pillar of the nation, as a result of history, royal tradition, and legal convention.

Here, instead of considering the question of national security, and how an alleged violation of Article 112 of the Criminal Code might affect it, the court directly avoided it. The Constitutional Court instead redefined the rule of law in the Thai context to include special protection for particular individuals within the polity, that is, the king, queen, heir apparent, and regent. The Constitutional Court's understanding of the rule of law is in line with the actually existing rule of law identified by Thongchai Winichakul as one that rests on fundamental inequality between the rulers and the ruled.[67] The people and the king are not equal. The king cannot be impugned, and the people who dare to do so must be locked up.

The Constitutional Court examined Sections 29 and 45 (1, 2) together. Section 29 addresses rights, liberties, and human dignity in a broad sense. It states:

> (1) The restriction of such rights and liberties as recognized by the Constitution shall not be imposed on a person except by virtue of provisions of the law specifically enacted for the purpose determined by this Constitution and only to the extent of necessity and provided that it shall not affect the essential substance of such rights and liberties. (2) The law under paragraph one shall be of general application and shall not be intended to apply to any particular case or person provided that the provision of the Constitution authorizing its enactment shall also be mentioned therein. (3) The provisions of paragraph one and paragraph two shall apply mutatis mutandis to rules or regulations issued by virtue of the provisions of the law.

Section 45 then addresses freedom of expression specifically and states:

> (1) A person shall enjoy the liberty to express his or her opinion, make speeches, write, print, publicize, and make expression by other means. (2) The restriction on liberty under paragraph one shall not be imposed except by virtue of the provisions of law specifically enacted for the purpose of maintaining the security of the State, safeguarding the rights, liberties, dignity, reputation, family or privacy rights of other persons, maintaining public order or good morals or preventing the deterioration of the mind or health of the public.

In response, the Constitutional Court dismissed the concern about these sections and argued that Article 112 of the Criminal Code does not have any effect on freedom of expression. It further noted that freedom of expression must be in line with the constitution, and speech that defames, insults, or threatens the king, queen, heir apparent, or regent is not, and therefore Article 112 of the Criminal Code does not limit freedom of expression. The sheer fact that the Constitutional Court examined this petition while two men were behind bars for words others wrote and they circulated is an illustration of how Article 112 constricts freedom of expression. The broader fear of speaking against, or even querying, the monarchy is more difficult to quantify, yet the law is never far from the minds of all who write and publish in Thailand.

What made the Constitutional Court's action particularly concerning was that it was legally binding and stood as the interpretation of the highest covenant outlining the relationship between the ruler and the ruled in Thailand. This was not the first time that the court had commented on a case related to Article 112 in a fashion that raised serious questions about its role and the place of the constitution in the Thai polity.[68]

Since the Constitutional Court dismissed the petitions submitted by Somyot and Ekachai, the case against Somyot continued in the Criminal Court. A month after the Constitutional Court decision was read, the Criminal Court handed down its decision. On 23 January 2013 the Criminal Court found Somyot guilty of two counts of violating Article 112. The prosecution argued that even though he was not the author of the two articles in question, his work in editing, printing, distributing, and disseminating the two issues of *Voice of Taksin* that contained articles deemed by the prosecutor and the judges to violate Article 112 was a violation equal to authoring the two articles. For the prosecution and convicting judges in this case, as in other lèse majesté cases, the decision turned on the issue of intention. In the abbreviated decision released on the day the judgment was issued, the court made this argument: "The two Khom Khwam Kit articles in *Voice of Taksin* did not refer to the names of individuals in the content but were written with an intention to link incidents in the past. When these incidents in the past are linked, it is possible to identify that (the unnamed individual) refers to King Bhumibol Adulyadej. The content of the articles is insulting, defamatory, and threatening to the king. Publishing, distributing, and disseminating the articles is therefore with the intention to insult, defame, and threaten the king."[69] The king's past cannot be impugned, or even impugned by suggestion. Did putting Somyot behind bars make King Bhumibol, or his reputation, any safer? No. Instead, an editor and human rights defender was deprived of his liberty, and the invisible line that citizens cannot cross before being arrested and prosecuted for violating Article 112 was etched wider and deeper.

Yutthapoom: Loyalty Is More Important Than Evidence

In contrast to the high-profile prosecution of Somyot Prueksakasemsuk, in which fellow domestic and international labor and human rights activists and diplomats filled the courtroom as observers, the trial of Yutthapoom was a quiet prosecution of an ordinary citizen. The majority of the observers in the courtroom were related either to Yutthapoom or to the person who initiated his prosecution, his older brother Thanawat. Yutthapoom and Thanawat operated a business that manufactured and sold car shampoo. Amid what may have begun as ordinary sibling tension, their working relationship soured and they fought about the business and other matters. As the conflict between the two brothers intensified, Thanawat picked one of the most potent tools of punishment available, Article 112, and accused Yutthapoom of insulting the monarchy. Thanawat alleged that Yutthapoom had insulted the monarchy on two separate occasions: he uttered an anti-king statement and later wrote an obscene word in permanent marker on a compact disc (CD) about the king. Even though Thanawat was the only witness to the alleged crimes, which took place inside the house they shared, both the police investigator and the prosecutor advanced the case.[70] In a rare instance of a verdict of innocence being returned in an Article 112 case, Yutthapoom was found not guilty on 12 September 2013 after spending 360 days behind bars awaiting his trial and judgment. The assertion of loyalty, not the evidence of innocence, is what led to Yutthapoom's exoneration. Although Yutthapoom walked free, the adjudication of the case contributed to building a dangerous royalist jurisprudence in which loyalty to the monarchy is prioritized over evidence of having committed a crime.

The witness hearings were held over three days in August 2013 at the Criminal Court in Bangkok. The initial evidentiary problem that Thanawat was the sole witness to the alleged crimes multiplied rapidly as the contention between the brothers and Thanawat's clear enmity for his younger brother emerged as soon as he took the stand as the first witness for the prosecution.[71] One morning in August 2009, the two brothers were at home arguing about politics. Thanawat leaned yellow and Yutthapoom leaned red. The television was on as background noise, and Thanawat alleged that when the king appeared on the screen during a news program, Yutthapoom said, "He ought to die already and bring it all to an end."[72] Then he said, "He is elderly and ought to let his son ascend to the throne. I don't know why he continues on."[73] Thanawat was approximately five meters away from Yutthapoom when he spoke these words to the screen. Their cousin was home at the time as well but was on a different floor. Thanawat testified that he felt dissatisfied when he heard Yutthapoom make these comments, but filing an Article 112 complaint against him did not come to mind. Instead, he warned Yutthapoom that he should not say such things.

Yutthapoom did not heed Thanawat's warning. About five days later, the two brothers were again alone on the first floor of the house while their cousin was upstairs. Thanawat was again approximately five meters from Yutthapoom and noticed that he was using a permanent marker to write on something. He could not see what Yutthapoom was writing on at the time, but he later noticed that a CD that had arrived in the mail shortly before had been altered and left on the common table. The CD had pre-printed text that read "yut kao luang phrachaoyuhua newin kho thaksin" (Newin asks Thaksin not to infringe upon the king), and new text, added below the word "king," read "hua khuai" (dickhead) in parentheses. The writing on the CD made Thanawat uneasy. An echo of the Constitutional Court's claim that actions that impugn the monarch may upset the consciousness of the citizens is present in Thanawat's assertion of discomfort. Thanawat reiterated that he had warned Yutthapoom to cease such actions, but still he did not stop. At this point, he still did not plan to file a complaint against his younger brother.

A month later, Thanawat's wife brought him the CD and commented that the words in permanent marker looked like his younger brother's handwriting. Thanawat put the CD away for safekeeping, "and thought that if the defendant once again insulted the monarchy, then I would file a complaint for prosecution against him. If the defendant did not do it again, then I would just hold onto it."[74] Four or five months later, Thanawat moved out of the house because he felt his younger brother drank too much and did not respect him as the older brother. The modified CD was among the possessions that Thanawat took with him. He heard from a mutual friend that Yutthapoom said that Thanawat had stolen from him in their shared business, which Thanawat assured the prosecutor was untrue.

After a period of time, Yutthapoom invited Thanawat to come back to live in their shared house. But the contention between the two brothers soon became explosive. The brothers had dogs that did not like each other.

The dogs fought, and then they fought. Thanawat kicked through Yuttha-poom's bedroom door and shoved him. Yutthapoom then threatened him with a knife and challenged him to a fight that did not come to pass. Yut-thapoom filed a complaint against Thanawat for assault at the local police station, although Thanawat did not know it at the time. Five days later, the brothers fought again, and Yutthapoom called the police. Thanawat moved out.

This time Thanawat did not return to his brother's house. Instead, he filed a complaint of violation of Article 112 against Yutthapoom because "the defendant behaved badly toward me."[75] Thanawat attempted to file the complaint at three different police stations before it was accepted; the first two refused him on the basis of the weakness of the evidence. When he filed the initial complaint, he had a different recollection of what Yuttha-poom said when the king appeared on the screen than his verbal testimony to the court and thought it was a more pared down statement: "Why hasn't he died already?"[76] Thanawat further noted that he filed the complaint because "the defendant acted inappropriately but was unaware and did not reform himself into a good person. The institution of the monarchy never did anything bad to the defendant, but the defendant spoke ill of it."[77] As he continued, Thanawat defined what it might mean to be a good person in personal rather than political terms: "My testimony that I thought that the defendant was unaware and did not reform himself into a good person means that he did not realize that he should give respect to me as his older brother. I was displeased with the behavior of the defendant toward me and the institution of the monarchy, and so I decided to file a complaint against the defendant."[78] A year separates the two brothers. The bonds of brotherly love might have been enough to keep Thanawat from filing a complaint. Had Yutthapoom realized the error of his ways, Thanawat said that he would not have brought a case against him, as he is his younger brother.

On cross-examination by the defense, Thanawat admitted that he was not certain where he had been standing when the defendant committed the alleged crimes. Nor could he remember the precise words the defen-dant uttered when the king appeared on the television screen, but it had something to do with the king dying. He asserted that the defendant had spoken ill of the monarchy on other occasions, but he had no evidence.

The next witness for the prosecution was Kralamphak Phraekthong, an expert from the Royal Institute, which creates the official dictionary of the Thai language and carries out a range of other cultural, linguistic, and literary activities. She held the weighty Royal Institute dictionary in her arms as she testified. The prosecutor first asked her to interpret the meaning of the parentheses around the word "dickhead" on the CD. She said that she was unable to comment on the intention or the meaning of the parentheses, as they were used contra to correct usage in the Thai language. The prosecutor then asked her to define the word "dickhead." But she refused, as the word did not exist in the official lexicon compiled by the Royal Institute. She could define two constituent words individually, but not the compound word. She offered, "As the Royal Institute Dictionary separates these two words, as I have testified above, when the two words are brought together it is often as an obscenity or insult. This depends on the context and mood of the speaker. For example, if a close friend utters this word, it may only be an impetuous word, not an obscene one. But if it is spoken in anger, then it could perhaps be an obscenity."[79] Intentional or not, her defense of the integrity of the Thai language also operated as a defense of freedom of expression.

The next three witnesses for the prosecution were Yutthapoom's wife, a neighbor, and a handwriting expert. The first two witnesses both offered testimony about the tense relations between the two brothers and their arguments about their dogs and their business. The handwriting expert then testified that her analysis was inconclusive.[80] Given that the offending word had been written on a CD, it was difficult to analyze the force with which the person wrote on the CD, and therefore difficult to compare it to a sample created later. In terms of the shape of the letters and the method of linking the letters, however, she could confirm that it was likely that Yutthapoom was the person who wrote on the CD.

The first defense witness was Yutthapoom himself. His attorney focused on outlining the picture of a deep, thorny contention between the two brothers. Thanawat had physically assaulted Yutthapoom in the past, and their business relationship ended due to malfeasance on Thanawat's part. Yutthapoom testified that he had taken the CD in question from the mailbox and brought it into the house. There was no writing on it at that time, and he did not write on it. On learning that his brother had filed an Article 112 complaint against him, he was shocked and frightened. He testified that he was loyal to the monarchy and whenever he encountered photographs of the king in the newspaper or other printed material, he cut them out so that he could keep them. When he was cross-examined by the prosecutor, Yutthapoom elaborated on his loyalty, commenting, "I am loyal to the monarchy. If I were to discover that any person uttered obscene or inappropriate words against the king, I would file a complaint and bring a case against that person. Even if that person was Mr. Thanawat, my older brother."[81] Yutthapoom followed the lead of the police and prosecutor in bringing the case against him, and the court in accepting it, and defined his loyalty to the monarchy in terms of his readiness to see his own brother prosecuted. Yutthapoom's final comment to the court, in response to re-examination by his lawyer, revealed another layer of incorrect, and illegal, behavior by Thanawat. After he filed the first complaint against Yuttha-poom, he wrote a letter to the effect that if Yutthapoom did not give him fifty thousand baht, he would bring an additional Article 112 complaint against him. Thanawat gave this extortion letter to their mother to give to Yutthapoom.

The judge decided to call a final, unscheduled witness: Yutthapoom and Thanawat's mother. This was a strange decision, as she was present in the courtroom during all the previous testimony, so providing testimony now was in violation of the criminal procedure for witnesses. Nonetheless, she testified that Thanawat had taken advantage of Yutthapoom since the two were young. Over the past six years, Thanawat had never come home to visit her in Srisaket in northeastern Thailand, but Yutthapoom had come home and called often. When she learned of the case, she asked Thanawat why he had filed a complaint against his younger brother, and he said that Yutthapoom was a bad person who had to be put in prison. She confirmed that Thanawat gave her the extortion letter and said that Yutthapoom told her that he did not have the money to pay off Thanawat. The key segment of her testimony, however, focused on her sons' loyalty to the monarchy. She said, "I never heard the defendant say anything bad about the monarchy."[82] She explained further that on days of importance to the monarchy (Father's Day, Mother's Day, Coronation Day), Yuttha-poom returned home to Srisaket and they went to the local temple together to make merit. She noted, "I do not believe that the defendant committed the offence of defaming the institution of the monarchy."[83] She went fur-ther and hinted that her second son might lack excessive loyalty, which had become merely adequate in late-reign Rama IX Thailand: "Mr. Thanawat is loyal to the institution of the monarchy. But when he encounters an image of the king, he does not have a strong desire to possess it. This is different from the defendant, who very much wants the images of the king that he encounters."[84]

Less than a month after the end of hearings, Yutthapoom was found innocent on 13 September 2013. In the decision, the judges noted the contentious relationship between the brothers and the weakness of the evidence. But it was Yutthapoom's loyalty that was decisive. The judges noted that "the defendant and the mother of the defendant testified and maintained that the defendant revered and was loyal to the institution of the monarchy," and therefore the evidence was not doubt proof.[85] Neither the lack of witnesses to Yutthapoom's alleged crimes nor Thanawat's inconsistencies sufficed to secure his innocence, but his professions of loyalty did. This means that the allegation of actions for which there were no witnesses was enough for him to be charged and lose his liberty for nearly a full year and yet loyalty for which there could be no witnesses was enough for him to be exonerated. There is no litmus test for loyalty to the monarchy defined in the Criminal Code, at least not yet. But the case of Yutthapoom indicates that belief in he who cannot be impugned is more important than evidence. After the verdict was read, Yutthapoom went back to the prison to collect his belongings before being released. The CD, however, was confiscated by the court because it had been used in a crime. Although the prosecutor appealed, the Appeal Court upheld the verdict of innocence on 28 November 2014.

History against Oblivion

The cases of the prosecution of Somyot Prueksakasemsuk and Yutthapoom are clear examples of how the law can be used to punish those who have committed public crimes against authority (such as Somyot, who did not shy away from questioning the role of the institution of the monarchy in politics and dared to dissent as an activist and editor), as well as those who have committed private transgressions (such as Yutthapoom, who allegedly failed to treat the monarchy with proper respect but for whom it could only be proved that he did not treat his older brother with the deference he desired). These are only two examples out of a much larger, and growing, number of those who have lost their freedom in the stated service of protecting the institution of the monarchy.

In late-reign Rama IX Thailand, the effects of the prosecutions extended far beyond the individual lives of those prosecuted. In an introduction to the publication of the full decision of the Criminal Court in the case of Somyot Prueksakasemsuk, Thanapol Eawsakul wrote, "The inherent problem of Article 112 at present, then, is not only the law itself but that it is used as a political tool to destroy the spirit of the citizens."[86] By using phrasing that is very close to that of the Constitutional Court when it claimed that acts of lèse majesté destroy the spirit of the citizens, Thanapol underlined the centrality of the people as the object of Article 112. Rather than a measure that primarily functions to protect the institution of the monarchy, the use of Article 112 is pedagogical and the pupils are the Thai people. The prosecutions function as a warning and a form of intimidation deployed against those citizens who might dare to raise a question or express criticism of the institution or the figures within it. The use of this political and pedagogical tool expanded as Rama IX's reign came to an end and the uncertainty felt by those in the corridors of power—whether they wore a crown or hoped to wear a crown, judged from high above the defendants and the people in the court, were clad in military green, or simply aligned themselves with these figures—grew. What they do not yet realize is that placing individuals behind bars for alleged cases of lèse majesté will only reveal their weakness and cannot make them stronger.[87] If and how the use of Article 112 to limit speech and shape the polity will change during the reign of Rama X remains to be seen.

The accounts of the lives and prosecutions of Somyot and Yutthapoom are part of the real history, the history of inequality before the law, that Eduardo Galeano warns risks disappearing in the official history that relies on and produces oblivion. Simultaneous with the acceleration of prosecutions under Article 112, the process of holding Abhisit Vejjajiva and Suthep Thaugsuban to account for their roles in the deaths during the April–May 2010 crackdown on red shirt protesters has come to a halt. The Criminal Court was willing to detain a man for 360 days as he awaited his trial and a decision for allegedly uttering anti-king sentiments in the privacy of his own home, but it would not even convene witness hearings in the case of the premeditated murder of ninety-four people. More than fifty thousand soldiers were deployed and over a hundred thousand bullets were fired between 10 April and 19 May 2010.[88] Although the Abhisit government claimed that it only resorted to the use of the army when negotiations with red shirt leaders failed to secure a resolution, the evidence indicates that these efforts were halfhearted at best. In her introduction to the People's Information Center report, Puangthong Pawakapan is clear: "It was the intentional use of military operations in the city in order to disperse the protests and suppress the red shirt movement. It was not to apply pressure to open negotiations, but to destroy [them]."[89] Murder was not an accident but rather the explicit goal. The reason why the dismissal of the case against Abhisit and Suthep was important is because this, too, was pedagogical. Each time state officials publicly and brazenly get away with killing civilians—whether the figure in question is the prime minister who gives the order or the soldier who pulls the trigger—they learn that they can do it again with no concerns about possible sanctions. And so they do it again.

By taking the simultaneity of these two processes as an invitation to analysis, the foundational inequality underpinning who holds sovereignty in Thailand becomes visible. In both kinds of cases, the court sought recourse in permutations of the written law or departed from it altogether; these departures both signal and bolster inequality before the law. Those who are very powerful and those who are not at all powerful are the ones for whom the law can be bent. Citizens can be killed with impunity, but the king, and the institution of the monarchy, cannot be impugned. Recognition of this inequality is the beginning, not the end, of a new history.

CONCLUSION

History in a Time of Dictatorship

THE COUP FOMENTED BY THE NCPO on 22 May 2014 led to a return to military dictatorship after twenty-three years of civilian rule.[1] Some of the repression conducted under the NCPO has been detailed in this book, including arbitrary detention of dissidents, the promulgation and exercise of Article 44, and the extensive use of Article 112 of the Criminal Code to prosecute citizens for alleged lèse majesté. This is only a fraction of the total range of human rights violations carried out by the junta. In addition, for example, a significant number of those detained by the military under martial law and Article 44, particularly those accused in weapons cases, have alleged that they were tortured while in military custody before being formally charged and transferred to the criminal justice system.[2] Through a comprehensive Forest Master Plan, as well as use of Article 44 and the promulgation of numerous orders, the NCPO has expropriated the land of thousands of rural villagers.[3] Although the junta claims that these actions are in the service of forest preservation, they amount to dispossession of the homes and livelihoods of citizens who are already vulnerable and marginalized. Villagers have been arrested, prosecuted, and sentenced to prison terms for alleged forest encroachment for engaging in subsistence-level agriculture. At the same time, the NCPO and local officials across the country have facilitated the expansion of mining and other national resource extraction projects by Thai and multinational corporations and obstructed villagers' right to protest, or even question, the effects of these projects on their communities. Military courts are being used for the first time since the late 1970s to prosecute civilians for alleged crimes against the crown and state; early reports indicate that the rate of conviction is higher and punishments relatively harsher in the Military Court system compared to the civilian Criminal Court system.[4]

A sharp constriction of freedom of expression and assembly accompanies all the other abrogations of human rights by the NCPO. Political demonstrations of five or more people are criminalized under a junta order, and those who defy it can face prosecution for violation of the order, as well as Article 116 of the Criminal Code or sedition. The list of actions deemed to be criminal protest grows longer and longer as the junta extends its time in power. Standing still on a public street and giving flowers to activists have become crimes.[5] Organizers of academic and other public seminars must ask the military's permission before organizing their events. If they do not do so, the police or military can shut down the event. Even if organizers do secure permission, events may still be closed down, or, at a minimum, be attended by police or military officials, either in uniform or masquerading in civilian dress. Human rights defenders face harassment, threats, and prosecution for documenting and challenging rights violations.[6] The junta follows the print and broadcast media closely and threatens outlets that grow too critical with closure.[7] Due to alliances between many high-level university administrators and the junta, universities are not sites of refuge. Instead, students and academics who speak out face censure and intimidation, rather than support, from university administrators. Prosecution and other penalties for dissent are handed out in an arbitrary fashion, and so one does not know that one has crossed the line until the police or military send an arrest warrant, as they did in the case of six academics who read a declaration criticizing the militarization of universities and calling for support of academic freedom.[8] Surveillance, and the fear of surveillance, of social media platforms for organizing, protesting, and ordinary conversation, including the popular applications Facebook and Line, by both security officials and right-wing royalist-nationalist citizens groups functions as another form of repression.

The threat of being accused, detained, prosecuted, and imprisoned under Article 112 is always present over and above all other repressive mechanisms. Since the 22 May 2014 coup, a record number of people have been prosecuted for lèse majesté, they have been hit with exceptional sentences, and the actions and expression deemed criminal under the law have spiraled in multiple directions. Although the law only specifies that it is applicable to the king, queen, heir apparent, and regent, one person was accused and spent ninety-three days in pretrial detention before being granted bail for allegedly impugning the king's dog, and another two people were sentenced to three years and eight months for defaming one of the princesses.[9] Private communication has become a clear space of danger: taxi conversations and Facebook messenger conversations between two people are enough for one to be charged and prosecuted if the authorities obtain a record of the communication.[10]

Since the NCPO illegally seized power, the Supreme Court has ruled in both Chiranuch Premchaiporn's case under the Computer Crimes Act and the case of the disappearance of Somchai Neelapaijit, the juxtaposed cases with which this book began. Upholding the two lower court decisions, the Supreme Court judged that Chiranuch Premchaiporn was guilty of violating the Computer Crimes Act for not removing a comment deemed to contain lèse majesté on the Prachatai web board *quickly enough.* Although neither the law nor any of the three court decisions specified the precise amount of time she had to do so, the message was pointed and clear. Good citizens must go beyond compliance with the law to be ever vigilant in protecting the monarchy. The vagueness reinforces rather than diminishes this message. In the case of the disappearance of Somchai Neelapaijit, the Supreme Court upheld the decision of the Appeal Court, which reversed the decision of the Court of First Instance. All five police officers accused of being involved in the disappearance of Somchai—they were accused of theft and coercive assault as disappearance does not yet exist as a category of crime in Thai law—were fully exonerated. The Supreme Court also ruled that members of Somchai's family could not join the prosecutor as coplaintiffs, as the evidence did not confirm that Somchai was dead or injured to the degree that he was unable to act on his own behalf. The message of this ruling was also clear. A lawyer can be disappeared because state officials are disquieted when he performs his job of defending human rights. The state officials, including those who carried out the disappearance, those who ordered it, and those who were complicit, will not be held to account. The provision of impunity for individual perpetrators is not sufficient, and so barriers must be put in place to prevent relatives of victims from calling for accountability and participating in the judicial process.

These two cases illustrate the twin processes behind the history of impunity for state violence in Thailand. Any and all questioning, let alone criticism, of the monarch and other figures linked to him must be suppressed.

The reason stated by the jailers is that doing so will affect national security. The jailers do not specify the details of how, for example, a conversation between a taxi driver and his passenger impacts the security of the institution of the monarchy, let alone the security of the nation.[11] State officials, even those who assault, torture, murder, and disappear civilians, must not be held to account. A range of official and unofficial reasons are provided by perpetrators and their spokespeople. In the case of the *thang daeng* killings in 1972, this is because, even though citizens were arbitrarily arrested, detained, tortured, and burned to death in oil drums, the state investigation determined that *only* seventy to eighty people were killed. Punishing the state officials involved would only serve to discourage them in their important work of fighting the communists. The lives of the people are expendable in the preservation of the nation. During the rush to pass the first amnesty for the 6 October 1976 massacre and coup at the end of 1976, those who supported the amnesty cited the devotion and love of the monarchy of those who were involved in the violence that day as the reason why it should be passed. If those who kill the people do so out of loyalty to the institution of the monarchy, then they should be rewarded with exemption from prosecution for their crimes.

When a link to the monarchy could not be plausibly claimed in the case against former prime minister Abhisit Vejjajiva and former deputy prime minister Suthep Thaugsuban for ordering the use of deadly force against red shirt protesters in April–May 2010, the Criminal Court adapted a technique used to exonerate state officials who killed citizens in southern Thailand. Resonant with the findings in postmortem inquests in the cases of the Tak Bai massacre and the torture and murder of Imam Yapa Kaseng, which ruled that state officials were responsible for the deaths but they occurred while the officials were performing their civil service duties, the Criminal Court dismissed the case against Abhisit and Suthep with the claim that it was outside their jurisdiction.[12] The alleged crimes were committed while Abhisit and Suthep held political office, and so the only body that could examine their actions was the NACC. The decision was decried as both unjust and legally incorrect by the attorney general, the families of those killed, and, in a rare dissenting opinion, the chief justice of the Criminal Court. The decision, which the Criminal Court released three months after the coup by the NCPO, was both unjust and legally incorrect, but it was in line with the history of impunity in postabsolutist Thailand. The indictment of two former state officials for their role in a massacre of civilians, rather than their exoneration, was the aberration. Rather than being defined by holding a monopoly on legitimate violence, the exercise, repetition, and impunity for illegitimate violence is both the defining characteristic of the Thai state and the way it is formed.

Revealing the identities, interests, and networks of those behind the twin set of processes—the killing of people with impunity and the prohibition against impugning the monarch—remains impossible and may have reached its apogee under the NCPO.[13] In response, I traced the history of this impossibility in this book. Drawing primarily on documentary sources in the public record, I wrote a history of state violence and the evasion of accountability for it from the end of the absolute monarchy on 24 June 1932 up to the 22 May 2014 coup. Newspaper reportage, newsletters of human rights groups, and the memoirs of civil servants and state security officials contain enough information to piece together an account of state violence. State archival records, including those concerned with the drafting of laws, the examination of draft laws, and engagement in the international human rights regime, provide evidence of the changing perspectives on violence, accountability, and human rights within state agencies. Using sources already in the public record was a decision at once practical, political, and analytic. I have not cultivated the relationships necessary to obtain access to secret military, police, and other state records. Perhaps public access to these records will be possible in the future if a different, more just and democratic regime comes to power. The analytic reason, which is more important than the practical or political ones, is that the production of impunity and its history are public processes that take place in plain sight of all in the polity. Impunity engenders widespread fear because state officials evade responsibility in public ways. The glaring visibility of this process reinforces impunity's lessons of vulnerability. Drawing on sources already in the public record then makes it possible to write a history of impunity cognizant of this public pedagogy.

Although I completed my research several months prior to the 2014 coup, I drafted this manuscript during the first two years of rule by the NCPO. During these two years, my time and attention were divided between writing this history of impunity and lending support to colleagues by participating in the small ways a foreign academic can to oppose dictatorship, primarily aiding in writing and editing reports and appeals on rights violations committed by the junta and translating firsthand accounts and commentaries on repression. Particularly during the first six months after the coup, weeks went by when I was consumed with work that followed the day-to-day calendar of an activist, and I did not even pick up the book manuscript. But when I began to do so again, and spent my days reading and writing about Field Marshal Sarit's exercise of absolute power through Article 17 and my evenings reading and working to keep track of General Prayuth's copious orders under Article 44, I heard Alfred W. McCoy's call to do the detailed labor of writing histories of impunity anew.[14]

The pen of the historian cannot bring perpetrators of torture and disappearance to account or end extrajudicial killing. Nor can it force soldiers back to their barracks or unlock the prison cells where people are confined for daring to express their opinions. But what careful academic research *can* do is uncover and examine the conditions under which state security officials get away with torture, arbitrary detention, disappearance, and other forms of violence, over and over again. This repetition of state violence has come to structure the relationships between the rulers and the ruled in Thailand. The experience of being a state official is characterized by the ability to commit violent acts against citizens without being held to account, and that of being a citizen is characterized by the knowledge that state officials can assault, torture, disappear, or kill you and will likely get away with it.

The history of impunity for state violence from 1932 up to the present in Thailand demonstrates that the repetition of state violence over time creates the conditions for it to continue. These conditions include the passage of amnesty laws that protect state perpetrators and the passage of other laws that strip citizens of their rights. They also include courts that issue rulings that rely on a particular notion of morality, rather than law, as the foundation of jurisprudence; systematized intimidation of witnesses in the few cases of state violence that make it to the courts; and actions that seem to support accountability but result in its foreclosure, such as responding to petition letters from human rights activists demanding an end to torture. Not only does repetition cause violence to become entrenched, but the collection of ministries, departments, and other agencies that comprise the Thai state come into being and cohere by acting violently against citizens and other civilians and then evading responsibility for these actions.

In 1979, in "For Memory," the poet Adrienne Rich wrote about the struggle for liberation in life and politics: "freedom is daily, prose-bound, routine / remembering. Putting together, inch by inch / the starry worlds. From all the lost collections."[15] Her words are equally applicable to the writing of histories of impunity. I close with an explicit admission of partiality and a call for continued work. The "particular bundle of silences," to again use Michel-Rolph Trouillot's words, that I addressed in this book is the beginning of a history of impunity in Thailand rather than a comprehensive and definitive account.[16] The oblivion built into both state violence and the evasion of accountability for it means that the process of uncovering and writing about the many decades of impunity in Thailand since the end of the absolute monarchy is a recursive, ongoing process. Every day the NCPO commits new human rights violations and produces new evidence of violence. Some perpetrators and survivors are writing their own stories or may be willing to talk to people who are willing to listen. Hundreds of thousands more pages of newspaper, archival, court, and other printed documents await readers alert to inconsistencies, lacunae, and unanswered questions. These are the sources of the lost collections, and the starry worlds that activists and scholars assemble from them will shine with the possibility of justice.

APPENDIX

A New, Partial Chronology of Thai History

One of the premises of this book is that marking time by means of coups, constitutions, and kings suggests an instability that elides the underlying continuity of state violence and impunity. Without attention to state violence and impunity, the understanding of the recent past, and the relationship between the past and present, will remain fundamentally incomplete. In response, the chapters of this book offer a new chronology by placing both the production of impunity and challenges to it at the center of analysis. Here this information is presented in abbreviated, list form. The instances of impunity and challenges to it are listed alongside moments of regime change; the chapter in which an instance is discussed is noted in parentheses at the end of the relevant entry. This chronology itself remains partial both because only the violent events discussed in this book are listed and because the history of impunity is one that will continue to be written as long as state officials continue to perpetrate violence and violations of the human rights of the people.

24 June 1932 Transformation from absolute to constitutional monarchy by the People's Party.

27 June 1932 Temporary Charter for the Administration of Siam of 1932 is promulgated.

10 December 1932 Constitution of the Kingdom of Thailand of 1932 is promulgated.

20 June 1933   Coup by General Phraya Phahon against the civilian government of Phraya Manopakorn Nititada.

21 January 1945   Act for the Internment of Those who are a Danger to the Nation during Emergency Times is passed (1).

9 May 1946   Constitution of the Kingdom of Thailand of 1946 is promulgated.
    Act for the Internment of Those Who Are a Danger to the Nation during Emergency Times is repealed (1).

9 June 1946   Death of Rama VIII, King Ananda Mahidol.
    Beginning of the reign of Rama IX, Bhumibol Adulyadej.

8 November 1947   Coup by the *khana thahan* (military group).

25 November 1947   Constitution of the Kingdom of Thailand (Interim) of 1947 is promulgated.

6 April 1948   Coup by the *khana thahan* (military group) to replace the civilian prime minister it had selected, Khuang Aphaiwong, with Field Marshal Plaek Phibunsongkhram.

10 December 1948   The UDHR is adopted by the United Nations, with Siam as one of the signatories.

23 January 1949   Constitution of the Kingdom of Thailand of 1949 is promulgated.

29 November 1951   Autocoup by the *khana thahan* (military group).

10 December 1951   First celebration of the UDHR held in Thailand (2).

8 March 1952   Constitution of the Kingdom of Thailand of 1932 (revised 1952) is promulgated.

13 November 1952   The ACAA of 1952 is promulgated (3).

12 December 1952   Tieng Sirikhan, a member of parliament from Sakhon Nakhon, is disappeared (6).

24 March 1954   Porn Malitong, a politician who opposes General Phao Sriyanond, is disappeared (6).

13 August 1954   Haji Sulong, a dissident religious and cultural leader in southern Thailand, is disappeared (6).

16 September 1957   Coup by Field Marshal Sarit Thanarat against the government of Field Marshal Phibun Songkhram.

20 October 1958   Autocoup by Field Marshal Sarit Thanarat.

2 November 1958   Decree 21 for the arbitrary detention of "hooligans" is issued (1).

10 January 1959   Decree 43, giving further power to state officials to arbitrarily detain "hooligans," is issued (1).

28 January 1959   Charter for the Administration of the Kingdom of 1959 is promulgated. It contains Article 17, a measure that provides for the exercise of arbitrary, unchecked executive power by the prime minister (2).

26 June 1959   Sila Wongsin is executed with the authorization of an order issued under Article 17 for the alleged crime of presenting himself as a god and a king (2).

6 July 1959   Supachai Srisati is executed with the authorization of an order issued under Article 17 for the alleged crime of communism (2).

31 May 1961   Khrong Chandawong and Thongphan Sutthimat are executed with the authorization of an order issued under Article 17 for the alleged crime of communism (2).

29 August 1961   Liang Ho Sae Lao is executed with the authorization of an order issued under Article 17 for the alleged crime of heroin production (2).

24 April 1962   Ruam Wongphan is executed with the authorization of an order issued under Article 17 for the alleged crime of communism (2).

1963   Supreme Court rules that the extended detention of Mr. Yiem Phunman under Decrees 21 and 43 was illegal (1).

9 December 1963   Field Marshal Sarit Thanarat dies and dictatorship continues under Field Marshal Thanom Kittikhachorn.

20 June 1968   Constitution of the Kingdom of Thailand of 1968 is promulgated. No arbitrary, executive power provision is included (2).

12 February 1969   The ACAA of 1969 is promulgated (3).

17 November 1971   Autocoup by Field Marshal Thanom Kittikhachorn.

15 December 1972   Temporary Charter for the Administration of the Kingdom of 1972 is promulgated. It contains an expansion of Article 17 first found in the 1959 charter (2).

August 1972   The *thang daeng* killings begin in Phatthalung in southern Thailand (3).

14 October 1973   Dictatorship ends with the ouster of Field Marshal Thanom Kittikhachorn's government following a popular uprising.

24 January 1974   The village of Ban Na Sai in northeastern Thailand is burned to the ground (3).

February–March 1974   Activist and state investigations are conducted into the burning of the village of Ban Na Sai. Activists conclude that the village was burned by state officials, but the state refuses to release its conclusions (3).

7 October 1974   Constitution of the Kingdom of Thailand of 1974 is promulgated. No arbitrary, executive power provision is included (2).

1975   Transitions to communist governments occur in Vietnam, Cambodia, and Laos.

12 February 1975   Decrees 21 and 43 are nullified (1).

February 1975   The *thang daeng* killings are exposed by students and villagers, who then carry out their own investigation and call for a state investigation (3).

Late March 1975   A summary of the state investigation into the *thang daeng* killings is released. Although there is acknowledgment that state officials extrajudicially killed civilians, no one is held to account (3).

6 October 1976   Massacre of students at Thammasat University and coup by the NARC against the civilian government of Prime Minister Seni Pramoj. The student survivors, rather than the state perpetrators, are arrested, imprisoned, and charged with grave crimes (4).

13 October 1976   Order 22 for the arbitrary detention of those deemed a "danger to society" is issued (1).

22 October 1976   Constitution of the Kingdom of Thailand of 1976 is promulgated. Like Article 17 in earlier constitutions, Article 21 provides arbitrary, executive power to the prime minister (2).

24 December 1976   Amnesty for Those Who Seized the Administrative Power of the Country on 6 October 1976 Act is promulgated (4).

16 April 1977   The CGRS is formally established in Thailand and undertakes comprehensive documentation of human rights violations and support for political prisoners and other victims and survivors (5).

23 and 30 June 1977   Hearings on Human Rights in Thailand are held in Washington, DC, by the Subcommittee on International Organizations of the US House Committee on International Relations (5).

20 October 1977   Coup against the dictatorial government of Prime Minister Thanin Kraivichien by General Kriangsak Chomanan.

9 November 1977   Charter for the Administration of the Kingdom of 1977 is promulgated. Like Article 17 and other earlier measures, Article 27 provides arbitrary, executive power to the prime minister (2).

11 April 1978   With assistance and information provided by the CGRS, AI launches its first appeal for human rights in Thailand and calls for the release of political prisoners and an end to torture. In response, the MFA denies that torture or other rights violations take place (5).

16 September 1978   Amnesty for Those Who Committed Wrongdoing at Thammasat University between 4 and 6 October 1976 is promulgated. The charges against the Bangkok Eighteen are dropped and they are released from prison (4).

22 December 1978   Constitution of the Kingdom of Thailand of 1978 is promulgated. Like Article 17 and earlier measures, Article 200 provides arbitrary, executive power to the prime minister (2).

1 March 1979   The ACAA of 1979 is promulgated (3).

7 August 1979   Order 22 is nullified (1).

23 April 1981   Prime Ministerial Order No. 66/2523 is promulgated and communism is partially decriminalized (3).

23 February 1991   Coup by General Suchinda Krapayoon and the National Peace Keeping Council against the civilian government of Prime Minister Chatichai Choonhavan.

1 March 1991   Charter for the Administration of the Kingdom of 1991 is promulgated. Like Article 17 and earlier measures, Article 27 provides arbitrary, executive power to the prime minister (2).

19 June 1991   Thanong Pho-an, senator and labor activist, is disappeared (6).

9 December 1991   Constitution of the Kingdom of Thailand of 1991 is promulgated.

May 1992   Crackdown on democracy protesters, including the disappearance of a disputed number of people (6).

11 October 1997   Constitution of the Kingdom of Thailand of 1997 is promulgated.

2 June 2000   The ACAA 1979 is nullified (3).

February–May 2002   More than two thousand people are killed or disappeared as part of the so-called War on Drugs (6).

4 January 2004   Martial law is declared in southern Thailand. Up to seven days of arbitrary detention are permitted (1).

12 March 2004   Somchai Neelapaijit, a lawyer and human rights defender, is disappeared (6).

April 2004   Following actions by human rights activists and Angkhana Neelapaijit, Somchai's wife, five police officers are arrested and charged in relation to Somchai's disappearance. There is no crime of disappearance in Thai law, so they are charged with assault, theft, and coercion. Bail is granted (6).

19 July 2005   Emergency rule is declared in southern Thailand. An additional thirty days of arbitrary detention on top of the seven permitted under martial law are allowed, for a total of up to thirty-seven days (1).

12 January 2006   Court of First Instance finds one police officer guilty of coercion but fully exonerates the four other officers in the case of the disappearance of Somchai Neelapaijit (6).

19 September 2006   Coup by the CDRM against the civilian government of Prime Minister Thaksin Shinawatra.

1 October 2006   Constitution of the Kingdom of Thailand (Interim) of 2006 is promulgated.

19 August 2007   Constitution of the Kingdom of Thailand of 2007 is promulgated.

30 October 2007   Chumpon, Ranong, and Surat Thani provincial courts rule on limits to arbitrary detention in southern Thailand (1).

10 April–19 May 2010   Military crackdown on red shirt protesters under the government of Prime Minister Abhisit Vejjajiva. At least ninety-four people are killed and more than two thousand are injured (7).

11 March 2011   Appeal Court exonerates all five police officers in the case of the disappearance of Somchai Neelapaijit and rules that his widow and children cannot be coplaintiffs in the case (6).

30 April 2011   Somyot Prueksakasemsuk is arrested and charged with violating Article 112 of the Criminal Code (lèse majesté) for publishing two articles deemed to defame the monarchy in *Voice of Taksin*, a magazine he edited. Bail is denied (7).

7 August 2012   Yutthapoom (family name withheld) is arrested and charged with violating Article 112 of the Criminal Code after his older brother accuses him of committing lèse majesté within the walls of their shared home. Bail is denied (7).

10 October 2012   Constitutional Court rules that there is no conflict between the enforcement of Article 112 and the protection of rights and liberties as stipulated in the 2007 constitution (7).

23 January 2013   Criminal Court sentences Somyot Prueksakasemsuk to ten years in prison for violation of Article 112, plus an additional year from an earlier case (7).

12 September 2013   Criminal Court dismisses the Article 112 case against Yutthapoom, and he is released from prison (7).

28 October 2013   The OAG announces that it will bring criminal charges of premeditated murder against Abhisit Vejjajiva and Suthep Thaugsuban for their roles, as prime minister and deputy prime minister, in the crackdown on red shirt protesters. They are indicted in December 2013 and May 2014, respectively. Bail is granted (7).

17 April 2014   Porlachee "Billy" Rakchongcharoen, Karen activist, is disappeared (6).

22 May 2014   Coup by the NCPO.
   Arbitrary detention of dissidents begins, first under martial law, declared two days prior to the coup, and later under Article 44 of the 2014 interim constitution (1).

22 July 2014   Constitution of the Kingdom of Thailand (Interim) of 2014 is promulgated. Like Article 17 and prior measures, Article 44 provides arbitrary, executive power to the prime minister (2).

28 August 2014   Criminal Court dismisses the case against Abhisit Vejjajiva and Suthep Thaugsuban in relation to the 2010 crackdown on red shirt protesters. The OAG and the families of those killed appeal (7).

29 December 2015   Supreme Court upholds the decision of the Appeal Court to exonerate the police officers and deny family members the right to be coplaintiffs in the case of the disappearance of Somchai Neelapaijit (6).

13 October 2016   Death of Rama IX, Bhumibol Adulyadej. Beginning of the reign of Rama X, Maha Vajiralongkorn.

NOTES

PREFACE

1. Pakavadi Mai Mi Nam Sakun, "Memory, Fear, and Truth Following Dictatorship," *Aan* 3, no. 1 (October–December 2553 [2010]), 91.

2. See People's Information Center for Those Affected by the Dispersal of Protests in April–May 2010, *Truth for Justice: The Incident and Effects of the Dispersal of Protests in April–May 2010* (Bangkok: People's Information Center, 2555 [2012]).

3. Pakavadi, "Memory," 91.

4. Howard Zinn, *A People's History of the United States* (New York: Harper Perennial, 2005), 10.

INTRODUCTION

1. If one counts the transformation from absolute to constitutional monarchy by the People's Party on 24 June 1932 as a coup, then there were thirteen successful coups.

2. Max Weber, "Politics as a Vocation," in *Weber's Rationalism and Modern Society: New Translations on Politics, Bureaucracy, and Social Stratification*, ed. and trans. Tony Waters and Dagmar Waters (New York: Palgrave Macmillan, 2015).

3. Fred Riggs, *Thailand: The Modernization of a Bureaucratic Polity* (Honolulu: East-West Center Press, 1967); Duncan McCargo, "Network Monarchy and Legitimacy Crises in Thailand," *Pacific Review* 18, no. 4 (2005): 499–519; Eugenie Merieau, "Thailand's Deep State, Royal Power, and the Constitutional Court (1997–2015)," *Journal of Contemporary Asia* 46, no. 3 (2016): 445–66.

4. The name Siam was used until 1939, when it was changed to Thailand in one of the twelve *rathhaniyom*, or "statisms," decreed by Field Marshal Phibunsongkhram; Siam was used again from 1945 to 1949. See Thak Chaloemtiarana, ed.,

Thai Politics: Extracts and Documents, 1932–1957 (Bangkok: Social Science Association of Thailand, 1978), for a full translation of the twelve statisms.

5. Michel-Rolph Trouillot, *Silencing the Past: Power and the Production of History* (Boston: Beacon Press, 1995).

6. Verne Harris, "The Archival Sliver: Power, Memory, and Archives in South Africa," *Archival Science* 2, no.1 (2002): 64n3.

7. See Dawne Adam, "The Tuol Sleng Archives and the Cambodian Genocide," *Archivaria* 45 (1998): 5–26.

8. The story of the Brazilian project's genesis, operations, challenges, and successes can be found in Lawrence Weschler, *A Miracle, a Universe: Settling Accounts with Torturers* (New York: Pantheon, 1990). For the final activist report, in Portuguese, see Catholic Church and Paulo Evaristo Arns, *Brasil: Nunca mais* (Petrópolis: Vozes, 1986). In English, see Catholic Church, Joan Dassin, and Jaime Wright, *Torture in Brazil: A Report* (New York: Vintage, 1986), which was republished as Catholic Church, Joan Dassin, and Jaime Wright, *Torture in Brazil: A Shocking Report on the Pervasive Use of Torture by Brazilian Military Governments, 1964–1979* (Austin: Institute of Latin American Studies, University of Texas, 1998).

9. The story of the discovery of the archive and the initial work of making the documents usable can be found in Kate Doyle, "Letter from Guatemala—The Atrocity Files—Deciphering the Archives of Guatemala's Dirty War," *Harper's*, December 2007, 52–64. See an ethnographic account of the establishment of the archive in Kirsten Weld, *Paper Cadavers: The Archives of Dictatorship in Guatemala* (Durham, NC: Duke University Press, 2014). A partial collection of the archive's documents can be found online as the Archivo Histórico de la Policia Nacional at https://ahpn.lib.utexas.edu/home.

10. James C. Scott, *Domination and the Arts of Resistance: Hidden Transcripts* (New Haven, CT: Yale University Press, 1992).

11. Although the police and military archives are not open to the public, records in *some* cases, in particular the 6 October 1976 case and some cases of those accused under the Anti-Communist Activities Act, are available in the library at the Office of the Attorney General (OAG). Two important articles published on 6 October 1976 have drawn on these materials: Thongchai Winichakul, "6 October in Rightist Memories (1976–2006): From Victory to Silence (but Still Victorious)," in *Violence Hides/Seeks Thai Society*, ed. Chaiwat Satha-anand (Bangkok: Matichon, 2553 [2010]), 407–512; and Thanapol Eawsakul and Chaithawat Tulathon, "The Struggle of the Defendants in the 6 October Case under the (In)Justice Process after the 6 October 1976 Coup," *Fa Diew Kan* 12, nos. 2–3 (May–December 2557 [2014]): 296–333. Finally, a different person might have chosen to interview perpetrators instead, such as was done in Joshua Oppenheimer's very thought-provoking film about the 1965–66 killings of suspected communists in Indonesia, *The Act of Killing* (2012).

12. Robin Wagner-Pacifici, "The Innocuousness of State Lethality in an Age of National Security," *South Atlantic Quarterly* 107, no. 3 (2008): 465.

13. A *wai* is a Thai greeting of respect made by holding one's palms together and bowing slightly.

14. Alfred W. McCoy, *Torture and Impunity: The U.S. Doctrine of Coercive Interrogation* (Madison: University of Wisconsin Press, 2012), 218–19.

15. Diane Orentlicher, "Updated Set of Principles for the Protection and Promotion of Human Rights through Action to Combat Impunity," Commission on Human Rights, Economic and Social Council, 8 February 2005, E/CN.4/2005/102/Add.1.

16. Ibid., 12.

17. In his account of impunity for torture by US state security forces, McCoy further notes that "by reconstructing this past and recovering its patterns, history allows the public to discover a larger design, seeing torture as an ineffective instrument for national security, impunity as the means for its persistence, and, on occasion, the past as prologue to prevention." McCoy, *Torture and Impunity*, 218–19.

18. Karl Marx, "Theses on Feuerbach," trans. William Lough, in *Marx/Engels Selected Works*, vol. 1 (Moscow: Progress Publishers, 1969), 15.

19. Kathryn Sikkink, *The Justice Cascade: How Human Rights Prosecutions Are Changing World Politics* (New York: Norton, 2011), 5. The database can be accessed online at http://www.transitionaljusticedata.com.

20. Ibid., 13.

21. Ibid.

22. Ibid., 18.

23. This is particularly true if one begins the timeline before 1970, which is the starting point for Sikkink's and several other large-scale databases variously tracking amnesties, prosecutions, and truth commissions in which there has been some form of a transition to democracy. While Thailand surfaces in all of these databases, the information is often fragmentary. This is not surprising, given that the sources for the databases are primarily English-language sources, including newspapers and Amnesty International reports, which are themselves fragmentary and incomplete. My criticism is not meant to invalidate or discredit the databases, which provide an important broad picture, but rather to suggest that a different kind of analysis of impunity and accountability can emerge from finely grained historical research. The other two databases are the Amnesty Law database directed by Louise Mallinder (http://incore.incore.ulst.ac.uk/Amnesty/) and the Transitional Justice Database Project directed by Leigh Payne, Tricia Olsen, and Andrew Reiter (http://www.tjdbproject.com/).

24. Sikkink, *Justice Cascade*, 22–23.

25. Pridi Banomyong, *Pridi by Pridi: Selected Writings on Life, Politics, and Economy*, trans. Chris Baker and Pasuk Phongpaichit (Chiang Mai: Silkworm Books, 2000), 124–25.

26. Nattapoll Chaiching, *Dream the Impossible Dream: Counter-revolutionary Movements in Siam (1932–1957)* (Bangkok: Fa Diew Kan Press, 2556 [2013]), 16. Nattapoll's book is an excellent analysis of the many different forms of counter-revolution that animated the first twenty-five years following the transformation from absolute to constitutional monarchy. The examples I note here are only a small fraction of the many that he exposes through careful analysis.

27. Ibid., 11–12.

28. Ibid., 14–15.

29. Thongchai Winichakul, "An Experimental Proposal: Impunity and the Understanding of Human Rights in Thai-Style Rule of Law," *Fa Diew Kan* 14, no. 2 (May–December 2559 [2016]): 202.

30. Ibid., 201.

31. Ibid., 197. Thongchai uses the phrase *abhisit plod khwam phid* (privilege of exemption from guilt) to describe impunity rather than the more common *kan loy nuan phon phid* (floating [away] to escape guilt).

32. For example, the Constitutional Court justified the restrictions on freedom of speech under Article 112 on the basis of the unique love for the monarchy held by Thai citizens in response to a petition submitted by Somyot Prueksakasemsuk. See chapter 7 for a further discussion of this case.

33. Benedict Anderson, "Studies of the Thai State: The State of Thai Studies," in *The Study of Thailand: Analyses of Knowledge, Approaches, and Prospects in Anthropology, Art History, Economics, History, and Political Science*, ed. Eliezer B. Ayal (Athens: Center for International Studies, Ohio University, 1978), 197.

34. Ibid., 199.

35. Ibid., 197.

36. For example, see academic work published by Nidhi Eoseewong, Thongchai Winichakul, Somsak Jeamteerasakul, Kasian Tejapira, Attachak Sattayanurak, Saichol Sattayanurak, Prajak Kongkirati, Nattapoll Chaiching, and Thanavi Chotpradit. A significant body of work has also been produced outside universities, including the books and articles published by Fa Diew Kan and An, two progressive publishing houses established in 2003 and 2009, respectively. Two writer-translators who have made particularly significant contributions to thought are Pipob Udomittipong and Pakavadi Veerapaspong.

37. Giorgio Agamben, *State of Exception*, trans. Kevin Attell (Chicago: University of Chicago Press, 2005), 4.

38. David Streckfuss, *Truth on Trial: Defamation, Treason, and Lèse-Majesté* (New York: Routledge, 2011); and David Streckfuss, "The End of the Endless Exception? Time Catches Up with Dictatorship in Thailand," Fieldsights—Hot Spots, *Cultural Anthropology Online*, 23 September 2014, http://www.culanth.org/fieldsights/567-the-end-of-the-endless-exception-time-catches-up-with-dictatorship-in-thailand.

39. Research informed by this assumption then examines how fully principles have been implemented in matters such as, for example, women's rights. See Sally Merry, *Human Rights and Gender Violence: Translating International Law into Local Justice* (Chicago: University of Chicago Press, 2006).

40. The UDHR became the basis for two more legally binding treaties: the International Covenant on Civil and Political Rights (ICCPR); and the International Covenant on Economic, Social, and Cultural Rights (ICESCR). The ICCPR was adopted by the UN on 16 December 1966 and entered into force on 23 March 1976; Thailand became a state party to the ICCPR on 29 October 1996. The ICESCR was adopted by the UN on 16 December 1966 and entered into force on 3 January 1976; Thailand became a state party to the ICESCR on 5 September 1999.

41. Eight member nations abstained from voting on the UDHR.

42. Samuel Moyn, *The Last Utopia: Human Rights in History* (Cambridge, MA: Belknap Press of Harvard University Press, 2010), 81. For similar assessments, see Jan Eckel and Samuel Moyn, eds., *The Breakthrough: Human Rights in the 1970s* (Philadelphia: University of Pennsylvania Press, 2013); Akira Iriye, Petra Goedde, and William I. Hitchcock, eds., *The Human Rights Revolution: An International History* (Oxford: Oxford University Press, 2012); and Barbara J. Keys, *Reclaiming American Virtue: The Human Rights Revolution of the 1970s* (Cambridge, MA: Harvard University Press, 2014).

43. Moyn, *Last Utopia*, 42–43.

44. The *UN Human Rights Yearbook* contained information submitted by member nations about the passage of relevant laws, court decisions, and other material relevant to the exercise of human rights. It was published annually from 1946 until 1973 and then biannually until 1988. After 1988, individual treaty bodies set up reporting mechanisms for state parties. For analysis of Thailand's submissions to the yearbook in relation to arbitrary detention, see Tyrell Haberkorn, "An Uneasy Engagement: Political Crisis and Human Rights Culture in Thailand, 1958 to 1988," in *Rights to Culture: Heritage, Language, and Community in Thailand*, ed. Coeli Barry (Chiang Mai: Silkworm Books and Princess Maha Chakri Sirindthorn Anthropology Centre, 2013), 115–34.

45. Revolutionary Announcement No. 4 noted that the coup would "respect and protect human rights according to the Universal Declaration of Human Rights made by the assembly of the United Nations. [The revolution] will not do anything out of step or to violate the Declaration, other than if there are situations in which it is truly necessary to do so in order to ensure the safety of the nation." *Ratchakitchanubeksa*, special issue, book 75, part 81, 20 October 2501 [1958], 14.

46. Moyn, *The Last Utopia*, 47.

47. There is a relatively rich body of scholarship on the use of human rights in struggles *against* Soviet and other authoritarian communist and socialist regimes but little about the use of human rights by the same regimes. The paucity grows even more severe when one examines the scholarship focused on Asia. An important

exception is Brad Simpson's work on the use of human rights by and against the Suharto regime in Indonesia. See his "'Human Rights Are Like Coca-Cola': Contested Human Rights Discourses in Suharto's Indonesia," in *The Breakthrough: Human Rights in the 1970s*, ed. Jan Eckel and Samuel Moyn (Philadelphia: University of Pennsylvania Press, 2013), 186–203.

48. Moyn, *The Last Utopia*, 214.

49. See the appendix to this volume for a partial chronology of Thai history in which the typical markers of time (coups, reigns) are interspersed with the instances of state violence and production of impunity traced in this book.

50. Thak Chaloemtiarana, *Thailand: The Politics of Despotic Paternalism* (Bangkok: Social Science Association of Thailand, 1979), 127.

51. Leigh Payne, *Unsettling Accounts: Neither Truth nor Reconciliation in Confessions of State Violence* (Durham, NC: Duke University Press, 2007), 285.

CHAPTER 1. THE REPETITION OF ARBITRARY DETENTION

1. See, for example, two books published in both English and Thai (and translated into many other languages): Chris Baker and Pasuk Phongpaichit, *A History of Thailand* (New York: Cambridge University Press, 2005); and David K. Wyatt, *Thailand: A Short History* (New Haven, CT: Yale University Press, 1984).

2. See Thongchai Winichakul, "The Changing Landscape of the Past: New Histories in Thailand since 1973," *Journal of Southeast Asian Studies* 26, no. 1 (1995): 99–120; and Chris Baker, "Afterword," in *Pen and Sail: Literature and History in Early Bangkok*, by Nidhi Eoseewong (Chiang Mai: Silkworm Books, 2005).

3. The US government's detention without official charge of those deemed "terrorists" at the Guantánamo Bay Detention Center is a notable recent example. Other examples include South Africa during the apartheid regime; Argentina, Brazil, Chile, and Uruguay during the years of the dirty wars; and Egypt and Syria since 2010. The unending nature of the list indicates the gravity of the problem of arbitrary detention.

4. The ICCPR was adopted by the UN General Assembly on 16 December 1966 and entered into force on 23 March 1976. Thailand ratified it on 29 October 1996. The full text of Article 9 reads: "1) Everyone has the right to liberty and security of person. No one shall be subjected to arbitrary arrest or detention. No one shall be deprived of his liberty except on such grounds and in accordance with such procedure as are established by law. 2) Anyone who is arrested shall be informed, at the time of arrest, of the reasons for his arrest and shall be promptly informed of any charges against him. 3) Anyone arrested or detained on a criminal charge shall be brought promptly before a judge or other officer authorized by law to exercise judicial power and shall be entitled to trial within a reasonable time or to release. It shall not be the general rule that persons awaiting trial shall be detained in custody, but release may be subject to guarantees to appear for trial, at any other stage of the judicial proceedings, and, should occasion arise, for execution of

the judgment. 4) Anyone who is deprived of his liberty by arrest or detention shall be entitled to take proceedings before a court, in order that that court may decide without delay on the lawfulness of his detention and order his release if the detention is not lawful. 5) Anyone who has been the victim of unlawful arrest or detention shall have an enforceable right to compensation."

5. United Nations Working Group on Arbitrary Detention, "Fact Sheet #26 of the Office of the High Commissioner for Human Rights: The Working Group on Arbitrary Detention," http://www.unhchr.ch/html/menu6/2/fs26.htm. The Working Group on Arbitrary Detention, established by the United Nations Commission on Human Rights in 1991, submits annual reports to the UN, carries out research missions to countries suspected of employing arbitrary detention, and accepts complaints from individuals and communities that have experienced arbitrary detention. See http://www.ohchr.org/english/issues/detention/index.htm for more information, including a full online library of documents it has produced.

6. Judith Butler and Gayatri Spivak, *Who Sings the Nation-State? Language, Politics, Belonging* (New York: Seagull Books, 2007), 5–6. Judith Butler is concerned that the bluntness of Agamben's concept of the state of exception may obscure a range of forms of violence and repression and notes that it may "become unable to take on the representational challenge of saying what life is like for the deported, what life is like for those who fear deportation, who are deported, what life is like for those who live as *gasterbeiters* in Germany, what life is like for Palestinians who are living under occupation. These are not undifferentiated instances of 'bare life' but highly juridified states of dispossession." Ibid., 42.

7. Butler writes, "What distinguishes containment from expulsion depends on how the line is drawn between the inside and the outside of the nation-state. On the other hand, both expulsion and containment are mechanisms for the very drawing of that line. The line comes to exist politically at the moment at which someone passes or is refused rights of passage." Ibid., 34.

8. Manfred Nowak, "Report of the Special Rapporteur on Torture and Other Cruel, Inhuman or Degrading Treatment or Punishment," Human Rights Council, Geneva, Thirteenth Session, Agenda item 3, 2010, A/HRC/13/39/Add.5.

9. For an account of Thailand's participation in World War II that highlights the role of the Seri Thai movement, which opposed the occupation and alliance with the Axis powers, see E. Bruce Reynolds, *Thailand's Secret War: The Free Thai, OSS, and SOE during World War II* (Cambridge: Cambridge University Press, 2004). Khuang's government was closer to the Seri Thai movement than Phibun's.

10. *Ratchakitchanubeksa*, 10 December 2584 [1941], book 58, 1781–82.

11. *Ratchakitchanubeksa*, 21 January 2488 [1945], book 62, part 5.

12. Streckfuss, *Truth on Trial*, 126.

13. Ibid., 124.

14. *Ratchakitchanubeksa*, 9 May 2489 [1946], book 63, part 29, 279–82.

15. See NA (2) So. Kho. Ko. 1/Book 393, National Archives, Office of the Juridical Council, Drafts of Laws and Legal Opinions, Finished Matters, B.E. 2487
[1944], "Act for the Internment of Those who are a Danger to the Nation during
Emergency Times, B.E. 2488," 558–648.

16. Ibid., 574.

17. Ibid.

18. Ibid., 575.

19. Ibid., 576.

20. Ibid.

21. Ibid., 640. There is no information about the detentions and psychological training to produce "good people" carried out under this army order prior to
Khuang's government. Perhaps if the army's files are one day opened, it will become
possible to learn how many people were detained, where they were detained, and
the content of the psychological training programs.

22. Ibid., 564.

23. Ibid., 582.

24. Ibid.

25. Ibid.

26. Ibid., 583.

27. Ibid. The English in the original is in italics.

28. Ibid. Pichan uses English for the phrase "social danger."

29. Ibid.

30. Ibid.

31. Ibid., 585.

32. Ibid. The English in the original is in italics.

33. Thak, *Thailand*, 189.

34. *Ratchakitchanubeksa* (special edition), 2 November 2501 [1958], book 75,
part 89, 1.

35. Ibid. Which people, and whose homeland? The relationship between hooligans to their fellow citizens was left vague in Decree 21. The assertion that they
needed to be dealt with for the good of the people and the nation raises the question of whether hooligans are themselves members of the Thai "people" described
in the law.

36. Ibid., 2.

37. *Ratchakitchanubeksa* (special edition), 10 January 2502 [1959], book 76, part
5, 2.

38. Thak, *Thailand*, 191n51. Fifty-eight people were released after questioning.

39. Thak, *Thailand*, 190.

40. Thak, *Thailand*, 190.

41. Thak, *Thailand*, 191.

42. Department of Corrections, *Information on Department of Corrections* (Bangkok: Ministry of Interior, 1968), 7.

43. Ibid., 3.

44. Regarding the precarious position of the stateless before and after World War II, Hannah Arendt writes, "Since he was the anomaly for whom the general law did not provide, it was better for him to become an anomaly for which it did provide, that of the criminal. The best criterion by which to decide whether some-one has been forced outside the pale of the law is to ask if he would benefit by committing a crime." She later notes, "If a human being loses his political status, he should, according to the implications of the inborn and inalienable rights of man, come under exactly the situation for which the declarations of such general rights provided. Actually the opposite is the case. It seems that a man who is noth-ing but a man has lost the very qualities which make it possible for other people to treat him as a fellow-man. This is one of the reasons why it is far more difficult to destroy the legal personality of a criminal, that is of a man who has taken upon himself the responsibility for an act whose consequences now determine his fate, than of a man who has been disallowed all common human responsibilities." Hannah Arendt, *The Origins of Totalitarianism* (New York: Harcourt Brace Jova-novich, 1973), 286, 300.

45. Supreme Court decision, No. 105/2506, *Governor of Surin v. Mr. Yiem Phunman.*

46. *Ratchakitchanubeksa*, 19 February 2518 [1975], book 92, part 41, 43.

47. Ibid., 34.

48. These six categories were (1) to bully, harass, or commit unjust acts against another in order to cause them to be afraid; (2) to not have a permanent residence, to be vagrant, and to not earn an honest living; (3) to make a living in a way that disturbs the peace and order or good morals of the people; (4) to illegally stockpile weapons or other materials intended for wrongdoing and to give reason to believe that the person will engage in wrongdoing or behavior that indicates possession of something that resulted from wrongdoing; (5) to harass other people to such an extent that they cannot do their jobs or live normal lives; and (6) to be involved in the procurement of women or the organization of prostitution, forced or unforced.

49. *Ratchakitchanubeksa*, 19 February 2518 [1975], book 92, part 41, 33–43.

50. *Ratchakitchanubeksa*, 6 October 2519 [1976], book 93, part 120, 19; *Ratchakitchanubeksa* 7 October 2519 [1976], book 93, part 121, 1–2; *Ratchakitchanu-beksa* 9 October 2519 [1976], book 93, part 123, 1–5.

51. *Ratchakitchanubeksa* (special edition), 13 October 2519 [1976], book 93, part 128, 1.

52. Ibid., 1. Unlike reeducation in China or Cambodia, which was aimed toward embrace of the collective, counterinsurgent reeducation in Thailand instead de-manded, among other things, allegiance to the monarchy, which might be under-stood as an anticollective.

53. In the statement of the NARC abrogating the constitution and announc-ing the coup on the evening of 6 October 1976, direct reference was made to the

"Vietnamese Communist terrorists who fought the police." *Ratchakitchanubeksa*, 6 October 2519 [1976], book 93, part 120, 1.

54. These nine categories were (1) to bully, harass, coerce, or terrorize other individuals; (2) to not have a permanent residence, be vagrant, and not earn an honest living; (3) to make a living in a way that disturbs the peace and order or good morals of the people; (4) to illegally stockpile guns, bullets, or bomb-making supplies, for the purpose of either selling them or committing other illegal activities; (5) inciting, provoking, using, or supporting the people in order to create confusion or unrest in the homeland; (6) causing the people to respect or go along with a form of government that is not a democracy with the king as the head of state; (7) establishing an illegal casino or brothel or participating in gambling sweepstakes or illegal lotteries; (8) hoarding commodities in order to make a profit or illegally raising the price; and (9) organizing strikes or illegally stopping work. *Ratchakitchanubeksa* (special edition), 13 October 2519 [1976], book 93, part 128, 1–2.

55. Kongsak Liewmanont, ed., *Collected Orders and Procedures of the National Administrative Reform Council for Dealing with the Dangers to Society* (Bangkok: Ministry of Interior, 2520 [1977]), 19n.

56. *Ratchakitchanubeksa* (special edition), 13 October 2519 [1976], book 93, part 128, 1–5.

57. Department of Corrections, *Annual Report, 1976* (Bangkok: Ministry of Interior, 1977).

58. CGRS, *Human Rights in Thailand Report*, April 1977, n.p.

59. CGRS, *Human Rights in Thailand Report*, May–June 1977, 1–2.

60. *Sayam Rat Sabda Wichan*, 18 December 2520 [1977], 16.

61. John B. Haseman, "National Security," in *Thailand: A Country Study*, ed. Barbara Leitch LePoer (Washington, DC: Federal Research Division, 1989), 269.

62. The annual reports of the Department of Corrections are bilingual, and so the English words used here are in the original. The transition to a new category of criminal was not smooth. Although Order 22 was announced on 13 October 1976, it was not until 21 October that the Ministry of Interior sent an express letter to the head of the police department, the attorney general, the head of prisons, and every provincial governor with instructions on the order and how to use it. The ministry also sent two new pieces of paperwork: a document recording the number and kinds of people who posed a danger to society and a booking sheet for use at the place of arrest. Kongsak, *Collected Orders*, 29–44. K., a former detainee in Chiang Mai, told me that when she was taken to the police station shortly after 6 October, a form dating from the Sarit era was used. She was furious, for the label "hooligan" was at the top of the form. Roman letters—K., L., and M.—are used as pseudonyms to protect the identities of three people arbitrarily detained whom I interviewed or whose testimony I draw on in my analysis.

63. Department of Corrections, *Annual Report, 1976*, 75.

64. Department of Corrections, *Annual Report, 1977* (Bangkok: Ministry of Interior, 1978); Department of Corrections, *Annual Report, 1978* (Bangkok: Ministry of Interior, 1979; Department of Corrections, *Annual Report, 1979* (Bangkok: Ministry of Interior, 1980).

65. *Bangkok Post*, 20 October 1976, 1.

66. *Sayam Rat Sabda Wichan*, 18 December 2520 [1977], 15.

67. European Co-ordinating Committee for Solidarity with the Thai People, *Political Repression in Thailand* (London: Ad Hoc Group for Democracy in Thailand, 1978), 52.

68. *Bangkok Post*, 29 October 1976, 5.

69. This subject is taken up extensively in chapter 5.

70. The Karunyathep Center still stands in Chiang Mai. However, it is now used as office space for the Santiban, the Special Branch police. I am grateful to Tze May Loo for locating the center building in 2004.

71. For an excellent introduction to the ISOC, see Thak Chaloemtiarana, "ISOC: Lullaby for the Communist Specter," *Thammasat Journal* 10, no. 2 (2524 [1981]): 107–12.

72. CGRS, *Human Rights in Thailand Report*, May–June 1977, 33. Between 15 and 30 October 1976, 159 people deemed dangers to society were arrested in Chiang Mai, 132 men and 27 women (*Thai Niu*, 18 November 2519 [1976], 1, 12). People were detained on a range of charges across the nine categories of detention noted earlier, including gambling and hoarding commodities. The location(s) of their detention remains unknown and is an important subject for future inquiry.

73. *Thai Niu*, 15 October 2519 [1976], 1, 12.

74. *Thai Niu*, 28 October 2519 [1976], 1, 12; 16 November 2519 [1976], 1, 12.

75. *Thai Niu*, 17 October 2519 [1976], 1.

76. *Thai Niu*, 18 October 2519 [1976], 1, 12; 19 October 2519 [1976], 1, 12; 20 October 2519 [1976], 1, 12.

77. *Thin Thai*, 17 October 2519 [1976], 1.

78. *Thin Thai*, 21 October 2519 [1976], 11.

79. *Thai Niu*, 19 October 2519 [1976], 3. It is also likely that some people reported on their neighbors and enemies and called for searches of people's houses out of spite.

80. *Thai Niu*, 21 October 2519 [1976], 12.

81. *Thin Thai*, 23 October 2519 [1976], 1, 11.

82. *Thai Niu*, 28 November 2519 [1976], 12.

83. *Thai Niu*, 16 November 2519 [1976], 1, 11; 15 December 2519 [1976], 1, 11.

84. *Thai Niu*, 15 December 2519 [1976], 1.

85. *Thai Niu*, 15 December 2519 [1976], 11.

86. Ibid.

87. *Ratchakitchanubeksa*, 8 August 2522 [1979], book 96, part 135, 1–4.

88. The full name of the emergency decree is the Emergency Decree on Public Administration in State of Emergency, and is hereafter referred to as "emergency decree."

89. Broad assessments of the conflict can be found in Thanet Aphornsuvan, *Rebellion in Southern Thailand: Contending Histories* (Honolulu: East-West Center, 2007); John Funston, *Southern Thailand: The Dynamics of Conflict* (Honolulu: East-West Center, 2008); and Duncan McCargo, *Tearing Apart the Land: Islam and Legitimacy in Southern Thailand* (Ithaca, NY: Cornell University Press, 2008). Deep South Watch, a nongovernmental organization based at Prince of Songkhla University, maintains the Deep South Incident Database, which tracks violent events. Between January 2004 and September 2016, there were 15,896 violent incidents, which resulted in 6,745 deaths and 12,375 injuries. For most recent numbers, see the Deep South Watch website, http://www.deepsouthwatch.org/dsid.

90. International Crisis Group, "Thailand's Emergency Decree: No Solution," Asia Report No. 105, 18 November 2005, http://www.crisisgroup.org/home/index .cfm?id=3795&l=1 (accessed 9 January 2015).

91. This ISOC document comes from a confidential source. Documents related to these detentions were shared with human rights activists by sympathetic officials, which makes them leaked documents rather than the public documents relied on for the rest of the analysis in this book.

92. The use of the word *chun* (invite) rather than *chap* (arrest) significantly elides the arrestees' lack of agency or ability to refuse the invitation to submit to detention. This kind of language was used with detention under Order 22 following the 6 October 1976 massacre and coup and has been used since the 22 May 2014 coup as well.

93. Duncan McCargo notes that supporters of the existing judicial system highlight the relatively small number of suspects prosecuted in the courts as evidence of its justness. McCargo, *Tearing Apart the Land*, 89. Yet this typology of individuals in need of state attention by the ISOC indicates that the very position of the judicial system is in crisis. The real indictment of the criminal justice system may not be in the cases processed through it but in those forced outside it.

94. My description of his arrest, detention, and release is based on my translation of a testimony M. wrote for human rights advocacy purposes.

95. Fourth Army Region and ISOC documents (confidential source).

96. For the provisions of administrative detention under the emergency decree, see Article 11 of it in *Ratchakitchanubeksa*, 16 July 2548 [2005], book 122, part 58 Koh, 1–9. For the provisions providing immunity for state actors, see Article 17. For analysis of the implications of the decree, see International Commission of Jurists, *More Power, Less Accountability: Thailand's New Emergency Decree* (Geneva: International Commission of Jurists, 2005).

97. Asian Human Rights Commission, "UPDATE (Thailand): Hundreds of Detainees Released from 'Vocational Training' Camps," UP-154-2007, 20 November 2007, http://www.ahrchk.net/ua/mainfile.php/2007/2667.

98. Asian Human Rights Commission, "UPDATE (Thailand): Hundreds Released from Army Detention Prevented from Going Home," UP-143-2007, 2 November 2007, http://www.ahrchk.net/ua/mainfile.php/2007/2641.

99. These numbers are as of December 2016. They are updated monthly by iLaw, and the current figures can be seen at http://freedom.ilaw.or.th/.

100. Immediately after the coup, this included the formal summoning of Somsak Jeamteerasakul, Pavin Chachavalpongpun, Suda Rangkupan, Surapot Taweesak, Suthachai Yimprasert, Sawatree Suksri, and Worachet Pakeerut and the revocation of the passports of the first three when they chose not to report. See Human Rights Watch, "Thailand: End Crackdown on Academic Freedom," 20 September 2014, http://www.hrw.org/news/2014/09/20/thailand-end-crackdown-academic-freedom; and Asian Human Rights Commission, "THAILAND: Ongoing Criminalization of Thought and Expression," AHRC-STM-172-2014, 22 September 2014, http://www.humanrights.asia/news/ahrc-news/AHRC-STM-172-2014.

101. Military courts were activated following the coup for civilians who commit crimes against the crown or state in Announcements 37/2557 and 38/2557 on 25 May 2014. On 12 September 2016 the initiation of new civilian cases in military courts ceased, but those cases already being processed there remained.

102. "Military Court Sentences Anti-coup Protester to 6 Months in Jail; Worachet, Jittra Deny Allegations," *Prachatai*, 9 August 2014, http://www.prachatai.org/english/node/4326.

103. Thantawut Taweewarodomkul, "Why I Did Not Report Myself," translated by Tyrell Haberkorn, *Prachatai*, 28 July 2014, http://www.prachatai.org/english/node/4249. Thantawut was convicted of allegedly violating Article 112 and the 2007 Computer Crimes Act in March 2011 and sentenced to thirteen years in prison.

104. Thanapol Eawsakul, "An Account of Reporting Oneself," *Prachatai*, 3 June 2014, http://www.prachatai.org/english/node/4080.

105. McCoy, *Torture and Impunity*, 218.

106. Ibid., 217.

107. Ibid., 264.

108. Ibid., 265.

CHAPTER 2. THE BIRTH OF HUMAN RIGHTS AND THE RISE OF AUTHORITARIANISM

1. Thak, *Thailand*.

2. In a chapter aptly titled "The Good Dictatorship," about the legacies of Field Marshal Sarit, Federico Ferrara quotes Bhumibol and notes that in a speech given in 1977, "The King added that, if Western newspapers insisted on calling Thai military generals 'dictators,' it was the military's responsibility to make sure it would be a 'good dictatorship,' given that 'the Thai military has never ruled dictatorially in the manner of Western dictators.'" Federico Ferrara, *The Political Development of Modern Thailand* (Cambridge: Cambridge University Press, 2015), 180.

3. Quoted and translated in Thak, *Thailand*, 127.

4. Ibid., 127–28.

5. Thamrongsak Petchlertanan, "The Political Role of Field Marshal Thanom Kittikhachorn, 2506–2516" (PhD diss., Chulalongkorn University, 2550 [2007]), 684.

6. *Ratchakitchanubeksa* (special edition), book 75, part 81, 20 October 2501 [1958], 10–16.

7. For the published reports, see United Nations, *UN Yearbook on Human Rights for 1958* (Lake Success NY: United Nations, 1960); United Nations, *UN Yearbook on Human Rights for 1959* (Lake Success NY: United Nations, 1961); United Nations, *UN Yearbook on Human Rights for 1960* (Lake Success NY: United Nations, 1962); United Nations, *UN Yearbook on Human Rights for 1961* (Lake Success NY: United Nations, 1964); and United Nations, *UN Yearbook on Human Rights for 1962* (Lake Success NY: United Nations, 1964). Drafts of the reports for 1958, 1959, and 1961 are available in the National Archives in Bangkok. See NA (2) So. Kho. Ko. 1/Book 538, National Archives, Office of the Juridical Council, Drafts of Laws and Legal Opinions, Finished Matters, "Text for Printing the Yearbook on Human Rights for 1958 C.E."; NA (2) So. Kho. Ko. 1/Book 563, National Archives, Office of the Juridical Council, Drafts of Laws and Legal Opinions, Finished Matters, "Law Drafts and Legal Opinions for the Yearbook on Human Rights for 1959 C.E."; and NA (2) So. Kho. Ko. 1/Book 610, National Archives, Office of the Juridical Council, Drafts of Laws and Legal Opinions, Finished Matters, "Law Drafts and Legal Opinions for the Yearbook on Human Rights for 1961 C.E."

8. Article 10 of the UDHR states, "Everyone is entitled in full equality to a fair and public hearing by an independent and impartial tribunal, in the determination of his rights and obligations and of any criminal charge against him." Article 11 states, "Everyone charged with a penal offence has the right to be presumed innocent until proved guilty according to law in a public trial at which he has had all the guarantees necessary for his defense. No one shall be held guilty of any penal offence on account of any act or omission which did not constitute a penal offence, under national or international law, at the time when it was committed. Nor shall a heavier penalty be imposed than the one that was applicable at the time the penal offence was committed."

9. As part of the development of the Thai human rights movement in the late 1970s, a rich body of scholarship was created to track precursors to ideas about human rights within Thai history and Theravada Buddhist thought. Work in this tradition includes Saneh Chamarik, *The Development of Human Rights in Thailand* (Bangkok: Union for Civil Liberty, 2531 [1988]); and Thanet Aphornsuvan, *The Origins and History of Human Rights* (Bangkok: Khobfai, 2549 [2006]). My project here is different. This work may provide activists with a set of tools with which to counter critics who claim that human rights are Western or otherwise un-Thai, but it leaves this criticism and dismissal in place. In contrast, my aim in

this chapter is to historicize the long engagement, from the launch of the UDHR, of various Thai governments with the international human rights regime.

10. Thak, *Thailand*, 20.

11. Ibid., 22–25.

12. Ferrara, *Political Development*, 131; Thak, *Thailand*, 32.

13. Thak, *Thailand*, 30.

14. Ibid., 43.

15. Ibid.

16. Ferrara, *Political Development*, 138; Thak, *Thailand*, 70–71.

17. Thak, *Thailand*, 70–71.

18. Ferrara, *Political Development*, 135.

19. E. Thadeus Flood, *The United States and the Military Coup in Thailand: A Background Study* (Berkeley: Indochina Resource Center, 1976); Daniel Fineman, *A Special Relationship: The United States and Military Government in Thailand, 1947–1948* (Honolulu: University of Hawai'i Press, 1997).

20. Thak, *Thailand*, 59. For a discussion of specific cases, see Thak, *Thailand*, 57–62; and Chit Wiphatthawat, *Phao Tells All (The Iron Man of Asia)* (Bangkok: Phrae Phitthaya, 2503 [1960]).

21. Thak, *Thailand*, 60.

22. Ibid., 63.

23. Ibid., 64.

24. Craig Reynolds, *Thai Radical Discourse: The Real Face of Thai Feudalism Today* (Ithaca, NY: Southeast Asia Program, Cornell University, 1987), 34.

25. The organizing and repression during this period are discussed in Kasian Tejapira, *Commodifying Marxism: The Formation of Modern Thai Radical Culture, 1927–1958* (Kyoto: Kyoto University Press, 2001); and Suthachai Yimprasert, *The Plan to Plunder the Thai Nation: On the State and Opposition to the State during the Second Regime of Field Marshal Phibun Songkhram (2491–2500 BE)* (Bangkok: 6 October Commemorative Press, 2553 [2010]) (originally published in 2531 [1988]). For a personal account of imprisonment during this period, see Thongbai Thongpao, *Communists of Lad Yao* (Bangkok: Khon Num, 2517 [1974]).

26. Jit Phumisak first published *The Real Face of Thai Feudalism Today* under a pseudonym as Somsamai Sisuttharaphan, "The Real Face of Thai Feudalism Today," *Thammasat University Faculty of Law Yearbook*, The New Century Edition, 2500 [1957]. It has been reprinted many times since then and was translated into English and published in Reynolds, *Thai Radical Discourse*, in 1987.

27. Kulap Saipradit, *Until We Meet Again* (Bangkok: Suphapburut Press, 2493 [1950]); Kulap Saipradit, *Looking Ahead (Youth)* (Bangkok: Thai Samphan Press, 2498 [1955]); Kulap Saipradit, *Looking Ahead (Middle Age)* (Bangkok: San Sayam, 2518 [1975]).

28. The CPT was a Marxist-Leninist party aligned with the Chinese Communist Party (CCP). On communist, socialist, and other leftist organizing during

this period, see Kasian, *Commodifying Marxism*; and Somsak Jeamteerasakul, "The Communist Movement in Thailand" (PhD diss., Monash University, 1991). Chris Baker has translated an internal history of the CPT, which includes a reference to the second party congress. See Chris Baker, "An Internal History of the Communist Party of Thailand," *Journal of Contemporary Asia* 33, no. 4 (2003): 510–41. The first shots were fired by the CPT against Thai state forces on 7 August 1965. The party slowly dissolved during the 1980s, both after a break between the CPT and the CCP and after the government of General Tinsulanond provided amnesty to those willing to surrender, as I discuss in chapter 3.

29. NA (2) Ko. To. 12.3.7/4, National Archives, Ministry of Foreign Affairs, Department of the United Nations, Social Unit, Human Rights, "Celebration of Human Rights Day, 2493 BE [1950 CE]," 51.

30. Ibid., 56.

31. Ibid., 57.

32. Ibid.

33. Ibid., 71.

34. NA (2) Ko. To. 12.3.7/6, National Archives, Ministry of Foreign Affairs, Department of the United Nations, Social Unit, Human Rights, "Celebration of Human Rights Day, 2495, 2496, 2497 BE [1952, 1953, 1954 CE]," 63.

35. Ibid.

36. NA (2) Ko. To. 12.3.7/13, National Archives, Ministry of Foreign Affairs, Department of the United Nations, Social Unit, Human Rights, "Organizing a Performance for Human Rights Day, 2498 [1955]."

37. Ibid., 6–7.

38. Ibid., 9–10.

39. Ibid., 10.

40. Ibid., 11.

41. Ibid.

42. Thak, *Thailand*, 44.

43. Ferrara, *Political Development*, 146.

44. *Ratchakitchanubeksa* (special edition), book 75, part 81, 20 October 2501 [1958], 14.

45. Sarit Thanarat, "Address of Field Marshal Sarit Thanarat, the Prime Minister, on Constitution Day and Human Rights Day, 10 December 2503 [1960]," *Ratchasaphasan* 9, no. 1 (December 2503 [1960]): n.p.

46. Ibid.

47. Sarit Thanarat, *Collected Speeches of Field Marshal Sarit Thanarat, 2505–2506 [1962–1963]* (Bangkok: Cabinet, 2508 [1965]), 842.

48. This is an example of what Nick Cheesman astutely analyzes as the production of law and order masquerading as the rule of law in colonial and postcolonial Burma. See Nick Cheesman, *Opposing the Rule of Law: How Myanmar's Courts Make Law and Order* (Cambridge: Cambridge University Press, 2015). See also Fa

Diew Kan Editorial Collective, "The Insufficiency of Rule by Law," *Fa Diew Kan* 7, no. 4 (October–December 2552 [2009]): n.p.; and the other articles in the same issue of the journal.

49. Thamrongsak, "Political Role," 684–85. Those executed were Sang Sae Lim, Siu-yok Sae Chin, Siu-yin Sae Chin, Hon-sin Sae Chin, and Ung Silpangam.

50. Sarit Thanarat, quoted in Thak, *Thailand*, 123.

51. Sarit Thanarat, quoted in ibid., 124.

52. Ibid., 128.

53. Ibid., 181.

54. Chakrawan Channuwong, *Article 17 and the 11 Executed Prisoners* (Bangkok: Chak Banlue, 2507 [1964]), 120.

55. Sarit Thanarat, "Announcement of the Prime Minister on the Ordering of the Execution of Mr. Sila Wongsin or Ladlakhon," 26 June 2502 [1959]: n.p. All the orders issued under Article 17 during the regimes of both Sarit and Thanom are reprinted in Premchai Phringsunlaka, ed., *Article 17 in Murky Times* (Bangkok: Krung Sayam Publishers, 2517 [1974]).

56. Sarit, "Announcement."

57. Sarit, "Announcement."

58. Sarit Thanarat, "Order for the Execution of Mr. Supachai Srisati," 6 July 2502 [1959].

59. Chakrawan, *Article 17*, 144.

60. Kasian, *Commodifying Marxism*, 121–22. Of the several hundred arrested, fifty-four were officially charged with violating the Anti-Communist Activities Act of 1952 and forty-nine were sentenced to twenty years in prison on 15 March 1955. Forty-eight received a reduction in their sentences by one-third, to thirteen years and four months, and they were all released under an amnesty in 1957.

61. Sarit Thanarat, "Order for the Execution of Mr. Khrong Chandawong and Mr. Thongphan Sutthimat," 30 May 2504 [1961].

62. Chakrawan, *Article 17*, 161.

63. Ibid., 165.

64. Office of the Prime Minister, "Declaration of the Government on the Execution of a Person who Subverted National Security," 29 August 2504 [1961].

65. The sale and consumption of opium was criminalized in Revolutionary Order No. 37 issued on 9 December 1958. See *Ratchakitchanubeksa*, Special Issue, Book 75, Part 106, 9 December 2501 [1958], 1–3.

66. Office of the Prime Minister, "Declaration."

67. For a discussion of both Phao's and Sarit's involvement in the heroin trade, see Alfred W. McCoy, *The Politics of Heroin in Southeast Asia* (New York: Harper and Row, 1972).

68. Office of the Prime Minister, "Declaration."

69. Ibid.

70. Ibid.

71. Preedee Hongsaton analyzed the ways in which newspaper coverage of Article 17 executions during the Thanom regime operated as a form of "killing a chicken to scare the monkeys" and spread fear. Preedee Hongsaton, "'Killing a Chicken to Scare the Monkeys': The Thai State's Annihilation of Its Enemies," *Thammasat University Journal of History* 1, no. 2 (2558 [2015]): 53–99.

72. Office of the Prime Minister, "Declaration."

73. According to Chakrawan Channuwong, Liang Ho wrote letters to his children and wife urging them to use the money remaining in the family's bank accounts carefully and to avoid illegal activities. See Chakrawan, *Article 17*, 176–77.

74. Office of the Prime Minister, "Government Statement on the Traitorous Rebellion against the Nation of Mr. Ruam Wongphan and Others," 24 April 2505 [1962].

75. Ibid.

76. The government statement does not state whether cells were successfully established in *every* subdistrict.

77. Office of the Prime Minister, "Government Statement."

78. Ibid.

79. Ibid.

80. Ibid.

81. Ibid.

82. Ibid.

83. Ruam Wongphan was cremated almost thirty-three years after his death, on 23 April 1995, and a cremation volume about his life and the CPT was published. Cremation volumes are print books of various lengths published and distributed at Thai Buddhist cremations, or at funerals in cases in which a person is not cremated. The volumes may contain biographical information, recollections by friends and family, essays (by the deceased person or others), or other materials. In the introduction to his cremation volume, Pradit Sutthijit, Ruam's wife, who was imprisoned in the cell next to his, wrote that every evening after returning from his interrogation, Ruam recorded the details of the day. But these scraps did not survive. She had no prior notice that he was going to be executed; on the evening of his execution, she waited all day for him to return to eat the dinner of fried squid and fruits that a relative had brought them. He did not return, and the next morning she learned of his death and went to view the body. She was held for another three months before being released without having been charged. The cremation volume contains copies of letters from Ruam to the party, his family, and his friends, as well as remembrances by those close to him and those inspired by his life. The names of 196 people who were targeted (either imprisoned or killed) for opposing Sarit's dictatorship are listed. See Pradit Sutthijit et al., *Cremation Volume of Mr. Ruam Wongphan* (Bangkok: Wat Makudkasattriyam, 2538 [1995]). See also Kasian Tejapira, "'Party as Mother': Ruam Wongphan and the Making of

a Revolutionary Metaphor," in *Traveling Nation-Makers: Transnational Flows and Movements in the Making of Modern Southeast Asia* (Singapore: National University of Singapore Press in association with Kyoto University Press, 2011), 188–208.

84. Thamrongsak, "Political Role," 686–89.

85. Premchai, *Article 17*, 36.

86. Premchai, *Article 17*, 37.

87. Article 17 in the 1972 constitution noted that it could be used "to prevent, repress or suppress any act subverting the security of the Kingdom, the Throne, national economy or affairs of State, or any act disturbing or threatening public order or good morals, or any act destroying national resources or deteriorating public health and sanitation." Office of the Juridical Council's Welfare Fund, *Constitution of the Kingdom, B.E. 2515* (Bangkok: Office of the Juridical Council's Welfare Fund, 1972), 8.

88. Thamrongsak, "Political Role," 689–92.

89. Premchai, *Article 17*, 149.

90. The 1976 constitution was promulgated on 22 October under the government of Prime Minister Thanin Kraivichien, the 1977 constitution was promulgated on 9 November following the coup of General Kriangsak Chomanan, and the 1978 constitution was promulgated on 22 December while General Kriangsak remained prime minister.

91. CGRS, *Human Rights in Thailand Report* 5, no. 2 (April–June 1981): 5.

92. Ibid.

93. CGRS, *Human Rights in Thailand Report* 5, no. 4 (October–December 1981): 14.

94. *Ratchakitchanubeksa* (special edition), book 99, part 62, 30 April 2525 [1983], 1–9.

95. CGRS, *Human Rights in Thailand Report* 6, no. 2 (April–June 1982): 18; CGRS, *Human Rights in Thailand Report* 7, no. 1 (January–March 1983): 5.

96. The text of the 2014 temporary constitution was published in *Ratchakitchanubeksa*, book 131, issue 55 Ko, 22 July 2557 [2014], 1–17. This translation is by Pakorn Nilprapunt, "Unofficial Translation of the Constitution of the Kingdom of Thailand (Interim), B.E. 2557 (2014)," 23 July 2014, http://lawdrafter.blogspot .com/2014/07/translation-of-constitution-of-kingdom.html.

97. iLaw, "What Does the NCPO Have to Show for Their Two Years of Rule?," manuscript, 2559 [2016].

98. Thai Lawyers for Human Rights, "Public Statement against the Invocation of Section 44 of the Constitution of the Kingdom of Thailand (Interim), B.E. 2557 (2014)," 30 March 2015, https://tlhr2014.wordpress.com/2015/03/30/public -statement-against-the-invocation-of-section-44-of-the-constitution-of-the-king dom-of-thailand-interim-b-e-2557-2014/.

99. See the ongoing running list compiled by iLaw in its "Report on the Exercise of Power under Article 44 of the Interim Constitution," http://www.ilaw .or.th/node/3679.

100. Kasian Tejapira, "Article 17: Field Marshal Sarit's Dog-Head Zha Guillotine," *Matichon Sut Sabda*, 22 April 2558 [2015], 52.

CHAPTER 3. THE BURNING OF PEOPLE AND VILLAGES

1. Their fears were perhaps misguided but not unwarranted. See Kasian, *Commodifying Marxism*, for accounts of the unexpected alliances, novels, newspapers, and other forms of dissident cultural politics that arose in the service of a different and more just Thai society.

2. These measures included the following: Act on Communism of 2476 [1933], Amended Act on Communism of 2478 [1935], Anti-Communist Activities Act of 2495 [1952], Junta Announcement No. 12 (issued on 22 October 2501 [1958]), Junta Announcement No. 15 (issued on 27 October 2501 [1958]), Act on the Control of Anti-Communist Activities Defendants of 2505 [1962], Act Amending Junta Announcement No. 12 of 2506 [1963], Act (version 2) on the Control of Anti-Communist Activities Defendants of 2506 [1963], Act (version 3) on the Control of Anti-Communist Activities Defendants of 2511 [1968], Anti-Communist Activities Act of 2512 [1969], Junta Announcement No. 12 (issued on 22 November 2514 [1971]), Junta Announcement No. 78 (issued on 16 February 2515 [1972]), Junta Announcement No. 199 (issued on 10 August 2515 [1972]), NARC Order No. 5 (issued on 6 October 2519 [1976]), NARC Order No. 8 (ssued on 6 October 2519 [1976]), NARC Order No. 14 (issued on 6 October 2519 [1976]), NARC Order No. 25 (issued on 17 October 2519 [1976]), NARC Order No. 43 (issued on 21 October 2519 [1976]), Ministry of Interior Announcement on the Restriction of Printed Material (issued on 6 October 2520 [1977]), Anti-Communist Activities Act of 2522 [1979]), Ministry of Interior Announcement on the Restriction of Printed Material (issued on 6 June 2523 [1980]), and Ministry of Interior Announcement on the Restriction of Printed Materials (6 November 2523 [1980]). See Jaran Kosanan, *Law, Rights, and Liberties in Thai Society: Parallel Lines from 1932 to the Present* (Bangkok: Coordinating Group for Religion in Society, 2528 [1985]), 71–75.

3. *Ratchakitchanubeksa*, book 86, part 14, 18 February 2512 [1969], 162–77.

4. The ACAA of 1952 defined "communist activities" as including (1) toppling the form of government as democracy with the king as head of state; (2) changing the economic system by abolishing private ownership and collectivizing production and ownership; and (3) agitating in the service of, providing assistance or support to, or otherwise aiding in the aim to carry out the activities named in the first two parts of the definition. See the full text of the law in *Ratchakitchabeksa*, book 69, part 68, 13 November 2495 [1952].

5. Streckfuss, *Truth on Trial*, 239.

6. Thanet Aphornsuvan, "From Thang Daeng to Tak Bai: Experiences in Solving the State's Problems," paper presented at Thammasat University, 23 January 2548 [2005], 4.

7. *Ratchakitchanubeksa*, book 89, part 26, 16 February 2515 [1972], 3–5.

8. *Ratchakitchanubeksa*, book 89, part 123, 11 August 2515 [1972], 9–10.

9. Ibid.

10. Jaran, *Law*, 87.

11. See Sinae Hyun, "Indigenizing the Cold War: Nation-Building by the Border Patrol Police, 1945–1980" (PhD diss., University of Wisconsin–Madison, 2014), for a history of the genesis and varied roles of the BPP. The VDV are local armed defense volunteers under the administration of the Ministry of Interior. This places them outside the chain of command, and chain of responsibility, of either the police or the army. They are often unprofessional and poorly trained in the use of their issued weapons. During the Cold War, as well as in more recent times in southern Thailand, they were often suspected of carrying out some of the most egregious violations of human rights.

12. The father, Phan Mattaraj, was fifty at the time of his death; the mother, Sai Mattaraj, was forty; and their son, Aeb Mattaraj, was six.

13. Democracy propagation was the name given to the activities of student activists who went to the countryside after 14 October 1973 with the intention of educating rural people about democracy. In many cases, the opposite occurred and rural people educated the students about injustice, inequality, and violence.

14. Payne, *Unsettling Accounts*, 2.

15. Ibid., 281.

16. Boudreau writes, "Instrumental violence sets out directly to neutralize or displace a threat or challenge. Instrumental violence in state building targets rival centers of power. It puts down rebels and replaces rival authorities with state institutions and agents. Instrumental violence directly disrupts, disaggregates, or eliminates political targets. Authorities troubled by communists may round them up for detention or murder. . . . Violence that seeks to delineate proper modes of political conduct, and to advertise those sanctions that will be visited on those who ignore such modes, is exemplary." Vince Boudreau, "Interpreting State Violence in Asian Settings," in *State Violence in East Asia*, ed. N. Ganesan and Sung Chull Kim (Lexington: University Press of Kentucky, 2013), 24–25.

17. *Thai Rat*, 24 January 2517 [1974], 1, 12.

18. Chaiwat, *What Took Place*, 41. In contrast to the term "communist terrorists" used by Thai state officials and many newspapers, I use the official name of the party.

19. *Daily Niu*, 17 February 2517 [1974], 5. The choice of words used by the paper is worth highlighting: villagers *rabai* (vent) and the state *raingan* (reports).

20. *Thai Rat*, 16 February 2517 [1974], 3.

21. Chaiwat, *What Took Place in Ban Na Sai*, 41.

22. Ibid., 42.

23. *Chao Thai*, 15 February 2517 [1974], 1.

24. *Chao Thai*, 21 February 2517 [1974], 1.

25. *Sayam Rat*, 21 February 2517 [1974], 12.

26. Ibid.

27. Chaiwat, *What Took Place in Ban Na Sai*, 77. Perhaps the governor was offended because the assessment of tyranny veered too close to the truth.

28. Ibid., 46.

29. *Daily Niu*, 24 February 2517 [1974], 16.

30. Chaiwat, *What Took Place in Ban Na Sai*, 43.

31. Lom did not specify in his account whether they were VDVs, BPP, regular police, or army soldiers.

32. Chaiwat, *What Took Place in Ban Na Sai*, 78–82.

33. Ibid., 59.

34. Ibid.

35. *Sayam Rat*, 15 February 2517 [1974], 1.

36. Ibid.

37. The governor donated fifteen sacks of rice, food, and clothing on 15 February and twenty-eight bags of rice, two hundred cans of food, and two hundred blankets on 18 February. He estimated the value of the donation at one hundred thousand baht. Ibid.; *Thai Rat*, 20 February 2517, 16.

38. The committee was chaired by Chamnien Khantasweu, vice governor, and the members in addition to the governor himself were Captain Chothi Phrommanot, deputy commander of the Communist Suppression Operations Command (CSOC) in Nong Khai; Phaiboon Limpitip, deputy governor; and Police Lieutenant Colonel Chup Suksomboon, the deputy provincial police commander. *Daily Niu*, 15 February 2517 [1974], 12.

39. The Village Scouts were a royalist-nationalist paramilitary scout movement linked to the BPP. For an ethnography of the Village Scout movement during this period, see Katherine Bowie, *Rituals of National Loyalty: An Anthropology of the State and the Village Scout Movement in Thailand* (New York: Columbia University Press, 1997).

40. *Daily Niu*, 9 March 2517 [1974], 2.

41. Jaran, *Law*, 87.

42. *Sayam Rat*, 19 February 2517 [1974], 8.

43. *Sayam Rat*, 17 February 2517 [1974], 3.

44. *Daily Niu*, 17 February 2517 [1974], 1, 12.

45. *Sayam Rat*, 28 February 2517 [1974], 3; *Sayam Rat*, 2 March 2517 [1974], 3.

46. *Sayam Rat*, 4 March 2517 [1974], 1.

47. *Sayam Rat*, 28 February 2517 [1974], 3.

48. *Daily Niu*, 20 March 1517 [1974], 1.

49. *Sayam Rat*, 21 March 2517 [1974], 1.

50. *Daily Niu*, 2 April 2517 [1974], 3.

51. *Daily Niu*, 2 March 2517 [1974], 1.

52. *Sayam Rat*, 13 May 2517 [1974], 3.

53. *Sayam Rat*, 9 May 2517 [1974], 1.

54. A debate in the National Legislative Assembly about whether to appoint an additional committee to investigate the burning of Ban Na Sai also addressed the matter of impartiality. Sathap Sirikhan, a representative from Sakhon Nakhon province, noted that civil servants could not be the arbiters of impartiality because the differences between them and the people had caused the people to fear them. Many other representatives spoke out against establishing a committee, and the motion was defeated with 58 voting in favor, 103 against, and the rest of the 299 members abstaining. National Legislative Assembly, *Report of the Meeting of the National Legislative Assembly*, 22 February 2517 [1974] (Bangkok: National Legislative Assembly, 2517 [1974]), 275–407.

55. During the *thang daeng* killings in Phatthalung, accounts indicate that VDVs reported directly to the CSOC.

56. Yotthong Thabtiumai, *Thang Daeng, Na Sai, ISOC, Anti-Communist Activities Act* (Bangkok: Mitnara Kanphim, 2518 [1975]), 62–69.

57. *Prachathipatai*, 16 February 2518 [1975], 12.

58. *Thai Rat*, 7 February 2518 [1975], 1, 12.

59. *Thai Rat*, 8 February 2518 [1975], 1, 12.

60. John Value Dennis, "The Role of the Thai Student Movement in Rural Conflict, 1973–1976" (MS thesis, Cornell University, 1982), 142. Dennis's thesis examines the burning of Ban Na Sai and the *thang daeng* killings along with a struggle against a mine in Lampang. Although this volume examines the same incidents, the focus here is markedly different. While I am concerned with accountability, Dennis examines the three incidents in order to analyze the relationships between the countryside and the city and student activists as agents of these relationships.

61. Yotthong, *Thang Daeng*, 76–77.

62. Ibid., 72–78; *Sieng Puangchon*, 8 February 2518 [1975], 10.

63. *Prachathipatai*, 9 February 2518 [1975], 1.

64. Ibid., 12.

65. Ibid., 1.

66. *Sieng Puangchon*, 6 February 2518 [1975], 1, 2.

67. *Sieng Puangchon*, 8 February 2518 [1975], 1.

68. Ibid., 10.

69. *Sieng Puangchon*, 9 February 2518 [1975], 10.

70. *Sieng Puangchon*, 10 February 2518 [1975], 1, 10.

71. *Sieng Puangchon*, 15 February 2518 [1975], 1, 2.

72. Ibid., 2; *Prachachat*, 15 February 2518 [1975], 1, 12.

73. *Prachachat*, 16 February 2518 [1975], 1.

74. *Prachachat*, 15 February 2518 [1975], 1, 12. One of the right-wing groups active during the 1973–76 period, the Krathing Daeng was primarily composed of vocational students who were under the leadership of Major General Sudsai Hasadin of the ISOC.

75. *Sieng Mai*, 16 February 2518 [1975], 11
76. *Voice of the Nation*, 16 February 1975, 3.
77. *Prachathipatai*, 16 February 2518 [1975], 12.
78. *Voice of the Nation*, 17 February 1975, 1.
79. *Prachathipatai*, 9 February 2518 [1975], 12.
80. *Prachachat*, 9 February 2518 [1975], 12.
81. The family name of the two brothers was not made public by the newspaper.
82. *Daily Time*, 9 February 2518 [1975], 1.
83. *Prachathipatai*, 16 February 2518 [1975], 12.
84. *Prachathipatai*, 17 February 2518 [1975], 1.
85. *Prachathipatai*, 21 February 2518 [1975], 12.
86. *Sieng Puangchon*, 17 February 2518 [1975], 1, 2.
87. *Sieng Mai*, 17 February 2518 [1975], 12.
88. *Voice of the Nation*, 24 February 1975, 3.
89. *Prachachat*, 15 February 2518 [1975], 12.
90. *Sieng Puangchon*, 24 February 2518 [1975], 2.
91. *Prachathipatai*, 17 February 2518 [1975], 1.
92. *Prachathipatai*, 20 February 2518 [1975], 1, 12.
93. *Sieng Mai*, 22 February 2518 [1975], 1, 2.
94. Ibid.
95. *Prachathipatai*, 20 February 2518 [1975], 1. The use of "they" may have been a mistake of either the person who made the poster or the newspaper that reported it. If villagers created the poster themselves, would they not use the pronoun "we"?
96. *Sieng Puangchon*, 24 February 2518 [1975], 2.
97. *Daily Time*, 24 February 2518 [1975], 1, 12.
98. Payne, *Unsettling Accounts*, 170.
99. *Prachathipatai*, 4 February 2518 [1975], 12.
100. *Prachachat*, 4 February 2518 [1975], 12.
101. Payne, *Unsettling Accounts*, 285.
102. Ibid.
103. Beginning in late 1974 and intensifying in 1975, farmers, workers, and other activists were assassinated in increasing numbers. For an analysis of the series of assassinations of the leaders of the Farmers' Federation of Thailand, see Tyrell Haberkorn, "An Unfinished Past: The 1974 Land Rent Control Act and Assassination in Northern Thailand," *Critical Asian Studies* 41, no. 1 (2009): 1–43.
104. *Prachachat*, 16 February 2518 [1975], 12.
105. *Sieng Mai*, 25 February 2518 [1975], 2.
106. *Voice of the Nation*, 25 February 1975, 4.
107. *Thai Rat*, 25 February 2518 [1975], 1, 12.
108. *Chao Thai*, 28 March 2518 [1975], 2.

109. *Thai Rat*, 27 March 2518 [1975], 1, 12.

110. *Prachachat*, 11 February 2518 [1975].

111. *Sieng Puangchon*, 15 February 2518 [1975], 2.

112. Prime Ministerial Order No. 66/2523, "Policy for the Struggle to Win Over Communism," 23 April 2523 [1980].

113. The explanation given for the nullification of the law was based on the absence of necessity. The law "was passed in order to be a special measure in the protection against the danger from Communist activities in the country at that time. But the situation has changed in the present and therefore there is no need for the use of this measure." *Ratchakitchanubeksa*, 2 June 2543 [2000], book 117, part 41 Ko, 1–2. Unlike the nullifications of various arbitrary detention orders noted in chapter 1, for example, there was no acknowledgment that this law was used to excess and negatively impacted many lives.

114. Winyu Angkhanarak, *Heart of the Permanent Secretary* (Bangkok: Matichon Press, 2544 [2001]).

115. He writes, "In telling my other stories up to now, I have used the real given and family names. But as this account of the Ban Na Sai Fire involves many areas and sides, I therefore do not specify the real given and family names of some people." Ibid., 109.

116. Ibid.

117. Ibid., 111–12.

118. Ibid., 112.

119. Ibid., 113.

120. Royal Institute, *Royal Institute Dictionary* (Bangkok: Royal Institute, 2542 [1999]), 325. Two colleagues also noted that it is a word used by gangsters and offered an example. Suppose that Gangster A provided information to the police that caused Gangster B to go to prison. Following his release from prison, Gangster B killed the son of Gangster A in retaliation and said to him, "*Chao kan laew na*," or loosely, "We are done [with this matter] now." Bencharat Sae Chua and Ponglert Pongwanan, personal communication, 18 January 2016.

121. Winyu, *Heart of the Permanent Secretary*, 116–17.

122. Pallop Pinmanee, *I Was Wrong? The Seizure of Krue Se!* (Bangkok: Good Morning Press, 2547 [2004]). On 28 April 2004 clashes between state forces and Muslim men resulted in the deaths of 106 Muslim men and 5 members of the state forces. What is clear is that, while Muslim militants did launch initial attacks on state forces in some locations, they were outnumbered and outarmed. Many of the militants were armed only with machetes, while the soldiers were well equipped with automatic weapons, grenades, and other hardware. The event is referred to as the Krue Se mosque massacre because, although there was fighting between Muslim men and Thai army forces in various locations in the south, including Saba Yoi district in Songkhla province and Krong Pinang district in Yala province, the largest number (32 men) were killed at the Krue Se mosque in Pattani. General

Pallop was the highest-ranking army officer involved in the massacre. See special issue of *Fa Diew Kan* 2, no. 3 (July–September 2547 [2004]), for commentaries on the Krue Se mosque massacre, as well as details about many of those who died.

123. Neither in this chapter nor elsewhere in his book does General Pallop provide details on what he did in Laos.

124. Pallop, *I Was Wrong?*, 166.

125. Ibid., 167.

126. Ibid.

127. Ibid., 168.

128. Ibid.

129. General Pallop's admission of responsibility stands in contrast to the state officials involved in the *thang daeng* killings that Jularat Damrongviteetam interviewed, who felt shame and discomfort and did not want to talk about the past. She writes, "State officials linked to violent incidents during the period of communist suppression have self-inhibiting memories. They refused to grant interviews, and their reactions showed that they did not want to talk about the past again. The officer-narrators tried to block out the past and escape the shadow of the Red Barrel incident by focusing solely on their identities in the present day. The silence of the officers could be interpreted in two ways. First, they might believe that the Red Barrel incident was an act carried out to excess by the state that they would now like to forget. Memories of the incident have a profound impact on their feelings, and blocking them out might be a means of emotional self-preservation. Second, they might not want their memories to have an effect on the institutions for which they now work." Jularat Damrongviteetam, "Narratives of the 'Red Barrel' Incident: Collective and Individual Memories in Lamsin, Southern Thailand," in *Oral History in Southeast Asia: Memories and Fragments*, ed. Kah Seng Loh, Ernest Koh, and Alistair Thomson (New York: Palgrave Macmillan, 2013), 113. General Pallop's account suggests pride born of an awareness of the continued impunity exercised by those at the top. For Jularat's excellent analysis of the range of memories of the *thang daeng* killings by a wide range of figures in Phatthalung, see Jularat Damrongviteetam, *Thang Daeng: The Restoration/ Reconstruction of History and Haunting Memories in Thai Society* (Bangkok: Matichon, 2559 [2016]).

CHAPTER 4. THE HIDDEN TRANSCRIPT OF AMNESTY

1. For a broad picture of assassinations and other means of repression of progressive and radical activists, see David Morrell and Chai-anan Samudavanija, *Political Conflict in Thailand: Reform, Reaction, Revolution* (Cambridge, MA: Oelgeschlager, Gunn and Hain, 1981).

2. *Thai Rat*, 26 September 2519 [1976], 1.

3. Puey Ungpakorn, "Violence and the Military Coup in Thailand," *Bulletin of Concerned Asian Scholars* 9, no. 3 (1977): 5.

4. Thongchai Winichakul, "Remembering/Silencing the Traumatic Past: The Ambivalent Memories of the October 1976 Massacre in Bangkok," in *Cultural Crisis and Social Memory: Modernity and Identity in Thailand and Laos*, ed. Shigeharu Tanabe and Charles Keyes (Honolulu: University of Hawai'i Press, 2002), 249.

5. Puey, "Violence," 5.

6. Robert F. Zimmerman, *Reflections on the Collapse of Democracy in Thailand* (Singapore: Institute of Southeast Asian Studies, 1978).

7. An unofficial, civil fact-finding report was published in Ji Ungpakorn and Suthachai Yimprasert, *The Crimes of the State in the Crisis of Changes* (Bangkok: 6 October Fact-Finding Committee, 2544 [2001]).

8. Thongchai, "Remembering/Silencing," 243–86.

9. "Amnesty for Those Who Seized the Administrative Power of the Country on 6 October 1976 Act," *Ratchakitchanubeksa*, 24 December 2519 [1976], book 93, part 156, 42–45.

10. "Amnesty for Those Who Committed Wrongdoing in the Demonstrations at Thammasat University between 4 and 6 October 1976," *Ratchakitchanubeksa*, 16 September 2521 [1978], book 95, part 97, 1–4.

11. The Bangkok Eighteen included sixteen men and two women: Sutham Saengprathum, Anupong Phongsuwan, Apinan Buaphakdee, Surachart Bamrungsuk, Praphon Wongsiriphitak, Viroj Tangwanich, Mahin Tanboonpurm, Arom Phongpangan, Prayoon Akaraboworn, Sucheela Tanchainan, Attakarn Upathambhakul, Suchat Phatcharasorawut, Thongchai Winichakul, Kongsak Asapak, Somsak Jeamteerasakul, Orissa Airawanwat, Sa-ngiam Chaemduang, and Seri Sirinuphong.

12. Amnesties with obscure agendas are not limited to Thailand. In her study of large numbers of amnesties between 1974 and 2007, Renée Jeffery notes, "Interpreting the intentions of an amnesty law is not a straightforward task, especially given that stated intentions may act to disguise or window-dress other less desirable intentions." Renée Jeffery, *Amnesties, Accountability, and Human Rights* (Philadelphia: University of Pennsylvania Press, 2014), 38.

13. Benedict Anderson, "Withdrawal Symptoms: Social and Cultural Aspects of the October 6 Coup," *Bulletin of Concerned Asian Scholars* 9, no. 3 (1977): 13.

14. The opposite of this, when calling for justice itself becomes a crime, is evident in the case of Suderueman Maleh, who filed a complaint of being tortured while in police and army custody in January 2004. The disappearance of Suderueman's lawyer, Somchai Neelaphaijit, shortly after the complaint was filed is the subject of chapter 6. Due to evidentiary problems, the state officials in question were cleared of the complaint against them. But for several individuals this was insufficient, and they brought criminal charges against Suderueman for allegedly giving false testimony to state officials about being tortured. On 10 August 2011 he was convicted and sentenced to two years in prison. See Asian Human Rights Commission, "THAILAND: Court Demonstrates Contempt for Human Rights by

Jailing Torture Victim on Say-So of Alleged Perpetrator," 11 August 2011, http://www.humanrights.asia/news/ahrc-news/AHRC-STM-103-2011. This decision was later overturned and the case thrown out by the Supreme Court in October 2015.

15. Ranajit Guha, "The Prose of Counter-Insurgency," in *Subaltern Studies II: Writings on South Asian History and Society*, ed. Ranajit Guha (Oxford: Oxford University Press, 1983), 1–42.

16. Scott, *Domination*.

17. Thai citizens can obtain a National Archives user card by presenting their identification card and filling out an application. Foreign readers can obtain a three-week pass by presenting their passports and stating the nature of their research; for long-term access, they must file a formal request with the National Research Council of Thailand.

18. John Roosa, *Pretext to Mass Murder: The September 30th Movement and Suharto's Coup d'État in Indonesia* (Madison: University of Wisconsin Press, 2006). The September 30th Movement was the name of a group of soldiers allegedly behind the murder of six generals in Indonesia in 1965. These murders became the pretext by which General Suharto came to power and launched a reign of terror against the Partai Komunis Indonesia, or Communist Party of Indonesia. The premise of *Pretext to Mass Murder* is that the identities and actual motivations of the September 30th Movement have consistently been obscured, and therefore the understanding of what came later has as well.

19. The Department of the Judge Advocate General in the Ministry of the Defense oversees all aspects of the military's judicial processes, including the military court system. Those present at the meeting of the Krisdika committee included Serm Winichaikul (chair), Phoj Pusapakjom (member), Luang Wichai Nitinat (member), Art Wisutyothaphiban (member), Nam Phunwatthu (member), Sompop Notrakit (member and secretary-general of the Krisdika), and the guest, Major General Sawat Oorungroj. Also present were two members of the secretarial staff, Maitri Tanthemsap (secretary) and Sathit Sulkusaworn (chief assistant secretary).

20. A list of these laws can be found in Charnvit Kasetsiri, "Blanket Amnesty: Agree or Not," *Prachatai*, 19 October 2556 [2013], http://blogazine.in.th/blogs/charnvit-kasetsiri/post/4407.

21. NA (2) So. Kho. Ko, 1/Book 996, National Archives, Office of the Juridical Council, Drafts of Laws and Legal Opinions, Finished Matters, "Draft Amnesty for Those Who Seized the Administrative Power of the Country on 6 October 2519 B.E., Act B.E . . . ," 54, 87.

22. Ibid., 56.

23. "Amnesty for Those Who Seized the Administrative Power of the Country on 6 October 1976 Act," *Ratchakitchanubeksa*, 24 December 2519 [1976], book 93, part 156, 44.

24. For the amnesty for the 1947 coup, see *Ratchakitchanubeksa*, 23 December 2490 [1947], book 64, part 62, 741–44; for the amnesty for the coup that reinstated

the use of the 1932 constitution in 1951, see *Ratchakitchanubeksa*, 31 December 2494 [1951], book 84, part 80, 25–28; for the amnesty for the 1957 coup, see *Ratchakitchanubeksa*, 26 September 2500 [1957], book 74, part 81, 1–3; for the amnesty for the 1958 coup, see *Ratchakitchanubeksa*, 4 April 2502 [1959], book 76, part 41, 1–4; and for the amnesty for the 1971 coup, see *Ratchakitchanubeksa*, 26 December 2515 [1972], book 79, part 198, 234–37.

25. NA (2) So. Kho. Ko. 1/Book 996, "Draft Amnesty for Those Who Seized the Administrative Power," 87.

26. Ibid., 63.

27. Ibid., 67.

28. Ibid., 68.

29. Ibid., 71.

30. Ibid., 63.

31. *Ratchakitchanubeksa*, 26 December 2515 [1972], book 89, part 198, 234–37.

32. NA (2) So. Kho. Ko. 1/Book 996, "Draft Amnesty for Those Who Seized the Administrative Power," 67.

33. Ibid., 68.

34. Ibid., 72.

35. Francesca Lessa and Leigh Payne, "Introduction," in *Amnesty in the Age of Human Rights Accountability: Comparative and International Perspectives*, ed. Francesca Lessa and Leigh Payne (Cambridge: Cambridge University Press, 2012), 4.

36. NA (2) So. Kho. Ko. 1/Book 996, "Draft Amnesty for Those Who Seized the Administrative Power," 65. The representative from the Department of Defense was very clear about what he and his colleagues wanted from the amnesty: "Our objective is that we want [to] 'be not guilty'" (69).

37. Streckfuss, *Truth on Trial*, 122.

38. Somchai Preechasilpakul, "The Coup Rule of Law," in *The 19 September Coup: Coup for Democracy with the King as Head of State*, ed. Thanapol Eawsakul (Bangkok: Fa Diew Kan, 2550 [2007]), 192.

39. NA (2) So. Kho. Ko. 1/Book 996, "Draft Amnesty for Those Who Seized the Administrative Power," 74–75.

40. "Amnesty for Those Who Seized the Administrative Power of the Country on 6 October 1976 Act," *Ratchakitchanubeksa*, 24 December 2519 [1976], book 93, part 156, 43.

41. NA (2) So. Kho. Ko. 1/Book 996, "Draft Amnesty for Those Who Seized the Administrative Power," 65.

42. Ambiguity is rarely accidental. In the case of state violence, the use of ambiguity can be one aspect of a particular strategy of concealment that protects perpetrators, makes redress difficult, and causes further suffering for victims and survivors. For an analysis of ambiguity in relation to disappearance in Thailand, see Pratubjit Neelaphaijit, Anuk Pitukthanin, and Sorawin Sitthisan, "Research Report on the Vocabulary of Ambiguity: Victims of Forced Disappearance, Using

Nonviolence Abroad, and the Insights for Thai Society," Year 3 Report, Thailand Research Fund Project, Nonviolence and Violence in Thai Society: Knowledge, Secrecy, and Memory, 2556 [2013]; and chapter 6 of this volume.

43. National Administrative Reform Assembly, *Report of the National Administrative Reform Assembly, Meeting 1 to Meeting 5, Book 1, 1976 B.E.* (Bangkok: NARA, 2519 [1976]), 109–10.

44. Ibid., 110.

45. Ibid., 111.

46. Ibid., 110–11.

47. Ibid., 111.

48. Ibid.

49. Ibid.

50. The series of three ACAA acts passed in 1952, 1969, and 1979 provided extensive powers of arbitrary detention, denied habeas corpus, initiated proceedings in military tribunals, and avoided the usual postmortem investigations in cases of death in custody in areas declared to be communist controlled.

51. National Administrative Reform Assembly, *Report of the National Assembly*, 114.

52. Ibid., 115.

53. Despite her self-identification as an "ordinary citizen-housewife," Mrs. Chongkol was neither. She was politically active and had been appointed a senator in 1976 prior to the massacre and coup. She also played an active role in various organizations whose primary purpose was to arm and train citizens as part of counterinsurgent defense of the nation-religion-king.

54. See various accounts reprinted in her cremation volume, Phayap Srikanchana, ed., *Cremation Volume for Mrs. Chongkol Srikanchana* (Bangkok: Rongphim Krungthep 2533 [1984]). Her account raises other questions. Her description of 6 October 1976 and her active role in the defense of the nation and monarchy are worthy of further investigation.

55. National Administrative Reform Assembly, *Report of the National Assembly*, 115.

56. Ibid.

57. Ibid., 122.

58. Ibid., 124.

59. Ibid., 131.

60. The change from the harsh constriction of freedom under Thanin, evidenced by the NARC's orders and censorship, can be seen in the public response to the trial of the Bangkok Eighteen, which was described by one editorialist as follows: "One side was a cheering section that provided support for the students who were the defendants. The other side was the opposition, who were against providing an amnesty and wanted the defendants to receive a proper punishment." *Daily Time*, 19 January 2521 [1978], 4. This kind of public demonstration

would not have been possible in the immediate aftermath of 6 October while Thanin was in office.

61. For a description of growing domestic protests and calls for justice in 1978, see Thanapol and Chaithawat, "The Struggle," 330.

62. "Interview with Vasant Panich: Appealing on Behalf of 'Somyot,'" *Prachatai*, 1 April 2013, http://prachatai.com/journal/2013/04/46051.

63. Thanapol and Chaithawat, "The Struggle," 319–20.

64. This could mean that either the Krisdika was not consulted or the minutes of the meeting were not sent to the National Archives.

65. Zimmerman, *Reflections*, 110.

66. The NLA met about the amnesty law on 15 September 1978 at the request of the cabinet. On 11 October, after its passage, there was a closed meeting in the NLA about whether to make the minutes of that discussion public. A committee of ten people examined this question; of the ten, eight held military titles. The decision was to keep the minutes secret. This is the only record of the deliberations of the meeting, and beyond the day, time, and individuals present no further details are available. According to a librarian at the Parliamentary Library, there are no further records available about the second meeting, the one about what to do with the records from the first meeting, because, as the decision to keep it secret was made in the beginning, no minutes were recorded. As for the first meeting, she could only tell me that there were no records I could access. Whether this means they exist or were destroyed is unknown.

67. *Thai Rat*, 15 September 2521 [1978], 12.

68. *Sayam Rat*, 16 February 2521 [1978], 1.

69. He said, "The use of Article 27 with this case would not be good. It would be a subversion of the authority of the court. It would be better to use legal authority." *Sayam Rat*, 13 September 2521 [1978], 1.

70. *Ban Muang*, 15 September 2521 [1978], 2.

71. *Matichon*, 13 September 2521 [1978], 12.

72. *Sayam Rat*, 13 September 2521 [1978], 1. General Kriangsak's use of kinship terms here references the actions of Field Marshal Sarit Thanarat, who explicitly cast himself as the father of the Thai nation during his dictatorship (20 October 1958–8 December 1963). See Thak, *Thailand*, 1979.

73. *Siang Puangchon*, 15 September 2521 [1978], 16.

74. *Matichon*, 15 September 2521 [1978], 5.

75. *Sayam Rat*, 15 September 2521 [1978], 12.

76. *Ban Muang*, 16 September 2521 [1978], 16.

77. *Ratchakitchanubeksa*, 16 September 2521, book 95, part 97, 1.

78. Ibid., 2.

79. *Matichon*, 16 September 2521 [1978], 12.

80. *Ratchakitchanubeksa*, 16 September 2521, book 95, part 97, 3.

81. I include the caveat "perhaps" on the matter of whether those released as a result of the amnesty were legally prevented from doing so because no case of this kind has ever been brought in a Thai court. Thus the strictures of the provision in practice are unknown.

82. *Ban Muang*, 16 September 2521 [1978], 16.

83. Ibid.

84. *Thai Rat*, 16 September 2521 [1978], 16.

85. *Athit*, 16 September 2521 [1978], 12.

86. Ibid.

87. *Matichon*, 16 September 2521, 12. For example, General Sitthi Chirot, member of the NLA and the army's chief of staff, refused to make a substantive comment to any newspaper. He said that this was a matter for the assembly and he would bow to the voice of the majority. *Siang Puangchon*, 15 September 2521 [1978], 16.

88. *Matichon*, 16 September 2521 [1978], 12.

89. *Ban Muang*, 16 September 2521 [1978], 12.

90. *Matichon*, 15 September 2521 [1978], 12.

91. *Sayam Rat*, 19 September 2521 [1978], 1.

92. *Athit*, 22 September 2521 [1978], 2.

93. *Sayam Rat*, 27 September 2521 [1978], 12; *Siang Puangchon*, 27 September 2521 [1978], 12.

94. *Athit*, 14 September 2521 [1978], 3.

95. In his essay "Who Was Who in 6 October?" Somsak Jeamteerasakul uses a similar strategy of reading memoirs, letters, and newspaper and other accounts to ascertain who planned and gave the order to use violence on the morning of 6 October 1976. See Somsak Jeamteerasakul, "Who Was Who in 6 October?," in *Recently Constructed History* (Bangkok: Samnakphim 6 Tula Raluk, 2544 [2001]), 161–207. Somsak also builds on that essay and the questions raised about the precise series of events, orders, and state actors involved in a close reading of the report of the cabinet meeting on the morning of 6 October 1976. See Somsak Jeamteerasakul, "Dissecting-Settling the History of 6 October 1976: The Cabinet Meeting on 6 October 1976," *Silpawatthanatham* 24, no. 12 (October 2546 [2003]): 61–73.

96. Roosa, *Pretext*, 20.

97. Kathryn Sikkink, *The Justice Cascade: How Human Rights Prosecutions Are Changing World Politics* (New York: Norton, 2011).

98. For example, following the end of the civil war between government forces and the Frente Farabundo Martí para la Liberación Nacional in El Salvador in 1992, an amnesty law was passed that provided blanket protection for human rights violations committed during the years of the conflict. In 2013 the nation's Constitutional Court decided to hear a challenge to the constitutionality of the amnesty, and a decision is currently being awaited. If the law is overturned, it

could lead to prosecutions and the court-ordered opening of state records related to the violence that occurred during that period. See Washington Office on Latin America, "Amnesty, Impunity, and Archives in El Salvador," 7 December 2013, http://www.wola.org/video/live_stream_amnesty_impunity_and_archives_in_el_salvador.

CHAPTER 5. ACCOUNTING FOR HUMAN RIGHTS
AT THE END OF THE COLD WAR

1. Promulgated on 13 October 1976 and in force until 7 August 1979, NARC Order 22 permitted the arbitrary detention of individuals deemed to fall into one of nine categories of those who posed a "danger to society." Indefinitely renewable 90-day periods of detention were permitted under Order 22. Under the ACAA, individuals suspected of being communists could be held for up to 480 days without charge. Both measures allowed for detention by military and counterinsurgency officials in addition to police, and this detention could take place in unusual places not run by the Ministry of Justice or the Department of Corrections. This heightened the risk of torture, disappearance, and extrajudicial killing. See chapter 1 for further discussion of Order 22 and chapter 3 for further discussion of the ACAA.

2. Thanin Kraivichien held office between 8 October 1976 and 19 October 1977. General Kriangsak Chomanan held office between 20 October 1977 and 3 March 1980. General Prem Tinsulanond held office between 3 March 1980 and 4 August 1988.

3. This includes, for example, the assassination of Jit Phumisak, the leftist thinker and revolutionary, on 5 May 1966 and the assassinations of members of the Farmers' Federation of Thailand throughout 1974 and 1975.

4. For the exclusion of those detained by the US military at the Guantánamo Bay prison and others accused of being terrorists from human rights protections, see Judith Butler, *Precarious Life: The Powers of Mourning and Violence* (Durham, NC: Duke University Press, 2004); and *Frames of War: When Is Life Grievable?* (Durham, NC: Duke University Press, 2009).

5. See Thanin Kraivichien, *Using the Law to Protect against the Communists* (Bangkok: Armed Forces Security Center, 2517 [1974]), especially 111–14.

6. Moyn, *Last Utopia*, 7.

7. Ibid., 214.

8. Ibid., 121.

9. Ibid., 7; Stefan-Ludwig Hoffman, "Introduction: Genealogies of Human Rights," in *Human Rights in the Twentieth Century*, ed. Stefan-Ludwig Hoffman (Cambridge: Cambridge University Press, 2010), 4.

10. Flood, *United States*; Fineman, *Special Relationship*.

11. Thomas Lobe, *United States National Security Policy and Aid to the Thailand Police* (Denver: Graduate School of International Studies, University of Denver,

1977); Sinae Hyun, "Indigenizing the Cold War: Nation-Building by the Border Patrol Police of Thailand, 1945–1980" (PhD diss., University of Wisconsin–Madison, 2014).

12. Flood, *United States*, 1; William H. Mott, *United States Military Assistance: An Empirical Perspective* (Westport, CT: Greenwood Press, 2002), 236.

13. There were 37,644 Thais soldiers who fought on the side of the US Army. Richard Ruth, *In Buddha's Company: Thai Soldiers in the Vietnam War* (Honolulu: University of Hawai'i Press, 2011), 1.

14. United States House of Representatives, Committee on International Relations, Subcommittee on International Organizations, *Human Rights in Thailand*, Hearings, 23 and 30 June 1977, 95th cong. (Washington, DC: Government Printing Office, 1977), 7.

15. Flood, *United States*, 3.

16. Thak, "ISOC," 107–12.

17. Flood, *United States*, 5–7. See chapter 3, notes 39 and 74, respectively, for more on the Village Scouts and Krathing Daeng. The members of the Nawaphon included bureaucratic, military, and civilian elites led by Wattana Kiewvimol. There is an urgent need for additional basic research on these groups and their roles, especially the Krathing Daeng and Nawaphon, and the precise nature of their links to the CIA and other agencies of the US government. This is the kind of declassification project that would be ideal for the National Security Archive at George Washington University to take up.

18. Comptroller General of the United States, *Withdrawal of U.S. Forces from Thailand: Ways to Improve Future Withdrawal Operations, Report to the Congress* (Washington, DC: US General Accounting Office, 1977), 1.

19. Flood, *United States*, 4.

20. Jimmy Carter, "Inaugural Address," Washington, DC, 20 January 1977, https://www.jimmycarterlibrary.gov/documents/speeches/inaugadd.phtml.

21. Lynsay Skiba, "Shifting Sites of Argentine Advocacy and the Shape of the 1970s," in *The Breakthrough: Human Rights in the 1970s*, ed. Jan Eckel and Samuel Moyn (Philadelphia: University of Pennsylvania Press, 2013), 112.

22. Barbara Keys, *Reclaiming American Virtue: The Human Rights Revolution of the 1970s* (Cambridge, MA: Harvard University Press, 2014), 141.

23. Ibid., 5, 145.

24. Skiba, "Shifting Sites," 108.

25. Puey's account of leaving and being detained is included in his essay "Violence and the Coup of 6 October 1976," which has been published and anthologized multiple times. See Puey Ungpakorn, "Violence and the Coup of 6 October 1976," in *From 14 to 6 October*, ed. Charnvit Kasetsiri and Thamrongsak Petchlertanan (Bangkok: Thammasat University Press, 2541 [1998]), 49–79.

26. United States House of Representatives, *Human Rights*, 1.

27. The hearings were held from 10:30 to 12:15 on 23 June and from 2:30 to 6:00 on 30 June.

28. The paper was later published as William Bradley et al., *Thailand, Domino by Default? The 1976 Coup and Implications for U.S. Policy, with an Epilogue on the October 1977 Coup* (Athens: Center for International Studies, Ohio University, 1978).

29. United States House of Representatives, *Human Rights*, 3.

30. Ibid., 8.

31. Ibid., 15.

32. Ibid., 11.

33. Ibid., 41.

34. Ibid., 22.

35. Ibid., 11–12.

36. Ibid., 12.

37. Ibid., 28–29.

38. Ibid., 29.

39. The tiger cages were exposed to the US public after Don Luce, a World Council of Churches activist and translator, accompanied a US congressional delegation to Con Son Prison in 1970. Tom Harkin, an aide to the group who was elected to Congress in 1974, took photographs of the cages, which were published in *Life* magazine on 17 July 1970. See Holmes Brown and Don Luce, *Hostages of War: Saigon's Political Prisoners* (Washington, DC: Indochina Mobile Education Project, 1973), for a description of the cages and US government and business involvement in their construction. In 1974 Grace Paley wrote an account of Thieu Thi Tao, a woman incarcerated in one of the tiger cages at Con Son Prison for three years. Paley was moved by Thieu Thi Tao's story because she was the same age—twenty-three—as Paley's children. In her clarion voice, Paley noted, "And the money that trained the men who tortured her, the dollars that kept her in a cage, came from my country. They were American tax dollars. The brand name proudly printed on her shackles is Smith & Wesson. The cage she lived in was very likely made in America." Grace Paley, *Just As I Thought* (New York: Farrar, Straus and Giroux, 1998), 85–86.

40. United States House of Representatives, *Human Rights*, 29.

41. Ibid., 68.

42. Ibid., 41.

43. Ibid., 42.

44. Ibid., 42.

45. Ibid., 43.

46. Ibid., 49.

47. Ibid., 50.

48. Ibid.

49. Ibid.

50. I contacted the Center for Legislative Archives at the US National Archives in April 2013 to arrange to read these documents, but the staff could not locate the original copies. Puey's account of 6 October 1976 was also published in a 1977 issue of the *Bulletin of Concerned Asian Scholars* as "Violence and the Military Coup in Thailand."

51. United States House of Representatives, *Human Rights in Thailand*, 51.

52. Ibid.

53. Ibid., 55.

54. Ibid.

55. Ibid., 58.

56. Ibid., 59.

57. Ibid., 59–60.

58. Ibid., 67.

59. Ibid., 62–63.

60. The speech was given on 7 July 1977 and published in the original English and Thai translation in the quarterly journal of the National Defense College. See Kriangsak Chomanan, "Speech on 'Human Rights in Thailand,'" *Ratthaphirak* 19, no. 4 (1977): 53–60.

61. Ibid., 57.

62. Ibid., 60.

63. Kukrit Pramoj was in office from 14 March 1975 to 12 January 1976.

64. M. R. Kukrit Pramoj, "Rice Far from the Field," *Sayam Rat*, 24 February 2521 [1978], 7.

65. Ibid.

66. Ibid.

67. Ibid.

68. Ibid.

69. For a critical and moving analysis of Puey's influence on activism and thinking about human rights and accountability in the four decades following 6 October 1976, see Bencharat Sae Chua, "Thinking about Thai Human Rights through the (Non) Search for Justice and (Non) Accountability: Cases of State Violence against the Movement for Democracy," in *Puey and Thai Society in the Transitional Crisis*, ed. Prajak Kongkirati and Pokpong Junvith (Bangkok: Social Sciences and Humanities Textbook Foundation, 2559 [2015]), 111–46.

70. Phra Phaisan Visalo, "Ajarn Puey and the CGRS," n.d., http://www.visalo .org/article/person24Puay2.htm. Puey's testimony and the subsequent question and answer period was translated into Thai and published for the first time in 1981 and then reprinted another seven times. The latest is Puey Ungpakorn, *Testimony of Dr. Puey Ungpakorn about 6 October 1976* (Bangkok: Komol Keemthong Foundation, 2543 [1998]). This version is also available online at http://puey.in.th/ index.php/หนังสือ?task=view&id=12.

71. See David Banisar, *The Freedominfo.org Global Survey: Freedom of Information and Access to Government Record Laws around the World* (New York: Open Society Institute, 2004).

72. In August 1977 Clark and Wen-hsien Huang visited Thailand to assess the situation of political prisoners and human rights broadly. They left dissatisfied with the limited access they had been granted and wrote a letter of complaint to the MFA requesting additional information. There was copious correspondence between the Krisdika and the MFA about how to best respond to this request. See NA (2) So. Kho. Ko. 1/Book 1167, National Archives, Office of the Juridical Council, Drafts of Laws and Legal Opinions, Finished Matters, "English-Language Translations of Orders 22, 28, 29, 30, and 43 of the National Administrative Reform Council."

73. MFA Archive, I1002-699-405-712-2101, Department of International Organizations, Social Division, "Amnesty International and Petition Letters about Various Cases in Thailand, 2521–2522 [1978–1979]"; MFA Archive, I1002-699-405-712-2102, Department of International Organizations, Social Division, "Amnesty International Calls for the Thai Government to Release Political Prisoners in Thailand (Ordinary Cases aside from the 6 October 2519 Case and the Case of the Members of the Coordinating Group on Religion in Society), 2521–2522."

74. Amnesty International, "Appeal on Behalf of Political Prisoners in Thailand," 11 April 1978, AI Index: ASA 39/04/78.

75. MFA Archive, I1002-699-405-712-2101, "Amnesty International Calls for the Thai Government to Release Political Prisoners."

76. For an account of letter-writing between AI prisoners of conscience in Indonesia and AI activists, and how it was transformative for all parties, see Vannessa Hearman, "Letter-Writing and Transnational Activism on Behalf of Indonesian Political Prisoners: Gatot Lestario and His Legacy," *Critical Asian Studies* 48, no. 2 (2016): 145–67.

77. MFA Archive, I1002-699-405-712-2101, "Amnesty International Calls for the Thai Government to Release Political Prisoners."

78. Ibid.

79. Katherine Verdery, *Secrets and Truths: Ethnography in the Archive of Romania's Secret Police* (Budapest: Central European University Press, 2014), 60.

80. Ann Laura Stoler, *Along the Archival Grain: Epistemic Anxieties and Colonial Common Sense* (Princeton, NJ: Princeton University Press, 2010), 20.

81. MFA Archive, I1002-699-405-712-2101, "Amnesty International Calls for the Thai Government to Release Political Prisoners."

82. Ibid.

83. Ibid.

84. This is true on the occasions when AI takes up cases in Thailand. Although AI has been active since the 2014 coup, during the period between 2007 and 2013

the organization was notably silent on the imprisonment of people for allegedly defaming the monarchy.

85. In mid-1977 the CGRS became aware that it was being surveilled by the Special Branch because copies of its correspondence were being used by the Special Branch to pressure a monk who worked with the CGRS to join a counterinsurgency campaign. CGRS, *Human Rights in Thailand Report*, April 1977, 1. In late 1977 members of the CGRS were attacked in newspapers for allegedly having met with members of the Socialist Party and discussing the 6 October 1976 massacre in order to destroy the image of the country. CGRS, *Human Rights in Thailand Report*, November–December 1977, 49–50. Then, on 16 February 1978, three CGRS activists (Chaiwat Yao-wapongsiri, Sukhon Tanthakeyoon, and Boontham Chindawong) were arrested in Surat Thani. All three were accused of being communists and a danger to national security, and Sukhon, who was asthmatic, was charged with having too much medication with him. CGRS, *Human Rights in Thailand Report*, January–February 1978, 4–5. They were granted bail after thirty days of detention. On 4 February 1979 all the charges were dropped except for the medication charge against Sukhon, who had to pay a fourteen-hundred-baht fine for possession of his asthma medicine. CGRS, *Human Rights in Thailand Report*, March–April 1979, 20.

86. Nicholas Dirks, "Annals of the Archive: Ethnographic Notes on the Sources of History," in *From the Margins: Historical Anthropology and Its Futures*, ed. Brian Axel (Durham, NC: Duke University Press, 2002), 63.

87. I use "partial" here because an entire book could, and should, be written about the CGRS and the cases it followed and worked on during the 1970s, 1980s, and 1990s, as well as the ideological and political impact of its work on the Thai human rights movement and Thai society writ large.

88. Phra Phaisan Visalo, "Ajarn Puey."

89. Those involved from the beginning included Ajarn Sulak Sivaraksa (Buddhist), Dr. Koson Srisung (secretary-general of the Church of Christ in Thailand), the Reverend Somchart Cha-unthong (vice-moderator of the Church of Christ in Thailand), the Reverend Father Prasit Samanchit (executive chairman of Catholic Council for Development), Dr. Gothom Arya (Buddhist and founder of the Union for Civil Liberty), Phra Pracha Pasannathammo (Buddhist monk), and Nicholas Bennett (Buddhist and UNESCO chief adviser to the Ministry of Education). CGRS, *Human Rights in Thailand Report*, 15–31 March 1977, 2–3.

90. US House of Representatives, *Human Rights in Thailand*, 14.

91. The CGRS described its relationship with AI in the following terms: "Though there is no official link between Amnesty International and CGRS, because of shared objectives, there has always been the closest possible cooperation between the two organizations on matters involving the Thai situation. Thus when Amnesty International decided to have an international campaign to try to improve human rights in Thailand it was obvious that they would ask for suggestions about

the topics and strategies for the campaign from CGRS." CGRS, *Human Rights in Thailand Report*, March–April 1978, 43.

92. CGRS, *Human Rights in Thailand Report*, July–August 1977, 27.

93. CGRS, *Human Rights in Thailand Report*, 15–31 March 1977, 3.

94. CGRS, *Human Rights in Thailand Report*, January–February 1978, 11. Although I can only address the nature of the CGRS as an interreligious Buddhist and Christian organization for human rights in this passing mention, it is worthy of further research both in the context of Thai studies and comparatively.

95. CGRS, *Human Rights in Thailand Report*, July–August 1979, 18.

96. CGRS, *Human Rights in Thailand Report*, November–December 1979, 1.

97. Shortly after the Gwangju massacre in 1980, the CGRS sent a protest letter to the South Korean president and collected money to aid those injured. CGRS, *Human Rights in Thailand Report*, April–June 1980, 16. During a visit to Thailand by the South Korean president in early July 1981, members of CGRS and other human rights and student organizations leafleted in front of the embassy and called for justice for Gwangju and the release of political prisoners. A group of one hundred students also protested in front of the hotel where President Chun Doo-hwan gave a speech to the foreign press. CGRS, *Human Rights in Thailand Report*, July–September 1981, 27–28. On 21 December 1981 members of CGRS and the Union for Civil Liberty handed out an open letter calling for the release of political prisoners and protesting the use of martial law to restrict the Solidarity movement in Poland. CGRS, *Human Rights in Thailand Report*, October–December 1981, 16–17.

98. I am grateful in particular to Saowapha Viravong at the National Library of Australia for her help in locating these materials and to Craig Reynolds for the generous gift of his personal files on human rights.

99. Doreen Lee, *Activist Archives: Youth Culture and the Political Past in Indonesia* (Durham, NC: Duke University Press, 2016), 20.

100. This work was carried out with Jasmine Chia, Charissa Iloure, and Andrew Snyder.

101. These data were compiled from the following issues of CGRS, *Human Rights in Thailand Report*: December 1976–March 1977, 15–30 March 1977, April 1977, May–June 1977, July–August 1977, September–October 1977, November–December 1977, January–February 1978, March–April 1978, May–June 1978, September–October 1978, November–December 1978, January–February 1979, March–April 1979, May–June 1979, September–October 1979, November–December 1979, January–March 1980, April–July 1980, January–March 1981, April–June 1981, July–September 1981, October–December 1981, January–March 1981, April–June 1982, July–September 1982, October–December 1982, January–March 1983, April–June 1983, July–December 1983, January–March 1984, April–June 1984, January–March 1985, April–July 1985, August–September 1985, October–December 1985, January–March 1986, April–September 1986, October 1986–June 1987, July 1987–April 1988, and May–December 1988.

102. The Department of Corrections reported that there were 2,188 people detained at the end of 1976. Department of Corrections, *Annual Report, 1976*. At the other end of the spectrum, a source inside the ISOC said that arrest lists at the end of 1977 contained over 60,000 names. *Sayam Rat Sabda Wichan*, 18 December 2520 [1977], 16. See chapter 1 for further discussion of the wide discrepancies in numbers of detainees.

103. For background information on the Om Noi case, see Coordinating Group for Religion in Society, *The Om Noi Workers and the Problems of Human Rights* (Bangkok: Coordinating Group for Religion in Society, 2521 [1978]). For an account of the case and their release, see CGRS, *Human Rights in Thailand Report*, July–August 1979, 4.

104. For an account of the case and their release, see CGRS, *Human Rights in Thailand Report*, November–December 1978, 8; and September–October 1979, 5.

105. CGRS, *Human Rights in Thailand Report*, January–February 1978, 28.

106. CGRS, *Human Rights in Thailand Report*, July–August 1978, 13–14.

107. CGRS, *Human Rights in Thailand Report*, 15–31 March 1977, n.p.

108. CGRS, *Human Rights in Thailand Report*, May–June 1978, 22.

109. CGRS, *Human Rights in Thailand Report*, January–February 1978, 33.

110. CGRS, *Human Rights in Thailand Report*, March–April 1978, 31.

111. CGRS, *Human Rights in Thailand Report*, May–June 1978, 37.

112. Ibid., n.p.

113. Throughout the country during the Cold War and again after the declaration of martial law in southern Thailand in January 2004, the military set up temporary camps on the grounds of Buddhist temples. The temporary bases frequently served as places of detention, and reports of torture were and remain common.

114. CGRS, *Human Rights in Thailand Report*, May–June 1977, n.p.

115. CGRS, *Human Rights in Thailand Report*, September–October 1979, 7.

116. Ibid., 5.

117. Jan Eckel, "The Rebirth of Politics from the Spirit of Morality: Explaining the Human Rights Revolution of the 1970s," in *The Breakthrough: Human Rights in the 1970s*, ed. Jan Eckel and Samuel Moyn (Philadelphia: University of Pennsylvania Press, 2013), 247–48.

118. CGRS, *Human Rights in Thailand Report*, September–October 1978, 15.

119. Ibid.

120. CGRS, *Human Rights in Thailand Report*, May–June 1978, 25.

121. Ibid.

122. Ibid.

123. CGRS, *Human Rights in Thailand Report*, September–October 1979, 8–9.

124. Moyn, *Last Utopia*, 173.

125. Weschler, *A Miracle*, 237–38.

CHAPTER 6. DISAPPEARANCE AND THE
JURISPRUDENCE OF IMPUNITY

1. For a full list of Farmers' Federation of Thailand members known to have been assassinated, disappeared, or injured, see Tyrell Haberkorn, *Revolution Interrupted: Farmers, Students, Law, and Violence in Northern Thailand* (Madison: University of Wisconsin Press, 2011), 159–63.

2. Jean Sangsakul wrote for both the *Sieng Rat* and *Muang Thai* newspapers. He was arrested in late January 1977 and then disappeared. The CGRS noted that it was told that many others in Nakhon Sri Thammarat had been disappeared but it was not given names. CGRS, *Human Rights in Thailand Report*, 15–31 March 1977, 5, 17.

3. On 29 November 1975 five young men were killed by marines in Bacho district of Pattani province. A sixth young man survived to tell the story of what took place, and this sparked a call for an investigation into the killings and a protest outside the Pattani Central Mosque, which began on 11 December and continued for forty-five days with the number of participants rising to perhaps as many as one hundred thousand. See Daungyewa Utarasint, "Voices and Votes amid Violence: Voting Behaviour and Electoral Politics in Thailand's Deep South" (PhD diss. draft, Department of Political and Social Change, Australian National University, n.d.), chapter 5; and Surin Pitsuwan, *Islam and Malay Nationalism: A Case Study of Malay-Muslims of Southern Thailand* (Bangkok: Thai Khadi Research Institute, Thammasat University, 1985), 236–40.

4. CGRS, *Human Rights in Thailand Report*, November–December 1977, 26.

5. CGRS, *Human Rights in Thailand Report*, July–September 1982, 11.

6. The Working Group on Justice for Peace was founded by Angkhana Neelapaijit in June 2006 and became the JPF in December 2009 to work on issues of disappearance, human rights, and accountability. In the introduction to the report, the JPF authors wrote, "Where we found one case of an enforced disappearance or extrajudicial killing, we nearly always heard about several additional cases, some of which we were able to document. This leads us to believe that the cases documented in this report represent only a small portion of the real number of enforced disappearances in Thailand." Justice for Peace Foundation (JPF), *Enforced Disappearances in Thailand* (Bangkok: Justice for Peace Foundation, 2012), 5.

7. Many more cases remain to be uncovered. In the absence of access to the police and military archives, one method a researcher could employ would be to sift through daily newspapers for reports of missing persons, especially those last seen being arrested or otherwise held in military or police custody.

8. In both cases, the bodies were ultimately recovered and the perpetrators tried for murder in the Court of First Instance. See ibid., 11–12. For additional information about these cases, including reproductions of the court decisions, as well as the broad context of General Phao's violence and influence, see Chit, *Phao Tells All.*

9. No investigation into his disappearance has taken place. Justice for Peace Foundation, *Enforced Disappearances*, 11–12.

10. During events surrounding the protests for democracy and the crackdown during "Bloody May" of 1992, there were a number of cases of disappearance. The precise number remains unknown. The official report released by the government claimed 69 people had disappeared. Office of the Prime Minister, *A Record of Bloody May: Evidence to Prosecute the Murders of May* (Bangkok: Office of the Prime Minister, 2535 [1992]). Amnesty International reported 175 cases of missing persons. Amnesty International, *Thailand: The Massacre in Bangkok*, October 1992, AI Index: ASA 39/10/92. By 2002 the United Nations Working Group on Disappearance had taken up 31 cases of disappearance in relation to May 1992. United Nations Working Group on Enforced and Involuntary Disappearances, "Question of Enforced or Involuntary Disappearances," Commission on Human Rights, Fifty-Eighth session, 18 January 2002, E/CN.4/2002/79. More than 2,000 people were killed or disappeared as part of the so-called War on Drugs, announced by Prime Minister Thaksin Shinawatra in early 2002, to eradicate the drug trade in Thailand. Many of those targeted were not involved with the drug trade but had come into conflict with local officials over other matters. See Human Rights Watch, *Not Enough Graves: The War on Drugs, HIV/AIDS, and Violations of Human Rights* (New York: Human Rights Watch, 2004). The JPF documented 59 cases of disappearance between 2002 and 2012 primarily in the north and south of the country. Justice for Peace Foundation, *Enforced Disappearances*, 3. In March 2007 Human Rights Watch reported on 22 cases of disappearance in or related to conflict in the south, including the case of Somchai Neelapaijit. Human Rights Watch, *"It Was Like Suddenly My Son No Longer Existed": Enforced Disappearances in Thailand's Southern Border Provinces* (New York: Human Rights Watch, 2007).

11. Thanong Pho-an, a senator and labor activist, was disappeared in June 1991 under the military government of the National Peace Keeping Council. The JPF noted, "He was last seen by a colleague leaving his office on the evening of 19 June 1991. Thanong was an insulin-dependent diabetic and did not have his medication with him at the time of his disappearance. The following morning his car was found parked at a strange angle on the curb in front of his office with what appeared to be footprints of army boots on the backseat. Thanong has not been seen since." Justice for Peace Foundation, *Enforced Disappearances*, 13–14. Several government investigations into his disappearance were carried out, but the results were not made available to the public. Billy was a Karen activist in Kaeng Krachan National Park in Phetchburi province who disappeared on 17 April 2014 following a conflict with park officials.

12. Since the 22 May 2014 coup, activist friends in Thailand have also expressed a fear of being disappeared. An international activist outside the country asked me if I knew why this was such a persistent fear and one that seemed out of joint with

the numbers of people disappeared. My response was to point to the unresolved history of disappearance in Thailand.

13. Marguerite Feitlowitz, *A Lexicon of Terror: Argentina and the Legacies of Torture* (Oxford: Oxford University Press, 1998), 57.

14. Pratubjit Neelapaijit and Anuk Pitukthanin, "Enforced Disappearance and the Implications of Ambiguity," in *Nonviolence Space, Thailand Future: Knowledge, Secret, Memory*, ed. Chaiwat Satha-anand (Bangkok: Protestista, 2559 [2016]), 29–76.

15. Ibid., 40.

16. Carlo Ginzburg, "Checking the Evidence: The Judge and the Historian," *Critical Inquiry* 18 (Autumn 1991): 84–85.

17. See Carlo Ginzburg, *The Judge and the Historian* (New York: Verso, 1999); Tyrell Haberkorn, "When Torture Is a Duty: The Murder of Imam Yapa Kaseng and the Challenge of Accountability in Thailand," *Asian Studies Review* 39, no. 1 (2015): 53–68; on the assassination of Rama VIII, see Somsak Jeamteerasakul, "New Information about the Case of Regicide: Who Is the Real Suspect?," *Fa Diew Kan* 7, no. 3 (2552 [2009]): 60–93; and Somsak Jeamteerasakul, "The Puzzle of the Regicide," *Fa Diew Kan* 6, no. 2 (2551 [2008]): 116–49. Natalie Zemon Davis's *Fiction in the Archives: Pardon Tales and Their Tellers in Sixteenth-Century France* (Stanford, CA: Stanford University Press, 1987) is a different kind of reading against the grain of legal and archival documents for other accounts of excess not contained by the law.

18. See chapter 3 of this book for an example of this kind of analysis in the cases of the burning of Ban Na Sai and the *thang daeng* killings in Phatthalung. See also Samson Lim, "The Case of Volunteer 8: Proof, Violence, and History in Thai Society," *Critical Asian Studies* 43, no. 3 (2011): 399–420; and Rodolfo Walsh, *Operation Massacre*, trans. Daniella Gitlin (New York: Seven Stories Press, 2013).

19. Some scholars and critics are explicit about their concern with justice and others leave it implied, but, I would argue, their concern is visible in their choice of topic.

20. Craig J. Reynolds, "The Plot of Thai History: Theory and Practice," in *Patterns and Illusions: Thai History and Thought in Memory of Richard B. Davis*, ed. Gehan Wijeyewardene and E. C. Chapman (Singapore: Institute of Southeast Asian Studies, 1992), 329–30.

21. Ibid., 318.

22. Ibid.

23. Ibid.

24. See Working Group on Human Rights Defenders, *The Disappearance of Lawyer Somchai Neelapaijit Is a Reflection of the Culture of Authoritarianism in Thai Society* (Bangkok: Working Group on Human Rights Defenders, 2547 [2004]).

25. See Thanet, *Rebellion*; and McCargo, *Tearing Apart the Land*.

26. International Commission of Jurists, *THAILAND: Report on the Criminal Trial and Investigation of the Enforced Disappearance of Somchai Neelapaijit* (Bangkok: International Commission of Jurists, 2009), 12.

27. The petition is reproduced in ibid., 42–43.

28. The letter was published in full in Bunruam Thiemchan, *The Case of the Disappearance of Lawyer Somchai* (Bangkok: Samnakphim Mala Plus One, 2549 [2006], 30–32.

29. Angkhana Neelapaijit, *Reading between the Lines* (Bangkok: Working Group on Justice for Peace Foundation, 2009), 11.

30. The DSI is a state organization under the Ministry of Justice that was established in 2002 to investigate cases related to national security, cases of organized crime, and cases in which the police or other state officials are the suspected perpetrators. Although the police carried out the investigation that led to this prosecution, following requests from Angkhana Neelapaijit, the case was officially transferred to the DSI in July 2005. International Commission of Jurists, *THAILAND*, 39.

31. They were charged with violation of Articles 83, 309, and 340 of the Criminal Code.

32. International Commission of Jurists, *THAILAND*, 15.

33. Although there is an Office of Witness Protection in Thailand, witnesses often have difficulty obtaining protection, and the form of protection can be tenuous. In addition, the protection is generally provided by the police, which means that in cases such as the disappearance of Somchai Neelapaijit, the same organization that the accused perpetrators work for was responsible for protecting those testifying about their crimes. In the case of the initial protection provided to Angkhana Neelapaijit, the Asian Legal Resource Centre noted that the witness protection was more like a form of surveillance and harassment. See Asian Legal Resource Centre, *Protecting Witnesses or Perverting Justice in Thailand*, special issue, *Article 2* 5, no. 3 (2006).

34. For detailed trial observation reports, see International Commission of Jurists, *THAILAND*; and Asian Human Rights Commission, *The Disappearance of a Person and the Defects of a System: A Collection of Notes from the Trial of the Police over the Abduction of Thai Human Rights Lawyer Somchai Neelapaijit* (Hong Kong: Asian Human Rights Commission and Asian Legal Resource Centre, 2006).

35. International Commission of Jurists, *THAILAND*, 24.

36. The cause of these procedural technicalities was the failure of Police Major Ngern to appear in court for the reading of the verdict. On 19 September 2008 he was reported missing following a mudslide near the Khwae Noi dam in Phitsanulok province. His body was never found, even though those of all the other victims of the mudslide, which occurred in a confined area, were located. The lack of a body created doubts about the veracity of his status as a missing person and suggested that he may have changed his identity. Since he was one of the defendants in the case and did not appear for the reading of the verdict, a warrant to appear

had to be issued and sent by registered mail to his address of record and also posted in a public place before the verdict could be read in his absence.

37. I list the names of the judges in the text in order to emphasize that the decisions were authored by specific individuals, which is elided by using the phrasing "The court ruled that . . ." There is no open database of judges and their decisions, at least not yet, so it is not possible to track the perspective of a particular judge over time and in different matters of law. The version of the full verdict by the Criminal Court [Black case No. 1952/2547, Red case No. Oo.48/2549, 21 January 2006, Office of the Attorney General (and Mrs. Angkhana Neelapaijit, Miss Sudprathana Neelapaijit, Miss Pratubjit Neelapaijit, Miss Kobkuson Neelapaijit and Miss Krongtham Neelapaijit) v. Police Major Ngern Thongsuk, Police Major Sinchai Nimbunkampong, Police Sergeant Major Chaiweng Paduang, Police Sergeant Rundorn Sithiket, and Police Lieutenant Colonel Chadchai Liamsanguan] that I cite is the one that was published in Bunruam, *Case*, 90–186. Hereafter I cite this decision as "Criminal Court verdict," with the corresponding page numbers. Criminal Court verdict, 91–92.

38. Criminal Court verdict, 184–85.

39. Ibid., 148–49.

40. Ibid., 149.

41. Ibid., 150.

42. Ibid., 152.

43. Ibid., 153.

44. Ibid., 153–54.

45. Ibid., 155.

46. Police Major Ngern was easily identifiable compared to the others because he was relatively large and balding (personal communication, Nick Cheesman, 15 September 2016).

47. Criminal Court verdict, 176.

48. Ibid., 100.

49. Ibid., 100–101.

50. Ibid., 179.

51. Ibid., 103–4.

52. Ibid., 107.

53. Ibid., 108.

54. Ibid.

55. Ibid., 106.

56. Ibid., 109.

57. Ibid., 147.

58. Danthong Breen, "Appendix I: Issues Concerning Mobile Phone Evidence," in Asian Human Rights Commission, *The Disappearance of a Person*, 137.

59. Criminal Court verdict, 183.

60. Craig Reynolds identifies repetition, along with redundancy, perspective, exaggeration, and the use of protagonists, as the way writers of history sustain plot. Reynolds, "Plot," 328.

61. Criminal Court verdict, 184.

62. Ibid., 185 (my emphasis).

63. The version of the Appeal Court verdict that I cite [Black Case No. 4717–4718/2549, Red Case No. 10915–10916/2553, Office of the Attorney General (and Mrs. Angkhana Neelapaijit, Miss Sudprathana Neelapaijit, Miss Pratubjit Neelapaijit, Miss Kobkuson Neelapaijit and Miss Krongtham Neelapaijit) v. Police Major Ngern Thongsuk, Police Major Sinchai Nimbunkampong, Police Sergeant Major Chaiweng Paduang, Police Sergeant Rundorn Sithiket, and Police Lieutenant Colonel Chadchai Liamsanguan] is the official one issued and paginated by the court. Hereafter I cite this decision as "Appeal Court verdict," with the corresponding page numbers. Appeal Court verdict, 42.

64. Appeal Court verdict, 58.

65. Ibid., 37.

66. Ibid.

67. The version of the Supreme Court verdict that I cite [No. 10915, 22 September 2558 [2015], Office of the Attorney General (and Mrs. Angkhana Neelapaijit, Miss Sudprathana Neelapaijit, Miss Pratubjit Neelapaijit, Miss Kobkuson Neelapaijit and Miss Krongtham Neelapaijit) v. Police Major Ngern Thongsuk, Police Major Sinchai Nimbunkampong, Police Sergeant Major Chaiweng Paduang, Police Sergeant Rundorn Sithiket, and Police Lieutenant Colonel Chadchai Liamsanguan] is the official one issued and paginated by the court. Hereafter I cite this decision as "Supreme Court verdict," with the corresponding page numbers. Supreme Court verdict, 7–8.

68. "Angkhana Neelapaijit: The Case of the Enforced Disappearance of Somchai Neelapaijit and a New Norm in the Judicial Process," *Matichon*, 29 December 2558 [2015], http://www.matichon.co.th/news_detail.php?newsid=1451377162.

69. Thaksin is quoted in Bunruam, *Case*, 48.

70. In November 2006 the Office of the Attorney General claimed to have evidence of Somchai's death, and the commander in chief of the army and leader of the 19 September 2006 coup, General Sonthi Boonyaratglin, claimed, "I have received information from investigators that some individuals close to former prime minister Thaksin were behind the disappearance of Somchai." International Commission of Jurists, *THAILAND*, 40.

71. Department of Rights and Liberties Protection, Ministry of Justice, "Draft Act on the Prevention and Suppression of Torture and Enforced Disappearance B.E . . . ," 18 February 2558 (2015). This law builds on antitorture legislation drafted in 2010 by the Human Rights Lawyers Association and the Cross Cultural Foundation. For a copy of this draft, see iLaw, "Torture Law and the Prevention of Torture," 19 November 2553 (2010), http://ilaw.or.th/node/592.

72. There are reports that torture and disappearance are being used by military officials under the NCPO.

73. Department of Rights and Liberties Protection, "Draft Act."

74. Disappearance cases have been reopened and prosecuted in Chile and Argentina. If a law criminalizing disappearance is passed in Thailand in the future, this would be possible, at least in theory.

75. Sudprathana, "When [My] Father . . . Was Disappeared," in *The Disappearance of Persons Is the Disappearance of Justice* (Bangkok: Working Group on Justice for Peace, 2549 [2006]).

76. Justice for Peace Foundation, *Enforced Disappearances*, 5.

77. Ibid., 3–4.

78. John Roosa, "The State of Knowledge about an Open Secret: Indonesia's Mass Disappearances of 1965–1966," *Journal of Asian Studies* 75, no. 2 (2016): 281–97.

79. Ibid., 281.

80. Ibid., 292.

81. Ibid.

CHAPTER 7. WHO CAN BE KILLED WITH IMPUNITY
AND WHO CANNOT BE IMPUGNED?

1. Tyrell Haberkorn, "Collusion and Influence behind the Assassinations of Human Rights Defenders in Thailand," *article 2* 4, no. 2 (April 2005): 58–63.

2. See Pasuk Phongpaichit and Chris Baker, *Thaksin: The Business of Politics in Thailand* (Chiang Mai: Silkworm Books, 2004), for an analysis of Thaksin as a capitalist-cum-politician.

3. Some prominent human rights activists joined the PAD in calling for Thaksin's ouster. The rights abuses during his regime, which maintained the status quo of prior and future regimes, fails to explain the fundamental contradiction of why people who worked for human rights were willing to support a military coup.

4. See Charles Keyes, *Finding Their Voice: Northeastern Villagers and the Thai State* (Chiang Mai: Silkworm Books, 2014), for a sophisticated analysis of shirt color, geography, and the nation.

5. Bhumipol Adulyadej was born on 5 December 1927. He ascended the throne on 9 June 1946 following the death of his older brother, Ananda Mahidol. He died on 13 October 2016 and his son, Maha Vajiralongkorn, was named the new king.

6. On 3 December 2008 the Constitutional Court dissolved the red-shirt-aligned People's Power Party (PPP), which was formed after the dissolution of the TRT. All the members of parliament associated with the PPP, and therefore with prime minister Somchai Wongsawat, were removed from power. Abhisit Vejjajiva was then appointed prime minister by a parliament reduced in both size and political perspective.

7. Serhat Ünaldi, *Working towards the Monarchy: The Politics of Space in Downtown Bangkok* (Honolulu: University of Hawai'i Press, 2016).

8. Thongchai Winichakul, "Thongchai Winichakul on the Red 'Germs,'" *New Mandala*, 3 May 2010, http://asiapacific.anu.edu.au/newmandala/2010/05/03/thongchai-winichakul-on-the-red-germs/.

9. On 26 April 2010 Colonel Sansern Kaewkamnerd, spokesperson for both the CRES and the army, announced that the red shirt protesters were part of a wide-ranging network that was plotting the overthrow of the monarchy. He disseminated an elaborate drawing that linked the protesters to politicians, capitalists, activists, writers, academics, and media outlets. At the time, the revelation of this alleged plot aided in making the killings of red shirts seem necessary for the preservation of the institution of the monarchy. See *Matichon*, 27 April 2553 [2010], 1, 14, 15. Less than two years later, the DSI announced that there was no evidence suggesting that there was ever such a plot. By that point, the crackdown on the protesters was a fait accompli and many of those named had been targeted in witch hunts. For a critique of the dissemination of the plot story as a *talok marana* (deadly joke), see Kasian Tejapira, "The Postmortem of the 'Plot to Overthrow the Monarchy,'" *Matichon*, 27 April 2555, 6. For a visual critique in the form of a *phang sang jao* (plot to build the monarchy), see the cover and fold-out pages in *Fa Diew Kan* 10, no. 2 (2555 [2012]).

10. See Sikkink, *Justice Cascade*.

11. Nidhi Eoseewong, "The Past-Present-Future of the Judgment," *Matichon*, 8 September 2557 [2014], 20.

12. The original Thai-language judgment in Daranee Charnchoengsilpakul's case can be found in *Fa Diew Kan* 7, no. 3 (2552 [2009]): 200–231. *Fa Diew Kan* also published an English translation of the judgment in *Fa Diew Kan* 7, no. 4 (2552 [2009]), 130–51. Sasiwimol's is case No. 681 and can be found in the iLaw online Freedom of Expression Documentation Center, http://freedom.ilaw.or.th/en/case/681.

13. Amsterdam and Peroff LLP on Behalf of the National United Front for Democracy against Dictatorship, "Application to Investigate the Situation of the Kingdom of Thailand with Regard to the Commission of Crimes against Humanity," a report presented to the Office of the Prosecutor of the International Criminal Court, 31 January 2011. This report was simultaneously submitted to the International Criminal Court (ICC) as an independent referral and request that the ICC investigate the crackdown. Although Thailand is not a state party to the Rome Statute, the treaty establishing the ICC, the ICC could choose to launch an investigation if it determined that genocide, crimes against humanity, or war crimes had been committed and there was no satisfactory domestic investigation. The credibility of the report was reduced because, although the authors placed the April–May 2010 violence in the context of the history of state violence and impunity, the events of the Thaksin years, namely, the so-called War on Drugs and the

Tak Bai massacre, are not mentioned. During the Tak Bai massacre, a total of eighty-six people died as a result of the dispersal of a protest outside a police station in Narathiwat province on 25 October 2014. Eight people were shot and killed by state security officials, and the other seventy-eight were crushed and suffocated during the six-hour trip to a military base for detention following arrest. Approximately fifteen hundred people were arrested, but the authorities did not have enough vehicles to transport them all without stacking the people on top of one another. Those who were on the bottom were dead on arrival at the base.

14. People's Information Center for Those Affected by the Dispersal of Protests in April–May 2010, *Truth for Justice: The Events and Impacts of the Dispersal of Protests in April–May 2010* (Bangkok: People's Information Center, 2555 [2012]).

15. Truth and Reconcilitation Commission of Thailand, *Report of the Truth and Reconciliation Commission of Thailand, July 2010–July 2012* (Bangkok: TRCT, 2012).

16. National Human Rights Commission, *Report on the Investigation for Policy Recommendations about the Incident of the UDD Demonstrations between 12 May 2010 and 29 May 2010* (Bangkok: NHRC, 2556 [2013]).

17. The second of these premises refers to the presence of the so-called men in black, whose existence remains unconfirmed. Some allege that they were an armed wing of the red shirt movement, while others allege that they were an elite armed state force.

18. A full accounting of these differences is beyond the scope of this chapter. One sharp difference, though, is that the NHRC report treats the red shirt protesters as the perpetrators, not victims, of human rights violations. See Puangthong Pawakapan, "Voices of the Victims: Truth for Justice," in People's Information Center for Those Affected by the Dispersal of Protests in April–May 2010, *Truth for Justice: The Events and Impacts of the Dispersal of Protests in April–May 2010* (Bangkok: People's Information Center, 2555 [2012]), 12. In addition, see Duncan McCargo and Naruemon Thabchumpon, "Wreck/Conciliation? The Politics of Truth Commissions in Thailand," *Journal of East Asian Studies* 14, no. 3 (2014): 377–404, for a comparison of the TRCT and People's Information Center reports.

19. Two prominent cases in which this has occurred are the Tak Bai massacre and the murder of Imam Yapa Kaseng. Imam Yapa Kaseng was arrested on 19 March 2008 and died shortly afterward as a result of being tortured while in army custody. For further details on the murder of Imam Yapa, see Haberkorn, "When Torture Is a Duty."

20. See "Four Years of Bloody April–May: Summary of the Inquest Orders, Where Did the Bullets Come From," *Prachatai*, 10 April 2014, http://www.pracha tai.com/journal/2014/04/52648; and "Court Order in the Autopsy of Kriangkrai Khamnoi, Died Due to Massive Blood Loss, the Bullet Came from the Soldiers," *Prachatai*, 4 July 2014, http://www.prachatai.com/journal/2014/07/54421.

21. *Matichon*, 30 October 2556 [2013], 12.

22. Article 84 defines the instigation of others to commit a crime as a crime itself. Article 83 makes it possible to create a link between the person who requested a crime be committed and execution of the crime. Article 80 defines the attempt to commit a crime as a crime. Article 59 describes the presence of intention to commit a crime as premeditation.

23. *Matichon*, 30 October 2556 [2013], 12.

24. Between late October 2013 and the 22 May 2014 coup, Suthep was the primary leader of the People's Democratic Reform Committee (PDRC), which was engaged in extended street protests in Bangkok. He cited his role in the protests as the reason why he could not appear any earlier for his formal indictment at the court.

25. See *Ratchakitchanubeksa* (special edition), 7 April 2553 [2010], book 127, part 45 ngo, 1–2, for the declaration of the state of emergency and invocation of the emergency decree. See p. 7 for the establishment of the CRES and the appointment of Suthep Thaugsuban as director. Two orders from Suthep to the commanders of the military units in the streets authorizing the use of weapons against the protesters, on 10 and 13 April, were made public. See People's Information Center, *Truth for Justice*, 1335–37.

26. Somchai Preechasilpakul, an associate professor of law at Chiang Mai University, raised this issue following the dismissal of charges by the Criminal Court. In particular, he noted that the point that needed to be analyzed was whether the soldiers who shot and murdered the people did so of their own accord or because they were ordered to do so. *Matichon*, 31 August 2557 [2014], 11.

27. For example, the Military Court Act of 2502 [1955] places proceedings against soldiers for crimes allegedly committed while on duty within the military justice system. In cases of torture and disappearance, the lack of categories for these crimes within the existing Criminal Code creates challenges for victims and their lawyers. Even in cases in which individual state perpetrators have been prosecuted in the judicial system for violence against citizens, such as several cases of extrajudicial killing committed by the police, witnesses and families of victims report facing intimidation, harassment, and violence in retaliation for daring to bring the case or testify against the police.

28. For a full description of the NACC's mandate and functions, see the Organic Act on Counter Corruption of 2542 [1999].

29. Attaphon cited the final section of Article 143 of the Criminal Procedure Code, which stipulates, "In the case of murder where a person is killed by an official alleged to be on account of carrying out his duty, or has died while being kept in custody by an official alleged to be on account of carrying out his duty, the prosecution or nonprosecution order may only be given by the attorney general or the person in charge of his functions."

30. *Matichon*, 30 October 2556 [2013], 12.

31. *Sayam Rat*, 30 October 2556 [2013], 2.

32. It is difficult to read Abhisit's statement about the illegality of the protests without noting its disingenuousness. The ruling that he refers to was made on 5 April 2010 when the Civil Court dismissed a petition that Abhisit had submitted requesting that the court order the UDD to lead the red shirt protesters out of the Ratchaprasong area. In response, the Civil Court ruled that Abhisit already had the power under the Internal Security Act, which had been activated on 7 March 2010, prior to the beginning of the protests, to take appropriate and necessary action to protect, suppress, restrain, check and resolve or mitigate any situations affecting national security. In its dismissal of the petition, the Civil Court noted, "The facts from the examination show that the actions of the five leaders and the demonstrators have blocked and obstructed the transportation routes and use of the vehicles of ordinary citizens. This has had a significant impact on business, including creating hardship for ordinary citizens in making a living and carrying on with their lives. Therefore, the demonstrations are an obstruction of the free-dom of movement of the citizens who use public roads and impacts national security. It is a use of the right to demonstration that is in excess of that stipulated in Articles 34 and 63 of the 2007 constitution." The decision is quoted in Korakot Phiengjai, *The Martyrs of 10 April: Faces of the Dead, Lives of the Murdered* (Bang-kok: Heroes of Democracy Foundation, 2554 [2011]), 177. Abhisit did not petition the Civil Court to rule on the legality of the protests but on the authority of his own potential actions. In retrospect, given the violent crackdown that began five days after he confirmed his authority through the court's dismissal, it is difficult to not view the petition as a form of preventive protective legal action.

33. *Sayam Rat*, 30 October 2556 [2013], 2.

34. Ibid.

35. Such selective remembering, or selective valuation of certain lives, is also reflected in comments Abhisit made concerning the events of April–May 2010 during an interview with the BBC on 10 December 2012 in which he noted that "unfortunately some people died." See BBC, Hardtalk, "Interview with Abhisit Vejjajiva," BBC, 10 December 2010, http://www.bbc.co.uk/programmes/b0126g9c.

36. *Sayam Rat*, 30 October 2556 [2013], 2.

37. Ibid.

38. Ibid.

39. Ibid.

40. *Khao Sod*, 30 August 2557 [2014], 14.

41. Ibid., 3. *Khao Sod* published the entire text of Thongchai Senamontri's dis-senting opinion.

42. Ibid.

43. Ibid.

44. Article 157 stipulates, "Whoever, being an official, wrongfully exercises or does not exercise any of his functions to the injury of any person, or dishonestly

exercises of omits to exercise any of his functions, shall be punished with imprisonment of one to ten years or fined two thousand or to twenty thousand baht,
or both."

45. The full text of the appeal was printed in *Khao Sod*, 30 September 2557
[2014], 3.

46. *Khao Sod*, 30 August 2557 [2014], 14.

47. Ibid.

48. "The Appeal from the Injured—Families of the Dead—in the 'Abhisit-
Suthep' Order to Disperse the 2010 Red Shirt Protests Case," *Prachatai*, 1 October
2014, http://prachatai.com/journal/2014/10/55779.

49. Streckfuss, *Truth on Trial*, 5. Streckfuss offers an excellent analysis of the
genesis of Article 112 in the context of judicial and other repressive measures.
While official statistics from the Office of the Judiciary have not been made public
since 2010, the number of complaints filed under Article 112 rose from 33 in 2005
to 30 in 2006, 126 in 2007, 77 in 2008, 164 in 2009, and 478 in 2010. See "'Hid-
eous Bars': Display of LM Case Statistics in the Middle of Ratchadamnoen Road,"
Prachatai, 17 December 2011, http://prachatai.com/journal/2011/12/38371.

50. These case statistics are updated monthly by iLaw and can be found online
at https://freedom.ilaw.or.th/.

51. Pronthip Munkhong and Patiwat Saraiyaem were sentenced on 23 February 2015 to two and a half years in prison for performing in the satirical play *The
Wolf Bride*, which was deemed to insult the king. Uncle Opas (last name withheld)
was sentenced on 20 March 2015 to one and a half years in prison for writing
graffiti deemed to insult the king on the walls of a bathroom stall in a Bangkok
shopping mall.

52. These include specialized units set up by the police, army, and other state
agencies, as well as various uncivil society organizations. Primary among these is
the Rubbish Collection Organization established by Rienthong Nanna, a physi-
cian and former military officer, which launches online witch hunts against people
it believes are insulting the monarchy on social media and makes frequent formal
complaints of violation of Article 112 to the police. Rienthong led a campaign of
coordinated submissions of complaints to police stations around the country,
which led to the arrests of Pronthip and Patiwat noted above.

53. Thongchai Winichakul, "A Social Political Regime Which Resists Change
Is Truly Dangerous," lecture in support of the proposed amendment of Article 112,
Friends of the Constitution, Bangkok, 11 February 2555 [2012]; Thongchai Win-
ichakul, *Thailand's Hyper-royalism: Its Past Success and Present Predicament*, ISEAS
Trends in Southeast Asia, no. 7 (Singapore: Institute of Southeast Asian Studies,
2016).

54. Mo Noi, *The Karma of Those Who Topple the Monarchy* (Bangkok: Bangkok
Books, 2553 [2010]).

55. Nidhi, "Past-Present-Future."

56. Unlike Somyot, Yutthapoom is not a public figure. In reportage around his case, his family name is used, but activists have left it unstated in the service of partial protection of his privacy. I have chosen to withhold it here for this reason.

57. Under the emergency decree, which was in force between 7 April and 22 December 2010, individuals could be arbitrarily detained for up to thirty days before a formal criminal complaint had to be brought.

58. At the time Somyot was arrested, Jakrapob was living in exile in Cambodia.

59. Bail is routinely denied in Article 112 cases. The court cites the classification of the crime as one of national security that carries a potentially lengthy sentence, and therefore the possibility of flight by the defendant, as the reason for the denial.

60. The Constitutional Court was established by the 1997 constitution, and it has been retained in the subsequent constitutions. The Constitutional Court does not hold open sessions but rather offers comments and rules on a range of petitions submitted by different parties. One of the key differences between the roles of the Constitutional Court under the two constitutions is that in the 2007 version the Constitutional Court examines petitions from individual citizens alleging a violation of rights and determines whether a specific legal provision is constitutional. The Court holds "final authority over all matters of constitutional interpretation." Andrew Harding and Peter Leyland, *Constitutional Courts: A Comparative Study* (London: Wildy, Simmonds and Hill, 2011), 164.

61. On 28 March 2013 Ekachai Hongkangwan was found guilty of violating Article 112 and the 2008 Film and Video Act and sentenced to three years and four months in prison for allegedly selling compact discs that contained copies of Wikileaks documents and a copy of an ABC (Australia) news program critical of the Thai royal family. On 8 May 2014 the Appeal Court upheld the original verdict and sentence, but on 9 October 2015 the Supreme Court upheld the verdict but reduced the sentence by one-third to two years and eight months. Ekachai was released on 15 November 2015.

62. To be clear, my own position is that democracy and monarchy are not compatible.

63. For an alternative interpretation, see an essay by Thanapol Eawsakul, who notes, "We should interpret this measure to be in line with a constitutional democracy, not interpret it through the lens of absolutist ideology. [Absolutist ideology] means that the king is protected by Article 112 and 'is a sacrosanct figure that cannot be impugned." Thanapol Eawsakul, "Scorched by the Sky That Looms Above for Laughing at Illegitimate Traditions: Daranee Charnchoengsilpakul's Struggle and Her Unjust Punishment," *Fa Diew Kan* 7, no. 3 (2552 [2009]): 188.

64. Constitutional Court, Ruling No. 28–29/2555, Issues Examined Nos. 16 and 44/2555, 10 October 2555 [2012], On the Matter of Whether or Not Article 112 Is in Conflict with Articles 3 (paragraph 2), Article 29, or Article 45 (paragraphs 1 and 2), 4–5 of the Constitution.

65. Ibid., 6.

66. Ibid.

67. Thongchai, "Experimental Proposal."

68. In 2011, in a delayed response to a petition filed by Daranee Charnchoeng-silpakul, the Constitutional Court ruled that a closed trial does not impact the rights and liberties of a citizen because the accused and the accused's lawyer are allowed to be present. In Daranee Charnchoengsilpakul's case, the Constitutional Court noted, "Examination in secret does not mean that either side will not be treated fairly in the judicial process and does not in any way restrict the rights of the defendant in a criminal case. This is because with regard to examination in secret, Article 178 of the Criminal Procedure Code mandates that involved individuals have the right to be in the courtroom, such as the plaintiff and the plaintiff's lawyer, the defendant and the defendant's lawyer, the defendant's guards, witnesses, experts, interpreters, etc. This shows that Article 177 of the Criminal Procedure Code is an article in line with the basic rights of individuals in the justice system put in place by the Constitution even though it has some limiting effects on the rights and freedoms of individuals. *But this is a limiting of individual rights and freedoms only to the extent that it is necessary. There are no significant repercussions on rights and freedoms.*" Constitutional Court, Order No. 38/2552, Issue Examined No. To. 17/2552, 21 October 2552 [2009], On the Matter Regarding Miss Daranee Charnchoengsilpakul's (Petititioner) Request for the Constitutional Court to Rule, Using Article 212 of the 2007 Constitution of the Kingdom of Thailand, the Instance of Whether Article 177 of the Criminal Procedure Code Is in Conflict with Articles 29 or Article 40 (2) of the 2007 Constitution of the Kingdom of Thailand (my emphasis). Those deemed to be disloyal to the monarchy do not register as equal members of the polity protected by the constitution. Therefore, their rights and liberties do not register as in need of protection.

69. See "Release of the Abbreviated Judgment: Ten Years Imprisonment for Somyot as an Editor Guilty of Violating Article 112, Foreign Observation That This Sets a Norm of Self-Censorship," *Prachatai*, 3 January 2013, http://www.pra chatai.com/journal/2013/01/44842. The full decision (Criminal Court, Decision in Black Case No. Or. 2962/2554. Red Case No. Or. 272/2556, 23 January 2556 [2013], Office of the Attorney General V. Mr. Somyot Prueksakasemsuk) was printed in *Fa Diew Kan* 11, no. 1 (2556 [2013]), 237–63. In his introduction to the decision, Thanapol Eawsakul commented that only five days prior to Somyot's arrest, he had issued a press release calling for a campaign to reform Article 112, and that "this may have been the actual crime for which Somyot Prueksakasemsuk had to be put in his place behind bars." Thanapol Eawsakul, "Reading the Judgment of Somyot Prueksakasemsuk as a Political Instrument and Problem of 'Royal Authority' in a Democracy," *Fa Diew Kan* 11, no. 1 (2556 [2013]), 235.

70. Before the formal charges were filed by the prosecutor, there was an attempt at mediation. This was fictionalized in a short story by Thanthawut Taweewaro-domkul, who was imprisoned at the Bangkok Remand Prison while Yutthapoom

was awaiting trial. See Lao Sun, "From the Lèse Majesté Fiction Files," trans. Tyrell Haberkorn, *Prachatai*, 14 August 2013, http://www.prachatai.com/english/node/3668.

71. I observed the witness hearings in this case, and the quotes I use here are from my notes. I checked these against the daily record of witness testimony made by the court, which is cited in the subsequent notes. In addition, iLaw compiled a detailed record of the witness hearings, which can be found at its online bilingual Freedom of Expression Documentation Center, case no. 439, http://freedom.ilaw.or.th/en/case/439.

72. Thanawat (family name withheld), Witness Testimony, Red Case No. Or. 3434/2555, Office of the Attorney General V. Yutthapoom (family name withheld).

73. Ibid.

74. Ibid.

75. Ibid.

76. Ibid.

77. Ibid.

78. Ibid.

79. Kralamphak Phraekthong, Witness Testimony, Red Case No. Or. 3434/2555, Office of the Attorney General V. Yutthapoom (family name withheld).

80. Yutthapoom had been forced to write the word "dickhead" one hundred times with a permanent marker as part of this process at the CSD.

81. Yutthapoom (family name withheld), Witness Testimony, Red Case No. Or. 3434/2555, Office of the Attorney General V. Yutthapoom (family name withheld).

82. Orn (family name withheld), Witness Testimony, Red Case No. Or. 3434/2555, Office of the Attorney General V. Yutthapoom (family name withheld).

83. Ibid.

84. Ibid.

85. Criminal Court decision, Black Case No. Or. 3434/2555, Red Case No. Or. 3112/2556, 13 September 2013, Office of the Attorney General V. Yutthapoom (family name withheld).

86. Thanapol, "Reading," 235.

87. Writing about the constriction of freedom of expression in China under the CCP, Liu Xiaobo makes a point that is relevant to late-reign Rama IX Thailand as well: "If every person were to speak just one sentence of truth on major issues that affect society, the dictatorship would fail, no matter how brutal it might be. As resistance to public mendacity builds among the people, drop by drop, eventually the drops will come together to form a flood, and a dictatorship that needs lies in order to maintain itself will find it hard to continue." Liu Xiaobo, *No Enemies, No Hatred: Selected Essays and Poems*, edited by Perry Link, Tienchi Martin-Liao, and Liu Xia (Cambridge, MA: Belknap Press of Harvard University Press, 2012), 298.

88. Puangthong, "Voices," 14. See also Eduardo Galeano, *Upside Down: A Primer for the Looking-Glass World*, trans. Mark Fried (New York: Picador, 2000).

89. Puangthong, "Voices," 17.

CONCLUSION

1. The 19 September 2006 coup was a military coup, but it led to a series of illegitimate civilian governments rather than a military dictatorship.

2. International Commission of Jurists and Thai Lawyers for Human Rights, Submission to the Universal Periodic Review of Thailand, United Nations Human Rights Council, 25th Session of the Working Group on Universal Periodic Review, 21 September 2015.

3. Puangthong Pawakapan, "Thai Junta Militarizes the Management of Natural Resources," *ISEAS Perspective*, 3 September 2015.

4. Human Rights Watch, "Thailand: Deepening Repression One Year after the Coup," 22 May 2015, https://www.hrw.org/news/2015/05/22/thailand-deepen ing-repression-one-year-after-coup.

5. Preecha Kaewbanpaew, a retired teacher, was sentenced to a four-thousand-baht fine and three months in prison, suspended, for giving flowers to members of Resistant Citizen, a dissident cultural political group. "Elderly Teacher Gets 3 Months for Giving Flower to Anti-junta Activist," *Prachatai*, 23 May 2016, http://www.prachatai.com/english/node/6182. Anon Numpa, a lawyer and member of Resistant Citizen, has been charged for standing still in protest against the junta. "Update: Human Rights Lawyer Indicted with Showing Support for Junta Critics," *Prachatai*, 24 May 2016, http://www.prachatai.com/english/node/6186.

6. See, for example, World Organization against Torture, "Thailand: Human Rights Lawyer Sirikan Charoensiri Summoned to Appear before the Public Prosecutor," THA 001 / 0715 / OBS 055.5, 10 May 2016, http://www.omct.org/human -rights-defenders/urgent-interventions/thailand/2016/05/d23757/.

7. Anuthee Dejthevaporn, comments made during the program "How Free Is Thailand's Media Now?," Foreign Correspondents' Club of Thailand, Bangkok, 3 May 2016.

8. On 31 October 2015 Attachak Sattayanurak, Somchai Preechasilpakul, and four academic colleagues read a one-page statement titled "The University Is Not a Military Base" in Chiang Mai. Less than a month later, they were summoned to appear and informed that they had been charged with carrying out an illegal political protest consisting of five or more persons.

9. Thanakorn (family name withheld) is a factory worker who was arrested on 8 December 2015 and accused of violating Article 112 by defaming Thongdaeng, the king's deceased pet dog, on Facebook. He was detained by the military for seven days and then spent another eighty-six days in detention at the Bangkok Remand Prison before being granted bail. For more information on his case, see iLaw, "Documentation Center Case #702: Thanakorn: Clicked Like on Lèse Majesté

Facebook Page and Satirized Royal Dog," http://freedom.ilaw.or.th/en/case/702. For more information regarding the defamation case of the princess, see "Two Lèse Majesté Suspects Get 3 Years, 8 Months in Prison," *Prachatai*, 30 May 2016, http://www.prachatai.com/english/node/6205.

10. Yutthasak (family name withheld), a Bangkok taxi driver, was sentenced to two and a half years in prison on 14 August 2014 for violation of Article 112 after one of his passengers recorded their conversation and reported him to the police. See "Taxi Driver Jailed 2.5 Years for Lèse Majesté in Political Talk with Passenger," *Prachatai*, 14 August 2014, http://www.prachatai.org/english/node/4285. Patnaree Chankij, the mother of a prominent student activist, was accused of lèse majesté for a one-word Facebook reply of *ja*, a participle that can mean either assent, disinterest, or something else altogether. See Richard C. Paddock, "Activist's Mother in Thailand Faces Long Prison Term for One-Word Facebook Reply," *New York Times*, 8 May 2016, A8.

11. The monarchy and the nation are linked in official ideology, but in practical, material terms, what is the connection between a private conversation between two individuals and security of the monarchy, an institution whose wealth is greater than many small and medium-sized nations?

12. See chapter 7; and Tyrell Haberkorn, "Southern Thailand: Persistent Injustice and Extrajudicial Violence," in *Diminishing Conflicts in Asia and the Pacific*, ed. Anthony Regan and Edward Aspinall (London: Routledge, 2012), 189–200.

13. Whether this is this case will only be determined in retrospect.

14. "Though they write last and are little read, academic historians have the tools for critical analysis that can identify continuities in public policy from past to present and offer suggestions for correction. In the struggle to overcome the oblivion so central to impunity, historical narrative can appropriate other disciplines such as law and psychology, incorporating their strongest points, contextualizing their insights, and offering a comprehensive analysis." McCoy, *Torture and Impunity*, 266.

15. Adrienne Rich, *A Wild Patience Has Taken Me This Far: Poems, 1978–1981* (New York: Norton, 1981), 22.

16. Trouillot, *Silencing the Past*.

BIBLIOGRAPHY

This bibliography is organized by both language and type of material. In the Thai-language section, both the original bibliographic information and an English translation are included. I list and alphabetize the sources by the roman alphabet, as the English translation is the referent present in the notes. With respect to material published in print and online newspapers, news articles are not cited individually in the bibliography, but signed columns are included. The *Ratchakitchanubeksa* (Royal Thai Government Gazette) is treated as a periodical and details for materials published in it are included in the notes but not cited individually in the bibliography.

ENGLISH-LANGUAGE BOOKS, ARTICLES, AND OTHER PUBLISHED MATERIAL

Adam, Dawne. "The Tuol Sleng Archives and the Cambodian Genocide." *Archivaria* 45 (1998): 5–26.

Agamben, Giorgio. *State of Exception*. Translated by Kevin Attell. Chicago: University of Chicago Press, 2005.

Amnesty International. "Appeal on Behalf of Political Prisoners in Thailand." AI Index: ASA 39/04/78, 11 April 1978.

———. *Thailand: The Massacre in Bangkok*. AI Index: ASA 39/10/92, October 1992.

Amsterdam and Peroff LLP on Behalf of the National United Front for Democracy against Dictatorship. "Application to Investigate the Situation of the Kingdom of Thailand with Regard to the Commission of Crimes against Humanity." Report presented to the Office of the Prosecutor of the International Criminal Court, 31 January 2011.

Anderson, Benedict. "Studies of the Thai State: The State of Thai Studies." In *The Study of Thailand: Analyses of Knowledge, Approaches, and Prospects in Anthropology, Art History, Economics, History, and Political Science*, edited by Eliezer B. Ayal, 193–247. Athens: Center for International Studies, Ohio University, 1978.

———. "Withdrawal Symptoms: Social and Cultural Aspects of the October 6 Coup." *Bulletin of Concerned Asian Scholars* 9, no. 3 (1977): 13–30.

Angkhana Neelapaijit. *Reading between the Lines*. Bangkok: Working Group on Justice for Peace Foundation, 2009.

Anuthee Dejthevaporn. Comments made during the program "How Free Is Thailand's Media Now?" Foreign Correspondents' Club of Thailand, Bangkok, 3 May 2016.

Arendt, Hannah. *The Origins of Totalitarianism*. New York: Harcourt Brace Jovanovich, 1973.

Asian Human Rights Commission. *The Disappearance of a Person and the Defects of a System: A Collection of Notes from the Trial of Five Police over the Abduction of Thai Human Rights Lawyer Somchai Neelaphaijit*. Hong Kong: Asian Human Rights Commission and Asian Legal Resource Centre, 2006.

———. "THAILAND: Call for Observers in Freedom of Expression Case." AHRC-STM-214-2014, 26 December 2014. http://www.humanrights.asia/news/AHRC-STM-214-2014.

———. "THAILAND: Concern for Detainees of the Military Junta." AHRC-STM-102-2014, 25 May 2014. http://www.humanrights.asia/news/ahrc-news/AHRC-STM-102-2014/.

———. "THAILAND: Court Demonstrates Contempt for Human Rights by Jailing Torture Victim on Say-So of Alleged Perpetrator." AHRC-STM-103-2011, 11 August 2011. http://www.humanrights.asia/news/ahrc-news/AHRC-STM-103-2011.

———. "THAILAND: Human Rights Defender and Law Professor Charged by Junta." AHRC-STM-121-2014, 18 June 2014. http://www.humanrights.asia/news/AHRC-STM-121-2014.

———. "THAILAND: Ongoing Criminalization of Thought and Expression." AHRC-STM-172-2014, 22 September 2014. http://www.humanrights.asia/news/ahrc-news/AHRC-STM-172-2014.

———. "THAILAND: Revocation of Passports by Junta Restricts Freedom of Movement and Creates Spectre of Statelessness." AHRC-STM-135-2014, 12 July 2014. http://www.humanrights.asia/news/AHRC-STM-135-2014.

———. "THAILAND: Verdict in Landmark Freedom of Expression Case." AHRC-UAU-018-2012, 31 May 2012. http://www.humanrights.asia/news/urgent-appeals/AHRC-UAU-018-2012.

———. "THAILAND: Verdict on Somchai's Case—His Wife, Daughter Could Not Be Plaintiffs; Not Enough Evidence to Convict Accused." AHRC-UAU-017-2011, 17 March 2011. http://www.humanrights.asia/news/urgent-appeals/AHRC-UAU-017-2011.

———. "UPDATE (Thailand): Hundreds of Detainees Released from 'Vocational Training' Camps." UP-154-2007, 20 November 2007. http://www.ahrchk.net/ua/mainfile.php/2007/2667.

———. "UPDATE (Thailand): Hundreds Released from Army Detention Prevented from Going Home." UP-143-2007, 2 November 2007. http://www.ahrchk.net/ua/mainfile.php/2007/2641.

Asian Legal Resource Centre. "Persecution of Torture Victims and the Legalization of Impunity in Thailand." Submission to the Eighteenth Session of the United Nations Human Rights Council. A/HRC/18/NGO/35, 11 July 2011.

———. Protecting Witnesses or Perverting Justice in Thailand. Special issue, article 2 5, no. 3 (2006).

Baker, Chris. "Afterword." In Pen and Sail: Literature and History in Early Bangkok, by Nidhi Eoseewong, 361–84. Chiang Mai: Silkworm Books, 2005.

———. "An Internal History of the Communist Party of Thailand." Journal of Contemporary Asia 33, no. 4 (2003): 510–41.

Baker, Chris, and Pasuk Phongpaichit. A History of Thailand. New York: Cambridge University Press, 2005.

Banisar, David. The Freedominfo.org Global Survey: Freedom of Information and Access to Government Record Laws around the World. New York: Open Society Institute, 2004.

BBC Hardtalk. "Interview with Abhisit Vejjajiva." BBC, 10 December 2010. http://www.bbc.co.uk/programmes/b0126g9c.

Boudreau, Vince. "Interpreting State Violence in Asian Settings." In State Violence in East Asia, edited by N. Ganesan and Sung Chull Kim, 19–46. Lexington: University Press of Kentucky, 2013.

Bowie, Katherine. Rituals of National Loyalty: An Anthropology of the State and the Village Scout Movement in Thailand. New York: Columbia University Press, 1997.

Bradley, William, David Morrell, David Szanton, and Stephen Young. Thailand, Domino by Default? The 1976 Coup and Implications for U.S. Policy, with an Epilogue on the October 1977 Coup. Athens: Center for International Studies, Ohio University, 1978.

Breen, Danthong. "Appendix I: Issues Concerning Mobile Phone Evidence." In The Disappearance of a Person and the Defects of a System: A Collection of Notes from the Trial of Five Police over the Abduction of Thai Human Rights Lawyer Somchai Neelaphaijit, by Asian Human Rights Commission, 129–37. Hong Kong: Asian Human Rights Commission and Asian Legal Resource Centre, 2006.

Brown, Holmes, and Don Luce. Hostages of War: Saigon's Political Prisoners. Washington, DC: Indochina Mobile Education Project, 1973.

Butler, Judith. Frames of War: When Is Life Grievable? Durham, NC: Duke University Press, 2009.

————. *Precarious Life: The Powers of Mourning and Violence.* Durham, NC: Duke University Press, 2004.

Butler, Judith, and Gayatri Spivak. *Who Sings the Nation-State? Language, Politics, Belonging.* New York: Seagull Books, 2007.

Carter, Jimmy. "Inaugural Address." Washington, DC, 20 January 1977. https://www.jimmycarterlibrary.gov/documents/speeches/inaugadd.phtml.

Catholic Church and Paulo Evaristo Arns. *Brasil: Nunca Mais.* Petrópolis: Vozes, 1986.

Catholic Church, Joan Dassin, and Jaime Wright. *Torture in Brazil: A Report.* New York: Vintage, 1986.

————. *Torture in Brazil: A Shocking Report on the Pervasive Use of Torture by Brazilian Military Governments, 1964–1979.* Austin: Institute of Latin American Studies, University of Texas, 1998.

Cheesman, Nick. *Opposing the Rule of Law: How Myanmar's Courts Make Law and Order.* Cambridge: Cambridge University Press, 2015.

Comptroller General of the United States. *Withdrawal of U.S. Forces from Thailand: Ways to Improve Future Withdrawal Operations, Report to the Congress.* Washington, DC: US General Accounting Office, 1977.

Corrigan, Philip, and Derek Sayer. *The Great Arch: English State Formation as Cultural Revolution.* London: Basil Blackwell, 1985.

Daungyewa Utarasint. "Voices and Votes amid Violence: Voting Behaviour and Electoral Politics in Thailand's Deep South." PhD diss. draft, Department of Political and Social Change, Australian National University, n.d.

Davis, Natalie Zemon. *Fiction in the Archives: Pardon Tales and Their Tellers in Sixteenth- Century France.* Stanford, CA: Stanford University Press, 1987.

Dennis, John Value. "The Role of the Thai Student Movement in Rural Conflict, 1973–1976." MS thesis, Cornell University, 1982.

Department of Corrections. *Annual Report, 1976.* Bangkok: Ministry of Interior, 1977.

————. *Annual Report, 1977.* Bangkok: Ministry of Interior, 1978.

————. *Annual Report, 1978.* Bangkok: Ministry of Interior, 1979.

————. *Annual Report, 1979.* Bangkok: Ministry of Interior, 1980.

————. *Information on Department of Corrections.* Bangkok: Ministry of Interior, 1968.

Dirks, Nicholas. "Annals of the Archive: Ethnographic Notes on the Sources of History." In *From the Margins: Historical Anthropology and Its Futures*, edited by Brian Axel, 47–65. Durham, NC: Duke University Press, 2002.

Doyle, Kate. "Letter from Guatemala—The Atrocity Files—Deciphering the Archives of Guatemala's Dirty War." *Harper's*, December 2007, 52–64.

Eckel, Jan. "The Rebirth of Politics from the Spirit of Morality: Explaining the Human Rights Revolution of the 1970s." In *The Breakthrough: Human Rights in the 1970s*, edited by Jan Eckel and Samuel Moyn, 226–60. Philadelphia: University of Pennsylvania Press, 2013.

Eckel, Jan, and Samuel Moyn, eds. *The Breakthrough: Human Rights in the 1970s.* Philadelphia: University of Pennsylvania Press, 2013.

European Co-ordinating Committee for Solidarity with the Thai People. *Political Repression in Thailand.* London: Ad Hoc Group for Democracy in Thailand, 1978.

Feitlowitz, Marguerite. *A Lexicon of Terror: Argentina and the Legacies of Torture.* Oxford: Oxford University Press, 1998.

Ferrara, Federico. *The Political Development of Modern Thailand.* Cambridge: Cambridge University Press, 2015.

Fineman, Daniel. *A Special Relationship: The United States and Military Government in Thailand, 1947–1948.* Honolulu: University of Hawai'i Press, 1997.

Flood, E. Thadeus. *The United States and the Military Coup in Thailand: A Background Study.* Berkeley: Indochina Resource Center, 1976.

Funston, John. *Southern Thailand: The Dynamics of Conflict.* Honolulu: East-West Center, 2008.

Galeano, Eduardo. *Upside Down: A Primer for the Looking-Glass World.* Translated by Mark Fried. New York: Picador, 2000.

Ginzburg, Carlo. "Checking the Evidence: The Judge and the Historian." *Critical Inquiry* 18 (1991): 79–92.

———. *The Judge and the Historian.* New York: Verso, 1999.

Guha, Ranajit. "The Prose of Counter-Insurgency." In *Subaltern Studies II: Writings on South Asian History and Society*, edited by Ranajit Guha, 1–42. Oxford: Oxford University Press, 1983.

Haberkorn, Tyrell. "Collusion and Influence behind the Assassinations of Human Rights Defenders in Thailand." *article 2* 4, no. 2 (2005): 58–63.

———. *Revolution Interrupted: Farmers, Students, Law, and Violence in Northern Thailand.* Madison: University of Wisconsin Press, 2011.

———. "Southern Thailand: Persistent Injustice and Extrajudicial Violence." In *Diminishing Conflicts in Asia and the Pacific*, edited by Anthony Regan and Edward Aspinall, 189–200. London: Routledge, 2012.

———. "An Uneasy Engagement: Political Crisis and Human Rights Culture in Thailand, 1958 to 1988." In *Rights to Culture: Heritage, Language, and Community in Thailand*, edited by Coeli Barry, 115–34. Chiang Mai: Silkworm Books and Princess Maha Chakri Sirindthorn Anthropology Centre, 2013.

———. "An Unfinished Past: The 1974 Land Rent Control Act and Assassination in Northern Thailand." *Critical Asian Studies* 41, no. 1 (2009): 1–43.

———. *Voices of a Free Media: The First Ten Years of Prachatai.* Bangkok: Foundation for Community Educational Media and Heinrich Böll Foundation, 2014.

————. "When Torture Is a Duty: The Murder of Imam Yapa Kaseng and the Challenge of Accountability in Thailand." *Asian Studies Review* 39, no. 1 (2015): 53–68.

Harding, Andrew, and Peter Leyland. *Constitutional Courts: A Comparative Study.* London: Wildy, Simmonds and Hill, 2011.

Harris, Verne. "The Archival Sliver: Power, Memory, and Archives in South Africa." *Archival Science* 2, no. 1 (2002): 63–86.

Haseman, John B. "National Security." In *Thailand: A Country Study*, edited by Barbara Leitch LePoer, 225–86. Washington, DC: Federal Research Division, 1989.

Hearman, Vannessa. "Letter-Writing and Transnational Activism on Behalf of Indonesian Political Prisoners: Gatot Lestario and His Legacy." *Critical Asian Studies* 48, no. 2 (2016): 145–67.

Hoffman, Stefan-Ludwig. "Introduction: Genealogies of Human Rights." In *Human Rights in the Twentieth Century*, edited by Stefan-Ludwig Hoffman, 1–28. Cambridge: Cambridge University Press, 2010.

Human Rights Watch. *"It Was Like Suddenly My Son No Longer Existed": Enforced Disappearances in Thailand's Southern Border Provinces.* New York: Human Rights Watch, 2007.

————. *Not Enough Graves: The War on Drugs, HIV/AIDS, and Violations of Human Rights.* New York: Human Rights Watch, 2004.

————. "Thailand: Account for 'Disappeared' Political Activist." 18 June 2014. http://www.hrw.org/news/2014/06/18/thailand-account-disappeared-political -activist.

————. "Thailand: Deepening Repression One Year after the Coup." 22 May 2015. https://www.hrw.org/news/2015/05/22/thailand-deepening-repression-one -year-after-coup.

————. "Thailand: End Crackdown on Academic Freedom." 20 September 2014. http://www.hrw.org/news/2014/09/20/thailand-end-crackdown-academic -freedom.

Hyun, Sinae. "Indigenizing the Cold War: Nation-Building by the Border Patrol Police, 1945–1980." PhD diss., University of Wisconsin–Madison, 2014.

iLaw. "Documentation Center Case #702: Thanakorn: Clicked Like on Lèse Majesté Facebook Page and Satirized Royal Dog." http://freedom.ilaw.or.th/en/ case/702.

International Commission of Jurists. *More Power, Less Accountability: Thailand's New Emergency Decree.* Geneva: International Commission of Jurists, 2005.

————. *Ten Years without Truth: Somchai Neelapaijit and Enforced Disappearances in Thailand.* Bangkok and Geneva: International Commission of Jurists, 2014.

————. *THAILAND: Report on the Criminal Trial and Investigation of the Enforced Disappearance of Somchai Neelapaijit.* Bangkok: International Commission of Jurists, 2009.

International Commission of Jurists and Thai Lawyers for Human Rights. Submission to the Universal Periodic Review of Thailand. United Nations Human Rights Council, 25th Session of the Working Group on Universal Periodic Review, 21 September 2015.

International Crisis Group. "Thailand's Emergency Decree: No Solution." Asia Report No. 105, 18 November 2005. http://www.crisisgroup.org/home/index .cfm?id=3795&l=1.

Iriye, Akira, Petra Goedde, and William I. Hitchcock, eds. *The Human Rights Revolution: An International History*. Oxford: Oxford University Press, 2012.

Ivarsson, Søren, and Lotte Isager, eds. *Saying the Unsayable: Monarchy and Democracy in Thailand*. Copenhagen: Nordic Institute for Asian Studies Press, 2010.

Jeffery, Renée. *Amnesties, Accountability, and Human Rights*. Philadelphia: University of Pennsylvania Press, 2014.

Jularat Damrongviteetam. "Narratives of the 'Red Barrel' Incident: Collective and Individual Memories in Lamsin, Southern Thailand." In *Oral History in Southeast Asia: Memories and Fragments*, edited by Kah Seng Loh, Ernest Koh, and Alistair Thomson, 101–18. New York: Palgrave Macmillan, 2013.

Justice for Peace Foundation. *Enforced Disappearances in Thailand*. Bangkok: Justice for Peace Foundation, 2012.

Kasian Tejapira. *Commodifying Marxism: The Formation of Modern Thai Radical Culture, 1927–1958*. Kyoto: Kyoto University Press, 2001.

———. "'Party as Mother': Ruam Wongphan and the Making of a Revolutionary Metaphor." In *Traveling Nation-Makers: Transnational Flows and Movements in the Making of Modern Southeast Asia*, 188–208. Singapore: National University of Singapore Press in association with Kyoto University Press, 2011.

Keys, Barbara J. *Reclaiming American Virtue: The Human Rights Revolution of the 1970s*. Cambridge, MA: Harvard University Press, 2014.

Keyes, Charles. *Finding Their Voice: Northeastern Villagers and the Thai State*. Chiang Mai: Silkworm Books, 2014.

Kriangsak Chomanan. "Speech on 'Human Rights in Thailand.'" *Ratthaphirak* 19, no. 4 (October–December 1977): 53–60.

Lao Sun. "From the Lèse Majesté Fiction Files." Translated by Tyrell Haberkorn. *Prachatai*, 14 August 2013. http://www.prachatai.com/english/node/3668.

Lee, Doreen. *Activist Archives: Youth Culture and the Political Past in Indonesia*. Durham, NC: Duke University Press, 2016.

LePoer, Barbara Leitch, ed. *Thailand: A Country Study*. Washington, DC: Federal Research Division, 1989.

Lessa, Francesca, and Leigh Payne. "Introduction." In *Amnesty in the Age of Human Rights Accountability: Comparative and International Perspectives*, edited by Francesca Lessa and Leigh Payne, 1–18. Cambridge: Cambridge University Press, 2012.

Lim, Samson. "The Case of Volunteer 8: Proof, Violence, and History in Thai Society." *Critical Asian Studies* 43, no. 3 (2011): 399–420.

Liu Xiaobo. *No Enemies, No Hatred: Selected Essays and Poems.* Edited by Perry Link, Tienchi Martin-Liao, and Liu Xia. Cambridge, MA: Belknap Press of Harvard University Press, 2012.

Lobe, Thomas. *United States National Security Policy and Aid to the Thailand Police.* Denver: Graduate School of International Studies, University of Denver, 1977.

Marx, Karl. *Marx/Engels Selected Works.* Vol. 1. Translated by William Lough. Moscow: Progress Publishers, 1969.

McCargo, Duncan. "Network Monarchy and Legitimacy Crises in Thailand." *Pacific Review* 18, no. 4 (2005): 499–519.

———. *Tearing Apart the Land: Islam and Legitimacy in Southern Thailand.* Ithaca, NY: Cornell University Press, 2008.

McCargo, Duncan, and Naruemon Thabchumpon. "Wreck/Conciliation? The Politics of Truth Commissions in Thailand." *Journal of East Asian Studies* 14, no. 3 (2014): 377–404.

McCoy, Alfred W. *The Politics of Heroin in Southeast Asia.* New York: Harper and Row, 1972.

———. *Torture and Impunity: The U.S. Doctrine of Coercive Interrogation.* Madison: University of Wisconsin Press, 2012.

Merieau, Eugenie. "Thailand's Deep State, Royal Power, and the Constitutional Court (1997– 2015)." *Journal of Contemporary Asia* 46, no. 3 (2016): 445–66.

Merry, Sally. *Human Rights and Gender Violence: Translating International Law into Local Justice.* Chicago: University of Chicago Press, 2006.

Morrell, David, and Chai-anan Samudavanija. *Political Conflict in Thailand: Reform, Reaction, Revolution.* Cambridge, MA: Oelgeschlager, Gunn and Hain, 1981.

Mott, William H. *United States Military Assistance: An Empirical Perspective.* Westport, CT: Greenwood Press, 2002.

Moyn, Samuel. *The Last Utopia: Human Rights in History.* Cambridge, MA: Belknap Press of Harvard University Press, 2010.

Nowak, Manfred. "Report of the Special Rapporteur on Torture and Other Cruel, Inhuman or Degrading Treatment or Punishment (Addendum): Study on the Phenomena of Torture, Cruel, Inhuman or Degrading Treatment or Punishment in the World, Including an Assessment of Conditions of Detention." Human Rights Council, Geneva, Thirteenth Session, Agenda item 3, Promotion and Protection of All Human Rights, Civil, Political, Economic, Social and Cultural Rights, including the Right to Development. 2010. A/HRC/13/39/Add.5.

Office of the Juridical Council's Welfare Fund. *Constitution of the Kingdom, B.E. 2515.* Bangkok: Office of the Juridical Council's Welfare Fund, 1972.

Orentlicher, Diane. "Updated Set of Principles for the Protection and Promotion of Human Rights through Action to Combat Impunity." Commission on Human Rights, Economic and Social Council, 8 February 2005. E/CN.4/2005/102/Add.1.

Paddock, Richard C. "Activist's Mother in Thailand Faces Long Prison Term for One-Word Facebook Reply." *New York Times*, 8 May 2016, A8.

Pakorn Nilprapunt. "Unofficial Translation of the Constitution of the Kingdom of Thailand (Interim), B.E. 2557 (2014)." 23 July 2014. http://lawdrafter.blogspot.com/2014/07/translation-of-constitution-of-kingdom.html.

Paley, Grace. *Just As I Thought*. New York: Farrar, Straus and Giroux, 1998.

Pasuk Phongpaichit and Chris Baker. *Thaksin: The Business of Politics in Thailand*. Chiang Mai: Silkworm Books, 2004.

Payne, Leigh. *Unsettling Accounts: Neither Truth nor Reconciliation in Confessions of State Violence*. Durham, NC: Duke University Press, 2007.

Pridi Banomyong. *Pridi by Pridi: Selected Writings on Life, Politics, and Economy*. Translated by Chris Baker and Pasuk Phongpaichit. Chiang Mai: Silkworm Books, 2000.

Puangthong Pawakapan. "Thai Junta Militarizes the Management of Natural Resources." *ISEAS Perspective*, 3 September 2015.

Puey Ungpakorn. "Violence and the Military Coup in Thailand." *Bulletin of Concerned Asian Scholars* 9, no. 3 (1977): 4–12.

Reporters without Borders. "Appeal Court Upholds Website Editor's Wrongful Conviction." 7 November 2013. http://en.rsf.org/thailande-appeal-court-upholds-website-07-11-2013,45439.html.

Reynolds, Craig. "The Plot of Thai History: Theory and Practice." In *Patterns and Illusions: Thai History and Thought in Memory of Richard B. Davis*, edited by Gehan Wijeyewardene and E. C. Chapman, 313–32. Singapore: Institute of Southeast Asian Studies, 1992.

———. *Thai Radical Discourse: The Real Face of Thai Feudalism Today*. Ithaca, NY: Southeast Asia Program, Cornell University, 1987.

Reynolds, Craig, and Team. "Time's Arrow and the Burden of the Past: A Primer on the Thai Un-State." *Sensate: A Journal for Experiments in Critical Media Practice*, 2011. http://sensatejournal.com/2012/05/craig-reynolds-et-al-times-arrow/.

Reynolds, E. Bruce. *Thailand's Secret War: The Free Thai, OSS, and SOE during World War II*. Cambridge: Cambridge University Press, 2004.

Rich, Adrienne. *A Wild Patience Has Taken Me This Far: Poems, 1978–1981*. New York: Norton, 1981.

Riggs, Fred. *Thailand: The Modernization of a Bureaucratic Polity*. Honolulu: East-West Center Press, 1967.

Roosa, John. *Pretext to Mass Murder: The September 30th Movement and Suharto's Coup d'État in Indonesia*. Madison: University of Wisconsin Press, 2006.

———. "The State of Knowledge about an Open Secret: Indonesia's Mass Disappearances of 1965–1966." *Journal of Asian Studies* 75, no. 2 (2016): 281–97.

Ruth, Richard. *In Buddha's Company: Thai Soldiers in the Vietnam War*. Honolulu: University of Hawai'i Press, 2011.

Scott, James C. *Domination and the Arts of Resistance: Hidden Transcripts*. New Haven, CT: Yale University Press, 1992.

Sikkink, Kathryn. *The Justice Cascade: How Human Rights Prosecutions Are Changing World Politics*. New York: Norton, 2011.

Simpson, Brad. "'Human Rights Are Like Coca-Cola': Contested Human Rights Discourses in Suharto's Indonesia." In *The Breakthrough: Human Rights in the 1970s*, edited by Jan Eckel and Samuel Moyn, 186–203. Philadelphia: University of Pennsylvania Press, 2013.

Skiba, Lynsay. "Shifting Sites of Argentine Advocacy and the Shape of the 1970s." In *The Breakthrough: Human Rights in the 1970s*, edited by Jan Eckel and Samuel Moyn, 107–24. Philadelphia: University of Pennsylvania Press, 2013.

Somsak Jeamteerasakul. "The Communist Movement in Thailand." PhD diss., Monash University, 1991.

Stoler, Ann Laura. *Along the Archival Grain: Epistemic Anxieties and Colonial Common Sense*. Princeton, NJ: Princeton University Press, 2010.

Streckfuss, David. "The End of the Endless Exception? Time Catches Up with Dictatorship in Thailand." Fieldsights—Hot Spots. *Cultural Anthropology Online*, 23 September 2014. http://www.culanth.org/fieldsights/567-the-end-of-the-endless-exception-time-catches-up-with-dictatorship-in-thailand.

———. *Truth on Trial: Defamation, Treason, and Lèse-Majesté*. New York: Routledge, 2011.

Subramanyan, Arjun. "Reinventing Siam: Ideas and Culture in Thailand, 1920–1944." PhD diss., University of California, Berkeley, 2013.

Surin Pitsuwan. *Islam and Malay Nationalism: A Case Study of Malay-Muslims of Southern Thailand*. Bangkok: Thai Khadi Research Institute, Thammasat University, 1985.

Tausig, Benjamin. "Bangkok Is Ringing." PhD diss., New York University, 2013.

Thai Lawyers for Human Rights. "Public Statement against the Invocation of Section 44 of the Constitution of the Kingdom of Thailand (Interim), B.E. 2557 (2014)." 30 March 2015. https://tlhr2014.wordpress.com/2015/03/30/public-statement-against-the-invocation-of-section-44-of-the-constitution-of-the-kingdom-of-thailand-interim-b-e-2557-2014/.

Thak Chaloemtiarana. *Thailand: The Politics of Despotic Paternalism*. Bangkok: Social Science Association of Thailand, 1979.

Thak Chaloemtiarana, ed. *Thai Politics: Extracts and Documents, 1932–1957*. Bangkok: Social Science Association of Thailand, 1978.

Thanapol Eawsakul. "An Account of Reporting Oneself." *Prachatai*, 3 June 2014. http://www.prachatai.org/english/node/4080.

Thanet Aphornsuvan. *Rebellion in Southern Thailand: Contending Histories*. Honolulu: East-West Center, 2007.

Thantawut Taweewarodomkul. "Why I Did Not Report Myself." Translated by Tyrell Haberkorn. *Prachatai*, 28 July 2014. http://www.prachatai.org/english/node/4249.

Thongchai Winichakul. "The Changing Landscape of the Past: New Histories in Thailand since 1973." *Journal of Southeast Asian Studies* 26, no. 1 (1995): 99–120.

———. "Remembering/Silencing the Traumatic Past: The Ambivalent Memories of the October 1976 Massacre in Bangkok." In *Cultural Crisis and Social Memory: Modernity and Identity in Thailand and Laos*, edited by Shigeharu Tanabe and Charles Keyes, 243–86. Honolulu: University of Hawai'i Press, 2002.

———. *Thailand's Hyper-royalism: Its Past Success and Present Predicament*. ISEAS Trends in Southeast Asia, no. 7. Singapore: Institute of Southeast Asian Studies, 2016.

———. "Thongchai Winichakul on the Red 'Germs.'" *New Mandala*, 3 May 2010. http://asiapacific.anu.edu.au/newmandala/2010/05/03/thongchai-winich akul-on-the-red-germs/.

Trouillot, Michel-Rolph. *Silencing the Past: Power and the Production of History*. Boston: Beacon Press, 1995.

Ünaldi, Serhat. *Working towards the Monarchy: The Politics of Space in Downtown Bangkok*. Honolulu: University of Hawai'i Press, 2016.

United Nations. *UN Yearbook on Human Rights for 1958*. Lake Success, NY: United Nations, 1960.

———. *UN Yearbook on Human Rights for 1959*. Lake Success, NY: United Nations, 1961.

———. *UN Yearbook on Human Rights for 1960*. Lake Success, NY: United Nations, 1962.

———. *UN Yearbook on Human Rights for 1961*. Lake Success, NY: United Nations, 1964.

———. *UN Yearbook on Human Rights for 1962*. Lake Success, NY: United Nations, 1964.

United Nations Working Group on Arbitrary Detention. "Fact Sheet #26 of the Office of the High Commissioner for Human Rights: The Working Group on Arbitrary Detention." Undated. http://www.unhchr.ch/html/menu6/2/fs26.htm.

United Nations Working Group on Enforced and Involuntary Disappearances. "Question of Enforced or Involuntary Disappearances." Commission on Human Rights, Fifty-Eighth Session, 18 January 2002. E/CN.4/2002/79.

United States House of Representatives, Committee on International Relations, Subcommittee on International Organizations. *Human Rights in Thailand*, Hearings, 23 and 30 June 1977, 95th cong. Washington, DC: Government Printing Office, 1977.

Verdery, Katherine. *Secrets and Truths: Ethnography in the Archive of Romania's Secret Police*. Budapest: Central European University Press, 2014.

Wagner-Pacifici, Robin. "The Innocuousness of State Lethality in an Age of National Security." *South Atlantic Quarterly* 107, no. 3 (2008): 459–83.

Walsh, Rodolfo. *Operation Massacre*. Translated by Daniella Gitlin. New York: Seven Stories Press, 2013.

Washington Office on Latin America. "Amnesty, Impunity, and Archives in El Salvador." 7 December 2013. http://www.wola.org/video/live_stream_amnesty_ impunity_and_archives_in_el_salvador.

Weber, Max. "Politics as a Vocation." In *Weber's Rationalism and Modern Society: New Translations on Politics, Bureaucracy, and Social Stratification*, edited and translated by Tony Waters and Dagmar Waters, 129–98. New York: Palgrave Macmillan, 2015.

Weld, Kirsten. *Paper Cadavers: The Archives of Dictatorship in Guatemala.* Durham, NC: Duke University Press, 2014.

Weschler, Lawrence. *A Miracle, a Universe: Settling Accounts with Torturers.* New York: Pantheon, 1990.

World Organization Against Torture. "Thailand: Human Rights Lawyer Sirikan Charoensiri Summoned to Appear before the Public Prosecutor." THA 001 / 0715 / OBS 055.5, 10 May 2016. http://www.omct.org/human-rights-defenders/ urgent-interventions/thailand/2016/05/d23757/.

Wyatt, David K. *Thailand: A Short History.* New Haven, CT: Yale University Press, 1984.

Zimmerman, Robert F. *Reflections on the Collapse of Democracy in Thailand.* Singapore: Institute of Southeast Asian Studies, 1978.

Zinn, Howard. *A People's History of the United States.* New York: Harper Perennial, 2005.

Thai-Language Books, Articles, and Other Published Material

Bencharat Sae Chua. "Thinking about Thai Human Rights through the (Non) Search for Justice and (Non)Accountability: Cases of State Violence against the Movement for Democracy." In *Puey and Thai Society in the Transitional Crisis*, edited by Prajak Kongkirati and Pokpong Junvith, 111–46. Bangkok: Social Sciences and Humanities Textbook Foundation, 2559 [2015].

[เบญจรัตน์ แซ่ฉั่ว. "มองสิทธิมนุษยชนไทยผ่านการ(ไม่)หาความจริงและการ(ไม่)รับผิด: กรณีความรุนแรงโดยรัฐที่กระทำต่อขบวนการประชาธิปไตย." ใน *ป๋วยกับสังคมไทยในวิกฤตเปลี่ยนผ่าน*, ประจักษ์ ก้องกีรติ และ ปกป้อง จันวิทย์, บรรณาธิการ, 111–46. กรุงเทพฯ: มูลนิธิโครงการตำราสังคมศาสตร์และมนุษยศาสตร์, 2559.]

Bunruam Thiemchan. *The Case of the Disappearance of Lawyer Somchai.* Bangkok: Samnakphim Mala Plus One, 2549 [2006].

[บุญร่วม เทียมจันทร์. *คดีอุ้มทนายสมชาย*. กรุงเทพฯ: สำนักพิมพ์มาลาพลัสวัน, 2549.]

Chaiwat Suriwichai. *What Took Place in Ban Na Sai.* Bangkok: People for Democracy Group, 2517 [1974].

[ชัยวัฒน์ สุรวิชัย. *เหตุเกิดที่บ้านนาทราย*. กรุงเทพฯ: ประชาชนเพื่อประชาธิปไตย.]

Chakrawan Channuwong. *Article 17 and the 11 Executed Prisoners.* Bangkok: Chak Banlue, 2507 [1964].

[จักราวาล ชาญนุวงศ์. *ม. 17 กับ 11 นักโทษประหาร*. กรุงเทพฯ: จักร บันลือ, 2507.]

Charnvit Kasetsiri. "Blanket Amnesty: Agree or Not." *Prachatai*, 19 October 2556 [2013]. http://blogazine.in.th/blogs/charnvit-kasetsiri/post/4407.

[ชาญวิทย์ เกษตรศิริ. "นิรโทษกรรมเหมาเข่ง: เห็นด้วย-ไม่เห็นด้วย." ประชาไท, 19 ตุลาคม 2556. http:// blogazine.in.th/blogs/charnvit-kasetsiri/post/4407.]

Chit Wiphatthawat. *Phao Tells All (The Iron Man of Asia)*. Bangkok: Phrae Phittaya. 2503 [1960].

[ชิต วิภาสธวัช. เผ่าสารภาพ (บุรุษเหล็กแห่งเอเชีย). กรุงเทพฯ: แพร่พิทยา, 2503.]

Coordinating Group for Religion in Society. *The Om Noi Workers and the Problems of Human Rights*. Bangkok: Coordinating Group for Religion in Society, 2521 [1978].

[กลุ่มประสานงานศาสนาเพื่อสังคม. กรรมกรอ้อมน้อยและปัญหาสิทธิมนุษยชน. กรุงเทพฯ: กลุ่มประสานงานศาสนาเพื่อสังคม, 2521.]

Fa Diew Kan Editorial Collective. "The Insufficiency of Rule by Law." *Fa Diew Kan* 7, no. 4 (2552 [2009]): n.p.

[กองบรรณาธิการวารสารฟ้าเดียวกัน. "ความไม่พอเพียงของนิติรัฐ." ฟ้าเดียวกัน 7.4 (2552): ไม่มีเลขหน้า.]

iLaw. "Report on the Exercise of Power under Article 44 of the Interim Constitution." Regularly updated running list. http://www.ilaw.or.th/node/3679.

[iLaw. "รวมผลงานการใช้อำนาจมาตรา 44 ตามรัฐธรรมนูญชั่วคราว." http://www.ilaw.or.th/node/3679.]

———. "Torture Law and the Prevention of Torture." 19 November 2553 [2010]. http://www.ilaw.or.th/node/529.

———. ["กฎหมายทรมานกับการป้องกันซ้อมทรมาน." 10 พฤศจิกายน 2553. http://www.ilaw.or.th/node/529.]

———. "What Does the NCPO Have to Show for Their Two Years of Rule?" Manuscript, 2559 [2016].

———. ["2 ปี ยุค คสช. มีผลงานอะไรบ้าง. ร่างต้นฉบับหนังสือ." 2559.]

Jaran Kosanan. *Law, Rights, and Liberties in Thai Society: Parallel Lines from 1932 to the Present*. Bangkok: Coordinating Group for Religion in Society, 2528 [1985].

[จรัญ โฆษณานันท์. กฎหมายกับสิทธิเสรีภาพในสังคมไทย: เส้นขนานจาก 2475 ถึงปัจจุบัน. กรุงเทพฯ: กลุ่มประสานงานศาสนาเพื่อสังคม, 2528.]

Ji Ungpakorn and Suthachai Yimprasert. *The Crimes of the State in the Crisis of Changes*. Bangkok: 6 October 2519 Fact-Finding Committee, 2544 [2001].

[ใจ อึ๊งภากรณ์ และ สุธาชัย ยิ้มประเสริฐ. อาชญากรรมรัฐในวิกฤตการเปลี่ยนแปลง. กรุงเทพฯ: คณะกรรมการรับข้อมูลและสืบพยานเหตุการณ์ 6 ตุลาคม 2519, 2544.]

Jularat Damrongviteetam. *Thang Daeng: The Restoration/Reconstruction of History and Haunting Memories in Thai Society*. Bangkok: Matichon, 2559 [2016].

[จุฬารัตน์ ดำรงวิถีธรรม. ถังแดง: การซ่อมสร้างประวัติศาสตร์และความทรงจำหลอนในสังคมไทย. กรุงเทพฯ: มติชน, 2559.]

Kasian Tejapira. "Article 17: Field Marshal Sarit's Dog-Head Zha Guillotine." *Matichon Sut Sabda*, 22 April 2558 [2015], 52.

[เกษียร เตชะพีระ. "ม. 17: เครื่องประหารหัวสุนัขของจอมพลสฤษดิ์." มติชนสุดสัปดาห์, 22 เมษายน 2558, 52.]

———. "The Postmortem of the 'Plot to Overthrow the Monarchy.'" *Matichon*,
    27 April 2555 [2012], 6.
———. ["ชันสูตรพลิกศพ 'ผังล้มเจ้า.'" มติชน, 27 เมษายน 2555, 6.]
Kongsak Liewmanont, ed. *Collected Orders and Procedures of the National Admin-
    istrative Reform Council for Dealing with Dangers to Society*. Bangkok: Ministry
    of Interior, 2520 [1977].
[คงศักดิ์ ลิ่วมโนมนต์. รวมคำสั่งของคณะปฏิรูปการปกครองแผ่นดินและระเบียบข้อบังคับเกี่ยวกับการปฏิบัติ
    ต่อบุคคลที่เป็นภัยต่อสังคม. กรุงเทพฯ: กระทรวงมหาดไทย, 2520.]
Korakot Phiengjai. *The Martyrs of 10 April: Faces of the Dead, Lives of the
    Murdered*. Bangkok: Heroes of Democracy Foundation, 2554 [2011].
[กรกช เพียงใจ. วีรชน 10 เมษา: คนที่ตายมีใบหน้า คนที่ถูกฆ่ามีชีวิต. กรุงเทพฯ: มูลนิธิวีรชนประชาธิปไตย,
    2554.]
Kulap Saipradit. *Looking Ahead (Middle Age)*. Bangkok: San Sayam, 2518 [1975].
[กุหลาบ สายประดิษฐ์. แลไปข้างหน้า ภาคมัชฌิมวัย. กรุงเทพฯ: สารสยาม, 2518.]
———. *Looking Ahead (Youth)*. Bangkok: Thai Samphan Press, 2498 [1955].
———. [แลไปข้างหน้า ภาคปฐมวัย. กรุงเทพฯ: ไทยสัมพันธ์, 2498.]
———. *Until We Meet Again*. Bangkok: Suphapburut Press, 2493 [1950].
———. [จนกว่าเราจะพบกันอีก. กรุงเทพฯ: สำนักพิมพ์สุภาพบุรุษ, 2493.]
Mo Noi. *The Karma of Those Who Topple the Monarchy*. Bangkok: Bangkok
    Books, 2553 [2010].
[หมอหน่อย. กรรมคนล้มเจ้า. กรุงเทพฯ: สำนักพิมพ์แบงค์คอกบุ๊คส์, 2553.]
M. R. Kukrit Pramoj. "Rice Far from the Field." *Sayam Rat*, 24 February 2521
    [1978], 7.
[มรว. คึกฤทธิ์ ปราโมช. "ข้าวไกลนา." สยามรัฐ, 24 กุมภาพันธ์ 2521, 7.]
National Human Rights Commission. *Report on the Investigation for Policy
    Recommendations about the Incident of the UDD Demonstrations between 12
    March 2010 and 19 May 2010*. Bangkok: NHRC, 2556 [2013].
[คณะกรรมการสิทธิมนุษยชนแห่งชาติ. รายงานผลการตรวจสอบเพื่อมีข้อเสนอแนะเชิงนโยบาย กรณี
    เหตุการณ์การชุมนุมของกลุ่มนปช. ระหว่างวันที่ 12 มีนาคม 2553 ถึงวันที่ 19 มีนาคม 2553. กรุงเทพฯ:
    กสม, 2556.]
Nattapoll Chaiching. *Dream the Impossible Dream: Counter-revolutionary Move-
    ments in Siam (1932–1957)*. Bangkok: Fa Diew Kan Press, 2556 [2013].
[ณัฐพล ใจจริง. ขอฝันใฝ่ในฝันอันเหลือเชื่อ: ความเคลื่อนไหวของขบวนการปฏิปักษ์ปฏิวัติสยาม. กรุงเทพฯ:
    ฟ้าเดียวกัน, 2556.]
Nidhi Eoseewong. "The Past-Present-Future of the Judgment." *Matichon*, 8
    September 2557 [2014], 20.
[นิธิ เอียวศรีวงศ์. "อดีต-ปัจจุบัน-อนาคตของคำพิพากษา." มติชน, 8 กันยายน 2557, 20.]
Office of the Prime Minister. *A Record of Bloody May: Evidence to Prosecute the
    Murders of May*. Bangkok: Office of the Prime Minister, 2535 [1992].
[สำนักนายกรัฐมนตรี. บันทึกประวัติศาสตร์พฤษภาทมิฬ: หลักฐานฟ้องโทษฆาตกรพฤษภาคม. กรุงเทพฯ:
    สำนักนายกรัฐมนตรี, 2535.]
Pakavadi Mai Mi Nam Sakun. "Memory, Fear, and Truth Following Dictator-
    ship." *Aan* 3, no.1 (2553 [2010]): 90–97.

[ภัควดี ไม่มีนามสกุล. "ความทรงจำ ความกลัว และความจริงในชีวิตยุคหลังเผด็จการ." อ่าน 3.1 (2553): 90–97.]

Pallop Pinmanee. *I Was Wrong? The Seizure of Krue Se!* Bangkok: Good Morning Press, 2547 [2004].

[พัลลภ ปิ่นมณี. *ผมผิดหรือ? ที่ยึดกรือเซะ!* กรุงเทพฯ: สำนักพิมพ์กู๊ดมอร์นิ่ง, 2547.]

People's Information Center for Those Affected by the Dispersal of Protests in April–May 2010. *Truth for Justice: The Incident and Effects of the Dispersal of Protests in April–May 2010.* Bangkok: People's Information Center, 2555 [2012].

[ศูนย์ข้อมูลประชาชนผู้ได้รับผลกระทบจากการสลายชุมนุมกรณี เม.ย.—พ.ค. 2553. *ความจริงเพื่อความ ยุติธรรม: เหตุการณ์ และผลกระทบจากการสลายการชุมนุม เมษา—พฤษภา 2553.* กรุงเทพฯ: ศูนย์ข้อมูลประชาชนผู้ได้รับผลกระทบจากการสลายชุมนุมกรณี เม.ย., พ.ค. 2553, 2555.]

Phayap Srikanchana, ed. *Cremation Volume for Mrs. Chongkol Srikanchana.* Bangkok: Rongphim Krungthep, 2533 [1984].

[พยัพ ศรีกาญจนา, บรรณาธิการ. *อนุสรณ์งานพระราชทานเพลิงศพ นางจงกล ศรีกาญจนา.* กรุงเทพฯ: โรงพิมพ์ กรุงเทพฯ, 2533.]

Phra Phaisan Visalo. "Ajarn Puey and the CGRS." n.d. http://www.visalo.org/ article/person24Puay2.htm.

[พระไพศาล วิสาโล. "อาจารย์ป๋วยกับกศศ." ไม่ระบุวันและปี. http://www.visalo.org/article/ person24Puay2.htm.]

Pradit Sutthijit et al. *Cremation Volume of Mr. Ruam Wongphan.* Bangkok: Wat Makudkasattriyam, 2538 [1995].

[ประดิษ สุทธิจิตร และคณะ. *อนุสรณ์เนื่องในงานฌาปนกิจศพ นายรวม วงศ์พันธ์.* กรุงเทพฯ: เมรุวัดมกุฏ กษัตริยาราม, 2538.]

Pratubjit Neelapaijit and Anuk Pitukthanin. "Enforced Disappearance and the Implications of Ambiguity." In *Nonviolence Space, Thailand Future: Knowledge, Secrecy, Memories,* edited by Chaiwat Satha-anand, 29–76. Bangkok: Protestista, 2559 [2016].

[ประทับจิตร นีละไพจิตร และ อนรรฆ พิทักษ์ธานิน. "การบังคับบุคคลสูญหายและนัยยะของความคลุมเครือ." ใน *พื้นที่สันติวิธี, หนทางสังคมไทย: ความรู้, ความลับ, ความทรงจำ,* ชัยวัฒน์ สถาอานันท์, บรรณาธิการ, 29–76. กรุงเทพฯ: Protestista, 2559.]

Pratubjit Neelapaijit, Anuk Pitukthanin, and Sowarin Sitthisan. "Research Report on the Vocabulary of Ambiguity: Victims of Forced Disappearance, Using Nonviolence Abroad, and the Insights for Thai Society." Year 3 Report, Thailand Research Fund Project, Nonviolence and Violence in Thai Society, Knowledge, Secrecy, and Memory, June 2556 [2013].

[ประทับจิตร นีละไพจิตร, อนรรฆ พิทักษ์ธานิน, สวริน สิทธิสาร. "รายงานการวิจัยเรื่อง คำสาปของความ คลุมเครือ:เหยื่อการบังคับสูญหายกับการเลือกไม่ใช้ความรุนแรงในต่างประเทศและข้อคิดสู่สังคมไทย." ภายใต้ โครงการเมธิวิจัยอาวุโส สกว. ปีที่ 3, สันติวิธีและความรุนแรงในสังคมไทย: ความรู้ ความลับ และความทรงจำ, มิถุนายน 2556.]

Preedee Hongsaton. "'Killing a Chicken to Scare the Monkeys': The Thai State's Annihilation of Its Enemies." *Thammasat University Journal of History* 1, no. 2 (2558 [2015]): 53–99.

[ปรีดี หงษ์สต้น. "'เชือดไก่ให้ลิงดู': รัฐไทยกับการทำลายศัตรูด้วยนาฏกรรม." *วารสารประวัติศาสตร์ธรรมศาสตร์* 1.2 (2558): 53–99.]

Premchai Phringsunlaka, ed. *Article 17 in Murky Times*. Bangkok: Krung Sayam Publishers, 2517 [1974].

[เปรมชัย พริ้งศุลกะ, บรรณาธิการ. *มาตรา 17 ในยุคมืด*. กรุงเทพฯ: กรุงสยามการพิมพ์, 2517.]

Puangthong Pawakapan. "Voices of the Victims: Truth for Justice." In *Truth for Justice: The Incident and Effects of the Dispersal of Protests in April–May 2010*, by People's Information Center for Those Affected by the Dispersal of Protests in April–May 2010, 10-23. Bangkok: People's Information Center, 2555 [2012].

[พวงทอง ภวัครพันธุ์. "เสียงจากเหยื่อ: ความจริงเพื่อความยุติธรรม." ใน *ความจริงเพื่อความยุติธรรม: เหตุการณ์และ ผลกระทบจากการสลายการชุมนุม เมษา-พฤษภา 53*, โดย ศูนย์ข้อมูลประชาชนผู้ได้รับผลกระทบจากการสลายการชุมนุมกรณี เม.ย.–พ.ค. 53, 10–23. กรุงเทพฯ: ศูนย์ข้อมูลประชาชนผู้ได้รับผลกระทบจากการสลายการชุมนุมกรณี เม.ย.–พ.ค. 53, 2555.]

Puey Ungpakorn. *Testimony of Dr. Puey Ungpakorn about 6 October 1976*. Bangkok: Komol Keemthong Foundation, 2543 [2000].

[ป๋วย อึ๊งภากรณ์. *คำให้การของ ดร. ป๋วย อึ๊งภากรณ์ กรณีเหตุการณ์ 6 ตุลาคม 2519*. กรุงเทพฯ: มูลนิธิโกมล คีมทอง, 2543.]

———. "Violence and the Coup of 6 October 1976." In *From 14 to 6 October*, edited by Charnvit Kasetsiri and Thamrongsak Petchlertanan, 49–79. Bangkok: Thammasat University Press, 2541 [1998].

———. ["ความรุนแรงและรัฐประหาร 6 ตุลาคม 2519." ใน *จาก 14 ถึง 6 ตุลา*, ชาญวิทย์ เกษตรศิริ และ ธำรงศักดิ์ เพชรเลิศอานันต์, บรรณาธิการ, 49–79. กรุงเทพฯ: โรงพิมพ์มหาวิทยาลัยธรรมศาสตร์, 2541.]

Royal Institute. *Royal Institute Dictionary*. Bangkok: Royal Institute, 2542 [1999].

[ราชบัณฑิตยสถาน. *พจนานุกรมราชบัณฑิตยสถาน*. กรุงเทพฯ: ราชบัณฑิตยสถาน, 2542.]

Saneh Chamarik. *The Development of Human Rights in Thailand*. Bangkok: Union for Civil Liberty, 2531 [1988].

[เสน่ห์ จามริก. *พัฒนาการสิทธิมนุษยชนในประเทศไทย*. กรุงเทพฯ: สมาคมสิทธิเสรีภาพของประชาชน, 2531.]

Sarit Thanarat. "Address of Field Marshal Sarit Thanarat, the Prime Minister, on Constitution Day and Human Rights Day, 10 December 2503 [1960]." *Ratchasaphasan* 9, no.1 (2503 [1960]): n.p.

[สฤษดิ์ ธนะรัชต์. "คำปราศรัยของจอมพล สฤษดิ์ ธนะรัชต์ นายกรัฐมนตรี ในวันรัฐธรรมนูญและวันสิทธิมนุษยชน 10 ธันวาคม 2503." *รัฐสภาสาร* 9.1 (2503): ไม่ระบุเลขหน้า.]

Somchai Preechasilpakul. "The Coup Rule of Law." In *The 19 September Coup: Coup for Democracy with the King as Head of State*, edited by Thanapol Eawsakul, 190–202. Bangkok: Fa Diew Kan Press, 2550 [2007].

[สมชาย ปรีชาศิลปกุล. "หลักนิติรัฐประหาร." ใน *รัฐประหาร 19 กันยา: รัฐประหารเพื่อระบอบประชาธิปไตย อันมี พระมหากษัตริย์ทรงเป็นประมุข*, ธนาพล อิ๋วสกุล, บรรณาธิการ, 190–202. กรุงเทพฯ: ฟ้าเดียวกัน, 2550.]

Somsak Jeamteerasakul. "Dissecting-Settling the History of 6 October 1976: The Cabinet Meeting on 6 October 1976." *Silpawatthanatham* 24, no.12 (2546 [2003]): 61–73.

[สมศักดิ์ เจียมธีรสกุล. "ชำแหละ-ชำระประวัติศาสตร์ 6 ตุลาคม 2519: การประชุมคณะรัฐมนตรีวันที่ 6 ตุลาคม 2519." *ศิลปวัฒนธรรม* 24.12 (2546): 61–73.]

———. "Who Was Who in 6 October?" In *Recently Constructed History*, 161–207. Bangkok: Samnakphim 6 Tula Raluk, 2544 [2001].

["ใครเป็นใครในกรณี 6 ตุลา." ใน *ประวัติศาสตร์ที่เพิ่งสร้าง*, 161–207. กรุงเทพฯ: สำนักพิมพ์ 6 ตุลารำลึก, 2544.]

Somsamai Sisuttharaphan. "The Real Face of Thai Feudalism Today." *Thammasat University Faculty of Law Yearbook*, The New Century Edition, 2500 [1957].

[สมสมัย ศรีสุทรพรรณ. "โฉมหน้าศักดินาไทยในยุคปัจจุบัน." *นิติศาสตร์ฉบับศตวรรษใหม่ (มหาวิทยาลัย ธรรมศาสตร์)*, 2500.]

Sudprathana Neelapaijit. "When [My] Father . . . Was Disappeared." In *The Disappearance of Persons Is the Disappearance of Justice*, 63–70. Bangkok: Working Group on Justice for Peace, 2549 [2006].

[สุดปรารถนา นีละไพจิตร. "เมื่อพ่อ . . . ถูกบังคับให้หายไป." ใน *การสูญหายของบุคคลคือการสูญหายของ ความ ยุติธรรม*, 63–70. กรุงเทพฯ: คณะทำงานยุติธรรมเพื่อสันติภาพ, 2549.]

Suthachai Yimprasert. *The Plan to Plunder the Thai Nation: On the State and Opposition to the State during the Second Regime of Field Marshal Phibun Songkhram (2491–2500 BE)*. Bangkok: 6 October Commemorative Press, 2553 [2010]. Originally published in 2531 [1988].

[สุธาชัย ยิ้มประเสริฐ. *แผนชิงชาติไทย: ว่าด้วยรัฐและการต่อต้านรัฐ สมัยจอมพล ป. พิบูลสงคราม ครั้งที่ สอง (พ.ศ. 2491–2500)*. กรุงเทพฯ: สำนักพิมพ์ 6 ตุลารำลึก, 2553 (2531).]

Thak Chaloemtiarana. "ISOC: Lullaby for the Communist Specter." *Thammasat Journal* 10, no. 2 (2524 [1981]): 107–12.

[ทักษ์ เฉลิมเตียรณ. "กอ.รมน.: บทความเพื่อกล่อมผีคอมมิวนิสต์ให้หลับ." *วารสารธรรมศาสตร์* 10.2 (2524): 107–12.]

Thamrongsak Petchlertanan. "The Political Role of Field Marshal Thanom Kittikhachorn. 2506–2516." PhD diss., Chulalongkorn University, 2550 [2007].

[ธำรงศักดิ์ เพชรเลิศอนันต์. "บทบาททางการเมืองของจอมพลถนอม กิตติขจร พ.ศ. 2506–2516." วิทยานิพนธ์ ปริญญาเอก, จุฬาลงกรณ์ มหาวิทยาลัย, 2550.]

Thanapol Eawsakul. "Reading the Judgment of Somyot Prueksakasemsuk as a Political Instrument and the Problem of 'Royal Authority' in a Democracy." *Fa Diew Kan* 11, no. 1 (2556 [2013]): 227–36.

[ธนาพล อิ๋วสกุล. "อ่านคำพิพากษาสมยศ พฤกษาเกษมสุข ในฐานะเครื่องมือทางการเมืองและปัญหา 'พระราชอำนาจ' ในระบอบ ประชาธิปไตย." *ฟ้าเดียวกัน* 11.1 (2556): 227–36.]

———. "Scorched by the Sky that Looms above for Laughing at Illegitimate Traditions: Daranee Charnchoengsilpakul's Struggle and her Unjust Punishment." *Fa Diew Kan* 7, no. 3 (2552 [2009]): 184–97.

———. ["ที่ฟ้าแผดแดดเผาให้ไหม้เกรียมเย้ยจารีตธรรมเนียมไม่ชอบธรรม: การต่อสู้คดีนี้ ชาญเชิงศิลปกุล กับโทษที่ไม่เป็นธรรม." *ฟ้าเดียวกัน* 7.3 (2552): 184–97.]

Thanapol Eawsakul and Chaithawat Tulathon. "The Struggle of the Defendants in the 6 October Case under the (In)Justice Process after the 6 October 1976 Coup." *Fa Diew Kan* 12, nos. 2–3 (2557 [2014]): 296–333.

[ธนาพล อิ๋วสกุล และ ชัยธวัช ตุลาธน. "การต่อสู้ของจำเลยคดี 6 ตุลา ภายใต้กระบวนการ (อ)ยุติธรรมหลังการ
    รัฐประหาร 6 ตุลาคม 2519." ฟ้าเดียวกัน 12.2–3 (2557): 296–333.]

Thanet Aphornsuvan. "From Thang Daeng to Tak Bai: Experiences in Solving
    the State's Problems." Paper presented at Thammasat University, 23 January
    2548 [2005].

[ธเนศ อาภรณ์สุวรรณ. "จากถังแดงถึงตากใบ: ประสบการณ์ในการแก้ปัญหาของรัฐ." บทความที่เสนอที่
    มหาวิทยาลัยธรรมศาสตร์, 23 มกราคม 2548.]

———. *The Origins and History of Human Rights.* Bangkok: Khobfai, 2549
    [2006].

———. [ธเนศ อาภรณ์สุวรรณ. *กำเนิดและความเป็นมาของสิทธิมนุษยชน.* กรุงเทพฯ: โครงการจัดพิมพ์
    คบไฟ, 2549.]

Thanin Kraivichien. *Using the Law to Protect against the Communists.* Bangkok:
    Armed Forces Security Center, 2517 [1974].

[ธานินทร์ กรัยวิเชียร. *การใช้กฎหมายป้องกันคอมมิวนิสต์.* กรุงเทพฯ: ศูนย์รักษาความปลอดภัย, กระทรวง
    กลาโหม, 2517.]

Thongbai Thongpao. *Communists of Lad Yao.* Bangkok: Khon Num, 2517 [1974].

[ทองใบ ทองเปาด์. *คอมมิวนิสต์ลาดยาว.* กรุงเทพฯ: คนหนุ่ม, 2517.]

Thongchai Winichakul. *Democracy in Which the King Is Above Politics.* Bangkok:
    Fa Diew Kan, 2557 [2014].

[ธงชัย วินิจจะกูล. *ประชาธิปไตยที่มีกษัตริย์อยู่เหนือการเมือง.* กรุงเทพฯ: ฟ้าเดียวกัน, 2557.]

———. "An Experimental Proposal: Impunity and the Understanding of
    Human Rights in Thai-Style Rule of Law." *Fa Diew Kan* 14, no. 2 (2559
    [2016]): 191–218.

———. ["บททดลองเสนอ: อภิสิทธิ์ปลอดความผิด (Impunity) และความเข้าใจสิทธิมนุษยชนในนิติรัฐ
    แบบไทยๆ." ฟ้าเดียวกัน 14.2 (2559): 191–218.]

———. "6 October in Rightist Memories (1976–2006): From Victory to Silence
    (But Still Victorious)." In *Violence Hides/Seeks Thai Society,* edited by Chaiwat
    Satha-anand, 407–512. Bangkok: Matichon, 2553 [2010].

———. ["6 ตุลา ในความทรงจำของฝ่ายขวา 2519–2549: จากชนะสู่ความเงียบ (แต่ยังชนะอยู่ดี)." ใน
    ความรุนแรงซ่อน/หา สังคมไทย. ชัยวัฒน์ สถาอานันท์, บรรณาธิการ, 407–512. กรุงเทพฯ: มติชน,
    2553.]

———. "A Social Political Regime Which Resists Change Is Truly Dangerous."
    Lecture in support of the amendment of Article 112 proposed by the Khana
    Nitirat, Friends of the Constitution, Bangkok, 11 February 2555 [2012].

———. ["ระบอบสังคมการเมืองที่ขัดขืนการเปลี่ยนแปลงคืออันตรายที่แท้จริง." ปาฐกถาในรายการสนทนาเพื่อ
    หารายได้สนับสนุนการแก้ไข มาตรา 112 ตามข้อเสนอของนิติราษฎร์, กลุ่มเพื่อนรัฐธรรมนูญ, กรุงเทพฯ, 11
    กุมภาพันธ์ 2555.]

Truth and Reconciliation Commission of Thailand. *Report of the Truth and Rec-
    onciliation Commission of Thailand, July 2010–July 2012.* Bangkok: TRCT, 2555.

[คณะกรรมการอิสระตรวจสอบและค้นหาความจริงเพื่อการปรองดองแห่งชาติ. *รายงานฉบับสมบูรณ์ คณะ
    กรรมการอิสระตรวจสอบและค้นหาความจริงเพื่อการปรองดองแห่งชาติ, กรกฎาคม 2553–กรกฎาคม
    2555.* กรุงเทพฯ: คอป, 2555.]

Winyu Angkhanarak. *Heart of the Permanent Secretary.* Bangkok: Matichon Press, 2544 [2001].

[วิญญู อังคณารักษ์. *หัวหน้าปลัดกระทรวง.* กรุงเทพฯ: สำนักพิมพ์มติชน, 2544.]

Working Group on Human Rights Defenders. *The Disappearance of Lawyer Somchai Neelapaijit Is a Reflection of the Culture of Authoritarianism in Thai Society.* Bangkok: Working Group on Human Rights Defenders, 2547 [2004].

[คณะทำงานปกป้องนักต่อสู้เพื่อสิทธิมนุษยชน. *อุ้มทนายสมชาย นีละไพจิตร บทสะท้อนวัฒนธรรมอำนาจ นิยมในสังคมไทย.* กรุงเทพฯ: คณะทำงานปกป้องนักต่อสู้เพื่อสิทธิมนุษยชน, 2547.]

Yotthong Thabtiumai. *Thang Daeng, Na Sai, ISOC, Anti-Communist Activities Act.* Bangkok: Mitnara Kanphim, 2518 [1975].

[ยอดธง ทับทิวไม้. *ถังแดง นาทราย กอ.รมน. พรบ. คอมมิวนิสต์.* กรุงเทพฯ: มิทนราการพิมพ์, 2518.]

ENGLISH-LANGUAGE NEWSPAPERS AND PERIODICALS

article 2
Bangkok Post
The Economist
The Guardian
Human Rights in Thailand Report
Thai Bulletin
TIC News
UDT Report
Voice of the Nation

ENGLISH-LANGUAGE DATABASE

Internet Dialogue on Legal Reform (iLaw). Documentation Center. http://freedom.ilaw.or.th/en/case.

THAI-LANGUAGE NEWSPAPERS AND PERIODICALS

Athit (อาทิตย์)
Ban Muang (บ้านเมือง)
Chao Thai (ชาวไทย)
Daily Niu (เดลินิวส์)
Daily Time (เดลีไทม์)
Khao Sod (ข่าวสด)
Matichon (มติชน)
Prachachat (ประชาชาติ)
Prachatai (ประชาไท)
Prachathipatai (ประชาธิปไตย)
Ratchakitchanubeksa (ราชกิจจานุเบกษา)
Sayam Rat (สยามรัฐ)
Sayam Rat Sabda Wichan (สยามรัฐสัปดาห์วิจารณ์)
Sieng Mai (เสียงใหม่)

Sieng Puangchon (เสียงปวงชน)
Thai Niu (ไทยนิวส์)
Thai Rat (ไทยรัฐ)
Thin Thai (ถิ่นไทย)

Thai State Archival Materials

MFA Archive, I1002-699-405-712-2101. Department of International Organizations. Social Division. "Amnesty International and Petition Letters about Various Cases in Thailand, 2521–2522 [1978–1979]."

[หอจดหมายเหตุกระทรวงการต่างประเทศ, I002-699-405-712-2101. กรมองค์การระหว่างประเทศ. กองการสังคม. "องค์การนิรโทษ กรรมสากล (Amnesty International) มีหนังสือร้องเรียนเกี่ยวกับการดำเนินคดีต่างๆ ในประเทศไทย, 2521–2522."]

MFA Archive, I002-699-405-712-2102. Department of International Organizations. Social Division. "Amnesty International Calls for the Thai Government to Release Political Prisoners in Thailand (Ordinary Cases Aside from the 6 October 2519 Case and the Case of the Members of the Coordinating Group for Religion in Society), 2521–2522."

[หอจดหมายเหตุกระทรวงการต่างประเทศ, I002-699-405-712-2102. กรมองค์การระหว่างประเทศ. กองการสังคม. "องค์การนิรโทษกรรมสากล (Amnesty International) เรียกร้องให้รัฐบาลไทยปล่อยตัวนักโทษการเมืองในไทย (คดีทั่วไปนอกเหนือจากคดี 6 ตุลาคม 2519 และคดีสมาชิกกลุ่มประสานงานศาสนาเพื่อสังคม, 2521–2522)."]

NA (2) So. Kho. Ko. 1/Book 393. National Archives. Office of the Juridical Council. Drafts of Laws and Legal Opinions. Finished Matters, B.E. 2487 [1944]. "Act for the Internment of Those who are a Danger to the Nation during Emergency Times, B.E. 2488."

[หจช. (2) สศก. 1/เล่ม 393. หอจดหมายเหตุแห่งชาติ. สำนักงานคณะกรรมการกฤษฎีกา. ร่างกฎหมายและความเห็นทางกฎหมาย. เรื่องเสร็จ พ.ศ. 2487. "ร่างพระราชบัญญัติกักคุมผู้เป็นภัยแก่ชาติในภาวะคับขัน, พ.ศ. 2488."]

NA (2) So. Kho. Ko. 1/Book 538. National Archives. Office of the Juridical Council. Drafts of Laws and Legal Opinions. Finished Matters. "Text for Printing the Yearbook on Human Rights for 1958 C.E."

[หจช. (2) สศก. 1/เล่ม 538. หอจดหมายเหตุแห่งชาติ. สำนักงานคณะกรรมการกฤษฎีกา. ร่างกฎหมายและความเห็นทางกฎหมาย. เรื่องเสร็จ. "ข้อความสำหรับการพิมพ์ในหนังสือรายปีว่าด้วยสิทธิมนุษยชน ค.ศ. 1958."]

NA (2) So. Kho. Ko. 1/Book 563. National Archives. Office of the Juridical Council. Drafts of Laws and Legal Opinions. Finished Matters. "Law Drafts and Legal Opinions for the Yearbook on Human Rights for 1959 C.E."

[หจช. (2) สศก. 1/เล่ม 563. หอจดหมายเหตุแห่งชาติ. สำนักงานคณะกรรมการกฤษฎีกา. ร่างกฎหมายและความเห็นทางกฎหมาย. เรื่องเสร็จ. "ร่างกฎหมายและความเห็นทางกฎหมาย หนังสือรายปีว่าด้วยสิทธิมนุษยชนประจำปี ค.ศ. 1959."]

NA (2) So. Kho. Ko. 1/Book 610. National Archives. Office of the Juridical Council. Drafts of Laws and Legal Opinions. Finished Matters. "Law Drafts and Legal Opinions for the Yearbook on Human Rights for 1961 C.E."

[หจช. (2) สศก. 1/เล่ม 610. หอจดหมายเหตุแห่งชาติ. สำนักงานคณะกรรมการกฤษฎีกา. ร่างกฎหมายและ
ความเห็นทางกฎหมาย. เรื่องเสร็จ. "ร่างกฎหมายและความเห็นทางกฎหมาย หนังสือรายปีว่าด้วย
สิทธิมนุษยชนประจำปี ค.ศ. 1961."]

NA (2) So. Kho. Ko. 1/Book 996. National Archives. Office of the Juridical
Council. Drafts of Laws and Legal Opinions. Finished Matters. "Draft
Amnesty for Those Who Seized the Administrative Power of the Council on
6 October 2519 B.E. Act B.E. . . ."

[หจช. (2) สศก. 1/เล่ม 996. หอจดหมายเหตุแห่งชาติ. สำนักงานคณะกรรมการกฤษฎีกา. ร่างกฎหมายและ
ความเห็นทางกฎหมาย. เรื่องเสร็จ. "ร่างพระราชบัญญัติ นิรโทษกรรมแก่ผู้กระทำการยึดอำนาจการปกครอง
ประเทศเมื่อวันที่ 6 ตุลาคม 2519 พ.ศ. . . . ."]

NA (2) So. Kho. Ko. 1/Book 1167. National Archives. Office of the Juridical
Council. Drafts of Laws and Legal Opinions. Finished Matters. "English-
Language Translations of Orders 22, 28, 29, 39, and 43 of the National
Administrative Reform Council."

[หจช. (2) สศก. 1/เล่ม 1167. หอจดหมายเหตุแห่งชาติ. สำนักงานคณะกรรมการกฤษฎีกา. ร่างกฎหมายและ
ความเห็นทางกฎหมาย. เรื่องเสร็จ. "คำแปลภาษาอังกฤษคำสั่งคณะปฏิรูปการปกครองแผ่นดิน ฉบับที่ 22,
28, 29, 30, และ 43."]

NA (2) Ko. To. 12.3.7/4. National Archives. Ministry of Foreign Affairs. Department of the United Nations. Social Unit. Human Rights. "Celebration of
Human Rights Day, 2493 BE [1950 CE]."

[หจช. (2) กต 12.3.7/4. หอจดหมายเหตุแห่งชาติ. กระทรวงการต่างประเทศ. กองสังคม. สิทธิมนุษยชน.
"การฉลองวันสิทธิมนุษยชน ปี พ.ศ. 2493."]

NA (2) Ko. To. 12.3.7/6. National Archives. Ministry of Foreign Affairs. Department of the United Nations. Social Unit. Human Rights. "Celebration of
Human Rights Day, 2495, 2496, 2497 BE [1952, 1953, 1954 CE]."

[หจช. (2) กต 12.3.7/6. หอจดหมายเหตุแห่งชาติ. กระทรวงการต่างประเทศ. กองสังคม. สิทธิมนุษยชน.
"การฉลองวันสิทธิมนุษยชน ปี พ.ศ. 2495, 2496, 2497."]

NA (2) Ko. To. 12.3.7/13. National Archives. Ministry of Foreign Affairs. Department of the United Nations. Social Unit. Human Rights. "Organizing a
Celebration for Human Rights Day, 2498 [1955]."

[หจช. (2) กต 12.3.7/13. หอจดหมายเหตุแห่งชาติ. กระทรวงการต่างประเทศ. กองสังคม. สิทธิมนุษยชน.
"การจัดฉลองวันสิทธิมนุษยชน ปี 2498."]

COURT DECISIONS AND RULINGS

Mr. Yiem Phunman, Decree 21 case

Supreme Court decision, No. 105/2506 [1963], *Governor of Surin v. Mr. Yiem
Phunman.*

[คำพิพากษาศาลฎีกาที่ 105/2506, ระหว่างผู้ว่าคดีศาลแขวงสุรินทร์ และ นายเยี่ยม พูนมั่น.]

Somchai Neelapaijit, enforced disappearance case

Criminal Court verdict [Black case No. 1952/2547, Red case No. Oo. 48/2549, 21
January 2549 [2006], Office of the Attorney General (and Mrs. Angkhana

Neelapaijit, Miss Sudprathana Neelapaijit, Miss Pratubjit Neelapaijit, Miss Kobkuson Neelapaijit and Miss Krongtham Neelapaijit v. Police Major Ngern Thongsuk, Police Major Sinchai Nimbunkampong, Police Sergeant Major Chaiweng Paduang, Police Sergeant Rundorn Sithikhet, and Police Lieutenant Colonel Chadchai Liamsanguan.

[ศาลอาญา, คำพิพากษา, คดีหมายเลขดำที่ 1952/2547, คดีหมายเลขแดงที่ อ. 48/2549, 21 มกราคม 2549, ระหว่างผนักงานอัยการ สำนักงานอัยการสูงสุด ประกอบด้วยโจทก์ร่วม (นางอังคณา นีละไพจิตร นางสาวสุดปรารถนา นีละไพจิตร นาวสาวประทับจิตร นีละไพจิตร นาวสาวกอปร์กุศล นีละไพจิตร และนางสาว ครองธรรม นีละไพจิตร) และพันตำรวจตรีเงิน ทองสุก พันตำรวจโทสินชัย นิ่มปุญญกำพงษ์ จ่าสิบตำรวจชัยเวง พาด้วง สิบตำรวจเอกรันดร สิทธิเขต พันตำรวจโทขัดชัย เลี่ยมสงวน.]

Appeal Court verdict [Black case No. 4717–4718/2549, Red case No. 10915–10916/2553, 10 July 2553 [2010], Office of the Attorney General (and Mrs. Angkhana Neelapaijit, Miss Sudprathana Neelapaijit, Miss Pratubjit Neelapaijit, Miss Kobkuson Neelapaijit and Miss Krongtham Neelapaijit v. Police Major Ngern Thongsuk, Police Major Sinchai Nimbunkampong, Police Sergeant Major Chaiweng Paduang, Police Sergeant Rundorn Sithikhet, and Police Lieutenant Colonel Chadchai Liamsanguan.

[ศาลอุทธรณ์, คำพิพากษา, คดีหมายเลขดำที่ 4717–4718/2549, คดีหมายเลขแดงที่ 10915–10916/2553, 10 กรกฎาคม 2553, ระหว่างผนักงานอัยการ สำนักงานอัยการสูงสุด ประกอบด้วยโจทก์ร่วม (นางอังคณา นีละไพจิตร นางสาวสุดปรารถนา นีละไพจิตร นาวสาวประทับจิตร นีละไพจิตร นาวสาวกอปร์กุศล นีละไพจิตร และนางสาวครองธรรม นีละไพจิตร) และพันตำรวจตรีเงิน ทองสุก พันตำรวจโทสินชัย นิ่มปุญญกำพงษ์ จ่าสิบตำรวจชัยเวง พาด้วย สิบตำรวจเอกรันดร สิทธิเขต พันตำรวจโทขัดชัย เลี่ยมสงวน.]

Supreme Court verdict No. 10915, 22 September 2558 [2015], Office of the Attorney General (and Mrs. Angkhana Neelapaijit, Miss Sudprathana Neelapaijit, Miss Pratubjit Neelapaijit, Miss Kobkuson Neelapaijit and Miss Krongtham Neelapaijit v. Police Major Ngern Thongsuk, Police Major Sinchai Nimbunkampong, Police Sergeant Major Chaiweng Paduang, Police Sergeant Rundorn Sithikhet, and Police Lieutenant Colonel Chadchai Liamsanguan.

[ศาลฎีกา, คำพิพากษา ที่ 10915/2558, 22 กันยายน 2558, ระหว่างผนักงานอัยการ สำนักงานอัยการสูงสุด ประกอบด้วยโจทก์ร่วม (นางอังคณา นีละไพจิตร นางสาวสุดปรารถนา นีละไพจิตร นาวสาวประทับจิตร นีละไพจิตร นาวสาวกอปร์กุศล นีละไพจิตร และนางสาวครองธรรม นีละไพจิตร) และพันตำรวจตรีเงิน ทองสุก พันตำรวจโทสินชัย นิ่มปุญญกำพงษ์ จ่าสิบตำรวจชัยเวง พาด้วง สิบตำรวจเอกรันดร สิทธิเขต พันตำรวจโทขัดชัย เลี่ยมสงวน.]

Miss Daranee Charnchoengsilpakul, Article 112 case

Constitutional Court, Order No. 38/2552, Issue Examined No. To. 17/2552, 21 October 2552 [2009], On the matter regarding Miss Daranee Charnchoengsil-pakul's (petitioner) request for the Constitutional Court to rule, using Article 212 of the 2007 Constitution of the Kingdom of Thailand, the instance of whether Article 177 of the Criminal Procedure Code is in conflict with Article 29 or Article 40 (2) of the 2007 Constitution of the Kingdom of Thailand.

[ศาลรัฐธรรมนูญ, คำสั่งศาลรัฐธรรมนูญที่ 38/2552, เรื่องพิจารณาที่ ต. 17/2552, 21 ตุลาคม 2552, เรื่อง นางสาว ดารณี ชาญเชิงศิลปกุล (ผู้ร้อง) ขอให้ศาลรัฐธรรมนูญพิจารณาวินิจฉัยตามรัฐธรรมนูญแห่งราชอาณา จักรไทย พุทธศักราช 2550 มาตรา 212 กรณีประมวลกฎหมายวิธีพิจารณาความอาญามาตรา 177 ขัดหรือ แย้งต่อรัฐธรรมนูญแห่งราชอาณาจักรไทย พุทธศักราช 2550 มาตรา 29 และมาตรา 40 (2).]

Mr. Somyot Prueksakasemsuk, Article 112 case

Constitutional Court, Ruling No. 28–29/2555, Issues Examined Nos. 16 and 44/2555, 10 October 2555 [2012], On the matter of whether or not Article 112 is in conflict with Article 3 (paragraph 2), Article 29, or Article 45 (paragraphs 1 and 2) of the Constitution.

[ศาลรัฐธรรมนูญ, คำวินิจฉัยที่ 28–29/2555, เรื่องพิจารณาที่ 16/2555, เรื่องพิจารณาที่ 44/2555, 10 ตุลาคม 2555, เรื่อง ประมวลกฎหมายอาญา มาตรา 112 ขัดหรือแย้งต่อรัฐธรรมนูญ มาตรา 3 วรรคสอง มาตรา 29 และมาตรา 45 วรรคหนึ่งและวรรคสองหรือไม่.]

Criminal Court, Decision in Black Case No. Or. 2962/2554, Red Case No. Or. 272/2556, 23 January 2556 [2013], Office of the Attorney General v. Mr. Somyot Prueksakasemsuk.

[ศาลอาญา, คำพิพากษา, คดีหมายเลขดำที่ อ. 2962/2554, คดีหมายเลขแดงที่ อ. 272/2556, 23 มกราคม 2556 [2013], ระหว่างพนักงานอัยการ สำนักงานอัยการสูงสุด และ นายสมยศ พฤกษาเกษมสุข.]

Mr. Yutthapoom (family name withheld), Article 112 case

Criminal Court decision, Black Case No. Or. 3434/2555, Red Case No. Or. 3112/2556, 13 September 2556 [2013], Office of the Attorney General v. Mr. Yutthapoom (family name withheld).

[ศาลอาญา, คำพิพากษา, คดีหมายเลขดำที่ อ. 3434/2555, คดีหมายเลขแดงที่ อ. 3112/2556, 13 กันยายน 2556 [2013], ระหว่างพนักงานอัยการ สำนักงานอัยการสูงสุด และ นายยุทธภูมิ (สงวนนามสกุล).]

Other Thai State Documents

Department of Rights and Liberties Protection, Ministry of Justice. "Draft Act on the Prevention and Suppression of Torture and Enforced Disappearance B.E. . . ." 18 February 2558 [2015].

[กรมคุ้มครองสิทธิและเสรีภาพ, กระทรวงยุติธรรม. "ร่างพระราชบัญญัติป้องกันและปราบปรามการทรมานและ การบังคับบุคคลให้สูญหาย พ.ศ. . . ." 18 กุมภาพันธ์ 2558.]

National Administrative Reform Assembly. *Report of the National Administrative Reform Assembly, Meeting 1 to Meeting 5, Book 1, 2519 B.E.* Bangkok: NARA, 2519 [1976].

[สภาปฏิรูปการปกครองแผ่นดิน. *รายงานการประชุมสภาปฏิรูปการปกครองแผ่นดิน, ครั้งที่ 1 ถึง ครั้งที่ 5, เล่ม 1, พ.ศ. 2519.* กรุงเทพฯ: สภาปฏิรูปการปกครองแผ่นดิน, 2519.]

National Legislative Assembly. *Report of the Meeting of the National Legislative Assembly, 22 February 2517 [1974].* Bangkok: National Legislative Assembly, 2517 [1974].

[สภานิติบัญญัติ. *รายงานการประชุมสภานิติบัญญัติ, วันที่ 22 กุมภาพันธ์ 2517.* กรุงเทพฯ: สภานิติบัญญัติ, 2517.]

Office of the Prime Minister. "Declaration of the Government on the Execution of a Person who Subverted National Security." 29 August 2504 [1961].
[สำนักนายกรัฐมนตรี. "คำแถลงของรัฐบาล เรื่อง ประหารชีวิตผู้บ่อนทำลายความมั่นคงของชาติ." 29 สิงหาคม 2504.]

Office of the Prime Minister. "Government Statement on the Traitorous Rebellion against the Nation of Mr. Ruam Wongphan and Others." 24 April 2505 [1962].
[สำนักนายกรัฐมนตรี. แถลงการณ์ของรัฐบาล เรื่อง การกบฏทรยศต่อประเทศชาติของนายรวม วงศ์พันธ์ กับพวก," 24 เมษายน 2505.]

Sarit Thanarat. "Announcement of the Prime Minister on the Ordering of the Execution of Mr. Sila Wongsin or Ladlakhon." 26 June 2502 [1959].
[สฤษดิ์ ธนะรัชต์. "คำแถลงของนายกรัฐมนตรี เรื่อง สั่งประหารชีวิตนายศิลา วงศ์สิน หรือลาดละคร." 26 มิถุนายน 2502.]

―――. "Order for the Execution of Mr. Khrong Chandawong and Mr. Thongphan Sutthimat." 30 May 2504 [1961].
―――. ["คำสั่งให้ประหารชีวิต นายครอง จันดาวงศ์ กับ นายทองพันธ์ สุทธิมาศ." 30 พฤษภาคม 2504.]
―――. "Order for the Execution of Mr. Supachai Srisati," 6 July 2502 [1959].
―――. ["คำสั่งให้ประหารชีวิต นายศุภชัย ศรีสติ," 6 กรกฎาคม 2502.]

INDEX

Page numbers in italics indicate tables.

Abdulmanee Abdullah, 98

Abhisit Vejjajiva, and topics: 10 April–19 May 2010 military crackdown, x, 191; March 2010 protests, ix, 190–91, 281n32; brothers and sisters language, 197, 198; Criminal Division for Persons Holding Political Positions, 192, 199, 200; Democratic Party, 190, 191, 196; historical memory for accountability for state violence, 197, 281n35; impunity for state violence, 197; Internal Security Act of 2010, 281n32; political crime, 196–97, 281n32; prime minister appointments, ix, x, 190, 277n6; real history versus history of oblivion, 197, 281n35; TRCT, 191–92, 194. *See also* trial for 10 April–19 May 2010 military crackdown

absolutely decisive (*det khat*) approach, 34–35, 55, 56

absolute monarchy, 5–6, 14, 43, 60, 77, 193, 204. *See also* monarchy/constitutional monarchy

ACAA: Anti-Communist Activities Act of 1952, 55, 78, 247n60, 250n4, 260n50; Anti-Communist Activities Act of 1979, 247n60. *See also* Anti-Communist Activities Act (ACAA) of 1969

accountability for state violence: 6 October 1976 coup and massacre and, 110, 113; amnesties after 6 October 1976 coup and massacre and, 113–14, 132; and Ban Na Sai, burning of, 80–81, 83–84, 88, 91, 105, 108, 255n120; disappearances and, 167, 184, 188; documentation and, x, 11, 12, 105, 220; failure to secure, 82, 251n16; historical memory in, vi, 53, 54, 197, 221, 281n35; human rights activists and, 136; impunity and, 4–5, 13, 59, 104–8, 184, 256n129; laws and, 196, 280n27; production of impunity versus, 82–83, 188; progressive movements and, 80–81; by progressive movements and politics, 80–81, 84, 88;

313

Article 17, and Sarit: about, 55–56;
1959 interim constitution and, 55;
communists and, 55, 65, 67–68, 69,
70–72, 77, 247n60, 248n76, 248n83;
dehumanization of citizens under,
66, 69; ethnicities and, 69; executions under, 34–35, 55, 56, 64–72,
247n49; extrajudicial violence and,
65, 66; heroin production and, 65,
68–70; impunity for state violence,
56; monarchy's protection under,
66–67, 68, 70, 72; national security
and, 64, 68, 72, 235n44; parliament
and, 56, 57; pedagogy of impunity
and, 69–70, 248n71; prime
minister(s) and office and, 65, 66,
68, 69, 71, 72; production of law
under, 65, 66, 246n48; royalist-
nationalism and, 72. *See also* Article
17; Sarit Thanarat, and topics
Article 21, 74, 75
Article 27, 74, 75, 127, 261n69
Article 29, 114, 115, 117, 119, 121
Article 44, 28, 51, 75, 216, 221
Article 59, 195, 280n22
Article 80, 195, 200, 280n22
Article 83, 195, 200, 280n22
Article 84, 195, 200, 280n22
Article 112: about, 3, 201–2, 282nn50–
52; amnesties and, 127; arbitrary
detention and, 203, 217–18, 283n57,
286n9; bail under, 203, 217–18,
283n59, 286n9; CCA of 2007 and,
x, 3, 51, 218, 243n103; Constitutional
Court on, 204–7, 283n63, 284n68;
freedom of speech versus, 207, 211,
214, 234n32, 245n28; imprisonment
under, 3–4, 13, 51, 193, 202, 243n103;
impunity for state violence under,
13, 193; intimidation under, 213–14,
285n84; monarch as free from
being impugned and, 11, 15, 193–94,

202, 206, 207–8, 213, 215, 283n63;
under NCPO, 201–2, 212, 217–18,
282n52, 286n9, 287n10; pedagogy of
impunity and, 213–14, 215;
political crimes and, 193; reform
campaign for, 284n69; rulers and
ruled relationship and, 15, 284n68;
trials and, 3–4, 209. *See also* social
media, and Article 112; trials under
Article 112
Article 116, 217
Article 150, 195
Article 157, 200, 281n44
Article 177, 284n68
Article 178, 284n68
Article 200, 74, 75
Article 288, 195–96, 200, 201
Asa Monkholsiri, 99–100, 101
Asia: authoritarianism in, 235n47;
documentation of state violence in,
9, 49, 232n11; Gwangju massacre in
South Korea, 155; Indonesia, 113,
131–32, 155, 187, 258n18; international human rights, 235n47; justice
cascade in, 13, 132, 233n23
Asian Human Rights Commission, 49
assassinations, 14, 101, 109, 112, 134,
254n103, 263n3. *See also* executions;
extrajudicial violence
Attachak Sattayanurak, 286n8
Attaphon Yaisawang, 196, 280n29
Atthasit Sitthisunthorn, 97, 102
authoritarianism: documentation of
state violence under, x, xi, 9, 187,
201; human rights language as
concurrent with, 19–20, 56, 57, 72,
235n47; institutionalization of
human rights violations and, 18,
21–22. *See also* political power; rulers
and ruled relationship
autopsies (postmortem inquests), 78,
79, 108, 195, 260n50

Communist Party of Thailand
(*continued*)
members of, 104, 134; Article 17
and, 70–72, 248n76, 248n83; burning of Ban Na Sai suspects and, 77,
78, 80, 84, 86, 245n28, 251n18;
human rights activists as members
of, 154; red drum murders and,
100; socialists/socialism and,
245n28. *See also* Anti-Communist
Activities Act (ACAA) of 1952; Anti-
Communist Activities Act (ACAA)
of 1969; counterinsurgency against
communism
communists (communism): arbitrary
accusations of being, 51, 71, 77, 78,
79, 91–94, 98–99, 110, 158–59, 219;
arbitrary detention for, 29, 41, 44,
78–79; arbitrary detention for those
accused of being, 42–43; Article 17
and, 55, 65, 67–68, 69, 70–72, 77,
79, 247n60, 248n76, 248n83; autopsies restrictions for, 78, 79, 108,
260n50; counterinsurgency against,
39–40, 59, 78–79, 134; definition
under ACAA of 1952, 78, 250n4;
elites' fear of, 77, 78, 250n1; executions and, 34–35, 55, 56, 64–72, 77,
79, 94, 247n49; heroin production
and, 69; human rights versus threat
of, 19; imprisonment of, 55; institutionalization of human rights violations and, 55, 62, 65, 67–68,
247n60; legal measures against,
77–78, 79, 81–82, 250n2; "semi-free,
semi-unfree" society and, 59, 60;
UDHR and, 62. *See also* Anti-
Communist Activities Act (ACAA)
of 1969; Communist Party of
Thailand (CPT); Communist
Suppression Operations Command
(CSOC)

Communist Suppression Operations
Command (CSOC): about, 137;
burning of Ban Na Sai investiga-
tions/reports and, 89, 252n38;
Karunyathep Center and, 42; red
drum murders and, 92, 93–94,
95–96, 98–99. *See also* Internal
Security Operations Command
(ISOC)
compensation and reparations:
amnesty law of 1978 and, 129,
262n81; justice and, 12, 82–83, 85,
88, 90, 101, 252n37
Computer Crimes Act (CCA) of 2007,
x, 3, 50–51, 218, 243n103. *See also*
Facebook posts
congressional hearings on human
rights, US. *See* United States congressional hearing on human rights
Constitutional Court: about, 283n60;
Article 17 and, 73; Article 112 and,
204–7, 283n63, 284n68; on disloyal/
un-Thai individuals, 205, 209, 214;
freedom of speech and, 206–7,
234n32; letter of the law and, 204,
205, 206; petitions under Article 112
charges and, 203–5, 207, 234n32,
283n61, 283n63, 284n68; PPP dissolution by, 277n6; on secrecy and
closed trials, 284n68
Constitution Day, 60, 61
constitution(s): 10 December 1932
Constitution, 14, 58; 8 March 1952
Constitution, 34; 28 January 1959
interim Constitution, 55, 65, 73; 20
June 1968 Constitution, 73; 15
December 1972 interim constitution, 73, 74, 249n87; 7 October
1974 constitution, 74; 22 October
1976 constitution, 74, 114, 249n90;
9 November 1977 constitution, 74,
127, 249n90; 22 December 1978

and, 162, 163–64. *See also* citizen(s), ordinary

democracy: arbitrary detention as danger to, 29, 37–38, 46; Article 17 and, 73–74; contentious coexistence and, 81–82, 91, 108; extralegal opposition to, 14; institutionalization of human rights violations and, 62; legal opposition to, 14; political rights and, xiii, 17; propagation of, 8, 80, 83, 94–95, 251n13; red shirt movement support for, ix; rulers and ruled relationship under, 14, 204, 283nn62–63. *See also* freedom of (expression) speech; freedom of thought

Democratic Party, 190, 191, 196

Department of Corrections arbitrary detention statistics, 39, 40–41, 240n54, 270n102

Department of Police, 7. *See also* police officers

Department of Rights and Liberties Protection, Ministry of Justice, 184

Department of Special Investigation (DSI): 10 April–19 May 2010 military crackdown, 192, 195, 198, 199, 200, 278n9; Somchai's disappearance, 173, 183, 274n30

Department of the Judge Advocate General, 114, 121, 127, 132, 258n19

detainees. *See* arbitrary detention

detention camps/centers, 42, 43–44, 47, 48–49, 79, 165, 187, 270n113. *See also* arbitrary detention

det khat (absolutely decisive) approach, 34–35, 55, 56

dictatorship(s): 14 October 1973 movement and, 37, 109; 22 May 2014 coup, 75; after 6 October 1976 coup and massacre, xi, 74, 81; human rights as term of use and, 18; human

rights language as concurrent with, 19–20; NCPO's return to, 26; post-dictatorship memories of, ix; truth versus, x, xi, 214, 285n84. *See also specific dictators*

Dirks, Nicholas, 153

disappearance(s): about, 24–25, 187–88, 271nn6–8; accountability for state violence and, 167, 184, 188; ambiguity and, 169, 171, 175, 176, 180–81, 182, 186, 187, 259n42; arbitrary detention and, 29, 41–42; CED and, 165, 167–68, 184; CGRS and, 156, *156*, 157, 166, 271n2; of citizens, ordinary, 166–67, 169, 188; criminal court system and, 185; under Criminal Procedure Code, 173, 195, 199, 280n29, 284n68; "disappeared" as term of use, 169; dissidents and, 167, 272n9; human rights activists and movements and, 4, 166, 167, 186–87, 271n6, 272nn10–12; impunity for state violence and, 167, 175, 188; intimidation and, 166, 168, 272n12; jurisprudence against impunity and, 171, 185; justice norms/justice system and, 13, 25, 165, 167, 183, 186; law and, 4, 168, 173, 176, 193, 218, 280n27; law drafted for, 171, 184–86, 277n72; May 1992 movement and, 272n10; newspaper accounts and, 166; Phao and, 59; police officers and, 4, 167, 271n8, 272n9; political will and, 167, 175, 184; public knowledge and, 165–66; red drum murders and, 82, 95, 99, 100, 101, 166, 186; reopened cases of, 185, 277n74; of Somchai, 4, 13, 169, 173, 183–84, 276n70; statistics, 156, *156*, 157, 166, 167, 186, 271n2, 271nn6–7; *UN Human Rights Yearbook* and,

ethnicities and cultural rights, 17, 33, 69, 134. *See also* Muslims

European Co-ordinating Committee for Solidarity with the Thai People, 41

executions: and communist, arbitrary accusations of being, 34–35, 55, 56, 64–72, 77, 79, 94, 247n49; human rights versus, 7. *See also* assassinations

executive orders for arbitrary detention: Article 44 and, 51; Decree 21, 35–36, 37, 39, 45; Decree 43, 35–36, 37, 39, 45; Emergency Decree of 2005 and, 46, 242n88; repetition of, 73. *See also* arbitrary detention; Order 22, and arbitrary detention

executive orders for executions, 55, 65, 247n49

exile, x, 50–51, 110, 154

exoneration(s), 4, 168, 174, 181

exposure of state violence, 80, 81, 83, 98, 101, 103–4, 126–27

extrajudicial violence: about history of, 6, 20; under Article 17, 65, 66; assassinations and, 14, 101, 109, 112, 134, 254n103, 263n3; justice norms and, 13; by police officers, 11, 58–59, 66, 110, 157, 280n27; statistics, 156, *156*, 157; *UN Human Rights Yearbook* and, 134

extralegal measures, 14, 131

Facebook posts, 15, 51, 193, 201, 217, 218, 286n9, 287n10. *See also* Computer Crimes Act (CCA) of 2007

familial brothers and sisters language, of state leaders, 197, 198. *See also* father and children familial language, of state leaders; rulers and ruled relationship

Farmers' Federation of Thailand, 166, 263n3

Fast, Henri, 60

father and children familial language, of state leaders: Kriangsak, 126, 127, 197, 261n72; Sarit, 34, 36, 63, 65–66, 67, 197, 261n72. *See also* brothers and sisters familial language, of state leaders; rulers and ruled relationship

fear and uncertainty, production of (intimidation). *See* intimidation (production of fear and uncertainty); safety, and arbitrary detention

Federation of Independent Students of Thailand (FIST), 85

Feitlowitz, Marguerite, 169, 174–75

Ferrara, Federico, 243n2

FIST (Federation of Independent Students of Thailand), 85

Flood, E. Thadeus, 237–38

Forest Master Plan, 216

Forgotten 200, 74–75

14 October 1973 movement: compensation for damages and, 74; dictatorships forced out of power and, 37, 109; progressive movements and politics and, 81, 84, 88, 109, 133; state violence and, 20, 27

Fraser, Donald, 135, 138, 139, 142, 144, 145. *See also* United States congressional hearing on human rights

freedom of (expression) speech: Article 112 versus, 207, 211, 214, 234n32, 245n28; CCA of 2007 and, x, 3, 50–51, 218, 243n103; Constitutional Court, 206–7, 234n32; Facebook posts and, 51, 193, 201, 217, 218, 286n9, 287n10; inequality/equality and, 15; Kriangsak and, 125–26, 260n60; under NCPO, xi, 217, 285n84, 286n5; Phibun and, 58, 63; Sarit and, 63

Khamphon Klinsukhon, 85, 87–88, 252n27

khana thahan (military group). *See* military group (*khana thahan*)

Khrong Chandawong, 68, 77, 79

Khuang Aphaiwong, 30, 58, 238n21

king(s): Chakri dynasty, 190, 277n5; loyalty under premodern, 193; Sukhothai Kingdom, 204; as term of use, 14. *See also* absolute monarchy; monarchy/constitutional monarchy; *and specific kings*

Kit Phonlachan (pseud. Jakrapob Penkair), 203, 283n58

Kobkuson Neelapaijit, 173–74

Krathing Daeng (Red Guars), 97, 137, 253n74, 264n17

Kriangsak Chomanan, and topics: 11 November 1977 coup, 125, 263n2; 1977 constitution, 249n90; 1978 constitution, 249n90; amnesty law of 1978, 126–27, 128, 129, 130; arbitrary detention, 157; dissidents, 133; father and children language, 126, 127, 197, 261n72; freedom of speech, 125–26, 260n60; Order 22 nullification, 45; US congressional hearing on human rights, 144–45

Krisdika (Office of the Council of State): about, 7; amnesty law of 1976 and, 113, 114–15, 116–17, 121, 131; amnesty law of 1978 and, 127, 261n64; on arbitrary detention, 32–33, 37; human rights and, 147; MFA's correspondence with, 147, 267n75; psychological training schools and, 31–34, 238n21; *UN Human Rights Yearbook* and, 56, 133–34, 147

Kris Sivara, 88–89, 95, 99, 105

Krom Phrathammanun, 114

Krongtham Neelapaijit, 173–74

Krue Se mosque massacre in 2004, 106, 255n122

Kukrit Pramoj, 103, 137, 145–46, 266n63

Kulap Saipradit, 59–60

Labor Coordinating Center, 163

labor rights and activists, 157–58, 162–63, 272n11

Laos, 78, 110, 134

Latin America, 132, 163, 262n98. *See also* Southern Cone

law(s) and legal system: accountability for state violence and, 196, 280n27; CAT and, 184; CED and, 184; dehumanization of citizens and, 25–26; disappearance and, 4, 168, 173, 176, 193, 218, 280n27; disappearance draft law and, 171, 184–86, 277n72; extralegal measures versus, 14, 131; iLaw and, 50, 243n99; individuals free from being impugned, 11, 15, 25–26, 193–94, 202–3, 206, 207–8, 213, 214–15, 283n63; individuals killed with impunity, 11, 25–26, 193–94, 202–3, 215, 219–20; lawyers/legal counsel and, 3, 4, 29, 40, 46, 168, 171–72, 218; letter of the law and, 9, 20, 52, 192, 193, 204, 205, 206, 215; opposition to democracy and, 14; red drum murders and, 96; rule of law and, 12, 14–15, 65, 206, 246n48 (*see also* rule of law); state of exception and, 16, 29; torture and, 280n27; torture draft law and, 184–86, 276n71, 277n72. *See also* justice; justice system (judiciary); *and specific laws*

lèse majesté. *See* Article 112; loyalty to monarchy; monarchy/constitutional monarchy

CAT and, 184; and communist, arbitrary accusations of being, 94; complaints filed about, 4, 24, 141, 142, 159–60; in detention camps/centers, 270n113; documentation of, 9, 151; justice norms and, 13; law drafted for crime of, 184–86, 276n71, 277n72; laws and, 280n27; MFA and, 136, 151, 159, 160; Ministry of Defense and, 151; Ministry of Interior and, 151; of Muslims, 172; observers of trials for, 11; Phao and, 59; police officers and, 157; public knowledge of, 160–61, 162; red drum murders and, 8, 93, 94, 95, 103; by state security forces, 25, 53; statistics, 136, 153, 155–56, *156*, 157, 159–60, 161–62; *UN Human Rights Yearbook* and, 134. *See also* interrogations during arbitrary detention; torture

training/occupational training (reeducation) during arbitrary detention: "danger to society," 39, 41, 44, 51, 239n52; hooligans and, 35, 37; Occupational Training Law of 1975 and, 37–38, 39, 239n48; Order 22 and, 39, 41; psychological training schools and, 31–34, 46, 238n21; red drum murders and, 93–94; terrorist category for Muslim southerners and, 47, 48–49, 242n92

TRCT (Truth and Reconciliation Committee of Thailand), 191–92, 194

trial(s): AI and, 135, 148; CGRS reports on, 154; and communist, arbitrary accusations of being, 159; justice cascade and, 13, 191; observers of, x, 11, 174, 175, 208; secrecy during closed trials and, 284n68; United States congressional hearings and,

140; witnesses' testimony and protection during, 174, 176–78, 208–12, 214, 274n33; Working Group and, 28. *See also* military court system; *and specific courts and trials*

trial for 10 April–19 May 2010 military crackdown: appeal and, 199, 200, 201; charges and, x, 192, 195–96, 280n22, 280n24; charges as dismissed in, 192–93, 196, 199–201, 215; coplaintiffs in, 196, 199, 201; corruption and, 192, 196, 199, 200, 201, 280n29, 281n44; dissenting opinion and, 199–200, 201; individuals free from being impugned and, 193–94, 202–3, 214–15; individuals killed with impunity and, 193–94, 202–3, 219; inequality/equality and, 193, 201; injustice cascade and, 192; institutionalization of human rights violations and, 193; jurisdiction and, 198–99; justice cascade and, 191, 199; letter of the law and, 192, 193, 215; NACC and, 192, 196, 199, 201, 219; OAG and, 192, 195–96, 199, 200, 280n29; political crime and, 192–93, 195, 196–97, 199–200, 201, 219, 281n32; witnesses and, 214

trials of police officers, for disappearance of Somchai: about, 4, 168, 218; alibis and, 178–80; ambiguity of disappearances and, 175, 176, 180–81, 182, 187; Appeal Court and, 174, 177, 181–82, 274n36; arrests and, 168; Chadchai and, 173, 179; Chaiweng and, 173, 179; charges and, 168, 173, 181, 274n31; coplaintiffs and, 173–74, 182, 183, 271n6, 274n30, 274n33, 275n37, 276n63, 276n67; disappeared as neither alive nor dead and, 168, 174–75, 181, 182–83, 276n60; exonerations and,

Dreams of the Hmong Kingdom:
The Quest for Legitimation in French Indochina, 1850–1960
MAI NA M. LEE

The Government of Mistrust: Illegibility and
Bureaucratic Power in Socialist Vietnam
KEN MACLEAN

Policing America's Empire: The United States, the Philippines,
and the Rise of the Surveillance State
ALFRED W. MCCOY

An Anarchy of Families: State and Family in the Philippines
Edited by ALFRED W. MCCOY

The Hispanization of the Philippines:
Spanish Aims and Filipino Responses, 1565–1700
JOHN LEDDY PHELAN

Pretext for Mass Murder: The September 30th Movement and
Suharto's Coup d'État in Indonesia
JOHN ROOSA

Hamka's Great Story: A Master Writer's Vision of
Islam for Modern Indonesia
JAMES R. RUSH

The Social World of Batavia: Europeans and Eurasians in
Colonial Indonesia, second edition
JEAN GELMAN TAYLOR

Việt Nam: Borderless Histories
Edited by NHUNG TUYET TRAN and ANTHONY REID

Thailand's Political Peasants: Power in the Modern Rural Economy
ANDREW WALKER

Modern Noise, Fluid Genres: Popular Music in Indonesia, 1997–2001
JEREMY WALLACH

www.ingramcontent.com/pod-product-compliance
Lightning Source LLC
Chambersburg PA
CBHW070841300326
41935CB00039B/1334